Routledge Revivals

Eclogues

Eclogues

Giovanni Boccaccio

Translated by
Janet Levarie Smarr

Volume II
Series A

First published in 1987 by Garland Publishing, Inc.

This edition first published in 2018 by Routledge
2 Park Square, Milton Park, Abingdon, Oxon, OX14 4RN
and by Routledge
52 Vanderbilt Avenue, New York, NY 10017

Routledge is an imprint of the Taylor & Francis Group, an informa business

© 1987 by Janet Levarie Smarr

All rights reserved. No part of this book may be reprinted or reproduced or utilised in any form or by any electronic, mechanical, or other means, now known or hereafter invented, including photocopying and recording, or in any information storage or retrieval system, without permission in writing from the publishers.

Publisher's Note
The publisher has gone to great lengths to ensure the quality of this reprint but points out that some imperfections in the original copies may be apparent.

Disclaimer
The publisher has made every effort to trace copyright holders and welcomes correspondence from those they have been unable to contact.

A Library of Congress record exists under ISBN:

ISBN 13: 978-0-367-17423-1 (hbk)
ISBN 13: 978-0-367-17427-9 (pbk)
ISBN 13: 978-0-429-05671-0 (ebk)

The Garland Library
of Medieval Literature

General Editors
James J. Wilhelm, Rutgers University
Lowry Nelson, Jr., Yale University

Literary Advisors
Ingeborg Glier, Yale University
William W. Kibler, University of Texas
Norris J. Lacy, University of Kansas
Fred C. Robinson, Yale University
Aldo Scaglione, University of North Carolina

Art Advisor
Elizabeth Parker McLachlan, Rutgers University

Music Advisor
Hendrik van der Werf, Eastman School of Music

Giovanni Boccaccio
ECLOGUES

translated by
JANET LEVARIE SMARR

Volume 11
Series A
GARLAND LIBRARY OF MEDIEVAL LITERATURE

Garland Publishing, Inc.
New York & London
1987

Copyright © 1987 by Janet Levarie Smarr
All rights reserved

Library of Congress Cataloging-in-Publication Data
Boccaccio, Giovanni, 1313–1375.
   Eclogues.

   (Garland library of medieval literature ; v. 11.
Series A)
   Translation of: Buccolicum carmen.
   Bibliography: p.
   I. Smarr, Janet Levarie, 1949–   . II. Title.
III. Series: Garland library of medieval literature ;
v. 11.
PQ4315.64.S6   1987   872'.03   87-104
ISBN 0-8240-8439-X (alk. paper)

Printed on acid-free, 250-year-life paper
Manufactured in the United States of America

Preface of the General Editors

The Garland Library of Medieval Literature was established to make available to the general reader modern translations of texts in editions that conform to the highest academic standards. All of the translations are original, and were created especially for this series. The translations attempt to render the foreign works in a natural idiom that remains faithful to the originals.

The Library is divided into two sections: Series A, texts and translations; and Series B, translations alone. Those volumes containing texts have been prepared after consultation of the major previous editions and manuscripts. The aim in the editing has been to offer a reliable text with a minimum of editorial intervention. Significant variants accompany the original, and important problems are discussed in the Textual Notes. Volumes without texts contain translations based on the most scholarly texts available, which have been updated in terms of recent scholarship.

Most volumes contain Introductions with the following features: (1) a biography of the author or a discussion of the problem of authorship, with any pertinent historical or legendary information; (2) an objective discussion of the literary style of the original, emphasizing any individual features; (3) a consideration of sources for the work and its influence; and (4) a statement of the editorial policy for each edition and translation. There is also a Select Bibliography, which emphasizes recent criticism on the works. Critical writings are often accompanied by brief descriptions of their importance. Selective glossaries, indices, and footnotes are included where appropriate.

The Library covers a broad range of linguistic areas, including all of the major European languages. All of the important literary forms and genres are considered, sometimes in anthologies or selections.

The General Editors hope that these volumes will bring the general reader a closer awareness of a richly diversified area that has for too long been closed to everyone except those with precise academic training, an area that is well worth study and reflection.

James J. Wilhelm
Rutgers University

Lowry Nelson, Jr.
Yale University

Acknowledgments

I wish to express my gratitude to those who helped me by checking my translation in whole or in part. Listed simply according to their temporal sequence, they are: Neda Jeny, John Kevin Newman, John Bateman, and David Bright. Any remaining errors are, of course, my own.

A fellowship at the University of Illinois Center for Advanced Study enabled me to complete this work. Research and production were also supported in part by the University of Illinois Research Board. Numerical Recipes Software is acknowledged for typographical and design assistance.

Boccaccio's text has its own dedication; my part of this work is dedicated to Rose McGuire Smith, who taught her love for Latin.

Contents

Introduction
    Life of the Author viii
    Artistic Achievement
        The Bucolic Genre xxiii
        Boccaccio's Pastoral Poetry xxix
        Boccaccio and Petrarch xli
        Judgments on Boccaccio's *Buccolicum carmen* l
    Sources and Influences
        Sources liii
        Influences lxi
    Editorial Policy for this Text and Translation lxxi
    Select Bibliography lxxiii

Text and Translation 1

Notes
    Historical Background 201
    Notes on the Eclogues 208

Introduction

Life of the Author

Giovanni Boccaccio was born in 1313, the illegitimate –but later legally legitimized – son of Boccaccino di Chelino, who had moved from Certaldo to Florence to pursue a career in banking.[1] Boccaccio's mother has never been identified, and Boccaccio does not seem to have known her. Possibly she died in childbirth. Attempted reconstructions of Boccaccio's life from romantic episodes within his fictions –episodes containing, indeed, autobiographical elements – had suggested that she was Parisian, but there is no real evidence for this. When Giovanni was about seven, his father married and had another son. Boccaccino did well for himself, economically and politically, and was elected prior in 1322-23. He had the young Boccaccio instructed in grammar by Giovanni da Strada, father of Zanobi da Strada; Zanobi was to become Boccaccio's successful and disdained rival for the position of literary man at the court of Naples. These lessons also introduced Boccaccio to some of Ovid's poetry and the realm of classical mythology. Boccaccio's step-mother was related to the family of Dante's Beatrice. Thus in early years Boccaccio made acquaintance with the two authors whose influence can be felt in everything Boccaccio wrote from the beginnings until the end of his life.

Boccaccio's father, however, did not conceive a literary education for his son. Rather he wanted to train Boccaccio for participation in the family business. Thus the study of grammar was followed by instruction in the arithmetic appropriate for commerce. During his early adolescence (the exact year is not known) Boccaccio moved with his father to Naples, where many Florentines lived and did business, and he worked as an apprentice in the banking company of the Bardi. There at the same time was another young Florentine from a different banking family, Niccola Acciaiuoli,

---

[1] Most of the information for this biography comes from Vittore Branca's "Profilo biografico," in Boccaccio, *Tutte le opere* (Verona: Mondadori, 1967), vol.1, pp.3-197. An English version can be found in V. Branca, *Boccaccio: The Man and His Works*, trans. Richard Monges (New York: New York University Press, 1976), pp.3-193. A briefer biography is contained in Thomas Bergin, *Boccaccio* (New York: Viking Press, 1981).

Life of the Author ix

whose spectacular rise to power in Naples figures largely in Boccaccio's eclogues. The business of lending money to the Neapolitan court was political as well as commercial; for the Angevin King Robert of Naples, head of the Italian Guelf party to which many Florentines traditionally belonged, was beleaguered by the Ghibelline ruler of Sicily, Frederick of Aragon, and threatened as well by the northern emperor Ludwig of Bavaria. Both Boccaccino and the Acciaiuoli were welcomed and trusted at the court of King Robert.

Both at court and through the banking business, Boccaccio was able to meet a wide array of people. The merchants and prostitutes of Naples recur in many tales of the *Decameron*, while the elegant diversions of the noble or well-to-do are described in several of his other writings, such as the *Caccia di Diana*, *Filocolo*, and *Elegia di madonna Fiammetta*, with their Neapolitan settings. Naples was a center of culture as well as of business, and Boccaccio was attracted to its men of letters. There were Barbato da Sulmona and Giovanni Barrili, friends of Petrarch, through whom Boccaccio came to know Petrarch's early writings. There was Cino da Pistoia, another Tuscan émigré, professor of law, poet, friend of Dante; Boccaccio took one of his courses. There was Graziolo de' Bambaglioli, one of the earliest commentators on Dante. The *Genealogiae deorum gentilium libri* (15.6) lists other friends and mentors: Andalo da Negro, "who was once my teacher of astronomy;" Francesco da Barberino, expert on canon law and "author of several essays in brilliant vernacular verse;" Barlaam, a Calabrian monk who knew Greek; Paulo da Perugia, King Robert's librarian, who began a collection of classical mythology (including Greek sources, with Barlaam's help), a work destroyed by Paulo's widow but revived in Boccaccio's own great handbook of mythology, the *Genealogia*; and others. Besides these men of letters, there came to Naples the great artist Giotto, whose paintings revolutionized the art world. Boccaccio praises him highly in the *Amorosa Visione* (4.13-18) and in the *Decameron* (6.5). Boccaccio recognized in Giotto the beginning of a new era, reviving a kind of art that had long been buried. Later (in his letter to Iacopo Pizzinga) he would speak similarly of Petrarch as one who cleared the path up Mount Parnassus that had long been overgrown from disuse.

Discontented with mercantile pursuits, Boccaccio enrolled in the study of canon law. From his father's point of view it was further vocational training which would lead to a secure income. From Boccaccio's view, its chief benefits were an increasing familiarity with Latin and acquaintance with some of the intellectuals just mentioned. As Boccaccio complained in his *Genealogia* (15.10): "Whatever the vocation of others, mine, as experience from my mother's womb has shown, is clearly the study of poetry. For this, I believe, I was born. I well remember how my father even in my boyhood directed all my endeavors towards business. As a mere child, he put me in charge of a great business man for instruction in arithmetic. For six years I did nothing in his office but waste irrevocable time. Then, as there seemed to be some indication that I was more disposed to literary pursuits, this same father decided that I should study for holy orders, as a good way to get rich. My teacher was famous, but I wasted under him almost as much time as before. In both cases I so tired of the work that neither my teacher's admonition, nor my father's authority, who kept torturing me with ever renewed orders, nor the pleas and importunities of my friends, could make me yield, so great was my one passion for poetry. It was not finally a sudden change of plan that sent me headlong into this pursuit, but rather a disposition of long standing...If my father had only been favorable to such a course at a time of life when I was more adaptable, I do not doubt that I should have taken my place among poets of fame. But while he tried to bend my mind first into business and next into a lucrative profession, it came to pass that I turned out neither a business man, nor a canon lawyer, and missed being a good poet besides."[2] The conflict between pursuit of wealth and intellectual or spiritual pursuits (for poetry and philosophy were intimately related in Boccaccio's mind) became one of the major themes of the bucolic poems, begun in Naples and finished many decades later in Certaldo.

While Boccaccio was fretting in misdirected studies, Niccola Acciaiuoli was astounding everyone by his rapid success. He had arrived at Naples in 1331, with one servant only. By 1333 he was providing furnishings for the royal family; by 1334 he was the person most trusted by the king's sister-in-law Caterina di Valois Courtenay, empress of Constantinople. By 1335, at the age of 25, he was chamberlain to the king and ennobled with the title of knight. As counselor to Caterina's son Louis, he managed in 1348 to arrange Louis's marriage to his cousin, King Robert's granddaughter and heir, Joan, and to reestablish the royal couple on their throne after the invasion of Naples by the King of Hungary. Thus Niccola ascended eventually to the position of Grand Seneschal, the most powerful man in the kingdom, rewarded by Louis with numerous titles and lands.

As Niccola was achieving increasing wealth and fame through business and politics (just the career Boccaccino would have loved for his son), Boccaccio began to write. The years at Naples witnessed the production of

---

[2] Trans. Charles Osgood, *Boccaccio on Poetry*, Library of the Liberal Arts (1930; rpt. Indianapolis: Bobbs-Merrill, 1956), pp.131-32.

the *Caccia di Diana* (1334?), a hunt by nymphs who are identifiable ladies at the court; the *Filostrato* (1335?), a verse narrative set in ancient Troy and adapted by Chaucer as *Troylus and Criseyde*; the *Filocolo* (1336), an ambitious long epic in prose that recounts Florio's search for his beloved Biancifiore and the conversion of western Europe to Christianity; and at least part of the *Teseida*, a stanzaic epic-romance in twelve books concerning the rivalry of two Theban knights for the love of an Amazon princess, culminating in a tournament arranged by Theseus (Chaucer found here the source for his "Knight's Tale"). These writings, along with the very early and brief "Allegoria mitologica," show an enthusiasm for classical literature and for Dante, and a desire to combine both by rewriting classical stories or genres in the new literary language. Boccaccio boasted in the *Teseida* (12.84) that it is the first martial epic in Italian. Moreover, most of these works are allegorically concerned either with the Christian religion or with the relations of reason and the passions, virtues and vices, in the soul. Boethius's image of Fortune holds a central place in the *Filostrato* and recurred in writings throughout Boccaccio's life to indicate the error of those who worship this world's goods.

Around 1340 the Bardi bank began to fail; and Boccaccino, who had recently left its employ, was also in personal financial difficulties. He summoned his son back to Florence in 1341, from an exhilarating and comfortable life among intellectual friends to a severely restricted one with a father who disapproved of his son's inability to contribute to the family finances. Boccaccio was now twenty-eight. Where Naples had offered a royal court as cultural center, an Angevin ruling family that delighted in French romances and Provençal poetry, and a university full of celebrated scholars, Florence offered a middle-class society run by the very businessmen that Boccaccio did not want to be; nor had the city established yet its university. Little wonder if Boccaccio felt initially depressed. For many years to come, even after he had entered into the public life of Florence with the trust and respect of his fellow Tuscans, he longed to return to live in the Naples of his youth. His hope was that Niccola Acciaiuoli, who desired for the sake of his own prestige to have a man of letters in residence at the court, would set him up in the style which he so fondly recalled. But when at last the invitation came, it was to be a bitter disappointment.

The move to Florence, however, did not interrupt Boccaccio's work. Within the year of his arrival in Florence, he finished the *Comedia delle ninfe fiorentine*, an allegory of vices and virtues, which not only made use of a pastoral setting, but also included two eclogues in Italian, written in terza rima. These two eclogues are moral and religious allegories and draw, like the *Comedia* which contains them, from Dante's *Commedia*, as their verse form makes clear. There was good reason for Boccaccio, who was continuing his revival and vernacularization of classical genres, to associate the pastoral with Dante as well as with Vergil; for Boccaccio had carefully copied into his notebooks a pastoral verse correspondence between Giovanni del Virgilio and Dante (see Sources).

The *Amorosa visione* (1342) was also composed shortly after Boccaccio's return to Florence. In a series of murals depicting the triumphs of Wisdom, Fame, Wealth, Love, and of Fortune which overturns them all, Boccaccio set his father in among the avaricious (14.34-45).

> Oltre grattando il monte dimorava
> con unghie adunche uno, ch'al mio parere
> in molte volte poco ne graffiava.
> Con ansietà quel poco poi tenere
> in borsa li vedea, ch'a pena esso,
> non ch'altro alcuno, ne poteva avere.
> Al qual faccendomi io più alquanto appresso
> per conoscer chi fosse apertamente,
> vidi ch'era colui che me istesso
> libero e lieto avea benignamente
> nodrito come figlio, ed io chiamato
> aveva lui e chiamo mio parente.

> [Also scratching at the heap with hooked nails was one who, as it seemed to me, scraped up little with many efforts. I saw how with anxiety afterwards he kept that little in his purse, so that barely he himself, much less anyone else, could have any of it. Drawing somewhat nearer to him to see who it was, I recognized that it was he who had kindly raised me as his son, free and happy, and whom I called and still call my parent.]

The passage reveals Boccaccio's ambivalent feelings, gratitude to the father who had raised him kindly, yet disgust for the life of money-grubbing which is rendered all the more pathetic by its lack of success. Boccaccio's own happiness is partly a cause for praise and thanks to his father, as well as a demonstration that Boccaccio chose the better way of life.

King Robert of Naples, the object of high praises in both the *Filocolo* and Latin eclogues, has his place too among the avaricious. Made anxious by Florentine overtures to the emperor, Robert and many of the leading Neapolitans had tried to withdraw their money from the Florentine banks.

The banks could not respond to this sudden large demand; their credit collapsed. The Bardi palaces were invaded and plundered by mobs. Clearly the important role of Fortune in the *Amorosoa visione* derived not only from Boccaccio's reading of Boethius but also from his own dramatic experiences.

The move to Florence had a notable effect on Boccaccio's style. He lost the abundant amplifications and periphrases expected perhaps by a courtly audience, and developed a much leaner style more readily appreciated by the busy and practical merchants of Florence.[3] Nonetheless, he set one more work in Naples and filled it with his memories of Neapolitan life: the *Elegia di madonna Fiammetta* (1343 or 1344). Narrated completely by the woman, it is a remarkable account of her psychological decline and ruin, beginning with a love affair and ending in suicidal madness and spiritual despair. Here Boccaccio showed his ability not only to work with allegorical ideas but also to portray with deep insight the motivations and self deceptions of another psyche. Most of the action takes place internally; brief events set off long inner monologues and debates. Boccaccio's use in this work of Ovid's *Heroides* and of Seneca demonstrates his continuing interest in developing classical models into a new vernacular literature. Similar in this regard is the *Ninfale fiesolano* (1344-46?), a delicately recounted myth about the metamorphosis of two lovers into two Tuscan rivers. A comparison of the language in this tale of a country lad and nymph with the language of the similarly pastoral *Comedia delle ninfe fiorentine* reveals a tremendous change towards the simple and direct.

Also soon after his return to Florence, Boccaccio made his first attempt at writing Latin poetry, producing two eclogues which would become the first two poems in his *Buccolicum carmen*.[4] Borrowing heavily from Vergil both ideas and phrases, he composed one dialogue and one monologue on basically the same theme: a lover rendered miserable by his lady's infidelity. Vergil had played conspicuously with the alternation of narrative and dramatic (or monologue and dialogue) forms in his *Bucolica*. Quite possibly Boccaccio was trying his hand at both methods without having yet the intention of writing a whole sequence of such poems. Or perhaps he did think of writing a set of ten like Vergil's, but felt unable to continue what he had begun.

In 1346 Boccaccio was living in Ravenna at the court of Ostagio da

---

[3] Branca, "Profilo," pp. 76 and 91, suggests also the influence on his style of translating Livy and rereading Dante.

[4] The dating is presumed from an allusion in the first to a speaker's move from Naples to Florence.

Polenta, for whom he translated the fourth decade of Livy. There he became friends with Donato degli Albanzani, the school teacher to whom the final set of Latin eclogues would be dedicated. In 1347-1348 Boccaccio had moved to Forlì under the patronage of Francesco Ordelaffi. Here he decided to imitate the pastoral correspondence of Giovanni del Virgilio and Dante, and wrote an eclogue to Checco di Meletto dei Rossi, a secretary of Ordelaffi, inviting him to participate. Checco responded, and Boccaccio wrote again, this time a long eclogue under the influence of a whole new pastoral model, Petrarch's "Argus."

Boccaccio did not yet know Petrarch personally, nor was he aware that the "Argus" was part of a sequence of bucolics; for Petrarch had circulated it separately, carefully guarding the rest of the work until he considered it polished enough to release in 1359. Until now Boccaccio had used the eclogue to discuss religious, moral, and literary topics. Petrarch's "Argus" is a political or historical allegory, dealing with the death of King Robert, the murder of Prince Andrew, and the ensuing turmoil and fear among the Neapolitans. The terrible turmoil in that city's current affairs certainly evoked strong emotional responses from Boccaccio. His host and patron, Francesco Ordelaffi, requested Boccaccio to accompany him in joining the Hungarian forces to punish those responsible for Andrew's death. Surely Boccaccio had never envisioned returning to his beloved Naples as an invader! He seems, in fact, not to have gotten that far, if indeed he left Forlì at all. Soon the vicious actions of the Hungarian king, a cousin of the Neapolitan ruling family, compelled Boccaccio to lose sympathy for what had initially seemed a just cause, for the Hungarians brought more violence than justice. Boccaccio continued to compose a sequence of eclogues on the events surrounding the murder of Andrew, the invasion by King Ludwig of Hungary, the beheading of Charles of Durazzo, and the triumphant return of Queen Joan and Louis of Taranto after their flight to southern France. (See the "Historical Background".) Thus, independently from Petrarch, he launched on the project of an eclogue sequence, a genre which had, with rare and obscure exceptions, lain fallow since Vergil and Calpurnius in the first century A.D. The revival of this genre was to have a tremendous success in the Renaissance.

In the spring of 1348 the infamous Black Death hit Florence. Boccaccio was probably there at the time, as he claims. For a writer already concerned with the figure of Fortune, the plague offered an unsurpassable example of its turnings. Among the thousands of dead were his father and step-mother, who left Boccaccio as the head of the family, in charge of his younger half-brother. Branca calculates that Violante, the child whose early death Boccaccio so tenderly celebrated in his fourteenth eclogue, was born at about this same time. Thus Boccaccio was thrust into a position of new responsibilities just as the two cities he cared most about were plunged into ruin, one by war and the other by plague. The *Decameron* on which he was working from 1348 until 1351, takes as one of its major themes the struggle between the power of Fortune and the strength of human will. It also continues his previous theme of the conflicts between human reason and the irrational aspects of the human psyche. The desire to establish some rational control within the individual is related by Boccaccio to problems of social health and sickness. If Petrarch had inspired Boccaccio to turn his mind to political topics, the desperate real need for reconstructing Florentine society after the plague further developed Boccaccio's interest in social and political affairs.

He began to be employed by the city on diplomatic missions: first in 1350 to Romagna, probably with regard to the threat of Visconti expansionism; then to Ravenna to present ten gold florins from the company of Or San Michele to the daughter of Dante, honored at last by his native town. A year later he was made treasurer of the Camera del Comune, and delegated to negotiate with Acciaiuoli the release of all Neapolitan claims to Prato. In the winter of 1351-52 he was sent farther afield, to Louis of Bavaria, count of Tyrol, to discuss possible measures against the Visconti.

During this time another momentous event occurred: Petrarch's visit to Florence in 1350 and the personal encounter of the two great authors. Boccaccio went to meet Petrarch outside the city gates and welcomed him into his own home. The circle of Florentine admirers who gathered there remained friends and correspondents with Petrarch long after. Petrarch stopped in Florence again a few months later, after his visit to Rome, and sent in gratitude to his new friends a copy of Cicero's "Pro Archia," a gift which encouraged both the pursuit of literary studies and the revival of classical culture. In 1351 Boccaccio was sent to Padua with official letters inviting Petrarch to reclaim the properties confiscated at his father's exile long before and to return to Florence as a professor in the new university. To the disappointment of his Florentine friends, Petrarch declined. Boccaccio in a letter to Petrarch ("Ut huic epistole," 1353) describes his visit to Padua, his eager copying of Petrarch's writings, and their conversations on subjects of mutual interest. Both men had the same goal at heart: to revive the glory of ancient literature in their own time. But until his eclogue project, Boccaccio had followed Dante's course of writing in Italian. Surely the matter of Latin eclogues, the most similar enterprise of the two poets, was a topic of conversation; but unfortunately we cannot know what they said or who gave what ideas to whom.

Two events, however, proved discouraging to Boccaccio. First Zanobi da Strada, although still in Florence for Petrarch's visit, had recently received from Acciaiuoli and had accepted an invitation to live at the Neapolitan court, an invitation which Boccaccio would dearly have liked to receive and certainly, as far as literary talents go, deserved much more. But what was much worse, Petrarch, that spiritual as well as literary guide, accepted an invitation from the dreaded Visconti and in 1353 moved to Milan. After Boccaccio's repeated political embassies against the Visconti and Petrarch's refusal of a post in Florence, this was too bitter a blow. Petrarch, despite previous speeches about the importance of liberty and the evils of the Visconti tyranny, was accepting payment from that very enemy of Tuscan freedom. Boccaccio sent him a letter of outrage, and so overwhelming was his fury that he declared openly his need to buffer the attack against his friend by the distancing device of allegory. This was his one pastoral prose epistle.

His political involvments continued, demonstrating the trust and respect of his fellow citizens; and in 1354 he was sent on a delicate mission to Avignon to sound out the intentions of the pope with regard to the descent of Charles IV from Germany into Italy to be crowned emperor at Rome. Sought out as an ally against the Visconti, Charles was nonetheless also feared by the traditionally Guelph Tuscan cities, which worried that his assumption of imperial power might mean the end of their civic liberties and autonomy. At Avignon he met old friends of Petrarch's, and possibly took a trip to visit the Vaucluse, the home Petrarch had celebrated as inspirational for his writings. In any case, the friendship of the two men continued despite the crisis of Petrarch's move to Milan. The issue of the impending coronation of Charles forms the subject of Boccaccio's seventh eclogue, while the coronation itself is treated in the ninth. Florence in these eclogues expresses its dismay that the crown of the great Roman emperors should be set on the head of a barbarian. Furthermore, at the request of Acciaiuoli, the emperor while in Pisa crowned Zanobi da Strada with laurel, an event that aroused Boccaccio's anger and disgust; for Zanobi was hardly a candidate to follow the great Petrarch as laureate. The dissociation between success and worth became a theme of Boccaccio's later poetry and probably part of the motivation for his increasing attraction to humanist ideas: that only the few really understand or value intellectual studies.

Zanobi soon afterwards left Naples for a job as secretary to Acciaiuoli's cousin, bishop of Florence and Montecassino. Once again the post of court poet was open at Naples, and Acciaiuoli, having vainly attempted to attract Petrarch, seems at last to have given the offer to Boccaccio. We know very little about Boccaccio's trip, but clearly something went very wrong. For between the eclogues about the emperor Boccaccio set a scathing attack on Acciauoli, accusing him of advancing his own ambitions without regard for law or morality. In the eclogue, a friend of Phytias warns him to turn back while there is still time, and not to trust the promises of thieving Midas.

Boccaccio, while writing his last Italian work of fiction, the *Corbaccio* (c.1355)[5] began to compose several scholarly works in Latin. The favorite theme of Fortune finds a prominent place in *De casibus virorum illustrium*, translated by Lydgate as *The Fall of Princes*, while Petrarch's volume on famous ancient men found a companion piece in Boccaccio's *De mulieribus claris*, the lives of famous women from ancient times to modern. Actually the *De casibus* ends with a woman too: not a royal figure but a lowly washerwoman who rose to a position of eminence at the Neapolitan court as the nurse for the royal children, but was tortured and killed when convicted of conspiring in the death of Prince Andrew. Thus the events in Naples which are so important for Boccaccio's eclogues offer also an example of the complete revolution of Fortune's wheel. At about the same time, he began work as well on the *De montibus*, a geographical dictionary of mountains, rivers, seas, and other places, and on the immensely important *Genealogiae deorum gentilium libri*, an encyclopedia of classical mythology with allegorical interpretations of various kinds: the myths are shown to refer to natural science, moral philosophy, or history, but never to Christian doctrine, as the ancient authors could not have intended such meanings. The work provides also Boccaccio's comments on the art and history of poetry in general. Besides these new and compendious works, which provided for the interpretation of classical literature the same kind of helpful reference book which had long existed for Scripture, Boccaccio was revising his Italian biography of Dante and his *Amorosa visione*. In sum, after several years of political activity, Boccaccio seems to have thrown himself into his research and writing with incredible intensity.

In 1359 Boccaccio went to visit Petrarch in Milan despite his criticism of Petrarch for accepting patronage from the dreaded Visconti. It was on the occasion of this visit that he was finally allowed to read Petrarch's entire *Bucolicum carmen*. Was this the impulse which turned Boccaccio from historical eclogues to eclogues of moral philosophy and more personal

---

[5] Giorgio Padoan, "Sulla datazione del *Corbaccio*," *Lettere italiane* 15 (1963), 1-27, argues for a later date around 1365 or 1366; Branca, "Profilo," p.140, supports this late dating. However, Tauno Nurmela ed., *Corbaccio, Annales Academiae Scientiarum Fennicae* vol.146 (1968), pp.18-21 and Anthony Cassell ed. and trans., *The Corbaccio* (Urbana: University of Illinois, 1975), pp.86-87 and 231, argue for the previously accepted date of approximately 1355.

topics? Certainly eclogues 12 (about the pursuit of poetry) and 15 (about the choice between this world and the next) are close in basic idea if not in execution to two of Petrarch's poems. And it is Petrarch who figures in both of Boccaccio's poems as literary and moral guide.

Another result of this visit was Boccaccio's project to study Greek with a Calabrian named Leonzio Pilato and with him to translate Homer for the first time. Boccaccio established for his tutor a professorship of Greek at the University of Florence, the very first chair of Greek studies in western Europe; and for all his usual humility, this is one action of which Boccaccio proudly boasted (*Genealogia* 15.7).

In 1360 the pope gave Boccaccio dispensation for his illegitimate birth so that he could receive an ecclesiastical benefice. It may surprise some who know Boccaccio only as the writer of the *Decameron* to think of him as an official in the church; yet he had studied canon law for years, and had written many works of Christian thought in his allegorical fictions.

Following an abortive Guelph conspiracy in Florence which caused the exile or punishment of a number of Boccaccio's friends and acquaintances, Boccaccio ceased for a while to participate in public life, and shortly withdrew to the hill town of Certaldo, the old family abode. Certaldo became for Boccaccio the same kind of fruitfully peaceful retreat that the Vaucluse had been for Petrarch years before. It was thus an ideal place to finish writing and revising pastoral poetry. The final eclogue of Boccaccio's sequence, which offers the little flock of sheep (or poems) to the grammarian Donato degli Albanzani, describes the poet years later, poor but happy and independent in his paternal dwelling.

Even here, however, not all was tranquil. A religious man named Pietro Petroni, who was reputed to have visions, sent a message in 1362 from his deathbed to Boccaccio and Petrarch exhorting them to turn away from literary pursuits. Perhaps he opposed their cult for pagan classics, or perhaps he simply considered the whole literary enterprise too worldly, entailing inevitably a desire for worldly fame. Boccaccio communicated his uneasiness to Petrarch, who hastened to assure him and to encourage him to continue his literary work. He even invited Boccaccio to come to live with him, an invitation which was not accepted.

Boccaccio received another invitation as well, which he did accept. Francesco Nelli, close friend of Petrarch and Boccaccio, had found employment at the Neapolitan court. He added his plea for Boccaccio to join him there, and once again Boccaccio succumbed to the temptation to return to the city of his youthful pleasures. The disastrous nature of this visit is

Life of the Author   xix

vituperatively registered in Boccaccio's long letter to Nelli. According to Boccaccio's account, he had made the journey expecting to be received honorably as a member of the court; instead he had been lodged disgracefully, fed with the servants instead of with his old acquaintances, ignored, expected to move continually with Acciauioli's entourage despite the difficulties of pursuing his work that way, and – the final blow– left behind and forgotten as the court throng traveled on again. Boccaccio mollified himself for a few months by staying with a dear friend Mainardo de' Cavalcanti and then, in the spring of 1363, headed back towards Certaldo, finished forever with dreams of being court poet at Naples.

Boccaccio had brought with him to Naples two finished volumes, the *De casibus* and the *De mulieribus* the latter dedicated to Acciauoli's sister, the former originally to King Louis but, since the king's death, intended perhaps for Niccola himself. After his experiences at court, however, he dedicated the *De casibus* to his more welcoming host, Mainardo. On his way home, he visited other friends, Barbato at Sulmona and Petrarch in Venice, whose reception surely made up for the offenses of Acciaiuoli. Petrarch even offered once again to share his home and library with his old friend; but Boccaccio, still smarting from the results of Acciauoli's invitation and anxious lest this most valuable friendship be spoiled by an attempt to live together, declined.

In 1365 and again two years later Boccaccio was sent by the city of Florence to the pope at Avignon to discuss the return of the papal court to Rome and to offer Florentine support as a way of preventing another descent into Italy by the emperor Charles IV. Thus Boccaccio was politically active in direct opposition to the aims of Petrarch, who had exhorted the emperor to return to Rome. At Avignon Boccaccio had occasion to converse with friends of Petrarch such as Francesco Bruni and Philippe de Cabassoles. The following year Boccaccio sent to Petrarch his completed Homeric translations. Thus their shared literary and spiritual interests survived their continuing political differences. And while the development of Boccaccio's humanism has generally been attributed to Petrarch's influence, Branca has argued that Petrarch's enthusiasm for his own Italian lyrics in the later years of his life as well as his work on the *Trionfi* reflects the reciprocal influence of Boccaccio, who had long insisted on the importance and potential greatness of vernacular literature demonstrated by Dante.[6]

Through Francesco Bruni, whom Boccaccio saw again in 1367 on a mission to the newly moved papal court at Rome, Boccaccio became ac-

---

[6] "Profilo," pp.138-39, 176.

quainted with the young Coluccio Salutati, who was to be so important for the continuation of the humanistic enterprise. Salutati admired Boccaccio ardently and eventually sent to him his own eclogues, now lost, for comment and correction. Boccaccio and Petrarch, together again in Padua in 1368, wrote a joint letter to the young literary enthusiast and to his mentor Bruni. This was the last encounter of the two great writers, with whom one can say the Renaissance began. Boccaccio consciously described his time as a new era in which both visual and literary arts had been reborn.[7]

We have few documents from the last years of Boccaccio's life. Sacchetti, one of the early imitators of the *Decameron*, reports a rumor that Boccaccio had become a monk at Naples (sonnet 150), a report seemingly corroborated by a letter of Boccaccio's from the monastery of Santo Stefano del Bosco, describing his enjoyment of the peace and quiet. But he was back in Certaldo by 1371. He was famous by now (the *Genealogia* was especially successful) and was sought after with offers of hospitality by Ugo di San Severino, backed by the persuasive efforts of Naples' Queen Joan, by the Queen's husband Giacomo di Maiorca, and, separately, by the Count of Nola. He refused them all, as he mentions in his final eclogue, preferring to live alone with his books in his own home. Despite his ultimate success, he was assailed by doubts about his value as a writer. His letter to Iacopo Pizzinga (1372), while proclaiming how Italian letters are reaching the level of the best ancient literature, describes himself as gazing upwards towards the peaks of Parnassus which domestic and public distractions have prevented him from reaching, too weary and discouraged to continue climbing yet ashamed to turn back. His later eclogues depict him in the same situation with regard to both the literary and spiritual quest: he is always near the bottom of the mountain, hesitatingly and unconfidently trying to follow Petrarch towards either Poetry or God.

Both Petrarch and Boccaccio were struggling with ill health. In a moment of respite in 1372, Boccaccio finished and sent out at last the *Buccolicum carmen* which he had written over many decades. The accompanying letter to Fra Martino da Signa gave brief explanations of the basic allegory in each poem, leaving many details to be worked out by the studious reader. Also at this time, he began to read and comment publicly on Dante's *Commedia* in a series of lectures in Florence, not at the university, which had as yet no place for vernacular literatures, but in a church near Dante's house. The lectures were well attended. The humanist leader Coluccio Salutati, the poet and story-writer Franco Sacchetti, Filippo Villani, Boccaccio's biog-

---

[7] See his letter to Iacopo Pizzinga about Petrarch and the *Decameron* 6.5 about Giotto as initiators of a new era.

rapher as well as Florentine historian, the poet Antonio Pucci, Benvenuto da Imola, commentator on the *Commedia* and on the eclogues of Petrarch, and other men of letters were in Florence at the time and probably attended these lectures. Certainly Boccaccio was still very much involved with and admired by the current literary circles. In his will Boccaccio bequeathed his books to the Augustinian monastery of Santo Spirito in Florence to be available as a kind of public library. Also in Florence during 1373-74 was Geoffrey Chaucer, whose works reveal an acquaintance with and a debt to nearly everything Boccaccio wrote in Italian. Could the two have met? We can only speculate fondly.

Recurring poor health, coupled with misgivings that he was prostituting the muses by trying to explain the *Commedia* to an audience unable to understand truly the lofty heights of poetry, caused Boccaccio to interrupt his Dante lectures, which were never resumed. Four sonnets (122-125) express regret for the whole enterprise.[8]   It is fitting, nonetheless, that Boccaccio's final large undertaking should be devoted to the author who, even more than Petrarch, had inspired Boccaccio's entire career, and whom Boccaccio had acknowledged (*Amorosa visione* 6.2-3) as "il maestro dal qual io/ tengo ogni ben" (the master/teacher from whom I have everything that is any good).

He used a similar phrase for Petrarch in a letter to Francesco da Brossano at the news of Petrarch's death in the summer 1374: "cui quantum habeo tantum debeo" (to whom I owe all that I have). Of Italy's "three crowns" Boccaccio was now the lone survivor, old and ill. Coluccio Salutati, who had become chancellor of the Florentine Republic, came to visit Boccaccio in Certaldo during his final year and to talk about Petrarch. In a letter to their common friend Donatus, Salutati described Boccaccio and Petrarch justly as the two lights of their age.

Boccaccio died in December 1375, having composed for himself a Latin epitaph which may be translated as follows:

> Beneath this mound lie the ashes and bones of Giovanni: His
> mind dressed in the merits of the labors of his mortal life
> sits before God. His father was Bocchaccius, his homeland
> Certaldo, his pursuit was nourishing poetry.

Salutati added some further verses in Latin which list and praise Boccaccio's Latin works, referring briefly to the popularity of his vernacular writings. The poet and short story writer Sacchetti too, in Italian, lamented

---

[8] *Rime*, ed. Vittore Branca (Padua 1958).

the loss of the last great poet of Italy (canzone 181): "un sol c'era rimaso,/ Giovan Boccacci, or è di vita fore" (One alone was left to us, Giovanni Boccaccio, who now is dead). It was appropriate that Boccaccio receive homage in both languages, Latin and Italian, and in both prose and poetry, and from two writers who reflected the lofty and the popular sides of Boccaccio's own writing.

Artistic Achievement

The Bucolic Genre

The words bucolic and eclogue have long been defined as a whole and its parts: Vergil's *Bucolica* contained ten eclogues. Commentaries had no trouble deriving *bucolica* from βουκολος or cowherd, but the word εκλογη was more problematic and gave rise to a variety of interpretations. The *Vita Monacensis* on Vergil gave the original meaning correctly as "excerpt" or "selection," from the Greek εκ λεγειν. [9] Thus the *Eclogarum libri* of Ausonius and others were volumes of short pieces not connected to each other.[10] The *Vita Gudiana*, however, derived the word from αιγο-λογος or "goat speech".[11] The association with the meaning of *bucolica* made this derivation irresistible, and it took over during the Middle Ages and Renaissance. It was supported not only by glosses to Vergil but also by the scholia on Horace, which referred to his satires as eclogues "since the speech comprises common and lowly words, or is called an eclogue, that is lowly speech. *Eglos* in Greek is *goat* in Latin: as a lowly and common song. In this book the matter it treats is the vices of men, which it intends to censure."[12] This definition contains already much of the development of the genre. The low style associated with goatherds is linked to the topic of moral satire. Linguistic proximity between "satire" and "satyr" further encouraged the connection. The "General Argument" to Spenser's *Shepheardes Calender* explicitly rejected a confused derivation from εκ-λογος or "extraordinary discourses of unnecessarie matter" in favor of the derivation as goatherds' tales.

---

[9] Iacobus Brummer, *Vitae Vergilianae* (Leipzig: B.G. Teubner, 1912), p.59.
[10] Doris Lessig, *Ursprung und Entwicklung der spanischen Ekloge bis 1650* (Geneva: Droz, 1962), p.30.
[11] Brummer, *Vitae Vergilianae*, p.64.
[12] Cited by Lessig, *Ursprung*, p.28; see also H.J. Botschauer ed., *Scholia ad Horatium* (Amsterdam, 1942), Vol.4, p.187.

A third term was quickly added to these two: that of comedy. The *Vita Monacensis* had followed its correct derivation with the further observation that "it could also be called 'colloquium' because of being a collection from many books or stories..."[13] The notion of "colloquium" became naturally associated with the dialogic nature of many of the poems. Servius' commentary on the Vergilian eclogues had pointed out its combination of narrative and dramatic modes. By the eleventh century Papias' *Elementarium doctrinae rudimentum* listed eclogue and comedy as two examples of drama, and in the twelfth century Alain de Lille's *Distinctiones* (*PL* 210, 776) gave Vergil and Theodulus as examples of dramatic verse. Renaissance theorists followed suit: Trissino and Minturno listed eclogues with comedy and tragedy as types of dramatic poetry, and Scaliger even suggested that the eclogue had been the source from which comedy developed.[14]

Around 1200 Geoffrey of Vinsauf described *argumentum* as "a not true but verisimilar fiction, such as eclogues and comedies. Eclogue is a discourse woven about the actions of lowly persons and is called stinking or goaty speech. And it is triple: for some consist in bitter reprehensions, and that part is satire, and is the kind used by Horace; some in the colloquy of lowly persons, as in the *Bucolics*; others in the colloquy of an honest person against a lowly one, as in Theodulus, where Pseustis, by whom we understand falsehood, disputes with Alithia, by whom truth is denoted."[15] Here all the associations are combined: dramatic dialogue, lowly persons and style, satire, and moral didacticism. The emphasis was not on reproducing peasant song but on using fictive or even allegorical peasants to comment on the mores of general human society. John of Garland's own proffered example in his *Parisiana Poetria* is an allegory about Coridon's loss of his beloved nymph to another lover; John explains: "By the nymph is signified the flesh; by the youthful seducer, the world or devil; by her proper love [Coridon], reason."[16] As Puttenham described the genre in his *Arte of English Poesie* (1.18) in 1589: "I do deny that the Eglogue should be the first and most aunctient forme of artificiall Poesie, being perswaded that the Poet devised the Eglogue long after the other dramatick poems, not of purpose to counterfait or represent the rusticall manner of loves and communication, but under the vaile of homely persons and in rude speeches to insinuate and glaunce

---

[13] Brummer, *Vitae Vergilianae*, p.59.
[14] Lessig, *Ursprung*, pp.32-34.
[15] "Appendix Two: Geoffrey of Vinsauf's *Documentum* in John of Garland, *The Parisiana Poetria*, ed. with transl. by Traugott Lawler (New Haven: Yale University Press, 1974), p.332.
[16] John of Garland, *Parisiana Poetria*, pp.24-25.

at greater matters, and such as perchance had not bene safe to have been disclosed in any other sort, which may be perceived by the Eglogues of Virgill, in which are treated by figure matters of greater importance than the loves of Titirus and Corydon. These Eglogues came after to containe and enforme morall discipline, for the amendment of mans behaviour, as be those of Mantuan and other moderne Poets."[17] The notion that political contents might make the poet hide his message in order to protect himself was not without foundation. Petrarch was in fact brought before the curia because certain prelates had suspected him of attacking them in his eclogues; and Petrarch referred to that event as his reason for omitting all names in the *Epistolae sine nomine* (Preface).[18]

Puttenham's initial argument is directed against the tradition, established by Donatus, that bucolics "very probably take their origin from the most ancient times, in which the pastoral life was led, and therefore in the simplicity of persons is perceived the appearance of the golden age..."[19] Besides suggesting the real primitiveness of early bucolics, Donatus fostered the idea of the pastoral realm as an idyllic image of life, which could authorize its innocent inhabitants to inveigh justly against the corrupted world.

Boccaccio's own descriptions of the genre in his *Genealogia deorum* echo the traditional poetics. The main mention of this genre comes fittingly under the chapter heading: "It is a fool's notion that poets convey no meaning beneath the surface of their fictions" (14.10). "Let any man, then, read the line in Vergil's *Bucolics*: 'He sung the secret seeds of Nature's frame,' and what follows on the same matter...This is poetry from which the sap of philosophy runs pure." Turning to the modern example of Petrarch, he continues: "Is there anyone sane enough to suppose that he devoted all those watches of the night, all those holy seasons of meditation, all those hours and days and years – which we have a right to assume that he did, considering the force and dignity of his bucolic verse, the exquisite beauty of his style and diction – I say, would he have taken such pains merely to represent Gallus begging Tyrrhenus for his reeds, or Pamphilus and Mitio in a squabble, or other like pastoral nonsense? No man in his right mind

---

[17] In G. Gregory Smith ed., *Elizabethan Critical Essays* (1904; rpt. Oxford University Press, 1971), vol.2, p.40.

[18] See also Robert Coogan, "The Nature, Artistry and Influence of Petrarch's 'Epistolae sine nomine'," *Acta Conventus Neo-Latini Turonensis (1976)* (Paris: Vrin, 1980), pp.114-15.

[19] Brummer, *Vitae Vergilianae*, p.13. See also Werner Krauss, "Über die Stellung der Bukolik in der ästhetischen Theorie des Humanismus," *Gesammelte Aufsätze zur Literatur und Sprachwissenschaft* (Frankfurt: Klostermann, 1949), 68-93.

will agree that these were his final object." In the bucolics and the *Remedies for all fortunes*, Petrarch has presented "all that is clear and holy in the bosom of moral philosophy." Finally, he concludes: "I would cite also my own eclogues, of whose meaning I am, of course, fully aware; but I have decided not to, partly because I am not great enough to be associated with the most distinguished men, and partly because the discussion of one's attainments had better be left to others."[20]   As the context is a discussion of literary interpretation, Boccaccio's focus is on the allegory or meaning of these poems, especially their moral meaning, rather than on their classification as satire or drama. Nonetheless, in his brief description of their typical pastoral contents, the dialogic, comic, and satiric qualities of the verses are implied.[21]

Boccaccio's letter to Fra Martino da Signa, accompanying a copy of the *Buccolicum carmen*, made an effort to distinguish Boccaccio's pastoral from Petrarch's. Describing three types of eclogue, Theocritus's superficial idylls, Vergil's occasionally but not persistently allegorical verses, and Petrarch's thoroughly allegorical poems in which every figure represents something else, Boccaccio identified his own eclogues with the Vergilian. His notes on the eclogues sometimes explain that a name has no special meaning, that a servant or a girl is simply that, without further significance. The early amorous eclogues are certainly the least allegorical, but they are also the ones about whose serious value Boccaccio felt most apologetic and uncertain. Thus allegory, while occasionally set aside, remained for Boccaccio one of the main means of justifying poetry's importance against the accusations of falsehood and frivolity. Where allegory subsides, moral example takes over, maintaining the didactic emphasis.

The assumed allegorical and didactic nature of bucolics raised a serious question about its proper stylistic level. Petrarch's eclogues were criticized by contemporaries precisely for being too lofty in style, although Petrarch considered their lofty content to deserve such treatment. In a letter to Boccaccio (*Seniles* 2.1, 1363) Petrarch complained of critics barking everywhere and discouraging him from showing his poetry at all. "They say that the style of my Bucolics is excessively more sublime than suits a pastoral mat-

---

[20] The translation is by Charles Osgood, *Boccaccio on Poetry* (1930; rpt. Indianapolis: Bobbs-Merrill, 1956), pp.52-54.
[21] Boccaccio copied into his zibaldone a gloss to Ovid's *Metamorphoses* (4.51-53) which identifies the whispering reeds of the Midas story as "fistule pastorum" or shepherds' pipes (Giorgio Padoan, "Giovanni Boccaccio e la rinascita dello stile bucolico," *Giovanni Boccaccio editore e interprete di Dante*, Florence, 1979, p.58). This might well imply a pastoral poetry satirically critical of ruling powers.

ter." But "as it seems to me, I said nothing in a style more sublime than what I wanted, and than befitted the nature of what was said." However, Thomas Bergin, for all the respectfulness of his translation and commentary, remarks: "And in truth, the *Carmen* produces on the reader of today something of the effect we might feel if a great statesman appeared before us, clad in a Roman toga, to speak in Shakespearean iambics on the subject of inflation or unemployment."[22]

The mix of high and low had felt problematic already to early readers of Vergil's *Bucolica*, who complained that a number of the eclogues were not truly pastoral. Vergil himself was conscious of going beyond the genre's traditional bounds, not only in presenting the elegiac poet in eclogue 10, but also in composing the central three elevated eclogues, introduced with the famous "paulo maiora canamus" [let us sing for a while of greater things] and with the replacement of humble shrubs by loftier forests (4.1-3).[23] Vergil's poems keep mentioning consuls and Augustus, though they remain off-stage; Boccaccio not only wrote nearly half of his eclogues about kings, a grand seneschal, and the emperor, but also included them as shepherd speakers. While the idea of a king as the shepherd of his people seemed natural enough, anyone who had written on the high, low, and middle styles knew that kings belonged to the highest genres, epic and tragedy. To set them forth among citizens as a shepherd among shepherds was already to degrade their authority. Nor is it surprising, therefore, that, apart from King Robert, none of these ruling figures is well treated by the poet.

If high political themes were lowered by satirical treatment, there was another lofty topic which Boccaccio treated with the utmost seriousness: religion. Here again the images of shepherd and sheep were sanctioned by tradition and by Scripture. Secondly, the humble style of the New Testament was explicitly acknowledged, e.g. in Petrarch's first eclogue, where he opposed it to the elegance of classical poetry. Thirdly, Donatus and Fulgentius, pairing Vergil's three works with the three kinds of life, identified the *Bucolica* with the contemplative, since shepherds have time to sit around thinking and watching the stars. Thus Boccaccio could justify to himself the use of pastoral for religious and philosophical topics. Indeed, part of the Christian message was that high and low would be confounded in a new

---

[22] Thomas Bergin, *Petrarch's Bucolicum Carmen* (New Haven: Yale University Press, 1974), pp.xiii-xiv.

[23] Charles Segal, *Poetry and Myth in Ancient Pastoral* (Princeton: Princeton University Press, 1981), p.264, further points out how "the larger potentials of the pastoral frame" are suggested also by invocations to Jupiter or Apollo and by the description of cups depicting Orpheus and astronomers.

order.

The final justification for the mix of high and low, I think, was Dante, whose *Commedia*, written in the vulgar tongue and making unabashed use of all levels of vocabulary, dared to encompass the entire universe and the vision of God. Boccaccio's *Trattatello in laude di Dante* [24] recounted the prophetic dream of Dante's mother before his birth; it is itself a pastoral allegory: "It seemed to the gentle lady in her sleep that she was beneath a very tall laurel on a green meadow beside a clear spring, and there she seemed to bring forth a son who, in very brief time, nourishing himself only with the berries that fell from the laurel and with the water from the clear spring, seemed to her to become a shepherd, and tried as best he could to pluck the leaves of the tree whose fruit had nourished him..." Already the rural scene and humble status of shepherd are linked allegorically to the loftiest literary education and ambition of a poet who will be through his poetry a spiritual guide and scribe of God. It is with Dante's *Commedia* that Boccaccio repeatedly associated Petrarch's eclogues as examples of a poetry of wisdom (*Genealogia* 14.10 and 22); for "Dante was a great theologian as well as a philosopher." To establish a basis for his view of poetry as a special discourse of holy wisdom, Boccaccio suggested its origins in the need of the ancients to create an elevated mode of speech for their prayers and praises to God; the creation of verses came about, reciprocally, "under the prompting stimulus of the Divine Mind" (*Geneal.* 14.8). Balduino has remarked that the bucolic poetry of Petrarch and Boccaccio fit this poetic theory better than most contemporary vernacular lyrics, including their own.[25] One might add that Boccaccio's Latin eclogues shifted ever closer to fulfilling his own theory, as the eclogues of emotional expression or historical commentary were succeeded by eclogues of moral and theological teaching. We should also point out, however, that his early vernacular eclogues in the *Comedia delle ninfe fiorentine* were already close to this goal with their clearly Christian educative content, and that Boccaccio's final eclogues can be seen in a way as a return to and Latin reworking of his original Italian pastoral. While writing both his earliest and his latest eclogues, Boccaccio had Dante clearly in mind, as we shall see, so that the *Commedia* curiously contributed to his conception of the bucolic genre.

---

[24] Ed. Pier Giorgio Ricci, *Tutte le opere* vol.3, Verona 1974), pp.441-42.
[25] Armando Balduino, *Boccaccio, Petrarca e altri poeti del Trecento*, Florence: Olschki, 1984, pp.38-39.

Boccaccio's pastoral poetry

Boccaccio's interest in the eclogue genre spans most of his writing career, from when he was a young man in his twenties until the end of his life. During those thirty years or so, his ideas about the genre changed radically several times, as did his choice of literary models. The obvious and chief model all along was Vergil, of course, but as one classicist has commented: "Vergil's eclogues do not easily yield a definition of pastoral."[26] Thus it was Boccaccio's problem to decide what he thought the genre was all about. The other writer whom Boccaccio sought humbly to imitate all his life was, of course, Dante, whose pastoral correspondence with Giovanni del Virgilio, with commentary, Boccaccio had copied into his notebooks previous to any pastoral composition of his own.[27]

Boccaccio's first two eclogues drew more from Dante than from Vergil; however, they looked not to the pastoral correspondence but to the *Commedia* for a model. The eclogues, one a monologue and one a dialogue, are inserted in the *Comedia delle ninfe fiorentine*, whose very title conveys its dependence on Dante's greatest work. Furthermore, the eclogues are written in Italian and in the terza rima verse form of Dante's *Commedia*. The framing narrative presents seven nymphs who turn out to be the virtues and who borrow for themselves (45.7) the line from Purgatory 31.106: "Noi siam qui ninfe, e nel ciel siamo stelle" (Here we are nymphs, and in heaven we are stars). The topics of the eclogues, too, seem more closely related to the *Commedia* than to the Latin pastoral epistles. In the first, Theoagapen expresses the desire to ascend to heaven, and then discusses the seven sins which must be avoided by anyone who wants to enter paradise. The second eclogue is a debate between the good shepherd Alcestus, who leads his small flock up to the healthful air of the high mountains, and the bad shepherd Acaten, who conveniently pastures his more numerous but sickly sheep in the lowlands. Clearly the meaning is both moral and religious, concerned with a choice of ways of life as well as a distinction between good ecclesiastics who care for the welfare of their charges and bad ones who care only for their own pleasure and profits. But the eclogue suggests literary meanings too, and has been interpreted by Hortis as a debate between two kinds of pastoral: the Theocritan (known to Boccaccio only from descriptions in the commentaries on Vergil's *Bucolica*), sensual and superficial, in contrast

---

[26] Eleanor Winsor Leach, *Vergil's Eclogues: Landscapes of Experience* (Ithaca: Cornell University Press, 1974), p. 19.

[27] See the discussion under "Sources".

to the Vergilian, allegorical and therefore more difficult and intellectual.[28] Boccaccio was clearly trying to write the Vergilian kind here, and to introduce lofty writing of this kind into the vernacular. So too his *Teseida*, written within a year of the *Comedia delle ninfe*, claims proudly to be the first martial epic in Italian. Thus his first eclogues, and indeed the whole pastoral narrative of the work into which they are set, can be seen as part of a general program to produce an Italian literature glorified by the various classical genres. While Vergil provided a model for classical genres, Dante provided the demonstration that a great Italian literature, as rich and glorious as the ancient Latin, was truly possible. This is one of Boccaccio's major differences from Petrarch, whose eclogues and epic were all in Latin and who disavowed the vernacular as an appropriate vehicle for great literature. The later Renaissance would vindicate Boccaccio's early view.

Boccaccio's next eclogues, although probably not much later in time of composition, were no longer part of this program of *translatio*. They, and all the rest of Boccaccio's bucolics, were written in Latin; and it is only the Latin eclogues that Boccaccio finally published together under the title of *Buccolicum carmen*. Eclogues 1 and 2 of this collection seem from their contents to have been written soon after Boccaccio's return from Naples to Florence in 1341, an event referred to also in the *Comedia delle ninfe*. They are heavily Vergilian, containing numerous echoes from various Vergil eclogues. The poems are not set into any external narrative context, as the previous ones had been; nor is it clear that Boccaccio as yet intended to compose an entire set of these poems. Rather the pair can be seen, at least

---

[28] Attilio Hortis, *Studi sulle opere latine del Boccaccio* (Trieste 1879), 66-67. His reading is supported by Aldo Rossi, "Boccaccio autore della corrispondenza Dante-Giovanni del Virgilio," in *Scritti su Giovanni Boccaccio*, ed. Rafaello Ramat et al. (Florence: Olschki, 1964), 50-53, and by Annabel Patterson, "Vergil's *Eclogues*: Images of Change," *Roman Images. Selected Papers from the English Institute 1982*, N.S. 8, ed. Annabel Patterson, 167-68. Enrico Carrara, *La Poesia pastorale* (Milano: Dottor Francesco Vallardi, n.d.), 160, disagrees, arguing that the general thrust of the eclogue is clearly moral rather than literary. Padoan, "Boccaccio e il rinascimento dello stile bucolico," 29, while conceding that Carrara is correct about the eclogue as a whole, nonetheless maintains that Hortis was not entirely wrong to see literary meanings sporadically introduced. He further supports Hortis' suggeston by noting that in Boccaccio's notebook the copy of Dante's first eclogue includes a gloss on lines 11-12 which interprets pastures and mountains as the bucolic style and its allegorical character. Verses from this poem – about the grass which keeps sheep fat but famished versus that which keeps them lean but truly nourished – reappear in Boccaccio's Latin eclogue 15, written much later, where the meanings are certainly religious rather than literary.

in part, as a rhetorical exercise in which the same basic topic is treated in two different ways: through dramatic dialogue, into which the author's voice never enters, and through a monologue framed briefly by the author's narrative. The variation of mode is itself an imitation of Vergil's art; for Servius had noted in his introductory comments on Vergil's third eclogue that Vergil intentionally mixed the narrative and dramatic modes in order to avoid monotony. The pair of eclogues in the *Comedia delle ninfe* consisted similarly in a monologue and a dialogue.

Boccaccio in the explanatory letter that accompanied his complete *Buccolicum carmen* says very little about these eclogues, which were his first two Latin poems of any kind, besides remarking that they "fere iuveniles lascivias meas in cortice pandunt" (openly bear on the outside my youthful lusts as it were).[29] Possibly they came to include other meanings as well, however. In their later position within the total sequence, they contrast with eclogues fourteen and fifteen about turning one's love from earthly to heavenly pursuits. Boccaccio in the fifteenth accuses himself of pursuing both money and women; those (or perhaps ambition rather than desire for money) can be seen as precisely the two pursuits of Tindarus and Damon in the first eclogue. Thus it would be possible to see them as part of a moral plot running through the entire sequence.[30]

There are also hints of literary meaning in this early poem. Damon, who had just begun to learn singing when he met his Galla, loses his girl to a superior singer, Pamphylus, for whom the woods and animals pause to listen.

> "O how much power, Pamphylus, did nature
> mother of all things, grant unto you!
> You know just how to weave the flower garlands,
> how by your singing to refresh the flocks
> and hush the rivulets, and how to move
> the sturdy mountain ash and even rocks,
> how to appease the gods and bend the mountains."

As this seemingly Orphic poet uses his song for purposes of seduction, it is not clear whether he really represents a loftier kind of poetry; but in

---

[29] These early Latin eclogues, written at roughly the same time as the Italian ones, show that Boccaccio was using both languages all along, and did not, as is sometimes claimed, switch from Italian to Latin later in life under the influence of Petrarch's humanism.

[30] Giacomo Lidonnici, "Il significato storico e psicologico del *Buccolicum Carmen* e la sua cronologia," in his edition of *Il Buccolicum Carmen* (Città di Castello, Casa Editrice S. Lapi, 1914), suggests a plausible storyline to the whole sequence.

any case, Damon's lament does imply a fearful praise of the sheer power of rhetoric and a rivalry in poetic power as well as in love. So too the *Filocolo* (5.8) had narrated the account of an unhappy novice poet, Idalagos, whose girl is lured away by the piping of a better musician. The *Filocolo* episode includes also a third singer, Calmeta, who represents truly lofty and intellectual poetry. In the *Buccolicum carmen* this lofty poetry is represented in the twelfth eclogue by Saphos. Thus the sequence may be seen to contain a literary plot as well as a moral one: a conversion from sensual song to intellectual poetry, from verse about the love for women to verse about the road to heaven. Eclogue two also seeks inclusion within this literary plot; for its line 84 "Nasilus taught me truly in the distant forests" implies Boccaccio's apprenticeship to Ovid (an influence apparent in most of his works) and the services offered by the abandoned lover include story-telling at bedtime, "to drive away heavy cares from the mind."

In 1347 Boccaccio wrote another Latin eclogue, this time in the epistolary mode of the Dante-Giovanni del Virgilio correspondence. It was addressed to Checco da Mileto (Francesco dei Rossi), another secretary at the court of Ordelaffi in Forlì. Like Vergil's first eclogue, it contrasts the bitterness of political realities with the sweetness of the peaceful bucolic world. Boccaccio's new twist is to invite Checco to join him for a walk in the pastoral landscape, that is, to join Boccaccio in turning away from the political world into the realm of poetic activity.[31] Boccaccio's poem describes the themes available to the bucolic genre:

> Indeed you know, my Moeris, the Muses love
> alternate songs; and let the loves of shepherds
> or Dyone's mighty weapons be the limit
> of our piping, not strong enough to sing
> of higher things. I too know Paphos and
> the flames of Venus, Cupid's savage blows,
> for wanton Galathea's gentle face
> keeps me in sighs, nor quells my fiercer flames;
> and if perhaps the sheep are not my care,
> yet goats have long been so. Then let us leave
> the works of men and gods to Mopsus, whom
> we saw binding green laurel on his brow.
> He's singing now upon the mountain top
> with his sistrum a song about the gods.
> A work at which I'm aiming speedily

---

[31] For an extended discussion of this poem and its relation to the Dante-Giovanni del Virgilio epistles, see Krautter, *Renaissance der Bukolik*, pp.69-80.

sees me weaving a fence of forest twigs."

The emphasis on erotic themes, picked up by Boccaccio from the ancient eclogue and not shared by Dante, Giovanni del Virgilio, or Petrarch, was to become a major part of later pastoral poetry. The explicit contrast between his humble poetry and Petrarch's (Mopsus's) epic ambition is also a new emphasis, underscored by his pursuit of a "myrtle" rather than a laurel crown[32] and his status as goatherd rather than shepherd. Is the work at which Boccaccio aims a pastoral sequence? The image of weaving twigs certainly derives from Vergil's metaphor for writing bucolic verse (Ecl.10.70-71); and coming, as it does, in the last of Vergil's eclogues, it may refer to the entire set. For Boccaccio, the weaving could suggest not only the weaving of words into a single poem or the connecting of individual eclogues into a *carmen* but also the alternation of songs with Checco. In sum, Boccaccio's contrast of real and idyllic worlds, his presentation of a coherent pastoral realm which is not an allegorical referent to real places but an autonomous albeit metaphoric space, his image of twig-weaving for his own poetic labor and his identification of goatherds' songs with love songs all place Boccaccio much closer to Vergil than either Dante or Giovanni del Virgilio had been. Whereas Dante had used an old genre in a new way for a personal occasion, Boccaccio was approaching a revival of the genre for itself. Given the dominance of the love theme in Boccaccio's list of possible topics, one can infer that the two love eclogues written earlier were intended as part of an ongoing project of classical revival. It is worth remarking the conceptual contrast present from the start between his Italian eclogues, which under the influence of Dante treat serious religious themes, and the Latin ones, which, closer to the ancient pagan model, concern themselves with love and poetry.

After these three Latin poems there came a sharp break in Boccaccio's ideas about the genre. Despite the rejection of public themes in his first poem to Checco, Boccaccio's second poem to this friend embraced the very political topics previously eschewed. This revolution in Boccaccio's concept of the genre was occasioned by the circulation of Petrarch's "Argus" eclogue. In the "Argus" Petrarch and two of his friends, under pastoral names, mourn the death of King Robert of Naples in a pair of songs based on Vergil's fifth eclogue for the death of Daphnis (usually glossed as Caesar). Within a year Boccaccio had produced his fourth Latin pastoral poem, a combination of Dantean and Petrarchan influences. Like Dante's it is again an epistle to his friend Checco, but the theme is political, closely following Petrarch's tracks, with a eulogy of the dead King Robert and an account of recent political

---

[32] Krautter, *Renaissance der Bukolik*, pp.75-76.

events involving Naples and Forlì, where Boccaccio was currently residing. The differences between this poem and its source of inspiration, however, are indicative of major differences between the two poets. There is no trace of the Vergilian model in Boccaccio's version. Instead, Boccaccio drew from Dante's pastoral epistle the dramatic structure of a dialogue interrupted by the arrival of a third speaker with news to report. Petrarch's lyrical emphasis has been replaced by a narrative which continues well beyond the events in Petrarch's poem. Furthermore the direct emotional involvement of Petrarch's two singers, who are residents of Naples, yields to the geographical and emotional detachment of Boccaccio's interlocutors, as perhaps befits a shift from lyrical to narrative modes. Boccaccio rewrote this poem as eclogue 3 of his final sequence, and followed it with six more political eclogues: three more on events in Naples, two on Florentine worries about the coronation of Charles IV as emperor and his descent into Italy, and one harsh diatribe against the crimes and corruption of Niccola Acciaiuoli, grand seneschal of the Neapolitan court. The events included take us up to 1355, although a few later passages were also added.

In these political eclogues, the pastoral realm ceased to represent a separate world of poetry and became, as for Dante, Giovanni del Virgilio, and Petrarch, a coded version of real places. Although previously the lovelorn shepherds and nymphs had not been specifically referent, now the characters represented identifiable historical persons or states. Once again drawing from Vergil via Servius rather than from Dante or what he knew as yet of Petrarch, Boccaccio used women to represent places: Forlì and Naples. Furthermore, following his own literary inclinations rather than any previous model, Boccaccio made of the series of Neapolitan eclogues a continuous narrative recounting the events from King Robert's death, through the King of Hungary's invasion and the flight of Louis and Joan, to their restoration as rulers of Naples. The linking of eclogues in the pursuit of a topic, which occurs for both Florentine and Neapolitan subjects, was a novelty in the genre which encouraged its incorporation into narrative.[33] Ultimately the entire sequence, with its multiplicity of themes, would similarly be given a narrative form.

The eighth eclogue with its harsh invective was another new mode for Boccaccian pastoral, and seems to be roughly contemporary with his equally harsh *Corbaccio*. It was a mode perhaps supported by the verbal connection between "satire" and "satyr." Certainly Petrarch acknowledged this link when discussing his own *Bucolicum carmen* in the preface to his scathing *Liber*

---

[33] Mantuan links even more smoothly his eclogues 2-3 and 7-8. Sannazaro sets his sequence of pastoral poems into a narrative that would connect them all.

sine nomine.[34] Petrarch's central bucolic blast was directed against the worldly papal court at Avignon, Boccaccio's against perceived corruption at the court of Naples.[35] Both poets had once hoped to establish themselves in comfortable posts at the courts they later blasted; no doubt personal disappointments lent fire to their tongues. In any case, Boccaccio had not yet seen Petrarch's invective eclogues when he first drafted his own.

In working with the Vergilian model of political pastoral, both Petrarch and Boccaccio faced the same problem: Vergil, for better or for worse, had written a poetry of empire; and the central eclogue was commonly considered to treat the death and apotheosis of Caesar. But in the fourteenth century, there was no Italian center of empire. Even the papacy no longer resided in Rome but, disgracefully, in Avignon. What, then, could be made of Vergil's political example? For Petrarch, the homeless wanderer and disappointed seeker of a new Rome, there were a variety of temporary solutions to the felt need for a political court center: 1) King Robert's death might be likened to the death of Caesar, but it was followed by years of war and chaos rather than by the firm establishment of any new order; 2) Cola di Rienzo offered a brief object of enthusiasm but failed all too rapidly; 3) the papal court at Avignon acted as an anti-ideal.[36] It is significant that Petrarch's central poems are devoted to a seething attack on that court; Vergil's central apotheosis of the worldly governor is replaced by a negative vision of the total corruption and immersion in worldliness of the governor of the city of God on earth.

Boccaccio's central poem too is a harsh attack on corruption: in Naples, the very court which had taken Rome's place as the locus of political events described in the *Eclogues*. It is flanked by two negative poems about the new German emperor, and Florentine dismay that the great Roman laurels should crown an impotent barbarian. As a Florentine, Boccaccio's allegiance was to a republic, and he served several times as envoy from the commune on missions involving Florentine fears about the increasing dominance of the Visconti and the possible effects of the emperor's coronation. Any praises of royalty were safely displaced to the kingdom of Naples where subsequent events were too disastrous for glorification. The eighth eclogue can be viewed as Boccaccio's farewell to the idea of a Neapolitan Rome.

---

[34] See also Krautter, *Renaissance der Bukolik*, pp.134-35 and 147.

[35] For a defense of Acciaiuoli against what is termed an injustice done by Boccaccio, see Emile Léonard, "Nicolas Acciauoli victime de Boccace," *Mélanges offerts à Henri Hauvette* (Paris: Les Presses Françaises, 1934), 139-48.

[36] See also Janet Smarr, "Petrarch: A Vergil without a Rome," in *Rome in the Renaissance. The City and the Myth*, ed. P.A. Ramsey (Binghamton, N.Y.: Medieval & Renaissance Texts & Studies, 1982), 133-40.

Although Boccaccio began, like Petrarch, by using Naples as a substitute for Rome, he ended by celebrating his own impoverished freedom from any great court and defiantly dedicated his sequence not to any lord but to a private scholar. In fact, Boccaccio wrote one other pastoral epistle, in prose: a letter to Petrarch expressing his horror at Petrarch's betrayal of Florentine freedom by accepting the patronage of the dreaded Visconti ("Ut huic epistole," 1353). In this allegorical letter the pastoral translation of people and events is consciously chosen to formalize Boccaccio's painful emotions of outrage and dismay, and thus to buffer his personal attack on a friend. Vergil's intention in the eclogues was commonly thought to be the praise of members of Rome's government who had restored to Vergil his property. Boccaccio took the pastoral ultimately as a means to celebrate the intellectual labors of the private man independent from any political powers. His final gesture is, like Dante's reply to Giovanni del Virgilio, a refusal of an invitation, even from Petrarch, lest it compromise his total independence. The pastoral form suitably celebrates this separation from political involvements even though he had used it also to veil his earlier political discussions. In this way Boccaccio's last Latin eclogue comes close to his first epistle to Checco, in which bucolic poetry is seen as an escape from or alternative to political troubles.

After the political poems came another break in Boccaccio's conception of the genre, and once again the subsequent eclogues were in an entirely new mode. By the later 1350's Boccaccio was weary of political intrigues, at the end of a period of intensive public service, eager to take up some major new scholarly enterprises, and invested with a clerical benefice. [37] Abandoning political and historical themes and reverting to religious and literary topics, he wrote the following eclogues: 10- a description of hell, 11- a retelling of the Old and New Testament in mythological disguise on the model of Vergil's sixth eclogue with its series of myths, 12- the poet's pursuit of Saphos or lofty poetry, 13- a singing contest or debate between a rich merchant and a poor poet about where true value lies, 14- a vision of his dead daughter descending from heaven in order to describe paradise and exhort her father to join her there, 15- the conversion of Boccaccio, under the influence of Petrarch, from worldly to spiritual pursuits, and 16- the presentation of the eclogues as a flock of fifteen scrawny sheep to a humanist friend and grammarian, Donato degli Albanzani.

By 1359 Boccaccio had at last read Petrarch's entire bucolic sequence

---

[37] See Branca, "Profilo biografico," pp.106-07; Boccaccio was beginning work on the *Genealogia*, the *De casibus*, and the *De montibus*. See also Thomas Bergin, *Boccaccio* (New York, Viking Press, 1981), p.52.

and found there some poems about literature and the life of literary pursuit which offered him a further topic to explore. This topic was not entirely new; earlier eclogues of Boccaccio's, including the very first Italian ones and the first three in Latin, had contained suggestions of literary meanings, celebratory of the power of poetry and possibly indicative of a preference for allegorical over straightforward verse. But if his reading of Petrarch's *Bucolicum carmen* impelled him to look again at his own earlier ideas, it led him back into the arms of his first love, Dante.

Eclogues 12 and 15 present two parallel conversions and parallel mountain ascents, one from popular to lofty poetry and one from worldly to spiritual goals. Although Petrarch is named as guide for both ascents, the interweaving of purgatorial and literary mountains does not derive from Petrarch; for Petrarch's eclogues, although emphatic about the poet's role as spiritual leader, include only a Parnassus and not a purgatorial mountain. Boccaccio's source is rather the *Commedia*. In Purgatorio 22, Statius, acknowledging Vergil as the source of both his poetry and his salvation, says that Vergil's fourth eclogue led him first to Parnassus and then to God:

> Ed egli a lui: "Tu prima m'inviasti
> verso Parnaso a ber nelle sue grotte,
> e poi appresso Dio m'alluminasti.
> . . .
> Per te poeta fui, per te cristiano. (64-66, 73)

Boccaccio pays a similar compliment to Petrarch, suggesting that Petrarch has been his guide in both literary and spiritual matters. Yet the unnamed inspiration of his poems is also Dante, who led Boccaccio's eclogues to God. Thus implicitly all three of Boccaccio's guides, Vergil, Dante, and Petrarch, are represented.[38]

---

[38] Boccaccio's *Decameron* opens with another reference to Dante's double-natured mountain. The preface describes the *Decameron* itself as a steep, harsh mountain with a delightful garden on top. Later the group of young narrators climb up from the dying city to a villa garden to tell the tales which are the garden of that first image. While the infernal conditions of Florence and their resolve to flee its moral as well as its physical corruption render their ascent a spiritual one, their ensuing production of narratives makes the hill also analogous to Parnassus, hence justifying Boccaccio's claim in the beginning of day 4 that he has not been so far from the Muses as some people think. The initial mountain, for all that it represents a work of literature, is clearly moral as well as literary; for the narrator's movement from passionate melancholy to rational freedom parallels both the reader's and the brigata's movement from plague-ridden city to hilltop and furthermore invites the lovesick lady readers to participate in a similar remove. In the bucolic poems, Boccaccio

In Purgatory 28.141 Matelda, explaining that the ancient poets dreamed of Eden when they wrote about the golden age, says to Dante "forse in Parnaso esto loco sognaro" (perhaps in Parnassus they dreamed of this place). The juxtaposition of Parnassus with "esto loco" or Eden suggests a parallel between the contemplative but pagan ascent of Parnassus and the Christian ascent towards redemption. It also suggests that for Dante the two processes –of becoming a great poet and of becoming a true Christian – have merged, for it is the Christian vision that can give Dante his poetic power and goal. Petrarch's first eclogue, in contrast, opposes the ways of poet and monk, opposes classical and Scriptural poetry, and identifies Petrarch as an epic poet in the classical mode. Petrarch's stance in the "Monicus" may have suggested to Boccaccio how he could, with the aid of Dante, mark out for himself a separate, un-Petrarchan identity as a pastoral poet of Christian verse.

Boccaccio's twelfth eclogue on the ascent of Parnassus, even though partly modeled on Petrarch's third, not only replaces Petrarch's triumphal winning of the laurel crown with Boccaccio's much humbler venture as a beginner, but also sets the whole aspiration towards lofty poetry in the context of poems about the afterlife –immediately following a poem on hell and closely linked to one about purgatory. Thus it may imply that the ascent of poetry should be not only from vernacular to Latin but also from classical or worldly to Christian. Petrarch's sequence remains much more throroughly rooted in this life, albeit offering a choice between material and intellectual or moral pursuits. Boccaccio's fourteenth and fifteenth eclogues, in which his long-dead and beloved daughter exhorts him towards heaven and in which a purgatorial ascent promises to lead him to a reconciliation with heaven's King, end the main body of his sequence and definitely imply an ascent right out of this world. The final stanzaic pastoral song, set into the poem on paradise, is a hymn, and a model for the future use of pastoral in this way. The final lovely Arcadian spot described is heaven itself. And in the final line of his fifteenth poem, to be followed only by the dedication to Donato, Boccaccio bids farewell to his laurel as he sets off to win the palm of Christian triumph.

Boccaccio's later eclogues include some of the least Petrarchan ones and show how Dante's *Commedia* superseded Petrarch as a formative influence even in the writing of eclogues. Numbers ten, fourteen, and fifteen have been called Boccaccio's own inferno, paradise, and purgatory.[39]   It is

---

separated the two strands, literary and spiritual, but kept both versions.
[39] Enrico Carrara, *Poesia pastorale*, p.128, calls it Boccaccio's "oltretomba bucolica;" the relation to Dante's *Commedia* is further discussed on p.129. See also W. Leonard Grant,

typical of Boccaccio– the *Amorosa visione* presented an earlier example – that he inverts the order to offer a glimpse of paradise and then to end with his own humble position at the base of the purgatorial mountain. Whereas Petrarch, in his third eclogue, celebrates his coronation as the success of his love for Daphne, Boccaccio ends his twelfth eclogue still at the beginning of a long hard journey toward the Saphos he adores. Similarly poem fifteen shows him merely starting up the arduous path towards personal salvation. More modestly than Dante, he puts the reports of heaven and hell into the mouths of other characters, while making himself a direct witness only in the purgatorial poem of reluctant conversion. The eleventh eclogue, with its retelling of the Old and New Testament is also entirely unlike anything in Petrarch's sequence. The religious and otherworldly emphasis in this last set of eclogues presents a clear divergence not only from Petrarch but indeed from any pastoral model, reflecting instead Boccaccio's endless admiration for Dante and his persistent aim of writing a kind of literature that would be Christian as well as classical.

In Dante's Statius episode, it is Vergil's eclogues which drew Statius to accept Christian teachings, while the *Aeneid* more simply offered a moral correction to Statius' prodigality. As if to emphasize the special importance of the eclogue, which by citing the Sybil offered a true albeit unwitting prophecy of Christ and thus persuaded Statius to accept the truth of Christian messengers, Dante identifies Vergil as "il cantor de' bucolici canti" (57) in immediate contrast to Statius' identification as the poet of two epics. Perhaps Dante meant to contrast the emphasis of both Vergil's and Statius' epics on history and death with the fourth eclogue's promise of an all-redeeming birth.

Possibly the influence of Dante enabled Boccaccio to see in Vergil the seeds for his new kind of pastoral. The prophetic value of Vergil's fourth eclogue was a common topic of debate. So too the sixth, with its mythological account beginning at creation, an account which Silenus claims he was taught by Apollo and which he teaches in turn to the laurels, could be revised by Boccaccio into Scriptural narrative. As for Vergil's fifth eclogue, not only did it demonstrate the soul's ascent to heaven after death, but John of Garland had observed that one could turn its lines about Daphnis into lines about Christ.[40]   In sum, the entire center of Vergil's *Bucolica*, the section marked off as a higher kind of song, could be wilfully reinterpreted by a Christian reader or poet as suggesting the birth of Christ, his death and

---

Neo-Latin Literature and the Pastoral (Chapel Hill: University of North Carolina Press, 1965), p.109.

[40] *Parisiana poetria*, pp.22-25; and see below, under "Sources".

resurrection as God, and the transmission of his divine message to human apostles and poets. Pastoral verse could be turned into Christian poetry. Boccaccio's fourteenth eclogue dramatically reverses the normal pastoral time by taking place at night and ending with daybreak instead of dusk. This reversal allows Boccaccio not only to present the light of heaven entering a darkened world, but also to end with a line in which Christian comedy pierces through Vergilian tragedy: "et mediis iam sol emittitur umbris" (and already the sun is shining forth amid the shadows). That final "umbris," the word with which Vergil had chosen to end both his first and final eclogues, is pierced through by the sunlight of Christian revelation.

Boccaccio himself was no young writer when he finally sent the sequence to his friends in 1372. Having excoriated the corruption of the court from which he had hoped for patronage, Boccaccio ended by proudly dedicating his work to a poor grammarian, not to a nobleman. It asks for no monetary support, but only for the welcome of someone with shared spiritual and intellectual aims. Boccaccio himself remains poor but content with his independence in Certaldo. Thus he ends his sequence with a double self-image: one at the bottom of mount Purgatory, struggling humbly upward at Petrarch's urgings and with Petrarch's help; the other at the top of the hill in Certaldo, independent and proudly refusing even Petrarch's invitations. That proud refusal marks not only the rejection of financial assistance from a friend but, I think even more, the rejection of literary dependence on a man whose influence had threatened to overwhelm him. By turning back to Dante, the poet whom Petrarch had scornfully set aside, Boccaccio found a counter-influence which helped him mark out a territory of his own, at the confluence of the classical and medieval. Thus even his Latin poetry does not cease to acknowledge the potential for great poetry in the vernacular.

Boccaccio's view of the eclogue had come full circle, back to the *Commedia*-inspired vision of his very first Italian eclogues. Dante offered Boccaccio a means of distinguishing himself from his friend and competitor, Petrarch. Indeed, it is Boccaccio, and not Petrarch, who became the model for religious as well as for amatory eclogues later in the Renaissance.[41]

Even though the poems were written over many years, Boccaccio presented them as a set rather than as separate poems and gave, as I see it, a narrative shape to the arrangement.[42]   Poems 1-6 show a hopeful involvement in worldly affairs; poems 7-9 show how worldly success attends

---

[41] Later amatory eclogues drew their language frequently from Petrarch's *Canzoniere*, but not from his bucolics. The pastoralization of love poetry came initially from Vergil through Boccaccio.

[42] For other descriptions of an organized pattern to the whole sequence, see Lidonnici,

the unworthy; poems 10-15 turn to otherworldly aspirations, a concern for immortality either through poetry or through salvation. Thus we have a cycle from false hopes through despair to new and truer hopes. Boccaccio's sequence moves away from its dark political center – the eclogue on hell provides the pivot–towards poems of hopeful effort for personal improvement. Vergil's ten-poem and Petrarch's twelve-poem sequences were both clearly symmetrical in their organization.[43] So too, the separation of Boccaccio's poems 7 and 9 (about the new emperor) by 8 suggests the definition of a center and flanking symmetries. This general form in turn supports a pairing of the first two poems, about love for"nymphs," with the last two poems (before the dedication) about the conversion of love from fallible objects to God. However, there is not always so obvious a poem-by-poem correspondence across the center. The narrative form dominates the symmetrical, allowing for a sense of progress rather than return. Both Boccaccio's "plot" with its narrative line and Petrarch's "theme" with its balanced oppositions owe a great deal to Vergil's central eclogue. Boccaccio may have seen in the pair of songs that mourn Daphnis' death and celebrate his apotheosis a model for his own narrative turn from lamentations for the world's affairs to a hopeful seeking of more spiritual certainties.

Boccaccio and Petrarch

Even when Boccaccio wrote on Petrarchan themes, differences between the two friends are readily apparent. Let us consider pair by pair some analogous eclogues of the two poets in order to highlight the basic differences between them. Boccaccio's own third eclogue, "Faunus," is clearly modeled on Petrarch's "Argus," yet just as clearly divergent from its model in a number of ways. First, what did Boccaccio adopt from Petrarch's poem? Most obviously, the theme, which is the death of King Robert of Naples and the appropriately pastoral praise of King Robert as a shepherd; more specifically, the tranquil opening scene with its sudden disruption. That is all. But already the differences emerge. Boccaccio's poem opens *comically* with a Vergilian trading of insults and an accusation of drunkenness. This levity is utterly foreign to Petrarch's mournful elegiac tone. Furthermore, the disruption in Petrarch's poem is caused by mighty forces: a terrible tempest reminiscent of the sudden storm in *Aeneid* I; like that epic storm, it is caused by angry gods and causes in turn the scattering of a once collected people. The opening words of the first speaker after this narrated opening

---

"Significato," pp.159ff., and Labagnara, *Il poema bucolico*, pp.31-41.

[43] Otto Skutsch, "Symmetry and Sense in the *Eclogues*," *Harvard Studies in Classical Philology* 73 (1969), 153-170. Krautter, *Renaissance der Bukolik*, pp.136-41.

are an appeal to Jupiter for mercy. In short, just as Petrarch in his "Monicus" presented himself chiefly as an epic poet rather than a pastoral one,[44] so too in this second poem he clearly has epic standards in mind. For Boccaccio, on the other hand, the sudden disruption of quiet is caused by an outcry of wife against husband, and the initial comic tone persists in the comment of Moeris about the well-known frequent quarrels of this couple. Thus the cause is not celestial but human, far less terrifying, and indeed almost farcical.

The detachment of tone, moreover, is possible because whereas Petrarch's poem takes place in the environs of Naples among friends of his who truly lived through its upheavals, Boccaccio's is set instead far from Naples, even though the quarrel turns out to be about Faunus' desire to involve himself in Neapolitan affairs. The issue of whether or not to become involved is the subject of dispute not only between Faunus, who represents Francesco Ordelaffi, lord of Forlì, and Testilis, who represents his state, but also between Palemon, who prepares to accompany his lord into action, and Pamphylus, who, like the Tityrus of Vergil's first eclogue, prefers to recline in the shade and sing. Here we come to another major difference which will recur in other pairs of poems: Petrarch's speakers are basically in agreement, while Boccaccio's speakers hold opposing attitudes which are never absolutely reconciled.

This presence of real conflict in Boccaccio's poems encourages another feature: a dramatic quality which Boccaccio derives not from Petrarch but from Dante. Petrarch's poem is modeled closely on Vergil's fifth eclogue, which it explicitly cites in ll.61-62: "Daphnis pastoribus olim,/ Et tibi nunc ingens merito cantabitur Argus" (Once Daphnis was sung by the shepherds, and now Argus mighty in merit will be sung by you). Following his model, Petrarch begins with a narrative introduction, leading into a pair of songs, the first a desolate lament, the other a consolatory song of eulogy and of the dead man's ascent to heaven. Boccaccio ignored this obvious model completely in his reworking of Petrarch's poem. Instead, he drew from Dante's pastoral epistle to Giovanni del Virgilio the dramatic structure of a dialogue followed by the arrival of a third speaker with news to report. After the initial altercation, the description of the peaceful scene and its interruption are narrated by one speaker to another, whereas Petrarch's introductory description is addressed solely to the reader by a speaker who does not participate in the ensuing scene. Thus it is non-dramatic.

Petrarch's pair of songs and even the introductory description and lament

---

[44] Krautter, *Renaissance*, pp.93-94.

are all parts of a lyrical response to a current situation. The discourse is predominantly emotional and effusive. Boccaccio's eclogue, in contrast, entails a historical narrative which extends beyond King Robert's death to subsequent events. A variety of causes and responses are discussed without great emotional intensity, and the narrative is further continued in the following poems. Boccaccio's speakers, rather than expressing grief at their own situation, want to know what is happening somewhere else. Thus the passing of time and the stream of events replace Petrarch's basically lyric focus on a particular moment.

One other of Boccaccio's eclogues may have drawn from Petrarch's "Argus," which remained for a while the only Petrarchan eclogue Boccaccio knew. His fifth, the "Silva cadens" or "Falling Forest," is a long and emotional lament for the ruin of Naples by war after King Robert's death. Like the "Faunus," it opens with an allusion to Vergil's first eclogue, as one speaker accuses the other of reclining contentedly and singing while terrible things are going on. The lament of Parthenope is set, again, within a dramatic context as it is reported by one speaker to another rather than simply to us. Whereas Petrarch's "Argus," like the Vergilian fifth eclogue, focuses its mourning and praise on the king, thus contributing to the tradition of using the eclogue to praise a ruler, Boccaccio's nymph subordinates the eulogy and lament for Robert (again named "Argus") in a much longer lament for the entire countryside and culture of Naples. Indeed, the mourning nymph bears the city's own classical name, much as Testilis represented Forlì. The emphasis on place rather than on ruler, an emphasis evident already in the titles, contributes to Boccaccio's later anti-court theme and his refusal to use his verse for the flattery of ruling powers. Petrarch, in contrast, used two of his eclogues to praise and address rulers, not only the dead King Robert but also the living Cola di Rienzo (ecl.5).

When Boccaccio did apply the model of Vergil's fifth eclogue to a ruler, in his "Alcestus" (ecl. 6), he used it to lament and rejoice at the flight and return of the royal couple from and to Naples during the Hungarian invasion; it remains notably in the political realm with no suggestion of deification or heavenward ascent for the rulers, about whom Boccaccio could indeed be quite critical elsewhere in the eclogues.

Both Parthenope's lament in Eclogue 4 and Amintas' joyful song at the return of Louis in Eclogue 6 make use of another Vergilian feature ignored by Petrarch: the refrain. In the case of Amintas's song, the refrain is certainly inspired by the love charm in Vergil's eighth eclogue which brings the straying lover back home. (As the lover's name was Daphnis, the connection to a ruler's return was implicit for anyone reading the Daphnis of Vergil's fifth eclogue as Caesar.) The refrain and its allusion cause two effects. One effect is the close association of pastoral song with real popular song: one might think, for example, of the contemporary *ballate* with their refrains. Petrarch, for all his lyric qualities, omits this musical feature, perhaps because of its more popular character. The other effect, through the echo of a love charm, is the domestication of political events, a tendency directly opposite their epic-like treatment in Petrarch's verses. The domesticating tendencies of Boccaccio's poetry are in turn related to the recurring comic tone, as in the case where the political decision of Ordelaffi to leave his own territory vulnerable and join the Hungarians is rendered as a domestic quarrel. We shall see other examples later.

Parthenope's lament for the fallen Naples depicts a golden Arcadian realm of tall forests, clear streams, fields of snowy sheep, and dancing nymphs and satyrs. It is a vision or a landscape absent from Petrarch's bucolics, about which the humanist Bruni rightly complained that they are in no way pastoral.[45] In keeping with her Arcadian scene, Parthenope addresses a prayer not to Jupiter (as in the "Argus") but to Priapus, "O ruddy god of gardens." Such a prayer is unimaginable in Petrarch's eclogues or indeed anywhere in his poetry. The idea of praising a real landscape in Arcadian terms would flourish later in the Renaissance. So would the theme, already Vergilian, of a pastoral world destroyed by invading human violence. As with the use of refrain, Boccaccio did not invent these notions, but used and emphasized them in a way quite foreign to Petrarch's concept of bucolic poetry; thus he offered later readers a path to Vergilian bucolic rather different from that offered by his admired but not too closely imitated friend.

Let us turn now to another pair: Boccaccio's thirteenth ("Laurea") and Petrarch's fourth ("Daedalus"). By the time Boccaccio composed his later eclogues, he had read Petrarch's entire sequence and realized that history was not its only theme. The "Daedalus" is a debate between Tyrrhenus, clearly representing Petrarch, and Gallus, some other inferior poet, possibly French, who wishes to obtain Tyrrhenus' lyre. He offers payment, which Tyrrhenus scornfully rejects, comparing the value of poetry to the paltry worth of material goods. Gallus is moreover too old to start learning how to play as well as the envied master of the lyre. The eclogue ends with the two speakers in total agreement about the superiority of Tyrrhenus as poet and about the hopelessness of Gallus' desire to be his equal. The topic of

---

[45] David Thompson and Alan Nagel, *The Three Crowns of Florence: Humanist Assessments of Dante, Petrarca and Boccaccio* (New York: Harper & Row, 1972), pp.37 and 50.

a debate between rival poets follows the model of Vergil's seventh eclogue, which according to Servius' interpretation showed a contest between Vergil and an inferior rival poet. Boccaccio's debate has a different focus. Perhaps inspired by the mid-section of Petrarch's eclogue, and also no doubt by his own past arguments with his father, Boccaccio's contest is between a poet and a merchant, each claiming the superiority of his own pursuits. Boccaccio claimed that the basis for the poem was a real discussion he had had with a merchant of Genoa. In any case, two aspects are surprising and totally un-Petrarchan. One is the friendliness between the two contestants; the other is their ultimate equality. From the beginning, the two are mirror images of each other, implying a balance as well as opposition. The merchant Stilbon, once busily traveling, is now at rest, and the poet Daphnis, once piping in his cave, is now wandering about. Daphnis offers to pause a while with Stilbon, and the other graciously responds with a welcome. As they compare their loves and as Stilbon scorns the poverty of the Muses (a theme not mentioned in Petrarch's poem), Daphnis suggests a song contest as a means of averting an argument ("ne vertantur in iram/ iurgia"). Whereas Petrarch's Tyrrhenus is the sole possessor of a lyre handed down to him by Daedalus, Boccaccio's Stilbon is quite as well equipped as the poet Daphnis; for although Daphnis has had Arcadian music teachers, Stilbon has a set of pipes handed him by Hermes. The very ambiguity of Hermes as a god both of eloquence and of commerce adds to the equivalence of the two contestants. Whereas Petrarch's Gallus agrees all along about Tyrrhenus' superiority, Stilbon never wavers in his self-confidence. Here again we see Petrarch using two speakers to express a unanimous opinion, while Boccaccio's two are involved in a real conflict to which there is no ultimate resolution. The judge (Critis) whom they agree to choose ends up awarding the wagered prizes to both singers: "Iurgia pastorum non est compescere parvum:/ et tu dignus eras vitula, tu dignus et hyrco" (It's no small thing to calm the shepherds' quarrels: you're worthy of the calf, you of the goat). One cannot imagine Petrarch leaving the debate unresolved like this, especially when we think of works such as his *Invecticum contra medicum*, very similar in topic to this eclogue. Boccaccio's humility not only prevents him from identifying himself too personally with the poet (in contrast with Petrarch's clear self-praise), but seems even to prevent him from assuring the claims of poetry against those of commerce. Both contestants are declared worthy of what the other can offer.

One more pair of eclogues will further support this difference between assured unanimity and real debate: Petrarch's ninth ("Querulus") and Boccaccio's fifteenth ("Phylostropos"). Petrarch's eclogue is the first of the three so-called "egloghe del dolore" (eclogues of sorrow) on the doleful losses from the great plague.[46] Although the names of the two speakers, Philogeus and Theophilus, lead one to expect some opposition of values, it never occurs. Philogeus opens with a lament for the long, hard, wasted labors of the farmer and, by implication, also of the poet. Asked by Theophilus about the origins of such pestilence, Philogeus answers literally with its geographical origins and morally by accusing the greed of merchants for carrying the plague back home from the orient. Theophilus declares that its source is the wrath of God and that the only hope for safety is the path to heaven. The difference is minor; for all his literal-mindedness, Philogeus has already spontaneously offered the interpretation that the plague was caused by sin. Thoroughly disenchanted with life on earth, Philogeus is immediately ready to follow his friend, who promises to help him on the way. Neither speaker is particularly well named: Philogeus never demonstrates the slightest love for the world and requires no persuasion to depart at once. Theophilus shows no evidence of love for God, who appears only as the wrathful God who has caused the plague and who threatens an eternal as well as a corporeal death. His brief mention of a "quiet region" atop lofty hills is followed by a more vivid warning about the perils of hell to be avoided. The emphasis of both speakers is negative: it is much clearer what they want to avoid than what they want to attain. It is also unclear what the role of poetry is here. On one hand it seems to be equated with the fruitless farming to be left behind; on the other hand it seems to be also identified with the pursuit of spiritual rather than material reward. The former identification is clearest in lines 31-35 of Philogeus' complaint:

> "Whither, alas, have ambition and blind desire of possessions
> Led me? How many other, more common vocations I might have
> Followed, how many different careers! Why chose I the worst one?
> Scratching the hostile earth, longing only to hear the cicada's
> Querulous rasp – it's a life of misery and hard labor."[47]

But the "right path...though extremely difficult and trod by few" (90-91) seems to echo the literary choice of a career apart from the common throng because of its difficulty and intellectuality. Sonnet 7 of the *Canzoniere*, for example, contrasts the vulgar pursuit of wealth to the poet's intellectual ascent, following the heavenly light within man, and exhorts the unidentified recipient to persevere although he will find few companions on the chosen way. In any case, the final lines of the eclogue call on Philogeus to exert

---

[46] Enrico Carrara, "I commenti antichi e la cronologia delle ecloghe petrarchesche" *GSLI* 28 (1896), p.146.

[47] Translated by Thomas Bergin, *Petrarch's Bucolicum Carmen* (New Haven: Yale University Press, 1974), p.131.

his own strength on the ascent. The suspicion that the path to salvation is partly literary is enhanced by the following eclogue with its catalogue of all the classical writers Petrarch had ever heard of. Certainly the call towards heaven does not signal an end to the writing of eclogues.

Boccaccio's "Phylostropos" is named for the speaker who, according to Boccaccio, represents Petrarch; the other speaker, Typhlus, represents Boccaccio himself and anyone else who is spiritually "blind." Unlike Petrarch's poem in its placement, it comes at the end of Boccaccio's sequence, followed only by the final presentation of this flock of poems to its dedicatee. Thus it seems to take the call towards salvation more religiously. At the same time, it offers a real debate, once again, between Phylostropos, whose name means a love-turning or conversion, and Typhlus, who, unlike the discouraged Philogeus, truly loves his present situation and has a hard time being persuaded to leave. Where Philogeus himself had complained about the farmer's hard life, Typhlus is happy with his life until Phylostropos mockingly points out to him the miseries of his endless labor. Typhlus in turn finds Phylostropos' urgings that he leave his present happiness for unknown goals "ridiculous" and ventures to cite Epicurus' view that the soul dies with the body. Phylostropos is shocked, as Petrarch certainly would have been. Indeed, the Epy cited sympathetically in Boccaccio's verse by the figure avowedly representing himself occurs in Petrarch's eclogues as the concubine of the Pope in Avignon, and thus as the object of a scathing and bitter attack. Although ultimately both poets were in agreement on the truth of Christianity, the attitudes towards Epicurus as presented in these eclogues could not be farther apart.

However, just as Typhlus truly loves the earth, so too the process of his conversion involves an emphasis on the love and mercy of God, not on his wrath. Thus both of Petrarch's negatives are reversed into positive representations. Without any warning description of hell, Phylostropos offers a lengthy inviting description of heaven as a pastoral place with crystal streams, tender grasses for the flocks, and breezy woods with satyrs, nymphs and dryads. Despite the obvious possibility of allegory here, the description is more or less like that of Naples in Parthenope's lament. Heaven is enticing because it is like earth without earth's troubles. But we should also realize that this is truly a conversion poem, about the conversion of pastoral as well as of the individual. Boccaccio's love of heaven gives it a place at the end of the sequence as the ultimate pastoral *locus amoenus*.[48]

---

[48] Might this indicate some influence of the *Roman de la Rose*, a work certainly known to Boccaccio and used in other of his writings?

The final section of the eclogue is also more Christian than Petrarch's. Peter and Paul are cited (through pastoral names) as examples of shepherds who had sinned against God but won his mercy. Typhlus, deciding to make the journey, appeals immediately in prayer to the Virgin Mary and to God (again through pastoral names). And, in one of the most notable departures from the Petrarchan model, Phylostropos promises not only his own aid but the aid of Soter, the Savior. This journey is not one more individual accomplishment separating one from the common herd. It is rather a path open to all who seek God's mercy. It is accomplished not by oneself but through Christ. The same generosity that enabled Boccaccio to be so kind to the merchant in eclogue thirteen, rather than insisting on his own superiority, similarly enables him to extend the invitation of salvation to the most recalcitrant and worldly rather than to the few and also to present a kindly rather than a wrathful God.

The poem ends with Typhlus bidding the laurels farewell and heading off towards the palms. Petrarch, whose Laura takes her place in heaven, causes a continued confusion of the two pursuits. But for Boccaccio, the goal of salvation is unambiguously separated from literary ambition however noble its conception. The insistent Christianity of this poem, with its references to the New Testament, its prayers, and its declaration of God's mercy to all repentant sinners, is quite unlike Petrarch's more classical poem, which omits prayer and treats the path towards heaven as the stoical path of virtue and intelligence. It is notable that the one Petrarchan eclogue with a truly unresolved debate is the opening poem about the divergent careers of himself and his monastic brother and that in this poem Petrarch takes the side of classical poetry against the claims of Christian and Scriptural verse.

It is Petrarch who Boccaccio's poet-figure hopes will show him the way up Parnassus and Petrarch who can turn his mind towards heaven. But through this very use of Petrarch Boccaccio offers another theme dear to later eclogue writers and unavailable in Petrarch's pastoral: the theme of love and admiration for a friend. Vergil's final eclogue to Gallus is undoubtedly a root of this tradition, but Vergil is still critical for all his evident affection. Boccaccio admires without hesitation. The eulogy of rulers is replaced by the personal eulogy of a friend and fellow poet. Similarly the dedication of the eclogue sequence shuns the opportunity for court flattery and and directs itself towards a private friend. In the same way –and again with great influence on future poetry – Boccaccio's great elegiac eclogue is not about a Caesar or a King Robert but about his daughter, dead at the age of five.

This poem (ecl. 14) sums up much of what is distinctive in Boccaccio's eclogues. Although it focuses on Boccaccio's own mourning for the death of his beloved daughter, the poem opens comically with a servant grumbling about his grouchy old master who will not let him sleep. A setting is quickly established: the shepherds' hut with its nearby fold and the surrounding forest. Domestic details, such as the dog's wagging its tail as if at the arrival of a friend, enliven the scene with touches of charming realism. In contrast, Petrarch's scene is given no particularized setting, but takes place as an abstract and formal tableau, a funerary monument beside a tomb. The female who descends from heaven in Boccaccio's poem is the spirit of his real daughter, and the old father greets her with convincingly personal emotion. The women in Petrarch's poem –all the speakers there are women – remain abstract figures of despair and enlightenment, as witnessed by their very names: Niobe, Fusca (dark), and Fulgida (shining). The vivid and comic domesticity of Boccaccio's verse is totally absent. The reality of Petrarch's grief for Laura, if that is whom the dead Galathea at least partly represents, is diminished by Petrarch's absence from the poem, in sharp contrast to the *Canzoniere* poems of lament; it is diminished further by the juxtaposition of this poem with the previous one, entitled "The fallen laurel," with its tediously riddling catalogue of classical authors. Even Boccaccio had once doubted that Laura was real.[49]

Much of the dramatic and expressive quality of Boccaccio's poem derives from his self-inclusion in a humble role broadly representative of worldly ignorance and blindness; he needs to be instructed and persuaded by his child. Petrarch, by remaining outside the poem, puts himself in the role of assured teacher through the words of the allegorical Fulgida and the mourners' ultimate agreement with her; thus once again, despite the appearance of conflicting attitudes, the resolution has clearly been worked out in advance. But whereas Petrarch's poem ends with an acceptance of consolation, Boccaccio's ends, as so often, with an inner conflict: the understanding has been enlightened, but the emotional self continues to grieve and protest. Yet despite Boccaccio's self-identification as an inhabitant of the dark woods of earthly error and despite the tenacity of his grief, the poem's major thrust is religious education. The central development of Christian teachings with its long descriptions of paradise were drawn not from Petrarch but from Dante. Petrarch offers a classically palatable consolation based on the necessity of

---

[49] His "De vita et moribus domini Francisci Petracchi de Florentia" (in Masséra's edition of the *Opere Latine Minori*, p.243) comments: "And however much in his many vernacular poems...he demonstrates that he ardently loved Lauretta, for that is no objection as I see it, I think that Lauretta is to be taken allegorically for the laurel crown which he soon attained." This work is an early one, however, composed before the two writers had ever met.

death for all and mentions Heaven without emphasis or specificity, as befits his classicizing tendency. Boccaccio elaborates a heavenly landscape filled with figures and activities, and rich in allusion to Dante and to Scripture. The heavenly visitors sing a stanzaic hymn before which human poetry is declared to fail. Boccaccio's final line, with its clear implication that Vergil can be overgone by a Christian poetics, is similarly Dantean for its sense of the modern poet's role in relation to the ancients.

Boccaccio's self-image in the eclogues is consistently different from Petrarch's. Where Petrarch as Tyrrhenus is the poet envied by incompetent rivals and as Stupeus (in ecl. 3) is the successful wooer of Daphne (thus implicitly surpassing even Apollo), Boccaccio's pursuit of the muses (in ecl. 12) is narrated with self-ridicule and its success left in doubt. Where Petrarch offers the figure of the poet ascending lofty peaks (ecls. 1 and 3), Boccaccio shows himself at the bottom of mountains (ecls. 12 and 15), longing to ascend but humble in the ascertainment of his own abilities. The possibility of treating the pastoral poet as a truly humble figure befitting the humble style, and thus also of treating himself and other themes with humor, also traditionally associated with the low style, was a possibility present in Vergil but scorned by Petrarch. It was Boccaccio who picked up that line of development, a line to be followed by Mantuan, Spenser, and others.

Judgments on Boccaccio's Buccolicum carmen

Judgments on the quality of Boccaccio's bucolic verses have varied considerably. Within the first century after their composition, they were generally well appreciated. Salutati spoke enthusiastically of them on several occasions. His letter to Francescuolo da Brossano (*Epistolae* 25) states: "He recently sang the pastures and flocks, which he has celebrated so elegantly in sixteen eclogues that we can easily equate or prefer them, I dare not only say to the *Bucolics* of our Francis [Petrarch], but to those of the ancients."[50] His epitaph for Boccaccio, which mentions individually only the Latin works, proclaims: "..In brilliant song/ You glorify the pastures." Giannozzo Manetti's *Life of Boccaccio*, written in the 1440's, declares the *Buccolicum carmen* "an excellent work."[51] Within the *Dialogues* of Leonardo Bruni, Niccolò Niccoli, picking an argument with Salutati, criticizes Petrarch's eclogues, saying "But he wrote in such a way that

---

[50] *Epistolario di Coluccio Salutati*, ed. Francesco Novati (Rome, 1891-1911), vol.1,p.226. See also Enrico Carrara, "Le vestigia bucoliche di Coluccio Salutati," *Studi Petrarcheschi ed altri scritti* (Turin: Bottega d'Erasmo, 1959), 207.

[51] Cited in David Thompson and Alan Nagel, *Three Crowns*, p.99.

in his bucolics there is nothing that smells of the pastoral or sylvan,..."; yet the same speaker lists Boccaccio's eclogues among other works in praising Boccaccio's "learning, eloquence, humor...and charm." [52] Filippo Villani's biography of Boccaccio a hundred years after his death calls the eclogues "very beautiful."[53]

Later writers qualified their praises, especially with regard to Boccaccio's Latinity. Paolo Cortese's work *On Learned Men* (1489) criticizes both Boccaccio and Petrarch for a poor Latin corrupted by medievalisms, characterizing our author's style as "disorderly, and limping, and weak. Yet one sees that he was trying many things, wanting much."[54] In a similar vein, Giuseppe Betussi's biography (1544) praises Boccaccio's Latinity with qualifying regard to the era when it was written. So too Marcantonio Nicoletti, in his sixteenth-century *Vite degli scrittori volgari illustri*, remarks carefully about Boccaccio: "in the Latin verses, albeit in this he freely yielded to Petrarch, he was very pleased...to have been nonetheless one of the first who, in the sea of barbaric and uncultivated discourse, labored to take lessons at least from the Roman splendor and eloquence."[55]

The argument has continued into more recent eras. Landau considered Boccaccio's eclogues of little poetic value, although their content was important for biographers.[56] Hortis, in his massive study of Boccaccio's Latin writings, declared: "It is good Latin; and whoever set himself to gather up all the errors of prosody in Boccaccio's Latin verses would have a very poor harvest."[57] To prove his point, he listed the examples he had found of long vowels treated as short ones, or vice versa. Körting, citing Hortis's judgment, disagreed, asserting that Boccaccio's Latin grammar and versification were terrible.[58] In Greg's opinion, Boccaccio's eclogues "show that as a metrist Boccaccio fell almost as far short of his friend in the learned as in

---

[52] In Thompson and Nagel, *Three Crowns*, pp.37, 50, and 51.
[53] Angelo Solerti ed., *Le Vite di Dante, Petrarca e Boccaccio scritte fino al secolo decimosesto* (Milan: Dottor Francesco Vallardi, n.d.), p.674.
[54] See Georg Voigt, *Pétrarque, Boccace et les débuts de l'humanisme en Italie*, trans. by A. Le Monnier (Paris: H. Welter, 1894), p.169n.; Thompson and Nagel, *Three Crowns*, pp.xi-xii.
[55] Solerti, *Vite*, pp.707 and 746.
[56] Marcus Landau, *Giovanni Boccaccio, sein Leben und seine Werke* (Stuttgart: Cotta, 1877), p.185.
[57] Attilio Hortis, *Studi* , p.68.
[58] Gustav Koerting, *Boccaccio's Leben und Werke* (Leipzig, Fues's Verlag, 1880), pp. 691, 698-700.

the vulgar tongue."⁵⁹

Certainly if one is looking for classical Latin, one may find Boccaccio's medieval style distasteful. But the interest of his verses lies beyond their mere (and perhaps unreliable) documentary value. The poetry is at times artificial and elaborate, at times truly beautiful and moving, at times charming and delightful. It reveals a serious attempt to come to terms with Vergil's mysteriously haunting eclogues, not to replicate but to transform them into a "modern" Christian poetry. In this regard, they are vastly preferable to the dull, albeit linguistically and prosodically purer, close imitations of Vergil's bucolics composed in the following centuries. Their experimental nature, revealed in the shifting generic conceptions of their author, in the humble manner of his self-presentation as a poet who is not accomplishing but essaying, and in their combination of a "low-style" classical model with the magnificent modern vernacular poem of Dante, made them a rich resource indeed for the literary Renaissance which they were consciously intended to help bring about.

---

⁵⁹ Walter W. Greg, *Pastoral Poetry and Pastoral Drama* (London: A.H. Bullen, 1906), p.24.

Sources and Influences

Sources

The most obvious model for anyone writing eclogues in the Middle Ages or early Renaissance was Vergil's *Bucolica*, and it remained the major source even after other influential pastoral poets had appeared. In the fourteenth century Theocritus was known only by name, and Servius' comment that he had written superficial idylls made him uninteresting to allegorically-minded poets. Servius pointed out various formal features of Vergil's work: the variety of kind and topic from eclogue to eclogue, the mixture or alternation of narrative by the author and dramatic dialogue among the characters, the use of rustic matter for comparisons and of appeal to rural deities, the significance of names, etc. The total form was not the eclogue but the sequence, within which variety could be exercised. It contained sundry topics: amorous complaint, funereal elegy and eulogy, poetic rivalry, mythological narrative, and comments on current events.

Servius's gloss on the *Bucolica* was as influential as the text itself, and certainly shaped the way Vergil was read. While asserting moderately that the poems are not everywhere allegorical, Servius nonetheless not only identified references to contemporary persons and events but also suggested many possibilities of allegorical interpretation: sometimes people represent places, for example, as when Tityrus's leaving one nymph for another signifies Vergil's change of city; sometimes elements of scenery represent people, as when (still in eclogue 1) a pine represents Rome, the murmuring streams are senators, and the fruitbearing trees are scholars. Other commentators were even less restrained in their hunt for meanings. Roughly four kinds of meaning were perceived. One kind of meaning was autobiographical and historical: the poems were about Vergil's loss of land or his love for a servant boy, or about the death of Caesar or birth of a consul's son. A second kind was moral – a reading especially encouraged by Dante, who used, for example, Vergil's 3.92-3 "Qui legitis flores et humi nascentia fraga/ frigidus, o pueri, fugite hinc, latet anguis in herba" (O youths who are gathering flowers and strawberries that spring from the earth, flee hence, a cold serpent lurks in the grass) to refer to God's hidden judgment in the circle of avaricious and prodigal sinners (Inferno 7.83-84). Boccaccio, who later glossed the Eurydice myth as signifying the damnation of natural concupiscence (Eurydice) through the deceitfulness (snake) hidden in worldly pleasures (grass and flowers), clearly read these lines in a similarly allegorical way. So too in Vergil's fourth eclogue, the blooming of flowers and death of the serpent are equated with the child's education in *virtus*.[60] Of course the serpent lurking in the flowers has a Biblical resonance; and the eclogues could also be read, despite Vergil's own paganism, as Christian allegory, especially in the case of the famous fourth eclogue. Dante cites it in connection with Statius's conversion to Christianity, implying an identification of the child with Christ. So too Boccaccio cites the opening line, "paulo maiora canamus," in the middle of his eleventh eclogue as he begins to narrate the life of Christ in mythological terms. A fourth kind of meaning concerned literary theory or criticism. The same "iam redit et virgo" cited for Statius's conversion was also used by Boccaccio in a letter to Iacopo Pizzinga (1372) to declare the rebirth of literature, the beginning of a new golden age of poetry. Autobiographical readings of the eclogues gave rise to literary ones as well: for example, the hostile *conflictus* in Vergil's seventh eclogue was glossed by Servius as an exchange between Vergil and a detractor or rival poet, and might consequently be viewed as a debate about two views of poetry. We will see that even Boccaccio's earliest Latin and Italian eclogues played with a combination of autobiographical, literary, moral, and religious meanings.

Boccaccio did not, as some later writers, closely imitate specific eclogues; but Vergilian phrases recur in a scattered manner throughout his *Buccolicum carmen*. Besides specific phrases, Vergil offered a source of tropes: invitations, rustic comparisons, lists of impossibilities, closure with nightfall, etc. Other classical poetry also finds occasional echo in Boccaccio's verses: the later works of Vergil, and the lyric poetry of Catullus, Ovid, and Horace.[61]

Two pastoral poets of later antiquity were also known to Boccaccio, although apparently not to Petrarch: Calpurnius (first century A.D.) and Nemesianus (third century A.D.).[62] Their eclogues were often paired

---

[60] The same lines might have offered Boccaccio a model for his political allegories, since the serpent was the sign of the dreaded Visconti and flowers the image of Florence's name.

[61] Silvia Labagnara, *Il poema bucolico del Boccaccio* (Rome: Luigi Ambrosini, 1970?), p.69. Pages 55ff. offer many examples of Boccaccio's borrowings from Vergil.

[62] Boccaccio certainly owned these texts, according to the catalogue *Mostra di manoscritti, documenti, e edizioni. Firenze, Biblioteca Medicea Laurenziana, 22 maggio -31 agosto 1975*, (Certaldo, 1975), vol.1, p.145. See also Helen Cooper, *Pastoral: Medieval*

together and sometimes all attributed to one poet. Calpurnius, in a patterned alternation of courtly and rustic poems, developed the panegyric of a contemporary ruler (in his case, Nero), a function which became major in the fifteenth and sixteenth centuries but which was not adopted by Boccaccio. His second eclogue, a contest between a shepherd and a gardener, may have suggested –along with medieval debate poems comparing soldier and cleric –Boccaccio's contest between poet and merchant in eclogue 13. Nemesianus' four eclogues do not allude to contemporary affairs, but focus on the timeless themes of death, love, and mythology. In his third eclogue, modeled on Vergil's sixth, Pan sings of the birth, power, and praises of Bacchus, described as "vera Iovis proles" (20) ["true offspring of Jove"]. In combination with Silenus's song in the Vergilian model, a song beginning with the creation of the world, it may have encouraged Boccaccio to turn that Vergilian sixth eclogue into a narrative of Scriptural history and the life of Christ.[63] After Nemesianus, writes Carrara in his history of the genre, "the pastoral pipes fell silent a long while."[64] The genre was revived during the Carolingian period, but it is not clear that those efforts were known to Boccaccio.[65]

Also unclear is the extent of Boccaccio's knowledge of another development spanning many centuries: the Christianized pastoral. It began in the fourth century with Lactantius's Christian reading of Vergil's fourth eclogue.[66] Several Christian eclogues were produced in the fourth and fifth centuries. Paulinus of Nola's "Natalicum 6" links a tale about a stolen sheep with the theme of Christ's nativity. Paulinus's younger friend Endelechius, also known as Severus Sanctus, wrote a "Carmen bucolicum de virtute signi crucis domini" [bucolic on the virtue of the sign of the cross of our Lord]; it is a dialogue between two shepherds, one of whom (Tityrus) has saved his flocks from pestilence through the power of the sign of the

---

into Renaissance(Totowa, N.J.: Rowan and Littlefield, 1977), pp.4, 36, 39.

[63] The texts of these two poets can be found in J. Wight Duff and Arnold M. Duff, ed., *Minor Latin Poets*, Loeb Classical Library (Cambridge, Mass.: Harvard University Press, 1935). For further discussion of their place in the history of pastoral poetry, see Enrico Carrara, *Poesia pastorale*, 28ff. and W. Leonard Grant, *Neo-Latin* , pp.71ff.

[64] Carrara, *Poesia pastorale*, p.37.

[65] For more information, see Carrara, *Poesia pastorale*, pp.43ff. and Francesco Macri-Leone, *La Bucolica latina nella letteratura italiana del secolo XIV* (Turin: Ermanno Loescher, 1889), pp.29ff.

[66] *De divina institutione*, PL 6.564-75. On the early medieval debates between pagan and Christian readings of Vergil, see Domenico Comparetti, *Vergil in the Middle Ages*, trans. E.F.M. Benecke (Hamden, Conn.: Anchor Books, 1966), pp.96-103.

cross. Tityrus's praises of Augustus as a "god" at Rome in Vergil's first eclogue are here transferred to the Christian God. Vergilian lines were frequently borrowed and shuffled by poets: to compose poems in honor of Christ, called "Tityrus", by Pomponius; to retell stories of Scripture, by Proba Faltonia; to sing of Christ's passion, by Marcus Victorinus; and to celebrate the incarnation, by Sedulius Scotus. Sedulius wrote several verse dialogues, naming himself Tirsi and referring to his pipes. One of them, for example, rewrites the love-charm of Vergil's eighth eclogue to summon the return of a bishop.[67]

The praise of rulers was turned to the praise of ecclesiastics as well as of Christ. In the ninth century, Paschasius Radbertus wrote an eclogue in which two nuns, Phyllis and Galathea, mourn the death of the abbot St. Adalard, alias Menalcas. The two speakers represent his former and more recent abbeys. Their descriptions of the abbot's newly founded abbey and its gardens take their place among the idyllic scenes of pastoral verse. A tenth-century bishop, Ratbodo, wrote an eclogue on the virtues of the Blessed Bishop Lebuinus. In the twelfth century, a monk named Metellus composed a twelve-eclogue sequence on the life and works of St. Quirinus. One should note that in all these cases, Metellus was the only poet to write a series rather than a single poem or two.[68]

Boccaccio, aware of the possible Christian reading of Vergil's fourth eclogue, would not have needed to know any of these writings in order to conceive his own Christian eclogues, which indeed have very little in common with earlier ones. Giovanni del Virgilio, whose writings were well known to Boccaccio, calls Dante the first to write bucolic verse since Vergil, implying either ignorance of or distaste for the intervening experiments.[69] Boccaccio similarly ignores them in his history of the genre in the letter to Fra Martino da Signa.

One tenth-century eclogue, however, probably was known to him, for it had become widely disseminated as a school text in the following centuries. Theodulus's poem is a dialogue between Pseustis (falsehood), representing pagan myth, and Alithia (truth), representing Scripture. Similar stories are

---

[67] Comparetti, *Vergil in the Middle Ages*, p.54; Carrara, *Poesia pastorale*, pp.39-53; Macri-Leone, *Bucolica Latina*, pp. 18-19. Wolfgang Schmid, "Tityrus Christianus: Probleme religiöser Hirtendichtung an der Wende vom vierten zum fünften Jahrhundert," *Rheinisches Museum für Philologie*, Neue Folge 96 (1953), pp.101-65.

[68] Lessig, *Ursprung*, pp.18-21; Carrara, *Poesia pastorale*, pp.53-58; Macri-Leone, *Bucolica Latina*, 34-38; Walter W. Greg, *Pastoral*, p.19.

[69] Greg, *Pastoral*, p.20n.

Sources and Influences

recited in parallel stanzas before the judge Fronesis (reason). Alithia is a royal and virginal shepherdess descended from David, but apart from this there is nothing pastoral about the verse. Clearly "eclogue" meant chiefly a dialogue or debate to Theodulus. The identification of pagan with Christian stories remained one of Boccaccio's favorite games, and recurs in the vernacular pastoral of the *Comedia delle ninfe* as well as in the Latin eclogues.[70]

Another Christianized eclogue with which Boccaccio was probably familiar is the example composed by John of Garland for his *Parisiana Poetria* (13th century).[71] John's eclogue, whose three speakers he identified as reason, the flesh, and the world or devil, has been mentioned already. Citing Vergil's epitaph for Daphnis (eclogue 5), John remarked that it is possible to speak in the same manner about Christ, identified both as shepherd and as mystic lamb. The lines he quoted to prove his point come from his own *Epithalamium Beatae Virginis* (7.261-62), demonstrating that Vergil's eclogue was a source not only for John's eclogue but also for his longer Christian poem, which is eclogue-like in including a debate (between Justice and Mercy) as well as in its imagery. Isaiah 59:14 supported the conflation of Vergil's Astraea with the Virgin Mary and the birth of Christ with the return of the Golden Age.[72] Theodulus, whom John mentions, also supported this merging of classical and Christian theme in a pastoral form.

Besides Vergil, the main initial inspiration for Boccaccio came from an exchange of pastoral verses between his adored Dante and Giovanni del Virgilio in 1319-21. Boccaccio copied this set of poems, with a gloss, into his notebook possibly as early as 1339.[73] Giovanni del Virgilio had initiated the exchange with an invitation to Dante and an expression of regret that Dante was not writing poetry in Latin. Dante replied with a pastoral epistle in which he masked himself and other friends as shepherds conversing about the message just received. Giovanni del Virgilio replied with a delighted continuation of the pastoral game, and Dante also wrote

---

[70] The text has been edited as *Theoduli eclogam* by Joannes Osternacher (Ripariae prope Lentiam, 1902). For further remarks on its relation to Boccaccio's poetry, see my notes to eclogue 11.

[71] John of Garland, *Parisiana Poetria*, ed. with a facing trans. by Traugott Lawler (New Haven: Yale University Press, 1974), pp. 24-27 and notes on pp.233-35.

[72] For a discussion of this poem, see Evelyn Faye Wilson, "Pastoral and Epithalamium in Latin Literature," *Speculum* 23 (1948), 35-57, and especially 43-52.

[73] Giorgio Padoan, "Giovanni Boccaccio e la rinascita dello stile bucolico," in *Giovanni Boccaccio editore e interprete di Dante* (Florence: Olschki, 1979), 25-44.

one more pastoral letter.[74] Boccaccio's two eclogues to Checco de' Rossi, the latter of which was revised to become part of his *Buccolicum carmen*, imitated this model in a number of ways, including the epistolary mode, the invitation to an exchange of pastoral verses, and the dramatic form of Dante's poem, in which a messenger arrives in the middle of an ongoing conversation. Dante's exchange of verses fostered the association between eclogues and debate poems, and encouraged the use of pastoral verse to refer to one's own acquaintances. By enacting a friendly disagreement between two poets, it developed the Vergilian theme of song contest as a debate about poetics. Furthermore, and importantly for Boccaccio, it associated the *Commedia* with the *Bucolica*, for Dante's defense of his vernacular poetry against the request for Latin verse drew from the introduction to Vergil's sixth eclogue, which rejects martial epic in favor of humble pastoral song.[75] Boccaccio was to make heavy use of the *Commedia* in his bucolics. Giovanni del Virgilio's use of the mode was somewhat different from Dante's, as Krautter has pointed out. For example, Giovanni took his verses seriously as a noble activity, while Dante wrote with considerable humor. That comic tone was also imitated by Boccaccio, even within some of his most serious poems. Moreover, whereas Dante's scenery in his first eclogue had referred to kinds of poetry (the lofty peaks, the humble valleys), Giovanni's referred to real places (Ravenna and Bologna). However, Dante's second eclogue excuses him from visiting Giovanni by referring to the fearful Polyphemus, usually interpreted as the politically hostile ruler of Bologna.[76] Boccaccio used both kinds of landscape in his eclogues, and took over Polyphemus to represent the hostile and destructive king of Hungary. Other details which he picked up from these poems include the use of Molossian hounds to signify attacking troops, and acknowledgement of the poet's desire for the laurel. The glosses Boccaccio copied with these texts not only identify historical

---

[74] The texts and some commentary can be found in several editions: P.H. Wicksteed and E.G. Gardner, *Dante and Giovanni del Virgilio* (Westminster, 1902); E. Bolsani and M. Valgimigli, *La corrispondenza poetica di Dante Alighieri e Giovanni del Virgilio* (Florence:Olschki, 1963); Giuseppe Albini and Giovanni Battista Pighi, *La corrispondenza poetica di Dante e Giovanni del Virgilio e l'ecloga di Giovanni al Mussato*. For further discussion of these poems, see especially Konrad Krautter, *Die Renaissance der Bukolik in der lateinischen Literatur des XIV Jarhunderts: von Dante bis Petrarca* (München: Wilhelm Fink, 1983).

[75] Thomas Rosenmeyer, *The Green Cabinet. Theocritus and the European Pastoral* (Los Angeles: UCLA Press, 1969), pp.273-74; Konrad Krautter, *Renaissance der Bukolik*, pp.35-37.

[76] Krautter, *Renaissance der Bukolik*, p.46, argues, however, that literary matters rather than— or perhaps as well as— political and geographical ones are at issue here.

persons but also support an allegorical reading in which, for example, a cave is a school and the flocks are students.

Half a dozen years later, after Dante's death, Giovanni del Virgilio tried to repeat the bucolic exchange with the poet laureate Mussato. The poem breaks in two, interrupted by Giovanni's dislocation from Bologna to the small town of Cesena; Giovanni calls the poem a sheep with a white head and black tail because of his unhappy turn of affairs. This poem is closer to Dante's, which Giovanni must have been studying, in its development of dramatic dialogue and humor.[77] It refers to its own genre as one which Dante had been the first to revive since Vergil's time. Justifying his presumption in addressing the famous Mussato by recalling his own interchange with Dante, Giovanni speaks implicitly for the glorious nature of the genre and the classicizing poetic enterprise. The poems of Dante and Giovanni del Virgilio were known not only to Boccaccio and to Petrarch and their friends, such as Donato degli Albanzani, but also in succeeding generations to Salutati and Sannazaro, both influential advocates of the genre.[78]

Dante was a major inspiration for Boccaccio all along, and the *Commedia* even more than the eclogues made its presence felt in Boccaccio's bucolics. The very presence of the three otherworldly eclogues on hell, heaven, and purgatory acknowledge the *Commedia* as a source; and many details and phrases echo the master's great work. But there are larger modes of imitation here as well. The peculiar mix of high subjects with low style was, as I have suggested, encouraged by Dante's use of the vernacular. Furthermore the recurring appearance, near the end of the sequence, of Boccaccio himself as a figure both historically individual and representative of humans in general, set in action within a dramatic fiction full of vivid detail, seems likely to have been an imitation of Dante's method. So is the posing of a self who needs divine assistance and instruction – a self quite different from the more assured Petrarchan figure. The very Christian emphasis of the later poems and the series's whole plot of conversion from human loves to God's love offer in a way a bucolic version of the *Commedia*. The intertwining of religious concerns with literary ones, and the desire to outdo the

---

[77] Guido Martellotti, "Dalla tenzone al carme bucolico: Giovanni del Virgilio, Dante, Boccaccio," *Italia Medioevale e Umanistica* 7 (1964), 333. The essay has been reprinted in Martellotti's volume *Dante e Boccaccio e altri scrittori dall'umanesimo al romanticismo* (Florence: Olschki, 1983),pp.71-89. That same volume also contains "La riscoperta dello stile bucolico (da Dante al Boccaccio)," pp.91-106.

[78] Giuseppe Billanovich, "Giovanni del Virgilio, Pietro da Moglio, Francesco da Fiano," *Italia Medioevale e Umanistica* 6 (1963), 226 and 234; Macri Leone *La Bucolica latina*, p.57.

much admired Vergil by being a poet of the holy truth also finds precedence in Dante's poem.

The last great source for Boccaccio, one which he encountered after having already composed two Italian and three Latin eclogues, was the bucolic poetry of Petrarch. For meanwhile, quite independently, Petrarch had decided –perhaps around 1346– to write a *Bucolicum carmen* of his own. His was clearly designed from the start as a complete sequence, or as he described it in a letter to his brother (*Fam.* 10.4), "a bucolic song divided into twelve parts." In 1347 Petrarch sent the "Argus" eclogue to a friend in Naples, and soon thereafter Boccaccio copied an incomplete version of it into his notebook.[79] In 1351 he became acquainted with Petrarch personally and read the letter *Familiares* 10.4 with its eclogue "Monicus" addressed to Petrarch's brother Gherardo. The rest of the eclogues Petrarch guarded carefully until he finally allowed Boccaccio to read and copy them in 1359. By then Boccaccio's own sequence was more than half written. Sending a copy of the whole Petrarchan sequence to their common friend Barbato da Sulmona, Boccaccio implies in his letter that Petrarch's best friends did not even know of the existence of the rest of the sequence apart from the "Monicus" and "Argus."[80] The "Argus" alone, however, suggested to Boccaccio a whole realm of meaning which he had hitherto ignored: the historical or political. Its lament for the death of King Robert of Naples spawned a stream of historical eclogues on the affairs of Naples and Florence. In 1359, after Boccaccio had read the entire *Bucolicum carmen* of his awesome friend, further imitations followed: poems on the pursuit of the laurel, on the death of someone beloved, and on the need to relinquish Earth's uncertainties for the certain good of Heaven. Petrarch is indicated in two eclogues as the guide who can show Boccaccio the way up Mt. Parnassus and who can persuade him to undertake the difficult ascent towards heaven. It was an influence that threatened to overwhelm Boccaccio, and from which only the counter-influence of Dante finally rescued him. Even when Boccaccio was following Petrarch's thematic lead, however, the two poets diverged widely in their writing, as the previous section has shown.

---

[79] Enrico Carrara, "Cecco da Mileto e il Boccaccio," *GSLI* 43 (1904), p.20.
[80] Giovanni Boccaccio, *Opere latine minori*, ed. Aldo Massèra (Bari: Laterza, 1928), pp.146: And do not think that it is only what you and many others have, the "Monicus" and "Argus;" for the whole is divided into twelve eclogues.

Influences

Between 1300 and 1700 more than two hundred poets wrote Latin eclogues, either singly or in series,[81] and many poets –the same ones or others–composed vernacular eclogues too. The first evidence of Boccaccio's influence is simply this enormous success of the genre's revival. Later poets who were imitating Mantuan or Sannazaro owed Boccaccio an indirect debt. And even those who were most consciously imitating Petrarch rather than Boccaccio owed their idea to Boccaccio's enthusiastic promotion of Petrarch's bucolic work, which Boccaccio not only copied and disseminated but also praised repeatedly in his extremely popular and respected *Genealogia* (14.10, 14.22, 15.6) as the model for excellent modern writing worthy of a place beside the ancient classics. His own eclogues, often together with his letters, remain extant in four fourteenth-century manuscripts and six fifteenth-century manuscripts; other manuscript copies referred to in documents can no longer be found.[82]

It was Boccaccio, too, who made the first anthology of pastoral verse, including that of Vergil, Giovanni del Virgilio, Dante, Petrarch, and himself. Thus he not only inserted himself into a noble literary company, but more importantly established the notion that bucolics were not simply imitations of Vergil's poem but a rich genre realizable in a variety of ways. His anthology went at his death with his other books to the Augustinian library of Santo Spirito in Florence, where it was recopied about fifteen years after his death by the friar Iacopo da Volterra[83] and possibly copied or read by others as well. By the fifteenth century a copy of this anthology, bearing the name of the son of Boccaccio's step brother, had found its way as far as Bohemia.[84] Boccaccio's eclogues were first published by Giunti in Florence in 1504 in an anthology including also the pastoral verse of Vergil, Calpurnius, Nemesianus, Petrarch, Mantuan, and Guarici. The pastoral anthology became a popular Renaissance form of publishing eclogues; and the most widely read anthology, that of Oporinus printed in Basel in 1546, included Boccaccio's

---

[81] W. Leonard Grant, *Neo-Latin* , p.62.

[82] Vittore Branca, *Tradizione delle opere di Giovanni Boccaccio I: Un primo elenco dei codici e tre studi* (Rome: Edizioni di Storia e Letteratura, 1958, pp.79-80; Giuseppe Billanovich and Frantisek Čada, "Testi bucolici nella biblioteca del Boccaccio," *Italia Medioevale e Umanistica* 4 (1961), 201-21. Of the ten manuscripts, four are outside Italy, in Oxford, London, Paris, and Bohemia.

[83] Giuseppe Billanovich, "Giovanni del Virgilio, Pietro da Moglio, Francesco da Fiano," *Italia Medioevale e Umanistica* 6 (1963), 224.

[84] Billanovich and Čada, "Testi bucolici," 201-221.

verses, perhaps with little awareness that the volume's very conception was due to him. E.K.'s dedicatory epistle to Spenser's "Shepheardes Calender" lists Boccaccio among a canonical series of pastoral poets (besides Boccaccio, he mentions Theocritus, Vergil, Petrarch, Mantuan, Sannazaro, and Marot) as those "whose foting this author every where followeth."[85]

The first famous imitator of Boccaccio's eclogues was Coluccio Salutati, who provided the important link between the aspirations of Petrarch and Boccaccio and the burgeoning humanist efforts of the following century. In 1372 he sent one of his eclogues to Boccaccio for comment.[86] He composed perhaps six such poems, of which only a few tiny fragments now remain. According to descriptions of them in Salutati's letters, they took up the theme established chiefly by Boccaccio: God's salvation of man. The first eclogue, of which we have the fullest notion, treated the love of Pyrgis, or ignited earth, for Caristes, or divine grace; the shepherd Silvis, representing Christ, shows the lover how to ascend the mountains, or virtues, in order to see his beloved. Thus the most immediate as well as the most lasting influence of Boccaccio lay in the establishment of the eclogue as Christian allegory. Certainly Vergil's fourth eclogue provided the initial hint; but it was a hint which Petrarch had chosen to ignore. Salutati was in turn sent eclogues by younger poets seeking his judgment, and he passed on to them the concept of the eclogue as spiritual allegory. Twenty years after he had sent his first eclogue to Boccaccio, he was still mentioning it in letters. Later he rejected his bucolics and perhaps destroyed them himself. Yet even this rejection contains an echo of Boccaccio's *Buccolicum carmen.* Salutati wrote to someone who had sent him an eclogue that he had thought of responding in kind, but then refrained because, although in youth he had been rapt with mad passion for bucolics, in older age his song had changed. To emphasize his point, he cited from his own earlier composition: "Nos tenet alter amor ac alia pascua cure/ sunt nobis" (Another love possesses me and other pastures are my concern). [87] The passage, both prose and verse, is clearly drawn from Boccaccio's eclogue 12.51-53.

---

[85] *Works of Edmund Spenser, A Variorum Edition. The Minor Poems* I, ed. Charles Osgood and Henry Lotspeich (Baltimore: Johns Hopkins University Press, 1943), p.10.

[86] Berthold Ullman, *The Humanism of Coluccio Salutati,* Medioevo e Umanesimo 4 (Padua 1963), 35-36.

[87] For the fullest treatment of Salutati as bucolic poet, see Enrico Carrara, "Le vestigia bucoliche di Coluccio Salutati," *Studi Petrarcheschi ed altri scritti* (Torino: Bottega d'Erasmo, 1959), 205-17. There is also a briefer, scattered mention of this topic in Ronald Witt, *Hercules at the Crossroads. The Life, Work, and Thought of Coluccio Salutati* (Durham, N.C.: Duke University Press, 1983).

Sources and Influences

The most important follower of Boccaccio in the fifteenth century was Battista Spagnoli, known as Mantuan. As his influence was enormous, he passed on to writers throughout Europe the lessons from his master. Those lessons covered both the large scale construction of a sequence and the small scale borrowing of details. Like Boccaccio's *Carmen*, Mantuan's series of eclogues moves from poems on love through social satire to the experience of religious conversion, followed then by a more Petrarchan attack on the corruption of the curia. Thus the work as a whole has a narrative flow and indeed a "plot" very similar to Boccaccio's. The narrative quality is enhanced by the linking of eclogues (2-3 and 7-8) in a continuous story.[88] As in Boccaccio's series, we find at the center three satirical poems, a reversal of the three central elevated poems in Vergil's *Bucolica*. The religious conversion in eclogue 7 is effected, as in Boccaccio's eclogue 14, by a female visitor from Paradise: not the dead daughter this time but the Virgin Mary herself. Her promise to Pollux of eternal life in a heaven filled with flower-crowned hamadryads, dryads, and nymphs is akin to the pastorally alluring presentation of heaven in Boccaccio's fourteenth and fifteenth eclogues. The following poem begins with a shepherds' debate about the relative merits of the mountains and the lowlands, influenced no doubt by Boccaccio's vernacular eclogue in the *Comedia delle ninfe*, and proceeds with a continued discussion of their friend's recent conversion. Describing the Virgin in classical terms as "superum regina, tonantis/ Mater" (queen of the gods and mother of the thunderer), a use of classical mythology for Christian meanings fostered by Boccaccio, it cites Pollux's long prayer to her for protection and aid; pastoral prayer is again one of the features of Boccaccio's poems. Finally it ends with a description of the cycle of Marian festival days to be observed.

Besides the Christianized mythology of Arcadia, Mantuan developed as well Boccaccio's comic and domestic tone, which he enhanced with anecdotes, homely images, and humorous turns of phrase. This comic and popularizing tendency was a fruitful one throughout the later Renaissance, for it allowed the eclogue to be at once serious and humble, or moral and delightful. Spenser was one of the inheritors of this trend. So too was Pontanus, whose eclogue "Quinquennio" (the five-year-old) mixes childish prattle, maternal promises of treats and admonitions to stop bedwetting with a discussion about God and the Boogeyman.

---

[88] Petrarch's *Bucolicum carmen* also includes one linked pair (6-7) at the center of the sequence, concerning the worldliness and corruption of the papal court; but the poems involved consist in debate and description rather than narrative, nor is there any narrative movement to the sequence as a whole.

Mantuan borrowed further details from Boccaccio as well: the unhappy lover's reiterated claim of victimization in the phrases "Quid meruere boni?" and "Quid merui?" (eclogue 3) echoes the opening phrase of the complaining lover in Boccaccio's eclogue 2. Similarly the lover rejects as useless all medicines, charms, and prayers. The opening lines of Mantuan's fifth eclogue, a disagreement between a poet and a wealthy miser, roughly echoes the opening of Boccaccio's thirteenth eclogue on a closely related topic. Moreover, the echo from Dante's *Commedia* in eclogue 6 shows that Mantuan adopted Boccaccio's merging of Dante's great Christian work with Vergil's humbler pagan one. Mantuan's poems were published first in 1498, six years before the first printed edition of Boccaccio's eclogues. Reprinted many times, they became a school text, and were translated into French in 1531, into English in 1567.[89]

Boiardo, Mantuan's contemporary who won fame for his chivalric romance rather than for his eclogues, wrote two pastoral sequences, one in Latin and one in Italian. The Latin sequence follows Vergil's model poem by poem; the Italian sequence, however, shows the influence of Boccaccio's Latin as well as his vernacular bucolics. These poems deal with the war between Venice and Ferrara of 1482-83 and with the poet's love for Antonia Caprara, whose name may well have suggested a pastoral tribute. All are in terza rima, the form established for vernacular eclogues by Boccaccio's *Comedia delle ninfe*. Eclogue 2, in which the nymph Galathea laments the ruin of her land by war, plague, and famine, may reflect the similar fifth eclogue of Boccaccio in which the nymph Parthenope laments the ruin of Naples. Moreover, as Boccaccio in his sixth, so Boiardo in his fourth eclogue used the model of Vergil's fifth with its pair of lamenting and rejoicing songs to comment on the exile and return (not death and apotheosis) of a political ruler. His eighth, like Boccaccio's fourteenth, is a lament for the death of a young girl, while consoling friends suggest that she is responding from heaven with assurance of her eternal life.

Boccaccio's elegiac eclogue for his daughter found numerous echoes. If, as has been suggested, it is a source for the Middle English "Pearl," then somehow it had found its way into the cultural backwaters of England in a remarkably short time. Castiglione's "Alcon" (1506), while drawing on Petrarch's "Argus" in some respects, follows Boccaccio's lead in treating the private loss of a personal friend rather than the public loss of a ruler.[90]

---

[89] Doris Lessig, *Ursprung und Entwicklung der Spanischen Ekloge bis 1650* (Geneva: Droz, 1962), p.24; David Norbrook. *Poetry and Politics in the English Renaissance* (Boston: Routledge & Kegan Paul, 1984), pp.59-60.

[90] For further discussion of Castiglione's "Alcon" in relation to Boccaccio's fourteenth

Sources and Influences   lxv

Pontano's lament for his wife (published in 1505, two years after his death) similarly continues the theme of personal and familial rather than public mourning. Sannazaro in turn set into the eleventh and twelfth chapters of his *Arcadia* an elegy for his mother and a recollection of Pontano's elegy for his wife, thus completing the array of possible close female relatives. Spenser's "Daphnaida" (1591) mourns at length the death of a daughter (though not his own), includes the dying girl's consolatory response about her heavenly bridal feast and place among the singing saints and angels, and continues, as Boccaccio's poem, with the father's unremitting grief.

The other great Italian disciple of Boccaccio's pastorals was, of course, Sannazaro. He was influenced mainly by Boccaccio's vernacular pastorals, the *Ninfale fiesolano* as well as the *Comedia delle ninfe fiorentine*, and was in turn a major influence on the vernacular composition of this classical form. From Boccaccio's *Comedia delle ninfe* he took the terza rima, which through him then became established as the preferred verse form for vernacular pastoral poetry. Along with the Dantean rhyme scheme, he took from Boccaccio the imitation of phrases from Dante's *Commedia*, a borrowing made more natural by the use of Italian.[91]   Furthermore, he adopted the elaborate prose style of Boccaccio's *Comedia delle ninfe* and learned from Boccaccio to mix verse and prose into a continuous narrative.[92]   From Boccaccio too, though perhaps through later writers as well, came the importance of setting, the creation and description of an Arcadian space. A shared Neapolitan experience made Sannazaro feel especially close to Boccaccio, although certainly the pastorals of Petrarch, Mantuan, Boiardo, and Pontanus also left their traces in his work.[93]

In recounting the history of pastoral poetry (*Arcadia* 10), Sannazaro lists Pan, Theocritus, Vergil, and then declares that since Vergil's time few have been able to play Pan's pipes though many have tried. This slighting of

---

eclogue, see Ellen Zetzel Lambert, *Placing Sorrow. A Study of the Pastoral Elegy Convention from Theocritus to Milton* (Chapel Hill, University of North Carolina Press, 1976), pp.69-73.

[91]   For uses of the *Commedia* within the *Arcadia* see William Kennedy, *Jacopo Sannazaro and the Uses of Pastoral* (Hanover: University Press of New England, 1983), pp.109, 113, 115, 124, 126, 146.

[92]   For the importance of Boccaccio as a source for Sannazaro's prose style and for the establishment of terza rima as the verse form for eclogues in Italian, see Walter W. Greg, *Pastoral*, pp.39-46.

[93]   William J. Kennedy, *Jacopo Sannazaro* , p.35. For further study of Sannazaro's sources, see Francesco Torraca, *La materia dell'Arcadia del Sannazaro* (Città di Castello: S. Lapi, 1888).

his own more recent sources not only serves to enhance Sannazaro's claim to novelty as a reviver of classical glories, but also imitates Boccaccio's own brief history of the genre in his letter to Fra Martino. There, although he does give credit to Petrarch, Boccaccio mysteriously omits any mention of Dante; in his life of Dante he had judged Dante's pastoral verses "very beautiful," yet the letter remarks that between Vergil and Petrarch "others wrote, but they are obscure and not worth caring about."[94] Sannazaro's account of the genre follows a description of a sacred statue of Pan holding two tablets on which are inscribed the *Georgics*. As the horned Pan with his two tablets clearly resembles a statue of Moses, the superposition of classical pagan "laws" for rural living and Scriptural law, of Pan and Moses, can also be attributed to Boccaccio's methods.

The theme of an unrequited lover whose friend tries vainly to console him (*Arcadia* 8) may have come to Sannazaro directly from Boccaccio or indirectly via Mantuan. Like Boccaccio, however, Sannazaro shifts towards the end of the *Arcadia* from love to death as the cause of pain and sorrow; and as Boccaccio's elegy for his daughter, so Sannazaro's elegy for his mother compares the rough song of shepherds to the lofty and beautiful singing in heaven. The popularity of the *Arcadia* was enormous: first published in 1504, it went through eighty-three editions by 1650.[95]

Simultaneously with the *Arcadia*, Sannazaro was writing his Latin *Piscatorial eclogue*, begun about 1490 and published in 1504. As is the case with Boiardo, Sannazaro seems to have applied the lessons of Boccaccio's pastorals, both Italian and Latin, to his own Italian writing while sticking more closely to the Vergilian model for his Latin bucolics.[96]

In 1481 Bernardo Pulci published at Florence a translation of Vergil's *Bucolics* along with a collection of vernacular eclogues by various authors;[97] influenced by Boccaccio's vernacular pastorals, the volume encouraged further development in this direction. Moreover, by this time, toward the end of the fifteenth century, Theocritus was becoming available as a source quite different from Vergil or from those fourteenth-century poets who had known only Vergil's bucolics. A complete Greek text of the *Idylls* was printed in 1495 and three Latin editions appeared in Italy before 1500.[98] Sannazaro, who had written the *Arcadia* without having read Theocritus, did begin to

---

[94] Attilio Hortis, *Studi*, p.67, notes this discrepancy.
[95] Kennedy, *Jacopo Sannazaro*, p.107.
[96] See Kennedy, *Jacopo Sannazaro*, pp.149-52.
[97] Greg, *Pastoral*, pp.30-31.
[98] Lessig, *Ursprung*, p.50; Kennedy, *Jacopo Sannazaro*, pp.7-8.

Sources and Influences lxvii

read his *Idylls* while composing the Piscatorial eclogues.[99] At about the same time, the genre began to take hold outside Italy as well. 1513 saw the publication of the first French translation of Vergil's *Bucolica*; 1531 Marot's first French eclogue.[100] From here on the sheer quantity of available models, both ancient and modern, and the recurrence of standard forms and themes make it much harder to trace direct influences of Boccaccio's work, which continued to be available, perhaps even more readily than before, in printed anthologies of pastoral verse.

Boccaccio was the main model for religious eclogues of the following centuries and possibly also for the use of Latin hexameters in writing hymns.[101] Petrarch had used two eclogues to attack corruption in the church, thus endearing him to the Protestant cause. But Boccaccio had used eclogues to sing Scripture and to persuade reluctant souls of the urgency and means of their salvation. Vergil's fourth eclogue and the presence of shepherds at the nativity combined to make the topic of Christ's birth one of the most obvious and popular religious topics. There were such eclogues by Francesco Patrizi of Siena to Pius II (1460), by Andrea Fulvio to Leo X, by the French François Habert (in the 1540's), by the Swiss Sebastian Castalio (1515-63), and at the beginning of the seventeenth century by the Spanish Lope de Vega.[102] Antonio Geraldini wrote a sequence of twelve eclogues on the life of Christ, Pentecost, the Credo, the Last Judgment, and the blessed life (Rome 1485).[103] It thus expanded the range of Boccaccio's eleventh eclogue, similarly using classical names for holy figures and varying the names of Christ to suit the context. Jan Aerts, an Augustinian prior at Louvain (d.1537), composed four eclogues on the three theological virtues and the death of Prince Charles.[104] A narrative about two friends, separated and reunited, links the series, which may have been inspired by Boccaccio's *Comedia delle ninfe*, especially as the first eclogue, opening with a lesson by Pan on how to be a good shepherd, continues with a disagreement between the two students about where to find better pastures.

---

[99] Kennedy, *Iacopo Sannazaro*, 7-8, 149-50.
[100] Lessig, *Ursprung*, p.24.
[101] W. Leonard Grant, *Neo Latin*, p.258, 108.
[102] Alice Hulubei, *L'Eglogue en France au XVIe siècle* (Paris: Librairie Droz, 1938), pp.63-64, 231, 237. Lessig *Ursprung*, pp.131 and 260n. In Spain, comments Lessig, religious themes were the first to be set in pastoral form. Most of Boccaccio's Latin works were well known in Spain by the 1400's. Castalio's work was included in the Oporinus anthology of 1546, published at Basel where Castalio was teaching Greek.
[103] It was reprinted several times and included in Oporinus.
[104] His work appears in Oporinus under the name Ioan. Arnolleti.

Like both the Italian and Latin pastorals of Boccaccio, these contain prayer in the form of pastoral song.

Both sides of the Reformation debates used the satirical and topically allegorical qualities of the eclogue. However, according to Hulubei's massive study of the eclogue in France, the Catholics tended to avoid discussions of dogma, preferring to strengthen their case by celebrating the king and the Guise family; Protestants, on the other hand, did write poems about doctrinal matters and used phrases from the Bible in their verse, as Boccaccio had done in composing the pastoral hymn of eclogue 14. Nonetheless, French Protestants rejected the use of classical gods to signify the Christian deity; the gods, satyrs, and nymphs of their verses tend to appear as representations of the saints of Catholic idolatry. [105] An English Protestant such as Spenser, however, was quite content to borrow Boccaccio's use of Pan for God (the notion may have come to him indirectly through Marot). Both he and Boccaccio liked especially the Biblical phrases pertinent to pastoral imagery: separating the sheep from the goats, or the wolf in sheeps clothing. Spenser also imitated several themes of Mantuan's which had come originally from Boccaccio: one is the debate between the mountain and lowland shepherds; another is the shepherd who seeks his fortune in a distant city, only to return home sorely disillusioned. For Boccaccio only the first of these two themes had been religious in its meanings; but Mantuan and Spenser after him, changing the city in the second theme from Naples to Rome, turned the poem into an attack on curial corruption, thus merging the thematic centers of Boccaccio's and Petrarch's sequences.

Both Boccaccio and Petrarch, unlike Vergil, introduced female speakers into their eclogues, but they used them and the other women they refer to in somewhat different ways. Both have a female speaker who represents the art of poetry as an object of desire (Daphne, Saphos); both also have contrasting female figures who represent worldly desires: Petrarch's Epy stands for the Epicurianism beloved by the pope, while Boccaccio's Crisis and Dyone represent the allures of wealth and sexual pleasure as the poet's own unwisely beloved. Both poets also followed Servius's idea in having women represent cities: Rome is the offstage mother of the speakers in Petrarch's fifth eclogue, while Forlì and Naples find their own female voices in Boccaccio's third and fifth. Apart from these, Petrarch's eleventh eclogue presents three women: Niobe is the mythical despairing mourner, while Fusca and Fulgida, whose names mean dark and light, represent dark and enlightened attitudes towards death. Unlike Petrarch, Boccaccio sometimes presents us with women who are simply real women. Olimpia, although her

---

[105] Hulubei, *L'Eglogue*, pp.544-52.

message is in part akin to that of Fulgida, is Boccaccio's own daughter; and the beloved women of the first two eclogues are unallegorically desired as human lovers. Ignoring the homosexual element of Vergil's second eclogue, Boccaccio imitated both that and Vergil's tenth, thus calling attention to a bucolic mode which was not allegorical either politically or morally but rather associated with the genre of love elegies. Vergil's tenth eclogue to the elegiac poet Gallus had reflected on just this connection. This became the preponderant mode of later pastoral verse in England (*England's Helicon* is almost entirely in this mode) and in Spain where Petrarch's *Canzoniere* rather than his eclogues became a popular source for pastoral material.

Boccaccio may have had a general influence also on the use of the annual cycle as an organizing principle for later poems, such as Marot's "Eglogue de Marot au Roy," or sequences, such as Spenser's.[106] Vergil's final eclogue had perhaps suggested winter, as Gallus's unfaithful lover has escaped north into colder regions. Boccaccio, in any case, made the winter ending much more explicit. His fifteenth eclogue, last except for the dedicatory poem, opens with a warning of approaching winter and the need to think about salvation. As the winter is clearly a reference to death, the human life cycle and seasonal cycle are both operative. So too Vergil had ended his ninth eclogue with travelers approaching a tomb. Just as Boccaccio's fourteenth eclogue had reversed the enclosing "umbra" of Vergil's *Bucolica* by ending his poem with dawn instead of dusk, so too the escape from wintry earth towards heaven implies a return to spring, for it closely follows Olympia's description of Paradise as an eternal springtime. Boccaccio's interest in the natural cycle to give a sense of form and closure, despite the uncalendrical number of poems in the sequence, works together with his delight in the pastoral place (both items being of notably less interest to Petrarch) to encourage attention to the presence of Nature in the pastoral world. Later poets, moving away from the allegorical eclogue, would pay this feature even greater attention. It is again a matter not so much of Boccaccio's inventing the idea as of his focusing on and developing certain aspects of Vergil's *Bucolica* different from those seized on by his partner in the enterprise of bucolic revival.

We can sum up some of the general tendencies of pastoral which Boccaccio encouraged, some in which he simply participated without providing a major source, and some which he omitted or rejected outright. Many of

---

[106] Merrit Hughes's appendix II on "Pastoral Sources" to the variorum edition of the "Shepheardes Calender" (*Variorum Minor Poems I*, ed. Charles Osgood and Harry Lotspeich, Baltimore: Johns Hopkins University Press, 1943, 596-632) suggests Boccaccio as a source for Spenser's winter eclogues.

these tendencies were present already in Vergil's work; but Boccaccio and Petrarch, launching first independently and then together a revival of the bucolic genre, stressed quite different aspects and thus created quite different avenues for its development. Encouraged by Boccaccio, and not by Petrarch, were themes of erotic love, of Christian doctrine, of personal elegy, of admiration for a poet-friend, and of the writer's independence and freedom. Boccaccio also contributed to themes for which Petrarch could provide another major source: historical allegory, political or social satire, public elegy, literary ambition, and the contrast of spiritual with material values. Themes which Petrarch fostered and which Boccaccio did not include the celebration of rulers and the attack on church abuses. Whereas Vergil and Petrarch both offered a symmetrical arrangement of poems, Boccaccio's organization was more narrative than geometric. The linking of eclogues into a continued story and the mixing of narrative with pastoral verse are his invention. The inclusion of humor, self-deprecation, domesticity, and stanzaic song contributed to the development of a popularizing tone, while the inclusion of prayer and hymn allowed the humble form a serious religious content. Finally, Boccaccio's promotion of the genre within a literary project of classical revival won the attention of humanists in the succeeding generation and of poets throughout the following centuries.

Editorial Policy for this Text and Translation

The Latin text used for this translation is that prepared by Aldo Francesco Masséra for his edition of Boccaccio's *Opere Latine Minori*, Scrittori d'Italia 111 (Bari: Gius. Laterza & Figli, 1928), pp.3-85. That edition was based, in turn, on the ms. Ricciardiano 1232, which has long been accepted as an original autograph, [107] and has been dated 1367-68.[108] Another late fourteenth-century manuscript, ms. Laurenziano XXXIX 26, is considered to be a copy of an earlier version of Boccaccio's work, and thus has offered some interesting points of comparison.[109] The less reliable edition by Giacomo Lidonnici, *Il Buccolicum Carmen* (Città di Castello: S. Lapi, 1914), nonetheless contains voluminous notes, which were a major source for my own annotations.

Some assistance for both notes and translation was provided also by Pier Giorgio Ricci's Italian version of eclogues 1, 3, 14, and 16 in his edition of *Giovanni Boccaccio: Opere in versi, Corbaccio, In Laude di Dante, Prose Latine, Epistole*, La Letteratura Italiana Storia e Testi 9 (Milano: Riccardo Ricciardi, 1965), pp.651-703. Arnaldo Bonaventura, *La Poesia Neo-Latina in Italia del secolo XIV al presente* (Città di Castello: S. Lapi, 1900), pp.49-57, includes an Italian translation of eclogue 12. The only eclogue ever translated into English is the fourteenth, because of its possible influence on the "Pearl": Israel Gollanz, *Boccaccio's Olympia* (London: Florence Press [Chatto & Windus], 1913). To my knowledge, no one has ever yet translated the entire sequence.

Although the original poetry is in hexameters, I have, after trying out both five- and six-foot lines, settled on pentameters as a more naturally flowing meter in English. Despite the use of meter, I have tried to remain as close as possible to the Latin text. My hope is that the availability of this

---

[107] The identification was made convincingly by Oskar Hecker in *Boccaccio-Funde* (Braunschweig: Georg Westermann, 1902), pp.43-77.

[108] Giuseppe Billanovich and Frantisek Čada, "Testi bucolici nella biblioteca del Boccaccio," *Italia Medioevale e Umanistica* 4 (1961), p.213.

[109] See Masséra's notes, pp.261-66.

work in English will help to reinsert it into discussions of the history and development of pastoral poetry, which have frequently neglected it unfairly. This volume also takes its place among some recent English translations of Boccaccio's other works, to increase the general understanding of this extremely influential author.

Select Bibliography

Bergin, Thomas G.. *Boccaccio*. New York: Viking Press, 1981, 257-68.

Billanovich, Giuseppe and Frantisek Čada. "Testi Bucolici nella biblioteca del Boccaccio," *Italia Medioevale e Umanistica* 4 (1961), 201-221.

Billanovich, Giuseppe, Frantisek Čada, Augusto Campana, Paul Oskar Kristeller. "Scuola di Retorica e Poesia Bucolica nel Trecento Italiano," *Italia Medioevale e Umanistica* 6 (1963), 203-234, and 7 (1964), 279-324.

Branca, Vittore. *Tradizione delle Opere di Giovanni Boccaccio I. Un primo elenco dei codici e tre studi*. Rome: Edizioni di Storia e Letteratura, 1958, pp.79-80.

Carrara, Enrico. "Cecco da Mileto e il Boccaccio," *Giornale Storico di Letteratura Italiana* [*GSLI*] 43 (1904), 1-27.

Carrara, Enrico. *La Poesia Pastorale. Storia dei Generi Letterari Italiani*. Milano: Dottor Francesco Vallardi, N.D.

Cooper, Helen. *Pastoral: Medieval into Renaissance*. Totowa, N.J.: Rowman and Littlefield, 1977. A. Foresti. "L'egloga ottava di Giovanni Boccaccio," *GSLI* 78 (1921), 325-43.

Faraglia, N.F. "Barbato di Sulmona e gli uomini di lettere della corte di Roberto d'Angiò," *Archivio Storico Italiano* 5th series, vol.3 (1889), pp.313-60.

Gerhardt, Mia Irene. *Essai d'analyse littéraire de la pastorale dans les littératures italienne, espagnole et française*. Diss. Rijksuniversitait. Leiden, 1950. Rotterdam: Van Gorcum & Comp., ND. Grant, Leonard. *Neo-Latin Literature and the Pastoral*. Chapel Hill: University of North Carolina Press, 1965.

Greg, Walter W. *Pastoral Poetry and Pastoral Drama*. London: A.H. Bullen, 1906.

Guidotti, Paola, "Un amico del Petrarca e del Boccaccio: Zanobi da Strada,

Poeta Laureato," *Archivio storico italiano* 7th series, vol.13 (1930), pp.249-93.

Hauvette, Henri. "Sulla cronologia delle egloghe latine del Boccaccio," *GSLI* 28 (1896), 154-175.

Hecker, Oskar. *Boccaccio-funde.* Braunschweig: Georg Westermann, 1902, pp.43-92. (Here Hecker established the identity of the autograph manuscript, with other very useful comments about it.)

Hortis, Attilio. *Studi sulle opere latine del Boccaccio.* Trieste 1879, 1-68. (This essay pioneered the turning of scholarly attention to Boccaccio's eclogues.)

Koerting, Gustav. *Boccaccio's Leben und Werke.* Leipzig: Fues Verlag, 1880.

Krauss, Werner. "Uber die Stellung der Bukolik in der ästhetischen Theorie des Humanismus," in *Gesammelte Aufsätze zur Literatur und Sprachwissenschaft.* Frankfurt: Klostermann, 1949, pp.68-93.

Krautter, Konrad. *Die Renaissance der Bukolik in der lateinischen Literatur des XIV-Jahrhunderts: von Dante bis Petrarca.* Munich: Wilhelm Fink, 1983. (An excellent study of the eclogues of Dante and Petrarch, and of Boccaccio's poems to Checco da Mileto, but not including his *Buccolicum carmen.*)

Labagnara, Silvia. *Il poema bucolico del Boccaccio.* Rome: Luigi Ambrosini (1967?). (Labagnara argues that the sequence forms an organized whole.)

Lambert, Ellen Zetzel. *Placing Sorrow. A Study of the Pastoral Elegy Convention from Theocritus to Milton.* Chapel Hill: University of North Carolina Press, 1976. (Discusses eclogue 14.)

Landau, Marcus. *Giovanni Boccaccio, sein Leben und seine Werke.* Stuttgart: Cotta, 1877.

Léonard, Emile G.. *Boccace et Naples.* Paris: Librairie Droz, 1944.

Léonard, Emile G.. *Histoire de Jeanne I, reine de Naples, Comtesse de Provence (1343-1382),* esp. vol.2. Paris: Librairie Auguste Picard, 1932.

Léonard, Emile G.. "Nicolas Acciaiuoli Victime de Boccace," *Mélanges offerts à Henri Hauvette.* Paris: Les Presses Françaises, 1934, 139-148. (Defends the character of Niccola Acciaiuoli against Boccaccio's defamation.)

Léonard, Emile G. "Victimes de Pétrarque et de Boccace, Zanobi da Strada," *Etudes Italiennes* N.S. 4 (1934), 5-19.

Lidonnici, Giacomo. "La Lupa e Polifemo nel 'Buccolicum carmen' di Giovanni Boccaccio," *Studi su Giovanni Boccaccio*. Castelfiorentino: Società Storica della Valdelsa, 1913, 175-186.

Lidonnici, Giacomo. "Il significato storico e psicologico del 'Buccolicum carmen' e la sua cronologia," *Il Buccolicum carmen* ed. Lidonnici. Citt di Castello, Casa Editrice S. Lapi, 1914.

Macri-Leone, Francesco. *La Bucolica Latina nella letteratura italiana del secolo XIV*. Torino: Ermanno Loescher, 1889. (Deals mainly with the poems by Dante and Giovanni del Virgilio, but is useful; a promised second volume on Petrarch and Boccaccio was never published.)

Macri-Leone, Francesco. "La Politica di Giovanni Boccaccio," *GSLI* 15 (1890), 79-110.

Martellotti, Guido. "Dalla tenzone al carme bucolico: Giovanni del Virgilio, Dante, Boccaccio," *Italia Medioevale e Umanistica* 7 (1964), 325-36.

Martellotti, Guido. "La riscoperta dello stile bucolico (da Dante al Boccaccio)," in *Dante e Boccaccio e altri scrittori dall'umanesimo al romanticismo* (Florence: 1983), pp.91-106.

Masséra, Aldo Francesco,ed. Giovanni Boccaccio *Opere Latine Minori*. Bari: Laterza & Figli, 1928. (Notes on the text, pp.261-86.)

Padoan, Giorgio. "Giovanni Boccaccio e la rinascita dello stile bucolico," *Giovanni Boccaccio editore e interprete di Dante*. Società Dantesca Italiana. Florence: Olschki, 1979, 25-72; also in *Il Boccaccio, le Muse, il Parnaso e l'Arno*. Florence: Olschki, 1978, 151-98.

Ramat, Raffaello et al. Società Storica della Valdelsa. Firenze: Olschki, 1964, 20-62. (Generally discredited. See the review by Padoan in *Studi sul Boccaccio* 2 (1964), 475-507.)

Ricci, Pier Giorgio, ed. *Giovanni Boccaccio: Opere in versi, Corbaccio, In Laude di Dante, Prose Latine, Epistole*. La Letterature Italiana Storia e Testi vol.9. Milano: Riccardo Ricciardi, 1965.

Rosenmeyer, Thomas G. *The Green Cabinet. Theocritus and the European Pastoral*. Berkeley and Los Angeles: University of California Press, 1969.

Rossi, Aldo. "Dante, Boccaccio, e la Laurea Poetica," *Paragone* N.S. 13, no. 150 (giugno 1962), 2-41. (Suggests that Boccaccio invented the Dante-Giovanni del Virgilio correspondence. See next item.)

Rossi, Aldo. "Boccaccio autore della corrispondenza Dante Giovanni del Virgilio," *Miscellenea Storica della Valdelsa* 69 (1963), 130-172. Also in *Scritti su Giovanni Boccaccio*. Ed.

Sabatini, Francesco. *Napoli Angioina, Cultura e Società*. Cava dei Tirreni: Edizioni Scientifiche Italiane, 1975.

Schmid, Wolfgang. "Tityrus Christianus. Probleme religiöser Hirtendichtung an der Wende vom vierten zum fünften Jahrhundert," *Rheinisches Museum für Philologie*, Neue Folge 96 (1953), p.101- 65; also in Klaus Garber ed. *Europäische Bukolik und Georgik*. Wege der Forschung 355. Darmstadt: Wissenschaftliche Buchgesellschaft, 1976, pp.44-121.

Servius Grammaticus. *In Vergilii Bucolica et Georgica Commentarii*. Ed. George Thilo. Leipzig: Teubner, 1887.

Thompson, David and Alan Nagel. *The Three Crowns of Florence: Humanist Assessments of Dante, Petrarca and Boccaccio*. New York: Harper & Row, 1972.

Torraca, Francesco. "Rileggendo le egloghe," in *Per la biografia di Giovanni Boccaccio*. Milano: Albrighi, Segati e C., 1912, 151-193. (Attempts to identify historical significances.)

Velli, Giuseppe. "L'Ameto e la Pastorale, il significato della forma," *Boccaccio: Secoli di Vita*, Atti del Congresso Internazionale Boccaccio 1975. Ed. Marga Cottino-Jones and Edward Tuttle. L'Interprete 4. Ravenna: Longo, 1977.

Villani, Matteo. *Cronica di Matteo e Filippo Villani*, vol. 2-3. Roma: Multigrafica Editrice, 1980. (reprint of 1825 ed.)

Walsh, Gerald Groveland. *The Emperor Charles IV* (New York: Appleton, 1924) (especially chap. on "The Imperial Coronation," pp.41-49).

Zumbini, B. "Le egloghe del Boccaccio," *GSLI* 7 (1886), 94-152. (Although alphabetically last, this essay is one of the classic founding studies on Boccaccio's eclogues.)

Text and Translation

I. GALLA

DAMON. Tindare, non satius fuerat nunc arva Vesevi
et Gauri silvas tenera iam fronde virentes
incolere, ac gratos gregibus deducere rivos,
quam steriles Arni frustra discurrere campos?
5 Quid stolidus moneo? Prudens es. Dic tamen, oro,
que te cura gravis iussit superare nivosas
alpes et fluvidas valles transire coegit?

TINDARUS. O Damon Damon, quantum sibi quisque beavit
qui potuit mentis rabidos sedare tumores
10 et parvas habitare casas, nemora atque remota!
Quod nequeam, dure de me voluere sorores.
Hinc igitur tauros curo deducere silvis
Alcesti: sic atra iubet voluitque cupido.
Sed quid tristis ades? Fervet nunc limpidus aer
15 et fugiunt virides inter spineta lacerti.
Quid tu solus agis? quid pascua torrida queris?

DAMON. Ne rogites: stat corde mori; mors ipsa quietem
sola dabit fesso. Mors est inimica laborum.
Tuque tuus facito sis, fac quoque semper amores
20 effugias volucres, et diras sperne pharetras.
Quo fortuna trahet miserum, moriturus abibo.

TINDARUS. Esne tui compos? Paulum requiesce sub antro;
est equidem veteris michi grandis copia bachi.
Perge, precor, Phorba, crateras fronde corona;
25 en pendant ansis patulam, si cernis, ad alnum.

I. GALLA

DAMON: Tindarus, would it not have been better
to inhabit now the green fields of Vesuvius
and tender leafing woods of Gaurus Mountain
and draw down streams so pleasing to the flocks,
than vainly roam the Arno's sterile plains?
But I'm a fool to be advising you!
You're prudent. Tell me, pray, what heavy care
compelled you to ascend the snowy Alps
and forced you to traverse the streaming valleys?

TINDARUS: O Damon, happy he who has been able
to calm the rabid swellings of the mind
and dwell in humble huts and groves remote!
That I cannot be such a man as this
the cruel sisters willed for me. Therefore
I am obliged to lead Alcestus' bulls
to pasture; thus calamitous desire
has ordered and commands. But why do you
come here in sadness? The clear air now is hot,
and the green lizards flee among the brambles.
Why walk alone? Why seek out torrid pastures?

DAMON: Don't ask! I have it in my heart to die!
Death alone can offer me repose.
Death is the foe of troubles. But may you
be your own master always and take care
to flee from winged loves and also shun
the deadly quivers. As for wretched me,
where fortune drags me, there I'll go to die.

TINDARUS: Are you in your right mind? Come rest a while
here in the cave; I even have on hand
a full supply of well-aged wine. Go, Phorba,
please crown the bowls with leaves; see where they hang
by handles on the spreading alder tree.

	Interea que dira lues michi pandito, Damon,
	te cruciet: leviat mentes recitasse dolores.
DAMON.	Quis neget? Audieram solitum cantare Menalcam.
	Ast ego si dicam, mecum lacrimaberis ipse.
TINDARUS.	Sic volo. Quem letis tantum dicemus amicum?
DAMON.	Nympha fuit silvis totis pulcherrima nostris;
	et quantum lauro cedit funesta cupressus,
	cupresso mirtus bicolor, mirtove mirice,
	Tindare, huic tantum cedit Galathea Miconis.
35	Hec facilem placidis quondam me cepit in annis
	has inter fagos, pulchris comitata napeis.
	Heu! quibus hec oculis, roseo suffusa rubore,
	impulit in pectus flammas quibus uror, et auxit
	blanda nimis! Nobis volucres nunc ferre sagictas,
40	nunc solita et catulos, nunc retia tendere cervis,
	dissuadere truces ursos ac dentibus apros
	ne sequerer sevos, lata et venabula furtim
	surripere, ut vacuo lenes apponeret arcus.
	Indignor memorans: quercus michi testis amorum est.
45	Amplexus centum cui iunximus, oscula centum,
	nunc alios, oblita mei, sic temperat ignes.
	ut moriar: permitte mori; moriemur amando!
	Sed videant silve montes arbusta fluenta,
	et memores nymphe reddant pro munere munus.
TINDARUS.	Absit, mi Damon! Nimium falluntur amantes.
	Quid nosti cur ista feras? Stat sepe sub umbra
	ignis. Dum pallet iuvenis, tum fervet Adonis.
DAMON.	Erras, non sic est: fraus hec notissima nobis.

I. GALLA

| | Meanwhile do you unfold to me, my Damon,
| | what deadly wasting grief torments you so.
| | The mind is lightened when its woes are told.
| DAMON: | That's undeniable. I heard Menalcas
| | used to sing that too. But if I tell you,
| | you yourself will weep along with me.
| TINDARUS: | That's just as it should be. Whom shall we call
| | a friend only in times of happiness?
| DAMON: | There was a nymph –in all our woods most beautiful!
| | As the funereal cypress to the laurel,
| | as the two-colored myrtle to the cypress,
| | or as the tamarisks yield to the myrtle,
| | so Micon's Galathea yields to her.
| | Ah Tindarus, in my once peaceful years
| | accompanied by lovely nymphs she captured me,
| | an easy mark, among these beeches here.
| | Alas! what eyes, what cheeks with rosy blush
| | thrust in my breast the flames with which I burn,
| | increasing them too much with her caress!
| | Now would she carry for me wingèd arrows,
| | now the little hounds, now spread the nets
| | for deer, and now beseech me not to hunt
| | ferocious bears or boars with savage tusks;
| | she'd steal away the broad-blade hunting spears
| | and hand to me, unarmed, the safer bow.
| | I am indignant now as I recall it!
| | The oak is witness for me of our loves:
| | a hundred hugs, a hundred kisses joined us.
| | Now she tends other flames, having forgotten
| | my love, in such a way that I am dying.
| | Then let me die! I shall have died of love!
| | But may the forests, mountains, bending trees,
| | behold my death, and may the nymphs, remembering,
| | give justice where it's due.
| TINDARUS: | Far be it, Damon!
| | Lovers are much deceived. What do you know
| | with certainty enough to cause your pain?
| | Fire often lurks beneath a shade; and while
| | the young Adonis pales, he then grows hot.
| DAMON: | Not so; you're wrong. Her fraud's well known to me.

55	Antrum grande manet silvis sub colle virentis Montis Ugi, quo forte greges contraxerat Egon, et pastos gracili solus refovebat avena. Huc ego dum, Phytia pecori custode relicto, errans advenio; sic me malus ardor agebat; presensi timuique dolos. Nam mixta puellis
60	Galla choros antro festos lasciva trahebat; nec secum Egoni quicquam cur luderet antro. Pamphylus interea dum cogeret inde capellas ad salices, tacitus meditans sub rupe sedebam invisus. Petit verum ille secreta salicti,
65	et stipula doctus pariter fidibusque canoris carmen inauditum cepit. Tunc sistere silvas cantu et stare capros et ludere saltibus edos vidisses. Quid multa feram? Iam certus amorum in longum tenuit, donec lasciva per umbras
70	venisset iuvenis. Timidos quis fallet amantes? Venit et illa quidem catulis sociata duobus, illis illudens manibus succinctaque ramis, voce ciens comites, ne forsan longius iret Pamphylus. At postquam coram lenique sub umbra
75	ylicis argute consedit, et ylice teste pastorem flagrans cepit spectare canentem, o! sibi quos oculos, actus quos quosque reflexus auricomi capitis, quos risus quosque rubenti obtulit amplexus facie! Vix illa profecto
80	abstinuit, quin visa prius se conderet altis in silvis. Nec plura loquar. Mors, eripe flammas.
TINDARUS.	Nequicquam lacrimas fundis. Narrare solebat Tytirus, heu! nobis quondam, dum dulcior etas: – Non lacrimis satiatur amor, non rore cicade,
85	non cythiso pecudes eque nec prata fluento. – Quid facies igitur? flebis? Quas sordidus ulmis abstulit autumnus cernis ver reddere frondes;

I. GALLA

There is a spacious cave within the woods
beneath the slope of green Mount Hugo, where
Egon by chance had brought his flocks, alone,
and was refreshing with his slender reed
the well-fed goats. I too came wandering there,
leaving my sheep for Phytia to guard;
thus my evil passion drove me forward
with fear and with presentiments of treachery.
For mingling with the girls, the wanton Galla
led on their festive dancing towards the cave;
nor had she an excuse for playing there.
Meanwhile as Pamphylus herded his goats
toward the willows, underneath the cliff
I sat unseen in silent meditation.
He sought a recess in the willow grove,
and, skillful both with reed pipe and with lyre,
began a melody unheard before.
You would have seen the woods stand still to listen,
the goats pause for the song, the blithe kids dance.
But why go on? Now certain of her love,
he kept on playing till the wanton girl
would join him in the shadows. Who'll deceive
a fearful lover? She, yes she indeed,
came crowned with boughs; two puppies at her sides
leapt at her teasing hands, while to her friends
she called aloud lest Pamphylus depart.
And then before my very eyes she sat
beneath the sweet shade of the rustling oak
and passionately —with the oak as witness—
gazed at the singing shepherd. O! for him
what eyes, what tossing of her golden hair,
what gestures, what laughter, what embraces
she offered with her face aglow! In truth
she scarcely cared to hide once she'd been seen.
I say no more. O Death, pluck out these flames!

TINDARUS: Your weeping's useless. Tytirus, alas,
once used to tell us when our life was sweeter,
"Love is not sated with tears, nor crickets with dew,
nor sheep with clover, nor fields with a stream."
What will you do then? Weep? The leaves dark autumn
stripped from the elm, you see the spring restore;

et zephyrus placat quas undas turbidus auster
miscuit; et pandos delphynes ludere sepe
vidimus in pelago quod sorbserat ante carinas.
Sic peragit fortuna vices: nunc livida vultu
prosternit miseros, relevat nunc fronte serena.
Est reditura dies qua dicas, non tibi primus
pastorum silvis sit: fletus hos pone, precamur.
Nam si non redeat, sunt et medicamina mille:
carmine sevus amor sacro revocatur et herbis;
carmina sunt nobis, et gratas novimus herbas.
Iamdudum veterem Phorbas iam portat hyacum.

DAMONS. Cum capreis pascetur ovis, lupus acer ybisco,
gurgite cum vultur vivet, cumque ethera piscis,
cum freta sulcabit vomer, cum pascua navis,
tunc servare fidem incipiet lasciva puella;
carmine tunc Gallam revocabimus, arte vel herbis.
Ydalium petii culmen sanctumque Cytheron
et Paphi mirteta dolens, oscillaque ramis
suspendi, pia thura dedi, precibusque potentes
tentavi nymphas, votis superosque vocavi;
postque preces supplex ingentia munera misi
in cassum: crudescit amor, crudescit et ipsa.

TINDARUS. Heu michi! nequicquam defers Amarillidis olim
castaneas, Phorba, nobis, bromiumque vetustum.
Frons cecidit viresque animi; precordia dirus
urit amor misero: saxis, heu! verba movemus.
Attamen expecta si cesserit impius ignis.

DAMON. O quantum natura parens tibi, Pamphyle, rerum
posse dedit nemori! Tu sertis nectere flores,
tu cantu recreare greges fluviisque quietem

I. GALLA

and zephyr calms the waves the wild south wind
aroused; and we have often seen curved dolphins
playing in the sea which recently
had swallowed ships. Thus fortune works by turns:
now with an angry brow prostrates the wretched,
and now with face serene upraises them.
The day will come when you'll declare no shepherd
in all the woods is better off than you.
I pray you, cease your weeping. If that day
does not return, there are a thousand medicines:
a cruel love's recalled by charms and herbs.
I know the songs, I know the pleasing herbs.
Now here comes Phorba bringing well-aged wine.

DAMON: When sheep eat goats, or when the ravening wolf
dines on hibiscus, or when vultures live
beneath the sea, and fish fly through the air,
or when a plough leaves furrows in the waves,
and ships plough fields, then will a wanton girl
keep faith, then only will we call back Galla
with song, with art, with herbs. I have sought out
the Idalian peak and sacred Cythaeron
and Paphos' myrtles, weeping, and have hung
the branches there with little votive masks;
I've offered pious incense, tried with prayer
the powerful nymphs, called on the gods with vows;
and after prayers, kneeling, I have sent
huge gifts, in vain: love only grows the crueler,
and she grows crueler too.

TINDARUS: Ah, woe is me!
In vain you bring to us the well-aged wine
and chestnuts, Phorba, once of Amaryllis.
His brow has fallen and his strength of soul;
this wretch's heart is burned with deadly love.
Alas, we speak to stones. Yet wait and see
if this unholy fire will abate.

DAMON: O how much power over the woods, Pamphylus,
did Nature, mother of all, grant unto you!
You know just how to weave the flower garlands,
how by your singing to refresh the flocks
and hush the rivulets, and how to move

ponere, tu validas ornos cautesque movere
novisti, et mulcere deos et flectere montes:
o quantum! Neque sevus amor sua iura negavit
ipse tibi; nam velle tuo, ni fallor, habenas
nunc manibus, nunc mente regis, quod forte Tonanti
non licuit quondam, silvis dum captus amaret.
Quis, nisi tu, placidam fusca sub veste per arva
Egonis Gallam nuper traxisset in antrum?
quisve inter salices et densa vepreta volentum?
Te, Silvane pater, precor hec: fac cernere possim
quos pectit croceos crines per tempora canos,
et rugis roseas plenas pallescere malas,
et tacitis nemorum iaceat neglecta sub umbris,
ut ludam tremulos gressus oculosque gementes.
Hoc si forte neges, patiaris ut ultima saltem
me rapiat mors atra, meo positura quietem
fervori, corpusque tegant sub cespite sicco
pastores miseri, signent et carmine bustum.

TINDARUS. Trux amor, et iuvenum semper certissima pestis.
Heu! cecidit. Lymphas manibus portate recentes,
o pueri, si forte queam revocare dolentem.

I. GALLA

the sturdy mountain ash and even rocks,
how to appease the gods and bend the mountains.
O how much! Nor has cruel love itself
denied you rights; for at your will, it seems,
you can direct love's reins, now with your hands,
now with your mind, a thing once not allowed
to even the mighty Thunderer himself
when he was seized by love within the forests.
And who but you could recently have drawn
the docile Galla in her dark attire
across the fields and into Egon's cave?
Who else could have allured her willingly
among the willows and dense bushes? Father
Silvanus, this I pray you: let me see
those yellow hairs she combs turn white upon her,
those ruddy apple cheeks grow pale and wrinkled;
in silent forest shadows may she lie
neglected, so that I may mock her trembling
steps and weeping eyes. Should you deny this,
then grant at least dark death at last to snatch me
and quench this burning pain. May the poor shepherds
bury my corpse and mark the grave with verse.

TINDARUS: Savage is love, the surest plague of youth.
Alas! he's fallen. Bring fresh water, boys,
so that I may revive the grieving lad.

II. PAMPINEA

PALEMON. Quid merui? Duris fustemne securibus olim
concessi, Silvane senex, aut fontibus ursos
segnes immisi, nymphas lesurus agrestes,
ut crucier misereque trahar moriturus in arvis?
5 Nunc tacet omne nemus; subeunt vineta cicade,
omne pecus radios cessat, cantare volucres
desistunt, et colla boum disiungit arator
fessus et umbrosos querit per rura recessus.
Me miserum male sanus amor per devia solum
10 distrahit, et longos cogit sine mente labores
ut subeam, victusque sequar vestigia nondum
cognita Pampinee. Dixi «sequar» inscius, imo
perscruter; nec cura potest retinere peculi
quin montes celsos densosque per invia lucos
15 discurram, tristique ferar referarque ferarque
quo iubet ire furor, prospectans undique nunquid
venantum turmas videam, nubemque per arva
surgere pulveream, seu capras vertice pulsas
currere et auritos lepores; si demere campis
20 retia, si sparsos eque revocare ministros
atque canes spectem. Sed frustra lumina tendo;
nusquam Pampineam video, vestigia nusquam.
Pampineam, o! quotiens nequicquam vocibus usque
in celum totis clamavi vallibus imis,
25 «Pampineam» et totiens valles dixere sonore!
O! quotiens deceptus ego surgentia longe

II. PAMPINEA

PALEMON: "What have I done wrong? Did I once yield
my staff to biting hatchets, old Silvanus,
or drive lumbering bears across the springs
to harm the rural nymphs, that I should suffer,
drawn wretchedly to perish in the fields?
Now all the wood is hushed; the crickets hide
among the vines; the herd yields to the rays;
the birds have ceased to sing; the weary plowman
unyokes the oxen's necks and seeks the shade.
Yet I alone am driven by mad love
through wandering ways, insanely to endure
long labors, wretched victim, and to follow
my Pampinea's as yet unfound footprints.
"Follow" I said, but still I search for them;
nor can the care of my own little savings
detain me now from running through high mountains
and through dense, pathless groves, from being sadly
driven back and forth and on again
wherever passion orders me to go,
forever looking whether I might see
the hunters, or their distant dustcloud rising,
or startled goats dashing from the summits
and long-eared hares; or whether I might see
the nets withdrawn upon the plains, or hear
called back the scattered servants and the dogs.
In vain I strain my eyes; for I see nowhere
my Pampinea, nowhere any traces.
How often have I called out "Pampinea,"
though fruitlessly with shouts up to the heavens
and called through every valley, "Pampinea,"
till all the vale was ringing with the sound!
How often from the hills I've seen, deceived,

arbusta aggeribus zephyro concussa putavi,
utque iubebat amor redeuntem credidi, et ultro
obvius in vacuum veni! Sic dirus amantes
fecit amor pronos ac omnia credere iussit.
Silvestres nymphe, colui quas sepe per umbras,
dicite cur homini reliquis animantibus alma
indulgens natura minus. Nam cetera possunt
indulgere suo, nimium si fervet, amori:
stant ducibus pecudes, tauro dilecta iuvenca;
turtur in arboribus socium, sociumque columba
turribus insequitur: pastori grata voluptas
tollitur, atque fugit miseros quos pulchra puella
traxerat in casses saviis et murmure dulci.
    Quid, dulces satyri, faciam, faunique potentes?
quid faciam? quid pulchra iuvant armenta? quid antra?
quid nemora aut valles? Uror sine mente sub umbra;
sole sub ingenti tristis tremor occupat artus.
Hinc amor infestat dubium, timor arguit illinc,
ne vel dura silex ictu vel belua morsu
leserit incautam, vel fessam seva viarum
asperitas grandisque labor fortasse moretur;
vel, quod fata vetent, non quis temerarius illam
traxerit invitam rapiatque per oscula mentem.
Novimus, insidias posuit persepe Cupido
silvarum in latebris, et longa silentia ruris
non sine labe manent. Quis nigras ire per umbras
succinctam et genibus nudam ventoque solutis
crinibus inspiciet nympham, mirtique virentis
conspicuam serto, qui non rapiatur in ignes
extemplo veneris, rapiatque quod optat in usum?
Dant aditus vires animis et opaca viarum.
Preterea non Egla fuit, non culta Neera
pulchrior; ac posito modicum sit fusca, quis alter
aptior est silvis color? His quoque Iuppiter olim

II. PAMPINEA

a rising tree far off by breezes shaken
and thought it her returning as love ordered,
and going out to meet her, met with emptiness.
Cruel love made lovers ever credulous.
You forest nymphs whom I have oft revered
among these shades, say why is nature kind
to other beasts, yet much less kind to man?
For every other can indulge its love:
for rams there are the ewes, and for the bull
the darling heifer; while the turtledove
follows his sweetheart in the trees, the dove
follows her cooing mate about the towers;
but to the shepherd pleasure is denied,
and shuns those wretches whom a pretty girl
has tangled in her snare with kiss and murmur.
What shall I do, sweet satyrs, potent fauns?
What shall I do? What help are lovely flocks?
what help the cave? what help the woods or valleys?
I burn insanely even in the shade;
in midday sun my limbs are shivering.
From this side love attacks me with fierce doubt;
from that side fear assails me, lest hard rock
by striking or wild beast by biting harm her
while she was off her guard, or the rough pathways
and weary toil delay her with fatigue;
or (may the fates forbid!) that someone bolder
has dragged her off against her will and steals
her mind with kisses. For we know how often
Cupid lays traps in woodland hiding places,
nor do long rural silences remain
unblemished. Who that sees the nymph pass through
black shadowed places, with her skirts tucked up,
knees bare, hair loosened to the wind, adorned
with garlands of green myrtle, would not then
be seized straightway with Venus' fires and seize
what he desired to use? The pathway's darkness
strengthens his intentions. Aegla, besides,
was not more beautiful, nor the refined
Neera; and if she is slightly dusky,
what color is more fitting for the forest?
By these even great Jove was often captured

sepius in lucis captus, sic Phebus et Argus.
Sed nullus timor iste michi: nunc atria celi
celicole servant; dubium non rufus Alexis
aut Coridon donis soliti hanc tentare vicissim
65 detineant: potuere deas iam flectere dona.
    Heu michi! cuncta meis obsunt venientia votis!
Exitium stabulis lupus est, sic messibus imber,
fructetisque novis grando, fetisque capellis
est boreas: michi sevus amor, quo distrahor uror
70 impellor crucior volvor rapiorque ferorque,
nec scio quid faciam; verum hec sententia cordis,
hanc animam exuere et placide hec dare membra quieti.
Heu michi! nonnunquam hos cornix expulsa labores
dixerat a quercu, sed mens hec leva neglexit.
75   O nostrum predulce decus, qua parte vagaris
hos inter montes? que te, mea, lustra ferarum
accinctam pharetra retinent? quas incolis umbras,
quave iaces longo forsan nunc victa labore?
O! utinam fortuna michi tam grata fuisset,
80 ut comes ire tibi possem! Quis retia cervis
ponere me melius, quisnam venabula porcis,
quis canibus dare lora magis, quis flectere retro
cornua dicteis olim lassata sagictis
et duros arcus validis curvare lacertis
85 ac telis agitare capros cognovit agrestes?
Nasilus in silvis docuit me nempe remotis.
O! michi si tantum cupido Phebeia faveret,
ut minimos inter pueros, dum solis ab estu
aufugis, unus ego possem numerarier unquam:
90 putre solum lymphis premerem, iuncoque palustri
tum specus omne latus strarem; post gramina pomis,
lacte novo et veteris bachi cererisque canistris
ornarem iussus; prestarent inde mirice
seu mirtus vel lenta salix in cespite lectum.

II. PAMPINEA

in the groves, and Phoebus too, and Argus.
But that is not my fear, for now the gods
keep to the halls of heaven; my worry is
lest Corydon or ruddy-cheeked Alexis
detain her, tempting her with wonted gifts:
for gifts have swayed even the goddesses.
    Alas! all is contrary to my prayers!
The wolf's the bane of stables, as the rain
is to the harvest, hail to tender orchards,
or as the northern wind to pregnant goats;
my bane is cruel love, by which I am
distracted, driven, burned, tormented, twisted,
seized and swept away; nor do I know
what I should do. But it's my heart's desire
to put away this care and give these limbs
some peaceful rest. Alas! the banished crow
sometime foretold these troubles from the oak,
but my unheeding mind ignored these omens.
    O sweetest jewel of mine, where do you wander
among these mountains? What wild creatures' lairs
detain you with your quiver far from me,
o dearest one? What shade do you inhabit,
or where do you now rest perhaps from toil?
O would that fortune had been kind enough
that I might go with you and be your comrade!
Who knows better than I to set the nets
for deer, or drive the spear into the boar,
whip on the dogs, pull back the antlers wearied
by Cretan arrows, bend the rugged bow
with my strong arms, or drive wild goats with spears?
Nasilus taught me in the distant forests.
O! If Diana would so favor me,
so eager as I am, that I might ever
count myself among your least of servants
while you find refuge from the midday sun,
I'd settle the dusty ground with freshest water,
with marsh reeds strew the cave in every part;
and afterwards, as bid, I would bedeck
the grass with fruits, fresh milk, baskets of wine
and bread; then supple willow, tamarisk,
or myrtle would prepare a bed for you.

O! tibi quot flores, violas quot quotque rubentes
narcissos ferrem! Quis flores non det amanti?
Inde graves animis didici depellere curas
et tenues somnos lepido revocare susurro
fabellisque novis, demum prohibere latratus
voce canum, et culices facie removere flabello.
Hec faceret Coridon, faceret vel rufus Alexis,
seu quem tu sequeris Glaucus quemque ipsa bubulcis
preponis campisque tuis? Cur ergo petenti
surripis optatos vultus? cur dulcia differs
oscula? cur tantos fugiens frustraris amores?
　　Quesivi persepe, miser! qua parte napeas
pastoresque pios ires; respondit Opheltes:
− Pampineam Glaucus nuper deduxit in antrum:
tu montes et fusca petis nunc lustra, Palemon. −
Heu miser! impulsus cecidi cessique dolori,
et victus iaceo scabrose vallis in imo.
　　Delia, virgineum potuit si flectere pectus
Endimïon, si sepe tuas celebravimus aras
sique tibi lentos fagis suspendimus arcus,
in me flecte tuas iras, me confice telis.
Quid prodest placidum calamis superaddere carmen?
quid labor assiduus? quid saltus ire per altos?
Excepit segnis Glaucus quem vepribus altis
excivi studio leporem, captoque potitur.
Ast ego delusus plorans effundo querelas
has inter cautes et saxa ruentia ripis
exesis, quas aura velox per inane resolvit.
　　O veteres quercus, ylex annosa nemusque
perpetuum, voces miseri Palemonis amaras
suscipite, et morte hos agiles mollite dolores!
En clausere dii, nymphe clausere procaces
supplicibus votis aures, clausere semones.

II. PAMPINEA

O! how many flowers I would bring you,
how many violets and bright narcissus!
Who would not offer flowers to a lover?
And then I've learned to drive off heavy cares
and summon gentle sleep with whispering
and with new stories, hush the barking dogs,
and brush away the gnats from your sweet face
with just a little fan. Would Coridon
do this, or would Alexis? or would Glaucus
whom you pursue and set above the farmers
and your own fields? Therefore why steal away
your much desired face from him who seeks you?
Why put off sweetest kisses? Why, by fleeing,
frustrate so great a love?
                                Ah, wretched me,
I've often asked the nymphs and pious shepherds
where you are headed; but Opheltes answered,
"Pampinea went off just now with Glaucus
into a cave; you search the mountain ranges
and shadowed woodlands, Palemon." Alas,
poor wretch! I fell as if I had been struck
and yielded up to pain; and so I lie
quite overcome in some rough valley bottom.
    Delia, if Endymion could sway
your virgin breast, if we have often honored
your altars and hung supple bows to you
upon the beech trees, bend your wrath on me,
finish me off with darts. What use is it
to add a quiet song above the pipes?
what use persistent labor? what use hunting
through thickets? Lazy Glaucus now has caught
the hare that I with zeal roused from the briars;
the captured prey is his. But I, deluded,
in tears pour out laments among these stones
and rough rocks fallen from the rain-worn cliffs:
laments the wind dispels in empty space.
    O ancient oaks, o ilex full of years,
eternal forests, hear the bitter words
of wretched Palemon: soften these pains
with death! Lo, gods and wilfull nymphs have closed
their ears to suppliant prayers, the rural spirits

Si qua igitur vobis pietas sub cortice duro est,
irruite, et grandi misero sub pondere mortem
130 ferte, precor, si dulce fuit sitientibus olim
exoptasse leves pluvias, servasse virentes
a pecorum morsu frondes, ramisque bipennes
obstasse; hec est sola meos que possit amores
et male complexos quondam dissolvere nexus.
135 Quid michi vita magis? Glaucus bona nostra moratur,
is tenet atque trahit. Quid vitam tristis in annos
extendis lacrimans? Negligis quid perfida tantum,
mors orata? Veni, venias precor, impia, nostros
exime quos nequeo iuvenis iam ferre furores.
140 Advenies tandem? Sed tu que dulcia falce,
dum tibi solus eram, signabas cortice fagi
furta, meos deflens, dum cogerer ire, recessus
amplexuque morans, summum iam munus amantis
tolle volens: facito iuvenis ne tempora perdas.
145 En redeunt flores, redeunt et gramina pratis;
tempora non redeunt, que dudum stulta Liquoris
in vacuum flevit moriens, ac obsita canis.
Nos morimur dum, dira, iubes, peiora futuris
linquentes, credo; flebit mea Testilis usque
150 vivet, et ornabit bustum lacrimosa corollis.
Tu flores titulumque necis concede dolenti,
si quondam placui, se te ferventer amavi.
Ast michi quod restat lucis te consequar, atque
dum montes silvasque coles et roscida rura,
155 ipse colam montes, silvas et roscida rura. –
   Hec secus umbrosas ripas quis defluit Arnus
lenis ad alpheos, prostratus mente Palemon
deflebat lacrimans: ast ocior Hesperus edos
egit ut ad septas traherem caprosque Melampus.

II. PAMPINEA

have likewise closed their ears. If you, therefore,
have any pity under that hard bark,
fall down on me and bring death to a wretch
beneath your mighty weight, I pray – if ever
you found it sweet in thirst to long for rain,
to save your green leaves from the nibbling herds,
to block the axe from chopping at your branches;
death only is what can dissolve my love
and that ill-tangled knot. Why should I live?
Glaucus detains our good, holds and attracts it.
Why, weeping, drag life on into sad years?
Why, faithless death, do you so disregard me,
o prayed-for death? Come, come, impious one,
pray take away my madness which, though young,
I am unable longer to endure.
Then won't you come? But you who with your blade
cut signs of sweet thefts in the beechtree bark
while I alone was yours, and when perforce
I had to leave, lamented my departure
while clinging to a lingering embrace,
now gladly take the last gift of a lover:
enjoy your youth before the time is lost.
Now blooms return and grasses to the fields;
but time comes not again, which some while past
Liquoris, foolish, white-haired now and dying,
bewept in vain. I'm dying as you bid,
you savage girl, and leaving worse things yet
for times to come. My Testilis will weep
her whole life long and tearfully adorn
my bust with garlands. May you grant death's flowers
and epitaph unto a woeful man,
if ever I did please or love you fervently.
But as for me in my remaining life
I'll follow you, and while you dwell apart
in mountains, woods, and dewy fields, I too
will dwell in mountains, woods, and dewy fields."
    These words did Palemon, prostrate in mind,
pour out, with weeping, by the shady banks
through which smooth Arno flows on to the Pisans;
but swifter Hesperus caused me, Melampus,
to drive the kids and goats to their enclosure.

III. FAUNUS

PALEMON. Pamphyle, tu patrio recubas hic lentus in antro,
dum fremit omne nemus pulsum clamoribus egre
Testilis, et parvi vacuus nunc omnia pendis?
PAMPHYLUS. Cantarus attrita nimium, puto, lapsus ab ansa
5 terruit hunc. I, siste sues, ne gramina campis
evellant rostris, et silvas mitte sonantes.
PALEMON. Marcidus externo credis tibi forsan hyaco
alloquar in somnum presso? Auribus accipe voces,
si patitur torpor, patitur si grata Licisca.
PAMPHYLUS. Pace precor nostra sedeas, ac ista sinamus;
ignaroque aperi, queso, percepta, Palemon.
PALEMON. Tempus erat placidum; pastores ludus habebat
aut somnus lenis; paste sub quercubus altis
ac patulis passim recubabant lacte petulcis
15 ubera prebentes natis distenta capelle.
Ast ego serta michi pulchro distinguere achanto
querebam, servanda tamen, dum fistula gratos
nostra ciet versus Mopso, cui tempora dignis
nectere concessum, lauro et vincire capillos;
ocia cum subito rupit vox improba meste
Testilis, – O! – clamans – que to vesania cepit?
Ursos quid sequeris montana per ardua, Faune?
Non te cura tui retinet? non parva tuorum
edis mixta cohors cornu ludentibus arvis

III. FAUNUS

PALEMON: Pamphylus, are you lying drowsy here
in your paternal cave, while the whole forest
trembles at the shouts of anxious Testilis,
and do you in your idleness consider it
unworthy of concern?

PAMPHYLUS: The tankard fallen
from its worn-out handle, as I think,
has terrified this man. Go, stop your pigs
lest with their snouts they tear up fields of grain,
and never mind about the strident woods.

PALEMON: Perhaps you think, while drowsing off to sleep,
that I speak as one drunk with foreign wine?
But listen, if your torpor lets you, listen,
and if pleasing Licisca will allow.

PAMPHYLUS: Sit down, I pray, and let's drop all these insults;
and tell an ignorant man what you have heard.

PALEMON: The day was clear; the shepherds played or slumbered.
Beneath the tall and spreading oaks, the shegoats
well-fed lay here and there, now offering
milk-swollen udders to their butting young.
But I was picking garlands of acanthus,
to be preserved as long as my reed utters
verses pleasing to Mopsus, who with laurel
has had his temples bound and locks entwined
by worthy men; when suddenly sad Testilis'
persistent voice broke in upon our leisure,
exclaiming, "O what madness has possessed you?
Why chase the bears through craggy mountains, Faunus?
Doesn't concern for safety hold you back?
Doesn't your little throng of children, mingled
in meadows with the playful, butting kids?

25	natorum? non matris amor? Dic, obsecro, nescis qualis in hos rabies circumstrepat atra luporum allobrogum? Credis tantis obstare periclis, femina sum, possim paucis sociata molosis? –
PAMPHYLUS.	Semper in adversos saltus fractasque ruinas
30	ire cupit Faunus, monstra atque minantia mortem querere. Quid tandem? Tenuit vox ire volentem?
PALEMON.	Hoc ego querebam veniens. Sed Meris, ut opto, ecce venit tardus baculoque innixus adunco, nescio quid secum meditans. Salveris, amice!
35	En optate venis. Quis nostris, obsecro, nuper rumor inest silvis? Nostin que Testilis ire?
MERIS.	Quid petis? Est usquam crebras qui nesciat iras Testilis et Fauni? Nequeunt subsistere quercus, depereunt fesse frondes clamoribus, et tu
40	si cantet phylomena petis, si ruminet hyrcus.
PAMPHYLUS.	Sepius has quondam memini risisse querelas. Sed tu, Meri decus nostrum, modo pone galerum et baculum, mecumque sede lucemque severam hanc fugito. Nulle veniunt de montibus umbre;
45	alta crepidinibus terre petiere lacerti. Hic nemus et gelidi fontes et mollia prata, hic hedere viridis tectum pictumque corimbis antrum, quo magnus quondam requievit Amintas; et pariter calamis una cantabimus omnes.
MERIS.	His ego cantabo silvis? Nemus omne cicadis, dedecus in nostrum, milvis corvisque relictum est.
PAMPHYLUS.	Quid tandem? Corvos observent mente subulci; nos equidem nobis Mopso Musisque canamus, et placidum gremio servabunt sydera carmen.
PALEMON.	Cura gregis parvi, quem forsan mergere lymphis, dum calor arva tenet, cupit, hoc nunc carmine Musis et nobis placuisse vetat: sine, queso, revisat delirus Cidypem tenuesque recenseat edos.

III. FAUNUS

	Doesn't their mother's love? Say, I beseech you, do you not know how Allobrogian wolves are howling in dark fury all around them? Or do you think I can resist such dangers, a woman with a few Molossian hounds?
PAMPHYLUS:	Faunus always seeks out hostile woods and broken ruins, and death-threatening monsters. What of it? Did this shouting hold him back?
PALEMON:	That's what I came to ask. But here comes Moeris, slow-paced and leaning on a crooked staff: he's pondering something. Greetings, friend! You come just as I wished. Say, what's the latest gossip? And do you know why Testilis is angry?
MOERIS:	How can you ask? Does anyone not know the frequent fights of Testilis and Faunus? The very oak trees can't stand up against it: their leaves fall off, worn out by all the din. You're asking if birds sing and if goats chew.
PAMPHYLUS:	I often used to laugh at all their squabbles, as I recall. But for a while, dear Moeris, set down your cap and staff, and sit with me out of this glaring sun. The mountains now produce no shadows; the lizards have sought out the highest banks of earth. Here are the forest, cold springs, and tender meadows; here a cave sheltered by green ivy and adorned with clustering ivy berries, where the great Amintas rested once; we shall all sing together while the reedpipes play along.
MOERIS:	Shall I sing in these woods? To our disgrace the woods are left to crickets, kites, and crows.
PAMPHYLUS:	So what? Let swineherds worry about the crows. And as for us, let's sing just for ourselves, for Mopsus, for the Muses; and the stars will keep the gentle song safe in their bosoms.
PALEMON:	My duty towards a little flock, which bids me bathe them in streams while all the fields are hot, won't let us please the Muses and ourselves with song right here and now; I pray that madman return to Cidypes and count his kids.

MERIS. Est Cidypes nobis niveos que contrahat agnos
in fontem cythisumque paret, vaccisque salicta;
et surgent celse salso de gurgite pinus
ante quidem, et blande venient ad ovilia tygres,
atque leo cevas fugiet, lupus atque capellas,
quam michi non animo Musis servire. Sed ecce,
si tibi tantus amor silvarum nosse tumultum,
expediam paucis, postquam consedimus antro.
Nescio si montes unquam nemorosaque plana
nostis que gemino resident contermina ponto
ausoniis, magno quondam disiuncta Peloro.
His Argus pastor, merito cantandus ubique,
vivus erat campis. Flavos hunc mille per arva
audivi servare greges; nec plenius usquam
et soles imbresque graves frondesque salubres
et pecori fetuque novo, seu flumina, quisquam
cognovit, tantusque fuit, dum carmine valles
tangeret, ut noster, Nyse cui summa dicamus,
amphrisus pastor vix quiret tendere secum
vocibus aut calamis vel nervis. Horrida tandem
parca virum rapuit meritisque recondidit astris.
Fleverunt montes Argum, flevere dolentes
et satyri faunique leves, et flevit Apollo.
Ast moriens silvas iuveni commisit Alexi,
qui cautus modicum dum armenta per arva trahebat,
in gravidam tum forte lupam rabieque tremendam
incidit impavidus nullo cum lumine lustrum
ingrediens; cuius surgens sevissima guctur
dentibus invasit, potuit neque ab inde revelli
donec et occulto spirasset tramite vita.
Hoc fertur. Plerique volunt quod silva leones
nutriat hec dirasque feras, quibus ipse severus
occurrens venans mortem suscepit Adonis.
Si nunc cuncta velim que tunc gessere propinqui
pastores narrare, dies non, lucis ab ortu
usque domum sature redeunt cum nocte capelle,
sufficeret spatio. Sed postquam Tytirus ista
cognovit de rupe cava que terminat Hystrum,

III. FAUNUS

MOERIS: I have a Cidypes who leads the lambs
to springs, prepares their clover, and brings willows
to feed the cows; but lofty pines will rise
from salty water, tigers tamely come
into their pens, the lion flee from deer,
the wolf from goats, before I have no will
to serve the Muses. Yet if you desire
to understand the tumult in our forest,
come sit down in the cave; I'll tell you briefly.
    Do you know the wooded plains and mountains
which lie in Italy between two seas
that separate the plains from great Pelorus?
In these same fields lived once the shepherd Argus,
who's worthy to be sung in every land.
I've heard he kept a thousand tawny flocks
throughout the countryside; and no one anywhere
knew better both the sun and heavy rains,
the leaves healthy for sheep and for their offspring,
or rivers. When with song he touched the valleys,
he was so grand that our Amphrysian shepherd
to whom we dedicate the peak of Nysa
could scarce compete with him in voice or pipes
or strings. However, horrid fates then snatched him
and hid him in the stars that he had earned.
The mountains wept for Argus, satyrs wept,
and nimble fauns, and even Apollo mourned.
He had bequeathed the woods to young Alexis,
who, careless as he led flocks through the fields,
proceeding without light into the forest,
encountered there by chance a pregnant wolf
swollen with rage; this savage beast sprang up
and plunged her teeth into his throat, nor could she
be pulled away until his life expired
upon that hidden path. That's what they say.
But many claim this forest shelters lions
and the ferocious beasts that killed Adonis,
as fierce himself when he was hunting them.
If I narrated all the shepherds' actions,
from sunrise till the sated goats come home
would not be time enough. When Tityrus heard it
in his hollow cliff beside the Hyster,

		flevit et innumeros secum de vallibus altis
		Danubii vocitare canes durosque bubulcos
		infrendens cepit; linquensque armenta suosque
100		saltus infandam tendit discerpere silvam,
		atque lupam captare petit flavosque leones,
		ut penas tribuat meritis: nam frater Alexis
		Tytirus iste fuit. Nunquid vidisse furentem
		stat menti ferro nuper venabula acuto
105		gestantem manibus, multos et retia post hunc
		portantes humeris, ira rabieque frementes,
		hac olim transire via silvamque per omnem?

PALEMON.   Calcidicos hystrosque refers. Quid, queso, tenenti
Eridanum secus arva queunt inferre laboris?

MERIS.   Ecce tene. Multi per devia Tytiron istum
ex nostris, canibus sumptis telisque, sequuntur,
inter quos Faunus, quem tristis et anxia fletu
Testilis in cassum revocat, clamoribus omnem
concutiens silvam: tendit tamen ille, neglectis
115   fletibus atque suis. Pulvis patet, aspice colles.

PAMPHYLUS.   Semper in adversum fertur male sanus, et egre
fert Faunus requiem. Veniet, ni sibilus austri
nunc aures fallit, tempus quo Testilis ibit
Hesperi in amplexus; dabitur nec posse volenti
120   sistere. Sed redeat cupio melioribus astris!

PALEMON.   Quis queat ardores iuvenum compescere frenis?
Apta quies senibus, sedeant in limine matres.
Naritius nullas potuit preponere laudes
quesitis peregre. Tibi si mens antra nemusque
125   est servare, precor, cum sim post ire paratus,
pasce greges nostros: et donec forte revertar
in silvas, nemeam Crisidem tu solus habeto.

PAMPHYLUS.   I felix, factumque putes rediturus, amice.

III. FAUNUS

he wept and summoned from the Danube valleys
innumerable dogs and toughened ploughmen,
gnashing his teeth; and leaving flocks and woods,
he headed out to tear down that vile forest,
and seeks to catch the wolf and tawny lions,
to punish those who merit it; for Tytirus
was brother to Alexis. Do you recall
not long ago having seen him raging,
carrying the sharp iron hunting spear,
and many men behind him bearing nets
upon their shoulders as, trembling with fury,
he crossed this way through the entire forest?

PALEMON: You mean the Hystrians and Chalcidians.
And what, pray, are they able to inflict
on him who holds the fields by Eridanus?

MERIS: Know this: many of our men follow Tytirus
with dogs and spears, among them Faunus, whom
the sad and anxious Testilis with tears
calls back in vain, her shouts shaking the woods.
He's going nonetheless, ignoring all
her tears and his own people's safety. Look:
you see the dust is rising on the hills.

PAMPHYLUS: A madman's always swept into misfortune;
Faunus can't stand repose. There'll come a time,
unless the south wind's whistle tricks my ears,
when Testilis will enter Hesperus' arms;
will he or nill, there'll be no way to stop it.
But may he come again with better stars!

PALEMON: Who ever can with reins control youth's ardors?
Let old men rest, let mothers sit in doorways.
The highest praises, said Naritius,
are praises won abroad. If you intend
to stay here in the forest and its caves,
since I'm preparing to go after him,
please feed my flocks; till I perchance return,
do you alone hold my Nemean Crisis.

PAMPHYLUS: Go with my blessing; and consider it done;
for surely you'll return to us, my friend.

IV. DORUS

MONTANUS. Quo te, Dore, rapis? nemorumne per herbida capros
scrutaris seu forte boves? Consiste parumper;
nondum tecta quidem fumant, non Hesperus ardet.
DORUS. Da veniam, Montane, precor, fugiamque iubeto.
5 Quod petis, hoc prohibet casus, nam cuncta pavesco,
MONTANUS. Dives abis, si cuncta times; requiescere mecum
hic fessus poteras. Nam si non tecta ligustris
antra michi videas, est nobis ignis et umbra:
et quanquam steriles agri sint, proxima capris
10 pascua non desunt; est grandi copia lactis
et veteris bachi nobis et farris acervus;
nec tibi quis tuscus prestabit tutius antrum.
DORUS. Ha! miserum rides; nescis quibus ipsa reservet
te fortuna dolis. Pastorum pascua quippe
15 nec bona nunc quero; magnum michi tuta latebra.
PHYTIAS. Si potius nil, Dore, petis, quid summere differs
oblatum? Spectare potes de vertice campos
alpheos tuscosque greges alpesque remotas
et ligurum saltus, Rhodanum rubrosque galeros
20 metiri, ac egram mentem revocare quiete.
Montani laudanda fides. I, summe. Quid obstat?
DORUS. Si laudas, faciam. Sperabam posse tumores

IV. DORUS

MONTANUS: Where are you rushing, Dorus? Looking for goats
or cows perhaps in grassy woodland spots?
Now pause a while: the roofs are not yet smoking;
indeed the evening star is not aglow.

DORUS: Forgive me, please, Montanus; let me flee.
What you request my circumstance forbids,
for I'm afraid of everything.

MONTANUS: You must
be going off with lots of money then
if you fear everything; yet you could rest
your weary self with me. I have a cave,
in case you haven't seen it, sheltered quite
with privets, and within are fire and shade;
and if the farmland's sterile, still the goats
don't lack for food; I have abundant milk
and well-aged wine, and there's a heap of grain;
no Tuscan offers you a safer cave.

DORUS: Ha! There you mock a wretch. You do not know
for what deceits fortune's reserving you.
I look not now for shepherd's pasture land;
the chief thing is a good safe hiding place.

PHYTIAS: Dorus, if that is all you're looking for,
then why refuse the offer? From this peak
you see the Pisan fields and Tuscan herds,
the distant Alps, and the Ligurian glades,
can trace the Rhône with all its redcapped folk,
and call a sick mind back in peacefulness.
Montanus' faith is praiseworthy. What hinders?
Go on, accept.

DORUS: If you advise, I will.
I hoped to lay my troubles down where flows

ponere quo placidus fesulanis defluit Arnus;
nam priscam tu sepe fidem cantare solebas
25 florigenûm, dum leta fuit fortuna, meorum.
PHYTIAS. Sic fateor: dammas nemorum vidisse luporum
rebus in adversis animos sumpsisse, labantem
prostravit mentem, et timeo quoscunque recessus.
MONTANUS. Sic est. Intremus. Postquam successimus antro,
30 tu dic, care puer, nobis, quibus anxius ultro
sic fugias; medioque cibos Galathea parabit.
DORUS. O tibi si memorem quantis inimica fatiget
me fortuna malis, non si per pascua tygres
immanes videas fetas agitare iuvencas,
35 in iugulumve rapi tauros, celoque maligno
omne pecus captum tristique putrescere tabo,
sic immite feres: utinam modo fata dedissent,
immemor ipse forem! Nam, dum mecum acta revolvo,
vix lacrimas cohibere queo, vix aspera verba.
MONTANUS. Quin tu pande, precor: magnos audire labores
non sumus insoliti, grandisque invictaque cordi
mens sedet, et nulli cedit, michi crede, labori.
DORUS. Que volsci coluere prius campanaque rura,
lucanos saltus, samnitum pascua, rupes
45 et montes brutios calabrûmque aspreta levesque
iam Dauni campos, peligno et flumina grata
olim Argus tenuit; princeps his omnibus unus
Argus pastor erat, cui fas complectere cuncta
viribus ac oculis, calamis et flectere quercus.
50 Hic abiit celoque senex se condidit alto,
defletus modicum. Verum presagia vatum
predixere quidem: – Lacrimas quas demitis Argo,
inferias poscet. – Post hunc miserandus Alexis,
qui gregibus nimium durus silvisque molestus

IV. DORUS

the Arno peacefully from Fiesole;
for you sang often of the ancient faith
of my dear Florentines, while fortune smiled.

PHYTIAS: And so I did. But to have seen the deer
take on a wolfish boldness in adversities
has thrown my tottering mind; I fear each cranny.

MONTANUS: That's how it is. Let's enter. In the cave
you'll tell, dear boy, from what you flee so anxiously,
while Galathea will prepare a meal.

DORUS: If I were to recount you all the evils
with which a hostile fortune wears me down,
not if you saw huge tigers in the pastures
alarm the pregnant ewes, the bulls' throats seized,
the whole herd stricken with a stinking plague
sent from a baneful heaven, would you think
such things so cruel. Would that the fates at least
allowed me not to think of it! For when
within myself I ponder the events,
I'm scarcely able to refrain from tears,
and scarcely able to hold back harsh words.

MONTANUS: Please do explain; we're not unused to hearing
of hardships, and a great unconquered mind
presides over the heart and yields, believe me,
to no calamity.

DORUS: Campanian fields,
and those the Volscians tilled, Lucanian groves,
and Samnite pastures, Bruttian cliffs and peaks,
and the Calabrians' rough territory,
the gentle fields that once belonged to Daunus,
and winding rivers pleasant to Pelignus,
Argus possessed; sole prince of all was Argus,
a shepherd granted to embrace all things
within his strength and sight, and even bend
the oaktrees with his reedpipe. As an old man
he went away and hid himself in heaven,
lamented not enough. Indeed the seers
predicted truthfully: "The tears you take
away from Argus, he'll demand from you
as offerings to the dead." Then poor Alexis,
who herded sternly, irksome to the woods,

imperitans, abiit crudeli funere pulsus.
Munere post Phytie pulchra est michi iuncta Liquoris,
et sub me septas Argi tenuere nepotes,
quas inter clarosque lacus pecorosaque tempe
calcidici veteres silvam posuere coloni
a Cumis, qua nulla prior dum floruit; in qua
dum nos iurgantes pueros agitaret Erinis,
ecce celer quondam patriis Poliphemus ab arvis
progenitus nostris et nostro sanguine, ripis
altus in extremis Hystri, puto, lacte ferino,
quo iaculo incertum, certo mutilatus ab ictu
parte sui, iusta rabie succensus et ira,
irruit ut torrens qui hybernis imbribus auctus
monte cadit celso et rumoribus omnia complens
hec arbusta rapit, quatit hec, ruit atque superbus
in rupes et saxa trahens ingentia volvit.
Nec sevo lacerasse prius sub vindice sontes,
nec post innocui Paphi fedasse cruore
sydereos vultus, truncum et iecisse cadaver,
aut vinclis gratos nymphis onerasse puellos,
immitis potuere gravem minuisse furorem.
Exuit infaustos ungues truculentior angue
frendens, et pomis foliis et cortice nudat
fructeta, et vitreos perturbans sanguine fontes,
dentibus infringens ramos pictasque volucres
murmure disperdens claustrisque repagula frangens;
omne pecus mungit, decerpit, vellera tondet,
absorbet natos, miseras eviscerat agnas:
si peiora nequit, rescindit cornua tauris.
Vix Cereri sacras quercus, vix antra Lyceo
intacta est passus; satyros nymphasque vetustas
et faunos lucis pepulit. Sic astra ferebant!

MONTANUS. Sic magnis prisci finem dare tristia rebus
iurgia cantabant nobis quandoque bubulci.
PHYTIAS. Quid lacrimis, Montane, mades? ubi pectu herile?

IV. DORUS

departed driven by a cruel death.
Then by the gift of Phytias fair Liquoris
was wed to me, and under me grandchildren
still kept the folds of Argus, which the ancient
Chalcidians from Cumae placed among
clear lakes and in a valley full of sheep;
no pasture was superior while it flourished.
There, while Erinys roused us brawling boys,
behold swift Polyphemus, our kinsman,
born from our fathers' fields, raised on the shores
of farthest Hyster on the milk, I think,
of wildest beasts, now maimed by a sure blow,
though by whose javelin it is not sure,
kindled with righteous rage and wrath rushed down
just as a torrent, swollen with winter rains,
sweeps down the lofty mountain, far resounding,
uproots these trees, shakes those, and proudly dragging
mighty rocks, hurls them upon the crags.
And not before with a ferocious vengeance
he'd torn apart the guilty, not before
he'd fouled the starry faces with the blood
and mutilated corpse of guiltless Paphus,
or heaped with chains the boys who pleased the nymphs,
could furor dwindle in that ruthless man.
Gnashing his teeth, more vicious than a snake,
he bares disastrous claws and strips the orchards
of fruit, of leaves and bark; perturbs with blood
the crystal springs; breaks with his teeth the boughs
and, roaring, scatters wide the colored birds,
and bursts through locks and bars. All sheep he fleeces,
or plucks away and shears; he swallows lambs,
he disembowels poor ewes; and at the least
he cuts the horns from bulls. Scarcely the oaks
sacred to Ceres did he leave untouched,
scarcely the caverns sacred to Lyceus;
He's driven from the woods the satyrs, fauns,
and nymphs of yore. The stars had this in store!

MONTANUS: Thus plowboys used to sing in days gone by
that sorry quarrels ruin great affairs.

PHYTIAS: Why weep, Montanus? Where's your mastering mind?

MONTANUS. O Phytia, fateor, quisnam sibi ponere leges
sic potuit prout ipse facis? Sum carneus, hercle!
Hec hodie, dum falce Lycas virgulta secaret,
intento gregibus Coridon narrabat Aminte;
etsi nulla fides illis, sum flere coactus:
95   quid veris faciam? Dorus sed cepta sequatur,
et me linque meis lacrimis: satiabitur istis,
heu! pietas et certa fides quibus angor amicus.

DORUS. Dum ruit omne decus nemorum, tunc ordine nullo
pastores pariterque greges armentaque passim
100   diffugiunt timidique ruunt; loca namque ministrat
ipse pavor: petit hic colles, petit ille cavernas
lustraque silvarum. Plures se iungere monstro
sunt ausi, et prestare fidem; quibus ipsa deûm vis,
si qua est, ut fertur, statuet pro munere munus.
105   Obscenas sevi pregnans vix squalida Nays
evasit tremebunda manus, onerata gemella
prole, per umbrosam noctem magalia tentans
passibus incertis. Lacrime non sponte tepentes
quas tu Montani, Phytia, sic ante monebas,
110   adveniunt; nec plura quidem iam dicere possum.

MONTANUS. Nec mirum: sed dura animum, mi Dore, precamur,
nec taceas reliquum. Iuvit narrasse labores.

PHYTIAS. Quis neget optatum iuveni? Mos nempe gerendus
Montano; dic, Dore, precor; nunc cura peculi
115   nulla tibi, trahimusque moras in vertice tuto.

MONTANUS. Quid Paphus, queso, cui centum brachia, centum
fama refert oculos, cui tanta licentia fandi
in superos hominesque fuit? Non cuspide lata
occurrit monstro? Quid tunc furibundus Asylas?
120   quid pecudum custos Phorbas? quid Damon amicus?
quid tu? quid Phytias? quid Pamphylus atque Molorcus?

IV. DORUS

MONTANUS: O Phytias, who can as well as you
impose laws on himself? I'm flesh, by Hercules!
Today while Lycas with his pruning hook
was cutting brushwood, Coridon was telling
these matters to Amintas as he watched
the flocks; and though I was incredulous,
I was compelled to weep; what should I do then
if what they said is true? Let Dorus narrate
and leave me to my tears; alas, they'll sate
the friendly pity by which I am anguished.

DORUS: While all the woodland's beauties crash to ruin,
in chaos shepherds, flocks, and herds all flee
hither and thither, rushing about in fear,
for fear now rules the realm; one seeks the hills,
another seeks the caves and forest dens.
Many have even joined the monster's force
and pledge him faith; to whom the powerful gods
–if there are any gods as it is said–
will give their just deserts. The pregnant Nays,
ragged and trembling, burdened with her twins,
barely escaped the cruel man's obscene hands
as through the shadowy night with unsure steps
she sought some shelter. Look, Montanus' tears
which you just now admonished, Phytias,
are pouring down warm and involuntary;
now I cannot go on.

MONTANUS: It is no wonder;
yet stiffen your courage, Dorus, pray, and don't
omit the rest. It helps to tell one's troubles.

PHYTIAS: Who would deny the young man's wish? Montanus'
request most certainly deserves compliance;
tell on, please, Dorus; now you have no care
for any flock; we tarry here in safety.

MONTANUS: What, I ask, of Paphus, who is famed
to have a hundred arms, a hundred eyes,
and spoke so freely against gods and men?
Does he assail the monster with his spear?
Or what of wild Asylas? what of Phorbas,
the shepherd? what of our old comrade Damon?
and what about you? what about Phytias?

	ac alii tecum tangentes alta boatu
	sydera, iactantes vario sermone palestras
	atque pedum cursus, cestus et fortia facta?
DORUS.	Iam satis ostensum. Phytias in litore solus
	invictus mansit, qui nunc peregrina per arva
	me profugum sequitur. Stabat mens currere contra
	ingens, et lectas pharetra de more sagictas
	abstuleram, nervusque levem iam flexerat arcum;
130	sed tenuit non sana fides numerusque meorum
	tunc nullus, Phytiasque boans: – Quo tendere frustra,
	stulte puer, tentas? Nequicquam flectere fata
	nitimur. Hoc celo placuit; sic Iuppiter equus
	viderat, et pensis dederat sua iura futuris. –
135	Hinc natale solum silvas armenta domosque
	liquimus, ac tenui lembo diffugimus ambo
	infandam monstri rabiem; nec defuit usquam
	dux fidus, placideque tulit quoscunque labores.
	Nos turbo fluctusque maris Thelamonis ad oras
140	impulit, inde tuos errantes venimus agros.
MONTANUS.	Ut vestros doleo casus, sit silva perennis
	hec nobis, parvumque pecus. Quod si tibi cure,
	summito: tu ducas. Sed, si michi nuntia veri
	ylice ab excelsa cornix fuit, ecce parantur
145	multa tibi graviora satis, reditusque propinquus.
	Spes te sepe trahet sterilis; quicquid modo perdis,
	vinces cunctando: sed non tibi delphyca laurus
	sertum leta dabit, donec tu manibus unum
	falce caput tribues pro cunctis. Nos quoque, diras
150	si tibi, Dore, placet faciles transire querelas,
	mittamus, Bachoque sacrum celebremus honorem.

IV. DORUS

or what about Pamphylus and Molorcus?
and others shouting with you to the stars,
discussing up and down the wrestling match,
the foot race, boxing gloves, and braver deeds?

DORUS: I've shown enough already. Phytias
alone remained unconquered on the shore,
who follows now my flight through alien fields.
His mighty mind was all set for attack,
and I had drawn the arrows from my quiver,
the bowstring had already curved the bow;
but perilous loyalty was wearing thin,
the number of my men by then was zero,
and Phytias was shouting, "Foolish boy,
now whither do you try to aim in vain?
In vain we strive to bend the fates. It's willed
by heaven; so just Jupiter foresaw,
and gave his laws to future undertakings."
Hence we have left our native soil, abandoned
the forests, flocks, and homes, and fled together
from the monster's rage unspeakable,
inside a fragile boat. I never lacked
a trusty guide; he calmly bore all blows.
The ocean's wave and eddy drove us to
the shores of Thelamon, from which we've come
by wandering to your fields.

MONTANUS: As your case grieves me,
so may this wood be ours perpetually,
so may the little flock – which, if you like,
do take them; you may lead them. If the crow
announced the truth from high atop the oak,
then things much weightier are still in store,
and soon you will return. Oft sterile hope
will lead you on; whatever you have lost,
you'll win back by delaying; don't expect
a garland from the happy Delphic laurel
until you offer to the shades one head
cut with a sickle on behalf of all.
Yet we too, Dorus, if it pleases you
that we pass lightly over dire laments,
will say no more; but let us celebrate
the sacred rites of Bacchus. Galathea

En Galathea vocat: redeunt cum matribus agni,
et nox cerulea iam terras denigrat umbra.

is calling; lambs and ewes are coming home,
the lands grow dark with night's cerulean shadow.

V. SILVA CADENS

CALIOPUS. Pamphyle, tu placidos tecum meditaris amores
Calcidie, viridi recubans in gramine solus;
ipsa dolens deflet miseras quas nescio silvas.
PAMPHYLUS. Unde, precor, nosti? Sis mecum: Phebus in altum
5 tollit equos; prosunt umbre, michi crede, capellis.
CALIOPUS. Sicilidum saltus et florida rura Pelori
forte pererrabam; vox venit tristis ad aures.
Attonitus tum firmo gradum, prospecto frequenter
si videam flentem. Video. Quid lilia falce
10 secta loquar, floresque malo iam sole reflexos?
Cespite sic nudo lacrimis oppleta iacebat
illa suis, questusque graves ex ore trahebat.
PAMPHYLUS. Heu michi! quid vivo? Iam tacte fulmine pinus,
et pecudes prostrasse canes, noctisque per umbram
15 ex septis ululare lupos audisse, nefandum
prodigium dederant. Sed dic, quas, obsecro, voces
illa dabat deflens? Tua presto stat tibi merces.
CALIOPUS. Quas ego concepi, referam. Tu, dulcis Aminta,
nunc oculos gregibus prestes servesque, precamur,
20 ne si damna satis faciant fortasse capelle,
hyrsutus Corilas, Bavio mittente, lacesset
hyrcos interea morsu vel terreat agnos.
PAMPHYLUS. Ne dubites, saxis sistet baculoque iuvabit.
CALIOPUS. Illa diu postquam faunos nymphasque vocavit

V. THE FALLING FOREST

CALIOPUS: Pamphylus, by yourself you meditate,
reclining on the green grass all alone,
the sweet love of Chalcidia; but she weeps
in sorrow for some wretched woods or other.

PAMPHYLUS: Where did you learn this, please? Here, sit with me:
Apollo's steeds mount high; the goats need shade.

CALIOPUS: As I was wandering through Sicilian woods
and through Pelorus' flowering countryside,
a sad voice reached my ears. I stop, astonished,
and looked about to try to find who's weeping.
I see her. Why should I speak of lilies mown
and blossoms drooping in the harsh hot sun?
So on the bare ground she lay choked with tears,
and heavy lamentations filled her mouth.

PAMPHYLUS: O woe is me! Why am I yet alive?
Already have the pines been struck by lightning,
the dogs have killed the sheep, and through night's shadows
I heard wolves howling from the folds; all these
had given horrid omen. Tell, I beg,
what words did she then utter in her weeping?
You'll be rewarded.

CALIOPUS: I'll tell you what I heard.
You, sweet Amintas, watch the flocks meanwhile
and take responsibility for them,
lest if the goats should happen to do damage,
shaggy Corilas, sent by Bavius,
might bite the goats and terrify the lambs.

PAMPHYLUS: Don't worry, he will stop the dog with stones
and also with a stick.

CALIOPUS: When she had called
the fauns and nymphs in vain for a long while,

in cassum, pectusque manu pulsavit et ora,
vocibus assiduis syrene in litore fractis
Parthenopes residens, misere singultibus inquit:
– Non fuit ausonicis campis, me iudice, silva hac
letior aut maior, nulla atque capacior evi.
Hec fagis celum tangebat et ylice multa,
quercubus insignis, viridi spectandaque lauro
ac cedro crebra, funesta et pulchra cupressu.
Non adeo quondam formosa Libistridos ursis
horrida, cui cessit magnorum Ercinia nutrix
silvestrumque boum gelido sub cardine celi,
Ydaque iudicio Paridis memoranda puellis,
bebritiumve nemus cessit, cessitque erimantum.
Floribus hec ramos et prata virentia semper
pingebat croceis roseisque et mille colorum,
colchida dum primum siccaret vellera Phebus.
Quid referam claros leni per gramina cursu
serpentes rivos fontesque lacusque recentes
antraque perpetuis non arte recondita tophis?
Hac picte nidos cuncte fecere volucres;
psytacus exustis usque huc accessit ab arvis,
captus amore soli, sic et pulcherrima fenix.
Nec fuit Ytalie que ferret silva leones
hanc preter: mites tulit hec iraque verendos,
ut taceam lepores, cervos et dente minaces
apros et capreas et grandes viribus ursos.
Hec niveas habuit pecudes, quibus inclita tantum
vellera prestabant reliquis, quantum aurea poma
glandibus aut sorbis. Referat quis grandia quantum
dudum armenta boum pavitque et texerit umbra,
quantum lactis eis fuerit, que copia prolis,
pascua dum magnus servabat Tytirus olim?
Heu michi! cognovit Ciclops. Ast Tytirus ille est
qui primus pecori leges nemorique salubres
carmine cantavit, quarum nec clarior usquam
copia docta fuit legum nec prisca tulere

V. THE FALLING FOREST

and beaten with her hands her breast and face,
then sinking down upon Parthenope's shore,
she moaned, her words broken by frequent sobs:
   "No forest in the Ausonian plains, I judge,
was happier or greater or more fit
for long life than was this. This wood touched heaven
with beechtrees and was thick with ilex too,
distinguished with its oaks, and worth beholding
for its green laurel, dense with cedar, lovely
with mournful cypress. Not so lovely once
were the Libistrian woods bristling with bears
to which Ercinia yielded, nurse of heroes
and of wild oxen under the frozen pole;
and to which Ida, memorable to girls
for Paris' judgment, the Brebycian wood,
and Erymanthian forest also yielded.
This forest always used to paint its branches
and verdant meads with flowers, yellow, pink,
and of a thousand colors, while first Phoebus
was drying the Colchian fleece. Why should I mention
the clear streams winding leisurely through grasses,
the springs, fresh lakes, and caves artlessly hidden
by limestone? Here the bright birds made their nests;
the parrot, much enraptured with the land,
came all the way here from her dried-up fields;
and so did the supremely gorgeous phoenix.
Nor were there any better woods in Italy
for breeding lions, mild or fierce with anger,
not to mention hares and deer and boars
threatening with the tusk, and goats and bears
of mighty strength. And she had snowy sheep
whose famous fleeces so surpassed all others
as a gold apple does acorns or berries.
Who can tell how many herds of cattle
she fed not long ago and offered shade,
or how much milk they gave, how many offspring,
while our great Tytirus once kept the pastures?
Ah woe! the Ciclops knew it. But it's Tytirus
who first sang laws salubrious to the sheep
and woods; the copious learning of those laws
was nowhere more illustrious, nor did

secula maiores, auro dum floruit etas
sanguine, si veri quicquam primeva vetustas
insculptum liquit fagis vel robore duro.
Me miseram! memini letis quibus ipsa choreis
saltantes vidi satyros facilesque napeas
floribus ornatas et sertis fronde revinctis
esculea, et gratos silvis expromere versus
nunc stipulis auctos, fidibus nunc arte canoris.
Sed quid tot refero? Complectar ut omnia paucis,
quantum cana salix alno quantumque mirice
quercubus et celsis cedunt vepreta cupressis,
huic omnis tantum cedebat silva nemusque.
Pro superûm virtus! quantum hec modo tempora distant
a priscis, quantumve malis dat Iuppiter astris
arbitrii! Fortuna quidem, quos ante fovebat
leta nimis, pavidos secum revoluta fatigat.
Plangite, silvani veteres, heu! plangite mecum.
Delapse quercus, grandes cecidere cupressus,
esculus exarsit summissis undique flammis,
pinus nulla sedet, virides albescere lauros,
heu! video, et bicolor passim iacet undique mirtus;
aret et omne solum pallens, arbustaque nuda
frondibus in nichilum tendunt; abiere volucres
antraque pastorum video deiecta, recessus
incultos, muscoque putri pallescere fontes
et nitidos rivos turpi sordescere limo,
ac circum ripas calamos crevisse palustres.
Quod meritum? quod triste nefas? quod crimen avitum
vel fortasse tuum potuit tot superis iras
iniecisse tua cum clade? Miserrima quis tam,
quis tam dira deus permisit lapsa? quis orco
eduxit pestes in te? quis, queso, labores
excudisse tuos potuit tristesque ruinas?
O ruber ortorum custos, cui pulcher achantus

V. THE FALLING FOREST

the primal centuries make better ones
while yet the golden age was flourishing,
if antiquity left any truth
incised in beeches or in hardest oak.
Ah wretched me! for I remember well
in what blithe dances I saw satyrs leaping
and gentle nymphs adorned with blooms and garlands
entwined with oakleaf, how they sang sweet verses
to the woodlands now with reeds and now with strings
made tuneful by their art. But why review
so many things? To sum it up in brief:
as much as the grey willow yields to the alder,
as much as lowly tamarisk to the oaks,
and as the thornbush to the lofty cypress,
so much did every other wood and grove
yield to this one. O power of the gods!
how different these times are from ancient times,
or how much rule Jove gives to evil stars!
And Fortune too spins down the frightened men
whom earlier she favored happily.
Weep, ancient woodsmen, weep with me, alas!
The oaks have crashed, the mighty cypress fallen,
the Italian oak is burning with set fires
in every part, no pine remains, alas!
I see the evergreen laurel has turned white,
the two-toned myrtle lies strewn here and there;
the whole pale soil is parched; the trees, denuded,
stretch into emptiness; the birds have gone;
I see the shepherds' caves have been cast down;
the quiet places lie uncultivated;
the springs are clogged with murky rotten moss;
the riverbanks once neat are foul with mire,
and all along the banks marsh reeds have grown.
What fault? what sad impiety? what crime
of your forefathers or perhaps your own
could have inspired in the gods such angers
along with your destruction? What god has
allowed so wretched and so cruel a fall?
Who introduced to you such plagues from hell?
Who could describe your troubles and sad ruins?
O ruddy lord of gardens, you for whom

95	aggere surgebat viridi canumque ligustrum,
	et quem puniceo quondam cum flore roseta
	et molles viole stabant et lilia circum
	ybleusque thymus, nigra et vaccinia tecum
	crescere sunt solita, an cernis quam creverit uncus
100	carduus, et vacuus surgat paliurus in ortis,
	ulvaque vel saturis onagris suspecta cicuta?
	Ha! faunûm pietas, fertis, dryadesve sorores,
	quis stipula totiens frondes virgultaque movi,
	hoc spectare nefeas? Video sine vitibus ulmos;
105	vix hedere vivunt. Solitos flavescere campos
	en vacuis plenos prospecto horrescere avenis;
	piscosique lacus, pontus fluviique quiescunt;
	cortex nullus inest, resonant nec litora tonsis,
	et passim video sparsas, heu! vasta per arva
110	infectas tabo pecudes morbisque capellas,
	pastoresque graves per sordida lustra ferarum
	dispersos, turpique fuga nemus omne relictum est.
	Alcestus trepidans abiit, tremebunda Liquoris
	in dubium liquit silvas evecta per altum.
115	Omne decus periit, luctusque laborque supersunt.
	Plangite, silvani veteres, heu! plangite mecum.
	Silva decus nostrum periit, pereamus et ipsi. –
	Hec ubi dicta dedit, manibus lacerasse capillos
	implicitos vidi; tandem quasi victa resedit.
PAMPHYLUS.	Heu miser, heu! video que sit sibi causa doloris:
	indignum facinus lacrimis revocare putabat
	previsum dudum superis, et pensa sororum.
	Errat stulta nimis: celo parere necesse est.
	Sed tu, dum fleret, nullis solatia verbis
125	perdita tentasti placidis reparare querentis?
CALIOPUS.	Non equidem, ne forte malus Poliphemus adesset
	indignans: celeri sed te per pascua passu
	quesivi. Tu verba dabis, tu nubila purga.

V. THE FALLING FOREST

the fair acanthus and white privet used
to rise from the green mound, whom with bright flower
the rosebeds and soft violets and lilies
encircled and the sweet Hyblaean thyme,
with whom dark blueberries were wont to grow,
do you not see how the barbed thistle's sprouted,
how useless bramble springs up in the gardens,
hemlock and sedge mistrusted by wild asses?
O piety of fauns or sister dryads,
whose leaves and thickets I have stirred so often
with reedpipes, can you bear it to behold
this foul abomination? I see elms
bereft of vines, the ivy barely living,
the fields once gold turned rough with worthless straw.
The fish-filled lakes, the sea and streams grow silent;
there is no fisher's float, nor do the shores
resound with any oars; I see dispersed
through desolate lands the plague-infected sheep,
the goats diseased, the woeful shepherds scattered
among the filthy lairs of savage beasts,
in shameful flight the forest all abandoned.
Alcestus has departed full of fear,
Liquoris, trembling, left the woods in doubt
and sailed away. All beauty here has perished,
bur grief and care remain. Weep, ancient woodsmen,
weep with me, alas! The woods our joy
have perished, let us perish too."
                                        I saw
her tear her tangled tresses as she spoke;
at last she sank down as if overcome.

PAMPHYLUS: Alas! ah wretch, I see her cause for grief!
she thought with tears she might revoke a crime
unworthy and previsioned by the gods
and spinning sisters. foolishly she errs:
for one must yield to heaven's will. But you,
did you not try to bring with gentle words
lost comfort to the mourner as she wept?

CALIOPUS: Oh no indeed, lest wicked Polyphemus
should happen near and be perchance offended;
but with swift step I sought you in the pastures.
You'll offer words, you clear away her clouds.

PAMPHYLUS.	Quid tibi mercedis statuam? que dona labori?
130	De grege nil possum; calamos accepit Opheltes. Sunt michi crescentes catuli, quos seva Licisca lacte domi nutrit; summas quem duxeris ipse.
CALIOPUS.	Dum grandes faciam. Sed tu modo quere gementem dilectamque tibi; pecudes mulsurus abibo.

V. THE FALLING FOREST

PAMPHYLUS: What shall I pay you? how reward your toil?
The flock's not mine to give. Opheltes took
my pipes away. I have some growing puppies
which wild Licisca nurses in my home;
do you yourself select the one you'll take.

CALIOPUS: I'll do so when they're big. But do you now
seek out the groaning girl and your beloved;
Meanwhile I will go off to milk the sheep.

VI. ALCESTUS

AMINTAS. Pastores transisse nives et frigora leti
 sub divo veteres stipula modulantur amores;
 esculeas hedera nectunt de more corollas,
 crateras Bromio statuunt et vina salutant
5 cantibus, et multo protendunt carmine sacrum.
 Tu, Melibee, quidem plangoribus omnia solus
 confundis. Que tanta tibi nunc causa doloris?
MELIBEUS. Silva vetus cecidit, lapsa est, cui prefuit Argus;
 custodes abiere gregum, periere sequaces.
10 Nostris an vivat nobis Alcestus in oris
 incertum, et clausas disiecit belua septas.
AMINTAS. Parcendum lacrimis, nam trux Poliphemus abivit.
 Alcestus rediit nobis, rediere vagantes
 pastores oviumque greges, rediere priores,
15 letitiaque virent silve vallesque resultant;
 omnis ager pubet, redeunt sua sydera pratis,
 frondes arbustis, edis quoque cornua surgunt,
 cornupetant campis lunata fronte iuvenci,
 Massicus et Gaurus florent, pulcherque Vesevus
20 innovat arbustis vites, stauratque Falernus
 ulmis iam colles, stringit Vulturnus et undas:
 surge ideo, letumque diem psallentibus auge.
MELIBEUS. Lenta fides magnis semper prestatur, Aminta,
 nec facile annosum falsis risisse subulcum est.
25 Pan deus a silvis oculos avertit et omne

VI. ALCESTUS

AMINTAS: Happy that the snow and ice have passed,
the shepherds pipe old lovesongs on their reeds
under the open sky; as is their custom,
oak garlands they entwine with ivy vines,
set bowls for Bacchus, honor the wines with songs,
and with much singing lengthen out the rite.
Yet Melibeus, you alone confound
it all with lamentations. What's the cause?

MELIBEUS: The ancient wood has fallen, it has crashed,
which Argus once ruled over; now the herdsmen
have left, and the attendants all have perished.
We are not certain where Alcestus lives,
and here a monster has thrown down the sheepfolds.

AMINTAS: No need of tears, for savage Polyphemus
has gone away. Alcestus has returned;
the wandering shepherds and their straying flocks
are all come back to us just as before;
with joy the woods grow green and valleys echo;
the fields are burgeoning; auspicious stars
return above the meadows; to the trees
fresh leaves return, and horns sprout on the kids;
the steers are butting with their horned brows;
both Massicus and Gaurus are in flower,
and fair Vesuvius renews the vines
in all its sloping vineyards, and Falernus
restores the hills with elms; Vulturnus calms
its waves: arise then, and augment the joy
this day for us who pluck the stringed lyre.

MELIBEUS: In greatest matters credence is lent slowly,
Amintas; at false tidings an old shepherd
does not easily muster up a smile.
Divine Pan turns his eyes from these our woods,

sevit in Alcestum dira vertigine celum.
Quis daret, heu! celeres pennas? quis, queso, volatum?
I, letis te dede, precor, sertisque corona,
30 meque meis lacrimis sinito miserisque querelis.
AMINTAS. Si Corinna meo sedeat, Melibee, sub antro,
vera loquor: vidi Cyrceum vertice flammis
fulgentem in reditu; sic et Garganus et ingens
Appenninus heri fumabant culmine summo
35 letitia, et, multis quod forsan credere durum,
Ethna quidem plausu fumos convertit in ignes.
Et si nulla fides dictis, hunc suspice collem
quam vireat, squalentem olim pallore. Quid ultra?
His oculis, iuro, calcantem litora vidi
40 euboica et matrem amplexu pulchrasque sorores
suscepisse pio, letis ac oscula dantem.
MELIBEUS. Quid verbis opus est multis, mi dulcis Aminta?
Floribus ut Titan nocturno frigore lapsis,
dictannus capreis pecorique favonius egro,
45 utque salus arvis estu sitientibus imber,
sic cordi tua dicta meo. Te, summe, precamur,
Phebe pater, te, leta Pales; da cepta secundent.
Non silvis unquam, nunquam pastoribus usquam
illuxit tam grata dies. Tu cespite vivo
50 erige propter aquas nobis altaria, Phorba,
et lauro et sertis hedere mirtoque corona;
inde et ydumeas fer palmas, postque bidentes
in sacrum niveas deduc ac omnia serva.
Tu mestas pecudes herbis et fonte, Lycophron,
55 et calamis refove: nosti quam turpis Orion
leserit has dudum, lacrimis dum tempora flerem.
Nosque diem celebrem cantu deducere, Aminta,
et delubra deûm festis ambire choreis,

VI. ALCESTUS

and heaven blasts with baneful revolution
Alcestus. Who, alas! might give swift feathers?
Who, pray, offers flight? Or who can suddenly
placate the raging gods? Go, give yourself
to joys and crown yourself with garlands, pray,
but leave me to my tears and sad laments.

AMINTAS: As I wish fair Corinna in my cave,
I'm telling you the truth, my Melibeus:
I saw Cyrceus' summit shine with flames
at his return; and likewise old Garganus
and mighty Appenninus yesterday
were smoking from their highest peaks with joy,
and –though it's hard for many to believe–
Etna applauded, turning smoke to flames.
And if you don't believe my words, look up:
how green this hill's become, once pale with mourning.
What shall I add? With these eyes, I do swear,
I saw him walk on the Euboean shores
and seize his mother and his pretty sisters
in loving arms, and kiss those happy women.

MELIBEUS: What need for many words, my sweet Amintas?
As sun to flowers drooping with night's chill,
as dittany to goats, as a west wind
to a sick flock, as saving rain to fields
thirsty from heat, so to my heart your words.
To you Phoebus, father supreme, we pray,
to you, o fruitful Pales; these beginnings
may you still favor. Never has so grateful
a day dawned for the woods and for the shepherds.
You, Phorba, build with living turf for us
some altars near the waters, and with laurel
and ivy wreaths and myrtle crown them all;
and then bring Idumaean palms, and after
lead in the snowy sheep for sacrifice
and do it all aright. You, Lycophron,
refresh the mournful sheep with grass and water
and with your pipes: you know how foul Orion
did harm them recently while I was mourning
the times with tears. But now this glorious day
we ought to spend in song, I think, Amintas,
and visit holy shrines with festive dances:

credo, decet: viridis foliis ornatus olive,
60 tu primus sacrum gracili perflabis avena;
ast ego, populea redimitus fronde, secundus
carmina cantabo. Stipulis et carmine docti
ambo sumus, nobis nemo nunc prevalet agris
in siculis, ni forte gravis certaret Yollas:
65 hic alios superat quantum vepreta cupressi.

AMINTAS. Ergo alacres dignum calamis et carmine festum
cantemus; tu primus eris, tu carmine maior.
Esculeo dudum descriptos cortice rastro
Phyllidis incipies, vel quos mage duxeris, ignes,
70 seu magis Alcesti laudes: non dignior ullus;
seu magnos Phytias quos pertulit ante labores,
qui meruit versus qua Stilbon flabat avena.

MELIBEUS. Phyllis in agresti se iactet cespite ludens;
expectet Phytias, cui credo magna paratur
75 posteritas, si vera sonat deus ethere levo;
nos tamen Alcesto dignas per secula voces,
ut dabitur, cantare decet: cantabimus ambo:
Libetrides nostrum tollant ad sydera carmen.

AMINTAS. Ecce, puer, placida pariter residemus in umbra,
80 et superis gratos mittunt altaria fumos;
ruminat omne pecus, pueri campique quiescunt.
Quid trahis in longum conceptos iam tibi versus?

MELIBEUS. Alcestum postquam silvis abstraxit amatis
fatorum predura lues, flevere dolentes
85 Parthenopes nymphe, nec vidit Daunia sulcos,
vitibus obstupuit Bachus, periere iuvence,
Vulturnusque senex ingentia saxa revolvens
excessit ripas, luteus demissus ab urna;
montibus obtectum nebulis fumoque cacumen
90 vidimus, et valles ululatu flere dolenti;
tunc, quos clara dedit tellus, rugire leones
non ausos, laqueosque graves sentire coactos
venantum primo, lyncis quoque lumen ademptum.

VI. ALCESTUS

adorned with olive leaves, you first will blow
a sacred song upon your slender reed;
I'll sing the second, crowned with poplar leaves.
We both are skilled in piping and in song,
no one in the Sicilian fields could beat us
unless perhaps grave Yollas contended:
he towers like a cypress over briars.

AMINTAS: Then eagerly let's sing fit celebration
with pipes and song; you first, for you sing better.
Begin with Phyllis' loves, writ long ago
in oak bark with your rake, or any loves
which you prefer; or even better sing
Alcestus' praises: no one is more worthy;
or the great trials which Phytias endured,
who earned some verses from the pipe of Stilbon.

MELIBEUS: Let merry Phyllis gambol on the turf;
let Phytias wait, for whom I think a great
posterity's prepared, if Jove presages
true things with that high thunder on the left.
However, we should sing unto Alcestus
something that's worthy for the centuries,
as will be granted: let's both sing; and may
the Muses raise our song up to the stars.

AMINTAS: Behold, we're sitting in the peaceful shade
together, boy, while from the altars rise
fumes pleasing to the gods; our flocks are all
chewing the cud, the lads and fields are still.
Why put off verses that you have in mind?

MELIBEUS: After too harsh calamity of fates
had drawn Alcestus from his cherished woods,
the sad Parthenopean nymphs were weeping,
Daunia saw no furrows, Bacchus drank
till he was senseless, and the heifers perished,
old man Vulturnus rolling heavy rocks
had quit his banks, and mud poured from his urn.
We saw the mountains veiled with fogs and smoke,
we heard the valleys weep with doleful howling;
then lions which the bright land had brought forth,
afraid to roar, were first compelled to feel
the hunters' heavy traps; the lynx went blind.

		Ha! quantum potuit de te fortuna, quibusque
95		casibus in dubios te traxit seva meatus!

          Ast ego, Phebe decus celi, posuisse labori
Alcesti finem et patriis post reddere silvis
dignatus, meritos nymphe tibi semper honores
carmine perpetuo resonent precor, atque bubulci.

AMINTAS. Non thymus est apibus, non agnis lenis ybiscus,
non cythisus capris, quantum tua carmina nobis.
Nunc ego restituam silvis silvisque tenebo.
    Plaudite iam colles, et vos iam plaudite, montes:
redditus est nostris Alcestus, redditus antris.
105 Litora iam plausu surgant et flumina certent
nunc plausu complere polos. Hic spernere terras
occiduas, solisque vias celumque serenum
cernere et obliquos Phebes mirarier orbes
cepit, et Astream silvis revocavit abactam:
110 hac tauris curru iunget cervis leones
armentisque lupos, serpentum sibila sulcis
auferet et meritos Musis concedet honores.
    Plaudite iam colles, et vos iam plaudite, montes:
redditus est nostris Alcestus, redditus antris.
115 Dum mare fluctivagos pisces tellusque tenebit
quadrupedes, aer volucres et sydera Olympus,
Alcestus silvis pastoribus atque puellis
sit lumen semperque decus, nec limina Ditis
conspiciat; moriens, superis sit Delphycus alter.
120   Plaudite iam colles, et vos iam plaudite, montes:
redditus est nostris Alcestus, redditus antris.
Non agnam mactare decet, nos cernat ovantes
Alcestus, taurumque sibi, dum tempora victor
umbrabit lauro: veniat lux illa, precamur,
125 et suris vinctis saltabimus inde coturno,
elicietque sonos stipulis tyrenus Asylas:

VI. ALCESTUS

Ha! How much power had fortune over you
and by what mishaps drew you cruelly on
to doubtful courses. But I pray, O Phoebus,
you jewel of the sky, who deigned to end
Alcestus' troubles and restore him to
paternal woods, may your deserved honors
be sung by nymphs in song perpetual
and by the farmboys too.

AMINTAS: Thyme's not more pleasing
to bees, nor to the lambs tender hybiscus,
nor clover to goats, than is your song to me.
Now I'll reply and keep it in the woods.
    Applaud now, hills, you too applaud now, mountains:
Alcestus is returned, returned to us.
Let now the shores surge with applause, and let
the waves strive with applause to fill the heavens.
Here he begins to spurn the sinking earth,
to observe the paths of sun and stars serene,
admire the slanted orbits of the moon;
Astrea, who was driven from the woods,
he has called back; his chariot he'll yoke
with bulls, join deer with lions, wolves with flocks;
he will remove the hissing snakes from furrows
and grant merited honors to the Muses.
    Applaud now, hills, you too applaud now, mountains:
Alcestus is returned, returned to us.
As long as water holds wave-wandering fish,
and earth four-footed beasts, and air holds birds,
and heaven stars, so may Alcestus be
the forest's light and joy forever, shepherds
and girls, nor may he see the doors of Dis,
but be another Sun among the gods.
    Applaud now, hills, you too applaud now, mountains:
Alcestus is returned, returned to us.
It's fitting that we slaughter now a lamb
and let Alcestus see us celebrating;
let him behold a bull just for himself
while, victor, he will crown his brows with laurel;
let that day come, we pray, and we will leap,
our legs laced up in buskins, and Tyrrhenian
Asylas make his pipes resound; and Damon

astabunt coram Damon Phytiasque canentes.
Plaudite iam colles, et vos iam plaudite, montes:
redditus est nostris Alcestus, redditus antris.
130 Vix, Alceste decus nostrum, vix credere fame
post nos ruricole poterunt, sed cortice duro
posteritas tua facta leget; te populus ingens,
te corilus sculptum, servabit te quoque fagus,
dum fluet Eridanus, dum montes vallibus umbras
135 prestabunt, dum grata salix, dum gratus ybiscus
nascetur capris. Crescent ea nomina quantum
ipsa quidem fagus crescet. Mirabitur Arnus
atque colet, gratis linquens tua facta futuris.
Plaudite iam colles et vos iam plaudite, montes:
140 redditus est nostris Alcestus, redditus antris.
MELIBEUS. Munera quis statuet pro tanto carmine digna?
Dulce viris quantum rusco prefertur amomum
atque rubis mirtus, laurus vel dignior alga,
tantum ego tu superes dicam cantando Menalcam,
145 et calamis. O! quantus eris, si prestet Yollas
te stipula perflare sua! Tunc saxa movebis.
Est michi conspicuum insignis quod condidit olim
Ylas spartanus, quamvis duo vasa fuissent,
dum placido nobis victus concessit amore.
150 Horum aliud nuper rapuit gratissima Phyllis;
tu reliquum, quanquam tanto sit munus agreste,
suscipe, sed noscas nulli tetigisse labellum.
AMINTAS. Sat video te cogat amor, dum munera tanti
concedis puero: non parva teneret Yollas.
155 Tu ne sperne, precor, baculum quem cyprius olim,
dum iuvenis frigias agitaret arundine dammas,
concessit Lycidas sumptum de rupe Camandri,
nodis insignem, nec non et cuspide fulva.
Sed sta, care, precor, modicumque adverte: quid, oro,
160 personuit silvis echo? Non, oro, latratus
concipis ipse canum? grandis non ille Melampus?
non gregis, heu! custos latrat? non illa Licisca

VI. ALCESTUS

and Phytias will stand before him singing.
  Applaud now, hills, you too applaud now, mountains:
Alcestus is returned, returned to us.
  O our joy Alcestus, later farmers
will scarce be able to believe report,
but our posterity will read your deeds
in the hard bark; your name will be preserved
by mighty poplar, hazeltree, and beech,
as long as Eridanus flows, as long
as mountains shade the valleys, or as willow
and hybiscus, pleasing to the goats, will grow.
Your names will grow just as the beech tree grows.
Arnus will wonder, reverent, and leave
your deeds for grateful future generations.
  Applaud now, hills, you too applaud now, mountains:
Alcestus is returned, returned to us.

MELIBEUS: Who'll say what gifts are worthy such a song?
As much as balsam is preferred to broom,
myrtle to brambles, or bay held more worth
than seaweed, by so much do you surpass
Menalcas, I declare, with song and pipes.
Oh, how great will you be if Yollas
will lend his pipes for you to play upon!
Then you'll move stones. I have an excellent thing
which once the famous Spartan Ylas made,
although there were two vessels when he gave them,
quite overcome with pleasing love, to me.
One of the two the lovely Phyllis snatched;
you take the other, rustic though it be,
but you should know that no one's lips have touched it.

AMINTAS: I see that love impels you when you give
a gift of such high value to a boy:
of no small worth would Yollas esteem them.
Please don't refuse a staff which Cyprian Lycidas
once gave me, taken from Camander's cliff
when as a youth he hunted Phrygian deer;
it's marked with knots and with a golden tip.
But stay, my dear, and hark a while, I pray:
what echoed through the woods? Do you hear barking?
That big one is Melampus, isn't it?
And isn't that, alas! the sheepdog barking?

Est equidem, nosco: timeo ne sevus ovili
nunc lupus insultet, seu belua sevior; ibo
ut videam, et manibus tollam ne ledat hiulcus.
Tu venias queso, si te fortasse ciebo.

VI. ALCESTUS

Isn't that our Licisca? Yes, it is,
I recognize the bark: a savage wolf,
I fear, is jumping at the sheepfold now,
or some more savage beast; I will go see,
I'll take the staff lest gaping jaws do harm.
You come too, please, in case I call for help.

VII. IURGIUM

DAPHNIS. Florida, quid stertens commissum linquis ovile?
Non satius fuerat dixisses: – Servet amicus
hoc saltem Daphnis – recubas dum victa lyeo?
FLORIDA. Tu servare gregem nosti, fur pessime Daphni,
5 cum veteres flectas fagos immersus hyaco?
DAPHNIS. Non ego quod vidi nuper, dum septa Phaselis
crinibus exires sparsis et veste soluta,
clam dicam: te tristis amet sine mente Lupiscus?
FLORIDA. Vir gregis impulsus rabie michi fugerat illuc.
10 An tibi liquissem, quem sevo vulnere capros,
alphei in medio nemoris, fetasque capellas
carpentem vidi? Quanquam plangore Phaselis
posceret in vacuum, tu per dumeta trahebas
infestus curva preaptas falce bidentes.
DAPHNIS. Nonne ego quo libuit poteram deducere nostras?
FLORIDA. Portasti tecum, credo. Quid, pessime, «nostras»?
Circius aut misit, seu forte Ercinia mater?
Quid fuit alpheis tecum? Vetus extat origo
his quidem ab Ellaida, tibi tristis et aspera patrem
20 barbaries inculta dedit. Quid, pessime, «nostras»?
DAPHNIS. Quid Galathea, precor, faciet, cum talia Lusca
audet, et infando deturpat gucture Daphnim?
Belua, me nemorum nuper pecorisque magistrum
silvicole fecere senes, omnisque potestas

VII. THE QUARREL

DAPHNIS: Why, snoring Florida, do you neglect
the fold entrusted to you? Wouldn't it
have been enough to say "Let my friend Daphnis
protect it" while you sleep off too much wine?

FLORIDA: Do you know how to guard the flock then, Daphnis,
you dreadful thief, when drunk you bend the beechtrees?

DAPHNIS: I won't tell what I saw not long ago
when you left secretly Phaselis' sheepfolds
with hair and dress undone. Would sad Lupiscus
still love you madly?

FLORIDA: There my ram had fled
by panic driven. Or should I have left him
to you, whom I saw in the Pisan wood
savagely wounding goats and pregnant nannies?
Although Phaselis begged with vain lamenting,
you, sickle-armed, were dragging through the thicket
the stolen sheep.

DAPHNIS: Did I not have the right
to take my own sheep anywhere I pleased?

FLORIDA: You took them with you, I believe, but what,
O wicked man, do you mean by "my own"?
Did Circius send you, or mother Ercinia?
What do you have to do, pray, with the Pisans?
Their ancient origin indeed goes back
to men of Elis; but to you a harsh,
uncultured foreign country gave a father.
O wicked one, what do you mean "my own"?

DAPHNIS: What, pray, will Galathea do when Lusca
dares say such things and shames Daphnis with insults?
Wild beast, the older farmers recently
made me the master of the sheep and pasture,

25 arbitrio commissa meo est. Quos Yndus inundat,
quosve Pyreneus collis seu celifer Athlas
quosque tenet Rhodopes silvis aut abluit Hebrus,
quosve niger garamas ferventibus urget harenis
arceo pastores; et tu, male sana, superbis!

FLORIDA. Et quos iam celo dederat decepta vetustas,
merserat aut orco, pariter dixisse decebat,
cum tibi sit parvus nemorum vix angulus unus,
iure cui possis fragiles iniungere leges.
Yndos Mosa secat, getulos abluit Albis,
35 atque tuas, Tybris, Rhenus nunc sulcat harenas!
I, decus arthoum, theutonos lude bilingues;
nos titulos vacuos et lentos novimus arcus.

DAPHNIS. Quid «titulos»? Non, orba, vides quibus ipse molosis
progrediar septus? Lauros Galathea reservat;
40 ornet et ut pexos nobis aliquando capillos,
flectere serta manu cepit. Tunc anxia dices:
«Nos titulos vacuos et lentos novimus arcus»!

FLORDIA. O miserum! tibi serta comis Galathea virentis
imponent lauri? Tedas extinguere flammas
45 tunc dicam, referetque diem tunc Hesperus et sol
inducet veniens umbras. Qui primus honores
hos tulit in silvis, poterit deposcere taxos
et lauri tristes porcis exponere frondes,
si te gestantem videat. Michi numina prestent
50 ante diem moriar, latiam quam cernere danem
sauromate possim crinesque caputque prementem.

DAPHNIS. Quid tantum, delira, tumes? quod iussit Apollo
tu renuis? Melius fuerat componere lites,
et quos iamdudum nostris antiquior etas
55 exhibuit sertis flores, tu candida letos

VII. THE QUARREL

and all authority has been entrusted
to my good judgment. I protect the shepherds
whom Indus floods, whom the Pyrenean hill
or heaven-bearing Atlas holds, and those
whom Rhodopean woods contain, whom Hebrus
washes, or whom the African drives over
the burning sands; and you, madwoman, act haughty!

FLORIDA: And those whom disappointed age already
had sent to heaven or had sunk to hell,
you should have added, since scarcely one tiny
real corner of the woods is yours, on which
you can by right inflict your fragile laws.
The Mosel crosses India, the Albis
now washes the Gaetulians, and the Rhine
furrows your sands now, Tiber! Go, you gem
of northerners, delude your two-tongued Teutons;
we know your empty titles and slack bows!

DAPHNIS: What do you mean by "titles"? Don't you see,
you blind one, how I come forth all encircled
with fine Molossian hounds? Now Galathea
is saving laurels; she's begun to bind
the wreaths so that one day she may adorn
my combed hair. Then you'll say uneasily,
"We know your empty titles and slack bows"!

FLORIDA: O wretch! will Galathea place green laurel
in garlands on your hair? Then I will say
that torches put out fires; Hesperus
will then begin the day; the rising sun
will bring on darkness. He who first did bear
these honors in the woods will bid the yews
cast his sad leaves of laurel to the pigs,
if he should see you wear them. May the gods
please let me die before the day I see
a Latian laurel pressing northern hair.

DAPHNIS: You raving girl, why are you so worked up?
Do you refuse the bidding of Apollo?
It would have been much better to allay
your quarrels and with gladness offer up
those flowers which our garlands long ago
displayed in ancient times, so that on high

FLORIDA.

60

65

70

75

DAPHNIS.

80

85

    prestares, ut sacra tuis Iovis ales ab alto
invigilet gregibus removens vulpesque luposque.
Hac ego te semper cognovi retia cervis
aut capreis laqueos, mediis in vallibus, arte
tendere, cum iaculo valeas nil, optime Daphni;
blandiris, cecamque putas includere claustris.
Nosceris; errasti. Nec tu, quibus inscia quondam
omne nemus septasque dedi taurosque caprosque
amplexusque meos ac oscula leta; nec illa
secula volvuntur nobis; nec vertitur ordo
qui dudum, quo grandis erat per compita Daphnis.
Absit et ut credam, de te modo sentiat, acer
qui fueras predo, tam sancte summus Apollo,
iusserit ut lauro tua cingas tempora sacra.
Sed cedam. Memini puerum dixisse Goliam
esse polos superûm, campos mortalibus esse
concessos, quos quisque sua dicione teneret.
Libera sum mulier, nullo sociata marito,
et thalamis ultro renuo iurique iugali;
sunt vires animique manent, arcusque trucesque
custodes ovium, peperit quos seva Licisca;
et moriar potius quam iactem lilia corvis.
Libera tu mulier? Quasi non viderimus ipsi
quot mechis prostrata iaces! Carecta Phaselis,
si tu forte neges, servant vestigia sulcis.
Venales tibi, stulta, manus mercede parasti:
hos fortes arcus, iacula hos tutosque recessus
esse putas? Fex nempe virûm servique fugaces
sunt, quos dirus amor seu forsan tristis egestas
e silvis pepulit nostris. Non, hercle! sagictam
eximerem pharetra: loris virgisque fugabo.
Ast tu summe colum calathosque, et pensa puellis

VII. THE QUARREL

FLORIDA:
    the sacred bird of Jupiter might watch
    over your flocks, removing wolves and foxes.
    I've always known you with this artfulness
    setting up nets for deer and snares for goats
    since with a spear you're worthless, O great Daphnis.
    You flatter and you think that you can shut me,
    all blind, in your enclosures. But you're wrong;
    you're recognized. Not you, on whom I once
    unwittingly bestowed the entire forest,
    the folds and bulls and goats, and my embrace
    and happy kisses, nor do those past ages
    come round again for me; nor does that order
    that formerly existed come again
    when Daphnis was a great man at the crossroads.
    Far be it that I should believe Apollo–
    so sacredly supreme– now feels about you
    so as to order you, a zealous pirate,
    to crown your temples with his sacred laurel.
    But let me yield. As I recall, Golia
    said that the heavens were given to the gods,
    the lands to mortals, so that each might have
    his proper jurisdiction. I am free,
    joined to no husband, and of my own will
    renounce the wedding bed and marriage right.
    My spirits still remain, and I have strength,
    and I still have my bow and my rough sheepdogs
    that wild Licisca bore; and may I die
    before I throw my lilies to the crows.

DAPHNIS:
    Free woman, you? As if I hadn't seen
    myself for how many adulterers
    you have lain down! Phaselis' sedgy marsh
    still bears the footprints, if you should deny it.
    You foolish woman, you have bought for pay
    armed bands that are for sale. Do you suppose
    these are safe refuges, strong spears and bows?
    They are the dregs of men and fleeing slaves,
    in truth, whom a fierce love or sorry need
    has driven from our woods. By Hercules,
    I wouldn't take one arrow from the quiver:
    with whips and rods I'll put them all to flight.
    But you take up the distaff and the basket

impartire tuis, et pascua linque bubulcis.
Spirantes tymbre tibi sint, mea Florida, cure,
90   atque roseta tuis aperi et violaria pande;
collige iam flores, pueris compone corollas
et natis occide sues, convivia pone;
da spatium barbas pectant, da stringere vestes,
da laqueis ambire femur, da tempora ludis,
95   da vitreos fontes, quorum testantibus undis
incedant compti; radios et findere Phebi
permitte, ut possint animos assummere grandes,
dum tenues ydolo, segnes se corpore cernent;
da graciles stipulas, umbras compone recentes,
100 sterne leves algas, nymphas immisce procaces,
da vina et somnos et vesca papavera lentis,
pelle canes silvis, arbustis pelle cicadas:
sed tandem videas miseris quid feceris, hercle!
Nos frigius lusit pastor, nos sprevit Osyris,
105 non impune diu; nec tu, si spreveris, inquam.

FLORIDA. Sic faciam, dum grata quies, dum floridus annus,
dum virides silve stabunt celumque serenum,
invidus ut doleas. Sed quid male sanus amores
obicis indecores? Nemo, stolidissime, credet:
110 mos vetus est mechis matronis turpia castis
obiecisse quidem; testis michi maxima quercus
sacra Iovi, quia falsa refers. Ast, inclite, quid tu?
quid «frigius pastor»? quid dicis: «sprevit Osyris»?
«non impune», miser? Quasi iam nemus omne canopum
115 videris et mysios colles vallesque Camandri
cum vix agnoscas, tibi celsos elicis ignes.
Hec stolidis stipula referes aliquando napeis,
dum tu pannonos victos cantabis agrestes.

VII. THE QUARREL

and share the chores of spinning with your maids;
and leave the fields to farmers. Make your care
the fragrant savory, my Florida,
and clear the rosebeds for your family
and spread the bed of violets; gather flowers,
make chaplets for the girls, then slaughter pigs
to serve your children, and prepare a feast;
allow your sons a chance to comb their beards
and change their clothes, put garters on their thighs;
allow them time for play, and glassy springs
by whose reflecting water they may pass
and split the rays of Phoebus, so they may
give themselves airs while they behold themselves
in image slender, sluggish in the flesh;
give them slim reedpipes and arrange for shade,
strew light seaweed, bring in the shameless nymphs,
and offer wines and sleep and slender poppies
to any who resist; shoo off the dogs,
and drive cicadas from the trees; but see
what you are doing to the wretched people
at last, by Hercules! The Phrygian shepherd
mocked us, Osyris scorned us, not for long
unpunished; nor will you be if you scorn us.

FLORIDA: I will do so, while quietness is pleasing,
while springtime is in flower, while the woods
remain in leaf and all the sky serene,
so that you may be pained with pangs of envy.
But why reproach me with scandalous loves,
sick man? No one will credit it, you fool.
It's an old habit for adulterers
to charge chaste matrons with such shameful things.
Jove's sacred mighty oak is witness for me
that you speak great untruths. But, famous man,
what about you? why say "the Phrygian shepherd"?
Why say "Osyris scorned"? Why "not unpunished,"
you wretch? As if you saw Canopus' forest,
the Mysian hills, and valleys of Camander
–although indeed you scarcely recognize them–,
you conjure up before yourself proud flames.
You'll pipe this on your reed to foolish nymphs
while singing of the conquered rustic folk

Nec taceas nuper signatum limen ab angue,
120 segnicieque tua pactum ex ferrugine sertum
in campis henetûm. Sunt hec purganda priusquam
excidium fagis, Daphni, septisque mineris
inflatus rabie. Satius tibi vertere passus
orbis in extremum, quo tu mulieribus arces
125 erigis ac onagris componis septa comatis,
vinitor et tensos resecat tibi vitibus antes.

DAPHNIS. Me miserum! raucis veni contendere ranis.
Te natis commendo tuis. Hi pectere crines
et faciem purgare tuam vestesque novare
130 et mores ornare tuos laudesque levare
noverunt. Primi facient, ni fallor, ut Arnus
nuntiet alpheis quoniam tua colla superba
calce premam victor, vacuatis sanguine fibris.

FLORIDA. Hesperidum michi poma dedit thirinthius heros,
135 asseruitque graves egris hec ponere somnos
freneticis. His ergo tuo postremo medebor
fervori: magnos memini pressisse furores.
Insuber atque ligus post hec tua somnia solvent.

VII. THE QUARREL

along the Danube. Sing too about the door
marked with a snake, and garland made of rust
thanks to your sloth in the Venetian fields.
Purge these before, inflated with your rage,
you threaten, Daphnis, to destroy the folds
and beeches. Better that you turn your steps
to the world's end where you erect a fort
for women and enclosures for wild asses,
and where the vinedresser cuts back for you
the rows of spreading vines.

DAPHNIS: Alas, poor me!
I've come here to contend with croaking frogs.
I commend you to your children. They have learned
to comb your hair and wash your face and dress you,
adorn your manners, and extol your praises.
They will first see to it, unless I err,
that Arnus tell the Alpheans how I
will press your proud neck with my heel, as victor,
your entrails being emptied of their blood.

FLORIDA: The hero of Thirinthia gave me
the Hesperidian apples, and he claimed
they bring deep sleep to sick and feverish men.
With these I will allay your future seething;
I do recall that they have calmed great ragings.
The Insubrian and the Ligurian
will afterwards shatter these dreams of yours.

VIII. MIDAS

DAMON. Tolle pecus, Phytia: nescis quibus inscius arvis
nunc sedeas. Midas si te vel forte Lupisca
viderit! Errasti; dubium quis promptius ultro
irruat in predam seu servet durius actam.
PHYTIAS. Quid verbis laceras grandes, venerande, bubulcos?
quid, Damon, suades fesso? Dum iussit egestas
hunc domini servare greges, hanc pensa Minerve
ducere per noctes, potuit fortasse timeri.
Nunc illis armenta boum per gramina servat
10 Aufidus, et vitulos deducit ab ubere marsus.
Non hostis venio; vult Midas ipse, daturus
pascua, si qua fides, fontesque umbrasque recentes.
DAMON. Coge pecus, dum tempus adest: ni fallor, amara
qua nolis venisse dies, michi crede, futura est,
15 et promissa quidem tenues dispersa per auras
in nichilum venient. Sed tu quid, stulte, putabas
hos magnos habuisse greges, ni fraude parassent?
Non hominum iusti quid possint ferre labores
novimus, et quantum septis augere peculi?
PHYTIAS. Me miserum! deceptus, inops, per saxa, per estus,
en iterum revocandus eras, grex anxie; nusquam
comperies quo grata quies tibi prestita fetus
gramine permittat leto deponere. Damon,
Pana deum testor, non herbida prata nec amnes
25 exhausti natale solum patriosque recessus

VIII. MIDAS

DAMON: Remove your sheep; you don't know, Phytias,
in whose fields you unwittingly are settled.
If Midas or Lupisca should perceive you!
You've gone astray; I don't know which of them
would rush more quickly at the driven prey
or more severely guard it.

PHYTIAS: Why, good sir,
do you wound mighty farmers with your words?
What counsel do you give a tired man?
While poverty commanded him to watch
his master's sheep, and her to spend the nights
plying Minerva's task, one might have feared.
But now Aufidus tends their herds of cows;
a Marsian takes the calves from off the udder.
I don't come as a foe; Midas himself
invites me, he will give me pasturelands,
if I can trust him, springs and cooling shade.

DAMON: Gather your sheep while there is still the time;
unless I err, a bitter day is coming,
believe me, which you'll wish had never come;
and promises dispersed into thin air
will come to nothing. But, you foolish man,
why did you think they had big flocks if not
that there had been foul play? Haven't we learned
how much the honest work of men brings in,
and by how much they can augment their folds? [heat,

PHYTIAS: Poor me! Deceived, in need, through stones, through
lo, anxious flock, you are again called back;
no place will you find out where pleasant rest
may let you lay your offspring on the grass.
Damon, I swear by Pan, not grassy meadows
nor dried streams made me leave my native soil,

		Archadie ut sinerem fecere, et querere campos

Archadie ut sinerem fecere, et querere campos
pastoris nimium cupidi, trucis atque Lupische.
Sola fides fallaxque nimis spes, alta Vesevi
atque sinus Gauri virides fontesque lacusque
30   ut peterem, potuere. Tamen, dum tristis Orion
alta tenet noctis prohibens cantare volucres,
sta, precor, atque doce miserum quo iure Lupisca,
quo Midas rapiant armentaque maxima ducant.

DAMON. Nympha decus nemorum placidis residebat in arvis
35   euboicis nuper, clara viduata mitella.
Hanc ardere quidem cepit, cum ferret ad urbem
lac pressum Midas, pecudum et de more cadentum
exuvias: cepto favit fortuna furori.
Nam gravis ere domum fervens dum forte redibat,
40   cespite pro viridi prostravit munere victam.
Hec huius iam capta leves e pectore curas
expulit ac animos immisit fervida grandes.
Cumque diem functus terras dimitteret Argus
et levo tandem fato cecidisset Alexis,
45   extemplo callens hic sese miscuit altis
pastorum rebus, dyrceaque semina passim
omnia complevit iactans; cumque impia virtus
in se discordes armasset cuspide fratres,
prosiliens avidus Midas pecudesque bovesque
50   occupat insidiis, et ne sibi tuta deessent
abdita, Melalcem studio coniunxit Ameto.
Quos postquam miseros undis retraxit avitos
in campos, lauro et flavos vincire capillos
et querno fecit dextras ornare bacillo,
55   primum se divûum titulis immiscuit altis,
cum pridem placido vix esset cognitus Arno.

PHYTIAS. O felix iam sorte sua! Quis plura requirat?

VIII. MIDAS

my ancestor's Arcadian retreats,
and ask for fields of a too greedy shepherd
and of savage Lupisca. Only trust
and too-deceiving hope could make me seek
Vesuvius' heights and the green bay of Gaurus,
the springs and lakes. Yet while baneful Orion
still rules the sky at night, prohibiting
the birds to sing, I pray you, stay and teach
a poor man by what right Lupisca and Midas
do seize and carry off the biggest herds.

DAMON: A nymph, the forest's jewel, dwelled recently
in Chalcis' peaceful fields, late widowed of
her shining diadem. Midas in fact
began to burn with love for her as he
was bringing to the town sheep-cheese and skins
as usual; fortune favored his madness.
For while he headed homeward money-laden,
he felled her, conquered by a gift, upon
the grassy turf. She, now his captive, drove
the light cares from his breast and, passionate,
instilled great boldness. And when Argus, dying,
had left the lands, and by unlucky fate
Alexis too had fallen, right away
this man, being experienced, mixed himself
in shepherds' high affairs and, sowing seeds
of discord here and there, filled every place;
and when impious valor had armed with spears
quarreling brothers each against the other,
then greedy Midas, leaping forwards, seized
the sheep and cows by treachery, and lest
he miss one safe in hiding, full of zeal
he joined up his Ametus to Melalces.
Then after he had drawn these wretches out
from ocean waves to their ancestral fields,
he made them bind his yellow hair with bays
and arm his right hand with an oaken staff,
and took on lofty titles of the gods,
though long before he had been scarcely known
by peaceful Arno.

PHYTIAS: Happy, lucky man!
Now who could ask for more? Though once a servant,

	Imperat ex servo, merces conflavit in aurum.
DAMON.	Saxeus es, Phytia, Video, coluisse napeas
60	et nemorum faunos eque nymphasque puellas
	thure pio credas, qui surripit undique capros;
	claustraque si frangat, felicem dicis avarum.
PHYTIAS.	Imo equidem dico: nemo, nisi Iuppiter equus
	iusserit, in celsos usquam conscendet honores.
DAMON.	Te Phytiam rebar: silve fecere Ligurgum,
	et superûm mentem, video, cessere subulco
	sulphurei colles et pascua grata Lyeo!
PHYTIAS.	Sum Phytias, Damon, Phytias sum pastor et archas,
	et calamis didici pastas mulcere capellas,
70	non mores hominum, sacra et monimenta Ligurgi.
	Tu miserum ridere potes: tibi grandis Apollo
	concessit cytharam, Pomona cadentia pomis
	arbuta; sic temnis summo de culmine lapsos.
	Sepe vices rerum verti cantabat Amintas
75	iam senior! Lacrimas mecum mors equa resolvet.
DAMON.	O Phytia, consiste, precor, mentemque resumme.
	Ante polos lyntres sulcabunt, nerea currus
	orbita, frondoso pandum delphyna Pelorus
	vertice suscipiet nantem, quam Damon amicum
80	contemnat Phytiam. Sed tu modo respice verum:
	huius quippe fuit mos semper vertere vultus,
	quodque velit validis se nolle infingere signis.
	Hinc, servus, pratis viridi contectus in herba,
	serpere et incautas cauda vincire capellas
85	atque edos morsu solitus lacerare tenellos;
	sed postquam vires auxit, compressa cathella,

VIII. MIDAS

he rules, he forges items into gold.

DAMON: You're dense, O Phytias. I see you think
he worshiped fauns and dryads of the woods
and likewise maiden nymphs with pious incense,
that man who pilfers goats from everywhere;
and if he breaks into the folds, you call him
a lucky miser.

PHYTIAS: Not at all, I say;
no one, unless just Jupiter so ordered,
will ever rise this way to such high honors.

DAMON: I thought that you were Phytias, however
I see the woods have made you a Lycurgus;
the sulphurous hills and fields that please Lyaeus
have granted godlike judgment to a swineherd!

PHYTIAS: I'm Phytias, Damon, Phytias I am,
the shepherd and Arcadian, and I've learned
to soothe the pastured goats with piping reeds,
but have not learned the many ways of men
nor learned the sacred records of Lycurgus.
But you can mock a poor man; for to you
the great Apollo gave a lyre, Pomona
an orchard bowed with fruits; therefore you scorn
men fallen from the summit of success.
Often Amintas, now an old man, sang
the changing fortunes of affairs! My tears
impartial death will end along with me.

DAMON: O Phytias, stop, I beg, and take new courage.
For boats will furrow wakes across the skies,
and chariots leave wheelruts in the sea,
Pelorus' leafy summit will receive
the swimming dolphin before Damon scorns
his good friend Phytias. But do you now
come to your senses; it has always been
your way to turn your gaze and willfully
refuse to be impressed by potent facts.
Hither as a slave he used to creep,
hidden among the grasses of the field,
to bind incautious shegoats by the tail
and tear the tender kidlets with his teeth;
but later on his boldness he increased,

insurgens coram, tauro qui ludat in ervo
persimilis cornu, celsas infringere pinus,
sternere prevalidas quercus silvasque boatu
terribili complere, leves pervertere septas
cepit, et horrendus rabie leo vertere magnas
in circum bubulas ursosque arcere frementes.
Quis putet? Et Bavio subtraxit subdolus hyrcos
pregnantesque boves, et pingues carmine tauros
eduxit stabulis, rauco latrante Melampo.
Quot faunos quondam, nymphas quot lusit agrestes,
quot satyros ficto calamis per devia cantu!
Seque Mecenatem magnumque deumque vocari
gliscit, et invitas dum servat rupe Camenas,
ascreum putat esse senem silvasque movere
castalias et plectra dei sacrasque sorores.
Quis queat insanos ausus, quis dicere sevas
et nemorum pecorumque simul iuvenumque ruinas
quas dedit, et pariter secum trux inde Lupisca?
Hec siliquas porcis et gramina subtrahit agnis,
emungit miseras turpi squalore iuvencas
ac matrum parvos subducit ab ubere natos,
terque die pecudes premit et ter vellere nudat,
si possit, tristique levem consistere lunam
carmine compellit celo, et sibi fascinat edos.
Nec vacat hec somno; virides ambire per agros
nocte etiam videas, et magnos vertice Gauri
enumerare greges. Quid multa? Hec omnia radit.
Ac ut nulla sinat silvis intacta vel agris,
arte nova pueros annosa per antra canentes
in venerem rapit illa suam, nudatque sequentes.

VIII. MIDAS

his chain suppressed, up rising openly,
and like a bull that's playing with its horn
among the bitter vetch, so he began
to break the lofty pines, pull down the oaks,
to fill the forests with a fearful roar,
to overthrow the hedged enclosures, and,
a terrifying lion in his rage,
to turn great oxen into the arena
and pen up growling bears. Ah, who would think it?
From Bavius the guileful man took goats
and pregnant cows, and with a song led out
the fat bulls from the stalls, while hoarse Melampus
kept barking all the while. How many fauns,
how many rural nymphs he once deceived,
how many satyrs in remoter places
he cheated with the false song of his pipes!
He burns moreover to be called Maecenas,
a great man and a god, and while he keeps
the Muses on a cliff against their will,
he thinks himself to be the old Ascrean
and that he moves the whole Castalian forest,
the plectra of the god and sacred sisters.
Who could recount his darings so insane,
or who the cruel destruction of the woods,
of cattle and young men which he effected,
and with him equally the fierce Lupisca?
She takes the husks from pigs, the grass from lambs,
smears poor young cows with shameful filth and pulls
the tiny newborns from their mother's udder,
and thrice a day she milks the sheep and thrice
she shears their fleece, if possible, and with
a dismal spell compels the fickle moon
to stop midcourse, and charms to her the kids.
Nor does she pause for sleep; even at night
you'll see her passing through the grassy fields
to count the flocks upon the peak of Gaurus.
Why many words? She scrapes at everything.
And to make sure that nothing goes untouched
in forest or in field, by some new art
she leads astray among the ancient caves
the singing boys into her lust, and strips

PHYTIAS.	Fur Midas igitur, mechus scelerumque satelles!
	O facinus! Meretrix anus est et avara Lupisca!
	Que nuper glandes oleasque legebat in agris,
120	nunc celum violat verbis et fascinat agnos.
	Quid tunc Melalces? tacuit? quid dixit Ametus?
DAMON.	Assensere: Dei sic ira et crimen inultum
	permisit miseri laqueo pereuntis Alexis.
PHYTIAS.	Heu! trepidans horresco solum suspectaque divis
125	pascua. Quid faciam? Minui post verba videntur
	nempe greges; dominam noverunt prata Lupiscam.
	Ast ego quid merui? Nolebam vertere vepres
	in lauros, fateor, neque celsum extollere Olympum
	degeneres calamis, divos cantare subulcos.
130	Hoc tam grande malum? Non rebar. Lusus et insons
	distrahor hinc pauper: videat Pan, deprecor, equum.
	E quercu veteri nuper michi garrula cornix
	hos cecinit lapsus; vetuit sed dira cupido
	noscere, et in dubios deduxit ab aggere campos.
135	Nec Coridon dudum silvis cantare solebat
	sic letis, dum tantus erat sub tegmine lauri.
DAMON.	Non Coridon, miserande, tibi, non fistula nota
	qua steriles, vobis blandus, cantabat amores;
	sensi ego quam tenues conflaret gucture versus
140	et modulos stipula, laqueos dum poneret arvis.
PHYTIAS.	Quid faciam, Damon? fugiam, dic, litus ineptum?
DAMON.	Summe quod in tristi veteres cecinere bubulci.

VIII. MIDAS

those whom she lures.

PHYTIAS: Then Midas is a thief,
adulterer and criminal accomplice!
O villainy! Lupisca's an old harlot
and greedy miser too! Just recently
she gathered acorns in the fields, and olives,
and now outrages heaven with her words
and does bewitch the lambs. What said Melalces?
Has he been silent? Or what said Ametus?

DAMON: They have assented: thus the wrath of God
permitted and the murder unavenged
of poor Alexis, dying in his noose.

PHYTIAS: Alas! with trembling I begin to dread
the soil and pastures suspect to the gods.
What shall I do? Since we have talked, in fact,
the flocks appear diminished; look, the fields
have recognized Lupisca as their mistress.
But what have I done wrong? I had no wish
to turn the brambles into bays, I grant you,
nor raise up to Olympus with my pipes
unworthy men, nor sing that swineherds are
divine. Is this so evil? I don't think so.
Deceived and innocent I was drawn hither,
a poor man: Pan, I pray, look to the right.
A chattering crow upon the ancient oak
sang of these errors to me recently;
but cruel desire forbade me learn from it
and led me from a safe place into fields
most perilous. Coridon was not wont
to sing this way before in the glad woods
while he was great beneath the laurel's shelter.

DAMON: Poor wretch, you don't know Coridon at all
nor know the pipe on which he'd celebrate
those barren loves, though flattering to the ears.
But I know well what feeble verses he
blew from his throat, what thin tunes from his oat,
while he was setting traps out in the fields.

PHYTIAS: What shall I do? Say, Damon, shall I flee
this pointless shore?

DAMON: Hear what the ancient ploughboys

PHYTIAS. Malo rudes habitare casas nemorosaque tesqua,
parrasii lambant malo iam saxa Lycei
145 he pecudes, quam pingue solum stimphalidis agri
tot plenum curis. Mecum cantabit Amiclas
rupe sub exigua tutus, cantabit et ingens
Silvanus placida componet pace furentes,
ylice sub prisca, bilem stolidamque dyonem.
DAMON. Nil melius: pecudes pridem dum forte lavarem,
omnis erat varia plenus vertigine gurges;
hinc sensi monitus venturi turbinis iras,
et Mide casum pariter pecorisque ruinam:
et repetet glandes veteres oleasque Lupisca.
153 Sunt in secessu nobis florentia rura
et gratum nymphis antrum, quod fronde recenti
sternet amica tibi Glaucis, mellisque parabit
inde favum: venias, quas conspicis, arbitror, umbras,
ante locum teneas, protendent arbuta longas.
PHYTIAS. Tende igitur, veniam: teneat sua prata Lupisca.

VIII. MIDAS

                sang in sad circumstances such as these.

PHYTIAS: I'd rather live in simple cottages
and wooded wastelands, and prefer my sheep
to lick the stones on Parrhasian Lycaeus
than the fat soil of the Stymphalian lands
so full of woes. Beneath the meager cliff
in safety will Amiclas sing with me,
and underneath the venerable oak
mighty Silvanus too will sing and calm
men's raging, wrath, and foolish stubborn lust
in quiet peace.

DAMON: There's nothing better.
Some time ago while I was washing sheep,
each eddy teemed with ever-changing whirls;
from this I heard a warning of the wrath
of future storm, the fall of Midas, and
destruction of his sheep; Lupisca will
seek once again the old acorns and olives.
In spots sequestered we have flowering lands,
also a cavern pleasing to the nymphs,
which your friend Glaucis will strew with fresh leaves,
and then she will prepare the honeycombs;
come: the arbutus will spread out long shadows
which you can see before you reach the place.

PHYTIAS: Lead on, I'll come; Lupisca, keep your fields!

IX. LIPIS

BATRACOS. Quis, precor, es, nostris in silvis exterus hospes?
ARCHAS. Archas eram quondam pastorque, et nominor Archas
incola Parthenii montis, nunc ductus in oras
has casu; video pecudes armentaque passim
5 pinguia, sed steriles agros et pascua nulla.
BATRACOS. Miraris fortasse, senex, nam causa latens est.
Nunc, ni cura vetet, nostris succedito claustris
et requiem longo paulum concede labori:
et que sit tibi causa, precor, prepone viarum.
ARCHAS. Sic ego parrasios umbris persepe viantes
suscepi fessos: prospectat gratus Apollo
in meritos. Sed prima refer que causa latens sit.
BATRACOS. Sunt in semotis colles silveque patentes
herbis insignes et grandia pascua rivis
15 irrigua: has celeri contendunt undique cursu
quas habeo fetas vacce, redeuntque volentes
uberibus plenis, que post pendentia natis
prebent et tenues cogunt pinguescere lacte.
ARCHAS. Est memoranda quidem grandis solertia vaccis.
20 Ast ego visurus cupiens Amarillida veni.
BATRACOS. Archades en nostram norunt Amarillida, queso?
ARCHAS. Quis fuit in terris qui non Amarillida norit?
BATRACOS. Quid secum tibi, care senex? Non cura sacrorum:
despicitis dori tracesque altaria nostra.
ARCHAS. Circius, aiebant, veniet sumpturus honores
quos vetus athletis dederat victoribus etas.

IX. ANXIETY

BATRACOS: Pray, who are you, a visitor in our woods?
ARCHAS: I once was an Arcadian and a shepherd,
Archas by name; on the Parthenian peak
I dwell, now led by chance to these your shores.
Here all around I see fat herds and sheep,
yet sterile fields and no good pastureland.
BATRACOS: You wonder, old man, for the cause is hidden.
Unless business forbids, come enter now
our folds and grant long labor brief respite;
and tell, pray, what's the reason for your journey.
ARCHAS: Thus weary wayfaring Arcadians
I've often welcomed underneath the shade.
Apollo looks with favor on the worthy.
But first explain about that hidden cause.
BATRACOS: There are in spots remote extended forests
and hills remarkable for grass and pastures
watered by streams; to these the fertile cows
hasten from all sides with swift gait and then
return all by themselves with swollen udders,
which afterwards they offer to their young
and make the slender calves grow fat with milk.
ARCHAS: Their cleverness is noteworthy indeed.
But I've come wishing to see Amarillis.
BATRACOS: Then do Arcadians know our Amarillis?
ARCHAS: Who is on earth that knows not Amarillis?
BATRACOS: My dear old fellow, what have you to do
with her? Not yours the care of sacred things.
You Dorians and Thracians scorn our altars.
ARCHAS: Some said that Circius will come to take
the honors which the ancient era gave

	Hac ego deductus fama vincire capillos
	pastori vidi. Post hec quis cultus agrorum,
	qui mores essent, qui ritus, queve bubulcis
30	artes servandi pecoris lactisque premendi,
	que nemorum leges, avidus cognoscere veni.
BATRACOS.	Et nobis quidam nuper referebat etruscus
	ornatum arthoum sertis, sed lenta ferenti
	prestita quippe fides: obstabat inertia Circi.
ARCHAS.	Sic, hera, sic factum: verum narrabat etruscus.
	Circius arripuit sertum; fuit Albula testis.
BATRACOS.	Inde novos alpes emittunt vertice fumos;
	hinc lupa cum geminis pressantibus ubera latrat,
	et vulpes ambire domos gallosque timentes
40	adverto, tristesque malas ululare per umbras
	audio pastores rutulos et cuncta timere.
	Cinnama nunc filices pariant et balsama taxus
	sudet cyrnensis, tristisque cicuta sabeos,
	postquam romuleis sic visum, prestet odores!
ARCHAS.	Indignans loqueris, video: tibi Circius egram
	commovit bilem; nolles redimitus adesset.
BATRACOS.	Quid non indigner? Potuit fors invida mundo
	crinibus arthois ytalas imponere lauros.
ARCHAS.	An possunt edos forsan saturare petulcos,
50	vel quid maius habent ytale quam syrmia laurus?
BATRACOS.	Non equidem nostros sentis satis, Archas, honores.
	Has frondes pharetris Phebus victricibus olim
	ac cytharis, lauro facta iam Dane, dicavit;
	hinc veteres ytalis sacras fecere triumphis.
ARHCAS.	Que, precor, acta virûm, quorum tam fulgida merces?

IX. ANXIETY

                to its victorious athletes. Drawn by the news,
I saw them wreathe the shepherd's hair, and then
grew eager to learn something of their ways
of cultivating fields, their customs, rites,
what arts the farmers had of keeping sheep
or making cheese, what were the forest laws.

BATRACOS: So an Etruscan recently reported
that Circius was decked with northern wreaths,
but only slow belief was lent the speaker,
for Circius' sloth made it improbable.

ARCHAS: Yes, lady, it was so; and the Etruscan
told you the truth. Circius snatched the wreath;
Albula witnessed it.

BATRACOS: That's why the Alps
send strange smoke from their peaks; that's why the wolf
with suckling twins is barking, and I see
how foxes skirt the homes and frighten roosters,
I hear gloomy Rutulian shepherds howling
through evil shades of night, afraid of everything.
Let ferns now proffer cinnamon, the yew
of Corsica drip balsam, and the dread
hemlock now offer Sabian perfumes
since such a thing has seemed good to the Romans!

ARCHAS: I notice that you speak with indignation:
that Circius has stirred your envious bile;
you wouldn't wish him present, wreath and all.

BATRACOS: Why shouldn't I be indignant? See how chance
unfavorable to the world has set
Italian laurels on that northern hair.

ARCHAS: Then are perhaps Italian laurels able
to glut the butting kids, or are they greater
than those of Syrmio?

BATRACOS: Archas, indeed
you don't appreciate enough our honors.
These leaves once Phoebus dedicated to
victorious quivers and lyres, when Daphne had
turned into laurel; hence the ancients made
them consecrated to Italian triumphs.

ARCHAS: What acts, I pray, won a reward so splendid?

BATRACOS. O! longum narrare, senex. Sed pauca reportes
Parthenii silvis volumus sacroque Lyceo.
Linternus lybicas pestes revocavit ab arvis
ausonicis, fecitque potens has fundere virus
60 in colles proprios, stomachis et mella falerna
immisit legesque suas servare coegit.
Rusticus arpinas sulcavit vomere montes
cyrtheos latio, grandesque olidosque per altum
hyrcos in Tyberim traxit, domuitque superbos
65 cymbrorum tauros et currus fregit inanes.
Hircanas tygres cursu superavit Opheltes,
armenosque equidem devictos arte leones
et curvos Syrie pressos sub fasce camelos
assyriosque greges et quos Eritrathalasson
70 litore servabat ratibus devexit in umbram
Tarpeii lapidis, cilicesque per alta volucres
cepit et in spolium rostrum portavit et alas.
Allobrogis heduisque bobus belgisque iuvencis
frontibus imposuit Daphnis virtute capistros,
75 et solitos errare iugis et ludere flexu
pastores tanto contrivit robore fessos,
ut iuga demissa faciles cervice subirent.
Gryphes yperboreas rapientes unguibus olim
quos nobis vitulos servabat maximus Hyster,
80 privavit pedibus iuvenis Corigillus aduncis.
Smirneus pastor, venetusque et grandis etruscus
meonios dudum tauros ytalosque leones
et tyrios apros stipulis domuere canoris.
Quid tam multa loquar? quid frustra cuncta revolvam?
85 Hesperidum qui poma tulit, quid duxit hyberas
in Latium vaccas, qui vellera longa britannis

IX. ANXIETY

BATRACOS: Oh! it would take me long to tell, old man.
But I'll give you a few to carry back
to the Parthenian woods and sacred mountain.
Linternus called back from Ausonian farmlands
the Lybian plagues and, powerful, made them pour
their poison on their own hills, introduced
Falernian honey to the palates, and
compelled men to obey his firm decrees.
Rustic Arpinas with a Latin plow
furrowed the Cyrthean mountains, dragged the smelly
large goats across the sea and up the Tiber,
and tamed proud Cymbrian bulls and shattered quite
their empty chariots.
 Opheltes surpassed
in speed Hyrcanian tigers; and by art
he subjugated the Armenian lions
and humpbacked camels pressed by Syrian bundles;
Assyrian flocks and those which the Red Sea
was guarding on its shores he carried off
in ships to where Tarpeia's rock casts shadow;
he seized the swift Cilicians on the deep
and carried back as spoils their prows and oars.
 Daphnis by valor imposed halters on
the Allobrogian and the Aeduan bulls
and Belgian calves, and wore down with such might
the weary shepherds used to wandering
in mountains and to playing as they roamed
that readily they passed their lowered necks
beneath his yoke.
 The young Corigillus
cut off the crooked feet of Hyperborean
griffins when once their claws were snatching calves
which mighty Hyster had reserved for us.
 The Smyrnian and the Venetian shepherd
and great Etruscan tamed some time ago
Maeonian bullocks and Italian lions
and Tyrian boars with their melodious reeds.
 Why should I list so much? why vainly go
through all these things? The man who took the apples
of the Hesperides, or he who led
Hiberian cows to Latium, he who took

	abstulit aut frixo nudavit vellere colcos,
	et niveos meruere Iovis conscendere currus
	et plebis plausus et tempora cingere lauro;
90	his Quiris veteri sancivit lege coronas.
ARCHAS.	Magna refers et laude quidem memoranda perenni.
	Sed quid turbaris? Possunt meruisse nepotes
	quod nequivere patres. Est magnus Circius, hercle!
BATRACOS.	Heu! michi dic, quando meruit, precor, iste nefastus
95	Circius, ut segnis nostros ambiret honores?
	Huius avos memini venisse securibus altas
	cesuros silvas latias, latioque molosis
	infestos pecori; cui nunc mea nescia mater
	sponte manu facili lauros concessit avitas.
100	Heu! quantum potuit celi vis plurima! Quondam,
	dum pastor luscus confringeret omnia ferro
	et nostras mactaret oves impunis et antra
	byrseo victor misere consummeret igne,
	non potuere duces flecti, cogente periclo,
105	ex gemino pastore gregis pereuntis ut alter
	esset campanus, cui par labor atque suorum
	exitium fuerat. Nunc unus Circius, hostis
	barbarus immanis, meritis nec laude refulgens,
	omnia solus habet, silvas pecudesque bovesque
110	ac insigne decus pastorum nobile sertum.
ARCHAS.	Erras; hoc latii quondam voluere coloni.
BATRACOS.	Confiteor; sic sepe dolor divertit inertes.
	Non veterum si fusca quidem sed sacra parentum
	hunc pietas miserum potuisset cernere finem,

IX. ANXIETY

                long fleeces from the Britons or who stripped
                the Colchians of the Phrixian fleece, they earned
                the right to mount the snowwhite chariots
                of Jove and be applauded by the people
                and bind their brows with laurel; to these men
                Rome consecrated crowns by ancient law.

ARCHAS: You tell great things and certainly things worthy
to be retold with praise perpetual.
But why are you perturbed? Descendants can
deserve what their own forefathers could not.
Circius is great, by Hercules!

BATRACOS: Alas! I pray you tell me when did that
accursed Circius merit that a sluggard
should dare pursue our honors? I recall
his ancestors with axes came to cut
the lofty Latian forests, and were hostile
to Latian sheep with their Molossian hounds;
to whom with ready hand my ignorant mother
has freely yielded the ancestral laurels.
Alas! how much the heaven's great power could do!
Once while the one-eyed shepherd with his sword
destroyed all things and slew our sheep unpunished
and as a victor piteously burned
the caves with Byrsian fire, even then
in danger's face, the leaders could not be
persuaded that one of the two chief shepherds
of the perishing flock be the Campanian
for whom the agony and the destruction
of his own people had been closely matched.
Now one barbaric monstrous enemy,
one Circius with neither praise nor merit
alone has everything, the woods and sheep
and cows and noble wreath, the glorious
adornment of great shepherds.

ARCHAS: You are wrong:
Latium's inhabitants once wanted this.

BATRACOS: I do confess it; so pain often turns
cowards aside. Yet if our ancient parents'
benighted but sacred piety could have seen
this wretched end, indeed, the man of Mars

115	Martius in stigias umbras se sponte dedisset
precipitem; senoni pardo nec credo dedissent
inferias patres animas cum sanguine silve,
et reor in vacuum iuveni cantasset et anser;
nec genitor genitusque parem sibi summere cladem
120	curassent, canibusque dari lanianda latinis
viscera. Quid repetam sanctos pulchrosque labores,
felices anime? Vitam pulchrumque cruorem
fudistis Rheno! Sibi fert Ercinia mater
insignes titulos, et per spineta nepotes
125	distrahit, heu! nostros; cedunt nunc sydera cymbris.
ARCHAS.	Quid veteres renovas, Batracos, nunc flendo querelas?
Dalmata pannonus graiusque et pessimus hostis
affer iamdudum iuga, que portaverat ipse,
imposuit vestris tauris, traxitque per arva.
130	Quid tandem? Silvis fuit hec et gloria nostris.
BATRACOS.	Quid «nostris»? Forsan vestros non novimus agros?
AMINTAS.	Crede equidem, nostis, sed non meminisse potestis
dum genus egregium campis effulsit Aminte
et cecidere trabes ex yndo culmine nigre,
135	et dum meoniis dixerunt iura colonis
limpidus Eurotas quondam pulcherque Aracinthus:
sed demum surrepta tuos devenit ad agros.
Nil sub sole novum: rapuistis, nunc rapit alter.
Sed tibi quid tanti, letos si summat honores
140	Circius aut viridi circumdet tempora lauro?
BATRACOS.	Egon erat latiis pastorum maximus et quem
preferrent homines cunctis mortalibus olim.
Parte alia Daphnis post hunc pregrandis, in ipsum
insultans, turbavit agros. Hos quisque secutus
145	pro votis. Egonis ego, quia iustior esset

IX. ANXIETY

would not have freely thrown himself headfirst
into the Stygian shadows; nor, I think,
would fathers have cast souls below with blood
to the Senonian panther in the forest,
and I believe the goose too would have sung
to the young man in vain; nor would the parent
and child have cared to welcome their disaster
equally to each other, and their entrails
be given to the Latin dogs to tear.
Why should I tell again the beautiful
and holy labors, happy souls? You poured
your noble blood into the Rhine. Now Mother
Ercinia wins herself noteworthy titles
and drags, alas! our grandsons through the briars;
and now they yield their stars up to the Cimbrians.

ARCHAS: Why, Batracos, renew ancient complaints
with weeping? The Dalmatian, the Pannonian,
the Greek, and your worst enemy the African
did long ago upon your bulls impose
the yoke which he himself had worn, and drew
your bulls across the fields. What of it then?
This also was the glory of my woods.

BATRACOS: Why "my"? Do I perhaps not know your fields?

ARCHAS: Indeed you know them, but you cannot have
remembered when the offspring of Amintas
shone forth outstanding in the battlefields
and black beams crashed upon the Indian peak,
when clear Eurotas and fair Aracinthus
pronounced laws once for the Maeonians;
but thievery came to your lands at last.
Nothing is new under the sun: you've stolen
and now another steals. But why is it
so much to you if Circius takes on
glad honors or with laurel crowns his brow?

BATRACOS: Egon was greatest of the Latin shepherds,
the one whom men once set above all mortals.
Daphnis, the second greatest, over him
triumphing threw the fields into confusion.
Each person chose to follow one of these.
I went to Egon's side because he was

partes intravi, quod propter credita semper
hostis eram Daphnis. Cui postquam Circius heres,
pertimeo, non forte velit renovare vetustas
iras maiorum memorans, vertatque secures
in silvas, gregibusque lupos immisceat acres.
Me miseram! que, queso, michi nunc tuta latebra?
quo fugiam? quo tristis eam? Michi terra dehiscat;
impia me coget genitrix intrare lupanar.
Me miseram! Furias educet Circius orco
inclitus hoc serto: corvi per inane volantes,
heu! rostris ventura sonant presagia veri.

ARCHAS. Debilis esne adeo, quin possis ferre priores
insultus? Facili solvuntur membra labore
rhenicolis; septas quo possis robore valla,
fac circum fossas et magnis cinge rubetis;
assint pastores sudibus, prepone molosos,
da pueris fundas ac obstrue sentibus arctos
introitus: persepe dii iuvere labores.

BATRACOS. Imbellis michi turba manet mollisque per umbras;
aspicis ut sterili nupsit me mater agello,
cui nec litus adest nec grandis defluit amnis
nec prerupta soli patiuntur devia currus.
Hincque meum robur iuvenes transcendere montes
coguntur pedibus, gregibusque referre iumentis
pabula: si veniant, timor usquam nullus adesset.

ARCHAS. Erige, fac, vires et firma robore mentem.
Vidi ego deflentem lacrimis Amarillida nuper,
quam tu sponte putas cupido posuisse coronam,
et nullis silvam letari floribus usquam.

IX. ANXIETY

more just, for on account of things believed
I always was an enemy of Daphnis.
Since his successor's Circius, I fear
lest he perchance wish to renew old grudges
of his ancestors and, remembering them,
set axes to the forests, send fierce wolves
among the flocks. Ah wretched me! I ask,
now what safe refuge will there be for me?
To what place shall I flee? where shall I go,
all sorrowful? May the earth swallow me;
an impious mother forces me to enter
a brothel. Wretched me! Circius now
made famous with this wreath will lead the Furies
from hell: crows flying through the air, alas!
sound with their beaks omens of truth to come.

ARCHAS: Are you so weak that you cannot endure
their very first attacks? For the Rhine-dwellers'
muscles have been relaxed by easy labor.
Just fortify as strongly as you can
the sheepfolds, and encircle them with ditches
and with great bramble thickets; let the shepherds
help out with stakes; put the Molossian hounds
in front, give the boys slings, and block with briars
the northern entrances: often the gods
have helped those who make effort for themselves.

ATRACOS: A crowd unwarlike and effeminate
is left for me in such a time of darkness.
You see to what a little sterile field
my mother weds me, with no shore and no
great river flowing by, nor do the steep
backroads of the terrain allow for chariots.
Therefore the young men who are all my strength
are forced to go on foot across the mountains
and bring food for the flocks on beasts of burden;
if they'd come back, I'd have no fear at all.

ARCHAS: Gather your courage, do, and fortify
your mind with strength. I have seen Amarillis
with flowing tears, who you believe has freely
bestowed the crown upon his eager head,
nor was the woodland gladdened with a flower

175 Fistula non cecinit, non era sonantia; Tybris
effuxit tacitus undasque retraxit in alvum,
atque graves tacuere senes, tacuere palestre
et tacuere nurus pariter, clausumque Lupercal
constitit et nullis monstravit gaudia ludis.
180 Post, dum sedisset scanno iam Circius alto,
conspicuas serti frondes prenubilus auster
eripuit sonituque gravi devexit ad arthos.
O monstrum! Frondes dum defert ille per auras,
exarsere quidem, tenuisque per alta favilla
185 vix est visa viris. Tunc qui pregrandis habetur
archadibus pastor confestim dixit Aruntes:
– Hic iter in silvas faciet tibi, Rhene, propinquas,
in quibus ipse diem claudet, condetque sepulcro
quod tam grande rapit nomen putridumque cadaver;
190 vel si iterum veniat, quia flexit flamma parumper
in reditum fumos, faciet memorabile nullum. –
BATRACOS. O nostris mea sacra Pales gratissima silvis,
fac firmes omen: repetat sua lustra bicornis
belua, nec nostros infestet cuspide campos.
195 En tibi, quam gemini sugunt mactabitur agna,
tuque, senex Archas, cui tantum cernere cure,
sis mecum: nox atra venit; iam sydera celo
surgere, nonne vides? abiens permittit Apollo.

IX. ANXIETY

in any spot. The reedpipe did not sing,
the trumpets did not sound; the Tiber flowed
in silence and drew back into its bed,
and all the solemn older men were silent,
all silent the gymnasia and silent
were equally the younger married women,
the Lupercal stood shut with no display
of joy in any games. When afterwards
Circius sat upon the lofty throne,
a cloudy southwind snatched away his wreath
of leaves illustrious and with low moan
did sweep them northward. O monstrous event!
While through the air it bore the leaves away,
they verily caught fire; the feeble spark
was scarcely visible across the air.
Aruntes then, held by Arcadians
in great esteem, immediately said:
"He'll make this journey to the woods near you,
O Rhine, in which he'll finish off his days,
and in the tomb beside his rotting corpse
he'll hide the famous name that now he snatches;
or if he should return, because the flame
a little while did backwards bend its smoke,
he will do nothing worth remembering."

BATRACOS: O sacred Pales, pleasing to our woods,
confirm this omen: let the two-horned beast
return into its lair and not infest
our fields with pointed horns. Behold to you
a ewe we'll slaughter whom twin lambs are suckling;
and you, Archas old man, who care so much
to see things, stay with me, for dark night comes;
already the retiring Apollo
allows – you see them?– heaven's stars to rise.

X. VALLIS OPACA

LYCIDAS. Dorile, seu pluvias terris immittat Orion
aut Amon flores vel Cancer rure cicadas,
auferat aut frondes Chyron, te fronte recurva
semper conspicio tristem lacrimisque madentem.
5   Quis dolor iste tuus? Periit tibi vitis in ulmo?
DORILUS. Iuppiter a celso prospectans cardine campos
prostravit feriens ignito fulmine fagum
his celebrem silvis: sonitu perterrita tellus
ingemuit, tremuere greges ac arbuta dumis;
10 pastores sese comperta fraude vicissim
in caveis clausere malis. Cui rustica cessit
libertas, turbare greges, disperdere capros
cepit. Crisifabro Iunoni sacra paranti
abstulit optatam frustra per tempora Rufam,
15 lascivusque mei formosam Phyllida ruris
eripuit Phytie nostro: quam magna supersunt
centauris obscena quidem, si dicere vellem!
Utque alios mittam, nostros damnavit amores
illecebris, pedicas ac antra carentia sole
20 imposuit, nulla mirto nec leta corimbis.
Hec tristis ploro. Sed tu fabrilia tractas,
centuculo tectus, nigra et fuligine tinctus?
LYCIDAS. Vera igitur tulerat fusca sub valle Menalcas
adveniens. Per Pana deum, non sordida ledunt
25 munera Plutarci quantum mala vota furentum

X. THE DARK VALLEY

LYCIDAS: My Dorilus, whether Orion sends
          rain to the earth, or Amon flowers, whether
          the Crab brings crickets to the countryside,
          or whether Chiron strips the leaves away,
          I always see you grieving with bent forehead
          and streaming tears. What is this grief of yours?
          Have all your grapevines died upon the elm?

DORILUS: Great Jupiter from high on heaven's pole
          has flattened the fields, with fiery thunderbolt
          striking a beech tree famous in these woods.
          In terror at the sound, earth groaned, the flocks
          and leaves all trembled mid the briars; in turn
          the shepherds shut themselves, with fraud disclosed,
          in evil caves. Then he whose rustic freedom
          has ceased began to throw the flocks in turmoil,
          and to disperse the goats. From Crisifabrus,
          who was preparing sacrifice to Juno,
          he stole the fruitlessly desired Rufa
          at the last moment; then, lascivious,
          snatched lovely Phyllis from our Phytias.
          What further great outrages by the centaurs
          I truly could report if I so wished!
          The rest I shall omit, but that he has
          condemned my charming love, bound me with chains
          in caves that lack the sunlight, all ungladdened
          by myrtle or by ivy. That is why
          I weep, so sorrowful. But you in patches
          and tinted with black soot, are you a workman?

LYCIDAS: Menalcas, coming down to the dark valley,
          spoke truly then. By Pan, the sordid gifts
          of Plutarch do not cause me so much pain
          as do the evil wishes of the madmen

quos genui calamos inter ranasque palustres!
DORILUS. Tune, precor, meus es Lycidas? Te nempe Podarcem
credebam. Quam leta dies! Spes lapsa resurgit;
tu celum campos fluvios armentaque nobis
30 restitues. Quernas superisque tibique coronas
post aras statuam! Placidam contingere dextram
mittito, quin subeas antrum. Non lacte tepenti
castaneis nucibus pomis bromioque fovebo;
omnia subtraxit Polipus: michi panis et unda,
35 algaque dat somnos mollis. Sic vivere divos
audivi in terris. Nec dedignere, precamur;
saltem que turbant faciem purgare tenebras
his poteris lymphis, et fessos inde cubili
hoc recreare artus; medio revocabimus ignes.
LYCIDAS. Erras. Prisca vides, non me, vestigia nostri.
Non ego plus vester, postquam cillenius Argus
surripuit virga radios ex ethere raptos
et crinem secuit Trivie iam falce dicatum.
DORILUS. Ha miserande puer! Periit spes alta salutis,
45 incertusque mei moriar, nomenque sub umbras
auferet atra dies. Pecudes ad prata Miconis
nunc Ylas pellit, manibus nunc ubera pressat;
hic cythisum salicesque novas frondesque recentes
apparat ac agnos recreat matresque per herbas;
50 hic alter mersat rivis et vellera tondet;
ille suos cantat calamis invisus amores
et corilos faciles mulcet celsaque cupressus.
Me solum miserumque tenet sine crimine victum,
heu! Polipus, dum seva tero nunc ocia planctu.
LYCIDAS. Castalie, dic, oro, puer, docuere sorores
te lacrimis transire diem? Quis nectere mentes
atque pios animos potuit vincire ginestis?

X. THE DARK VALLEY

whom I brought forth among the reeds and marsh frogs!
DORILUS: Pray tell, are you my Lycidas? Indeed
I thought you were Podarcis. Happy day!
My fallen hope rebounds; you will restore
the sky to me, the fields, the streams, the herds.
I'll set up crowns of oak behind the altars
for both the gods and you! Forget the handshake,
but come into the cave. I will not offer
warm milk, fruit, chestnuts, hazelnuts, and wine;
Polipus confiscated everything.
Water and bread are all I have to offer,
soft seaweed for a bed. I've heard the gods
themselves live thus on earth. So please don't scorn it;
at least you can wash off with this clear water
the dirtiness that darkens now your face,
and rest your weary limbs then on this bed,
while I revive the fire in the center.

LYCIDAS: You're wrong, you see my ancient vestiges,
not me. I'm yours no more since Hermes' wand
deprived me of the light of upper air
and cut the hair assigned to Hecate.

DORILUS: Ha wretched boy! My hope for safety's lost,
and I shall die uncertain of myself,
a dark day take my name down to the shades.
Now Hylas drives the sheep to Micon's meadow,
his hands now press the udders; someone else
brings clover, fresh leaves, and young willow shoots,
refreshing both the lambs and ewes with grasses;
another shears the fleeces, dipping them
into the streams; another man, unseen,
sings on his pipes his loves, charming the pliant
hazeltrees and lofty cypresses.
Me alone, alas! Polipus keeps
in misery and fettered for no crime,
while I wear out my cruel idleness
with lamentation.

LYCIDAS: Tell me, boy, I pray,
did the Castalian sisters teach you thus
to pass the day in tears? Who has been able
to fetter minds or chain up pious souls?

quis prohibet meliore tui quin parte peragres
gnosiacos saltus et menala pascua? quisve
pastores Yde videas fontesque bicornis
Parnasi et lauri dulces per culmina silvas?
Ha scelus infandum! Sic nondum vivere nosti
annosus tecum? Secum superavit Olympum
olim Argus, qui iura deûm viditque deditque;
pastores frigios orbatus lumine Mopsus
et danaos cecinit; sic Tytirus arva latina
non vidit, rutulus dum tinxit sanguine Turnus.
Has lacrimas nobis sinito, cui nulla potestas
ni damnosa manet: memor es, dum pascua solus
hec tenui, quam grandis eram? Nunc tristis egestas
arguit atque iubet miseris solatia prestem.

DORILUS. O Lycida, fateor, dure solamina vite
de te tot merui nunquam. Sed pande, precamur,
quis tibi Plutarcus, quas valles, quosve recessus
nunc habites, Archas divos postquam abstulit ignes.

LYCIDAS. Spelunca in medio stat Trenaros, inscia Phebo,
qua vehimur celo vetiti, cui limine primo
pervigil insultat canis ater et atria servat.
Blanditur cauda intranti morsuque fatigat
tentantes reditum, ni princeps iusserit. Inde
et lucos silvasque vides fluviosque lacusque.
Atra loci facies nebulis fumoque palustri;
perpetua sordent vallis fuligine rupes.
Semper hyemps glacialis inest, nox semper opaca;
cecus adest ignis, nemorum nec stipite vivus,
arte tamen superûm. Nec credas leta Pelori
pascua vel campos tyrios Libanive roseta,
tymbreos colles, iuga vel ridentia achanto,
Eridanique leves undas et amena colamus:

X. THE DARK VALLEY

Who keeps your better part from wandering
through Cretan forests and Sicilian pastures?
Who keeps you from the sight of Ida's shepherds
or from the springs on double-peaked Parnassus,
the fragrant laurel groves along its summits?
Ha crime unspeakable! With all your years
have you not learned yet how to live in peace?
Once Argus by himself, who saw and gave
the laws of gods, surmounted great Olympus;
the Phrygian shepherds and the Danaans
blind Mopsus sang; and Tytirus saw not
the Latin farmlands while Rutulian Turnus
was dyeing them with blood. Allow me tears,
to whom no power remains except self-ruin.
Do you recall how great I was when I
alone possessed these pastures? Now sad need
is plainly mine and bids me manifest
some consolation to the miserable.

DORILUS: O Lycidas, admittedly I never
deserved from you so many consolations
for my hard life. But please explain who is
Plutarchus to you, what retreats or valleys
you now inhabit, since the Arcadian
deprived you of the sight of heaven's fires?

LYCIDAS: At the center stands the cave Trenaros,
unseen by Phoebus, into which we're led,
prohibited the sky; at its first threshold
the black watchdog leaps up and guards the hall.
He coaxes with his tail the one who enters,
but with his bite assails the one who tries
to leave again unless the prince commanded.
From there you see groves, forests, streams, and lakes.
The place looks dark with fogs and marshy mist;
the cliffs are black with soot perpetual.
It's always icy winter, thickest night,
with fire invisible not kept alive
by forest kindling but by art divine.
Don't think we dwell in Pelorus' glad pastures
or Tyrean fields or Lebanese rose gardens,
the Thymbraean hills, acanthus-brightened ridges,
or mid the sparkling streams and lovely views

90	late sardoniis et taxo prata, locique
	omnes conspicui vepribusque et vimine torto.
	Implicite miseras reddentes flentibus umbras
	insurgunt silve; ceno sanieque fluentes,
	in medio maculant olidi de vertice rivi.
95	Non ibi sunt celeres capree cervique fugaces;
	serpentum locus ille ferax pestisque nefande
	telluris lybice, quorum nunc verbere caude,
	nunc acri morsu, nunc nexibus angimur egre.
	Syrene in scopulis vobis silvisque napee
100	cantantes aures mulcent ramisque volucres:
	ast nobis aliter resonare per omnia valles
	mugitu valido, turpes et frendere porcos
	dentibus et sevos rabie rugire leones
	audires, tristesque sonos ut reddat et echo.
DORILUS.	Quid dicis, Lycida? Potuit natura vel alter
	visceribus terre tam diram condere sedem?
LYCIDAS.	Quidni? Cuncta potest qui silvas fecit et astra.
	Sed paulum consiste, precor; peiora sequuntur.
	Plutarcus scopulo residet. Fusca atque marita,
110	frondibus umbrati nigris et vellere pullo.
	Stant squalens circum scabies morbique caduci
	omnes et pecoris pestis certissima frigus
	et sicce febres ac horrida mortis ymago.
	Has inter colubris hyrtus squamisque cruentis
115	trux pastor miseros leviat nec pectine pastos,
	nec calamis mulcet, sed cornu territat umbras
	atque greges surgens scopulo, et clamore sonoro
	irritat furias, vepretaque mandat amena
	lustrari taurosque iterum per inania verti.
120	Quot gemitus vox ista levet, tibi sydera pandent
	si numeres, seu fulva sali monstrabit harena.
	Concutit inde polos et sevo murmure replet
	Iuppiter iratus silvis ac fulmina vibrat;
	quassateque ruunt nubes, et grandine multa
125	frangitur omne nemus, nodosaque robora rumpit

X. THE DARK VALLEY

of Eridanus. Rather, far and wide
grow fields of yew and crowsfoot; every place
shows twisted twigs and briars. Tangled woods
rise up with shadows bleak for those who weep;
flowing with filth and venom, stinking streams
flow down to stain the midst. Not there swift goats
or fleeting deer; it is a savage place
unspeakable of serpents and of pests
from Lybia, that now with striking tail,
now with sharp bite, and now with knotting coils
torment us sorely. Here your ears are charmed
by sirens from the rocks, nymphs in the woods,
and birds on branches singing; but you'ld hear
quite differently our valley loud resounding
with mighty bellows, foul boars' gnashing teeth
and savage lions' roaring rage, so that
even the echo sends back gloomy noises.

DORILUS: What are you saying, Lycidas? Could nature
or something else establish such a place
so dreadful in the bowels of the earth?

LYCIDAS: Why not? He can do all who made the woods
and stars. But wait, I pray; worse follows.
Plutarcus sits beside his swarthy spouse
upon a boulder shaded with black boughs
and with a dark sheep's hide. Around them stand
foul mange and chill, the sheep's most certain plague,
and every mortal illness, and dry fevers,
and horrid shapes of death. Among them, prickly
with snakes and bloody scales, the savage shepherd
does not relieve the poor flocks with a lyre
nor charm them with a pipe, but with his horn
atop the rock he panics flocks and shades
and with a loud blast stirs the Furies up
and orders them to run among the briars
and bulls to turn again through desert places.
As many as the stars, if you could count them,
or as the yellow sands beside the sea,
so many groans that voice gives forth. Then Jove,
in anger strikes the poles and fills the woods
with furious rumbling, shakes his lightning bolt;
the shattered clouds pour down, the forest's broken

ventorum vis magna furens. Quid multa? Dolentes,
heu! quot tunc pavidos inter spineta videres
currere et oppositas sentes contundere dorso,
precipitesque dari celsis ex rupibus ultro!
130 Ast postquam Dyomedis equas, Gerionis et acres
iussit inire canes, omnis per devia turba
convenit, ac ydris agimur; tristesque ministri
componunt turmas avidi penasque minantur.
Nec pecudes credas: tauros hic arguit atros
135 et summa de rupe truces impellit ad ima;
convocat hic torvos angues, et fuste preusto
in glaciem cogit squamosaque tergora frangit;
isque lupos igni de vertice culminis alti
deicit. O! quotiens hos inter lapsus et ipse!
DORILUS. Siste, precor, Lycida. Quid? tu devolveris, oro,
immixtusque lupis e summo montis in ignes?
Quid sceleris? que dura trucem sententia movit?
LYCIDAS. Heu michi! iamdudum pecudes rapuisse Miconis
et, scelus infaustum! pueros traxisse per umbras
145 in vetitam venerem, melio dum vita maneret,
has sedes tribuere michi sub vindice iusto.
DORLIUS. Alcidem memini monstrum traxisse trifauce
cecropiumque ducem ex imo iam vallis opace;
vis rogitem, si forte queam quandoque movere,
150 Pana pium retrahat te nostras mitis in auras?
LYCIDAS. Dorile, ne facias; nequicquam tangere Olympum
iam precibus posses aut irrevocabile fatum.
Actum est de me deque illis quos iustus in orcum
Archesilas misit quondam. Nunc desine; quorsum
155 contendo veniam, et reliquos tibi carmine signem.
Setigeros trahit ille sues fortisque frementes
illidit scopulis et membra trementia quassat;

X. THE DARK VALLEY

                with heavy hail, the winds' great raging power
tears down the knotted oaks. Why say it all?
How many grieving souls you'd see, alas!
running in terror then through thorny brakes;
opposing briars lash them on the back,
and headlong from high cliffs they hurl themselves!
When he has ordered Diomedes' horses
and Gerion's fierce hounds to enter in,
the whole throng gathers through the pathless ways;
we're driven on with hydras; eager demons
assemble gloomy troops and threaten vengeance.
You'd not believe the cattle: wild black bulls
he drives down from the highest mountaintop;
grim snakes he summons, with a stake fire-sharpened
compels them all to writhe upon the ice
and breaks their scaly backs; he throws the wolves
from highest summits down into the fire.
Alas! how often I have been among them!

DORILUS: Stop, please, my Lycidas. What? Have you hurtled
among the wolves from peaks into the fires?
What crime, what sentence harsh evokes such cruelty?

LYCIDAS: Ah woe is me! the theft of Micon's sheep
long past, and –hapless crime!–the boys' seduction
into forbidden lust among the shadows,
while still a better life might have been mine,
have set me there under a just avenger.

DORILUS: I remember that Alcides dragged
the three-jawed monster and Cecropian leader
from out the very depths of that dark valley;
do you wish me to ask our pious Pan,
if I perchance may move him at some time,
to draw you back into our milder airs?

LYCIDAS: No, Dorilus; your prayers will not be able
to touch Olympus nor to change my fate.
What's done is done for me and for all those
whom just Archiselas once sent to Orcus.
Now quiet; let me get to where I'm hastening
and point the others out to you in song.
That one drags bristling hogs and with great strength
dashes them foaming on the rocks and shatters

summo alius studio ducit de montes molosos,
tabo et marcentes cogit gustare paludes;
immanes ursos ex lustris pellit ad undas
is tardosque onagros, et ferro tranat adunco;
fascinat hic lynces, demum per devia vertens
atque fame longa miseras hinc inde molestat.
Nequicquam tibi cuncta velim mala pandere versu:
vivimus inviti mortem per aprica cientes.
Nunc memor esto tui; fugientia sydera Phebum
adventare monent, michi nec fas cernere. Tandem
tunc Polipus, quercum dum scandet forte palumbas
perquirens, michi crede, ruet, nostrosque tumultus
adveniens auget, sic ducunt fila sorores,
teque tuis linquet campis: sic vincula solves.

DORILUS. Numen honoratum silvis, Pan, te precor, assis,
et veniat lux illa michi: tibi pinguior agnus
ex grege quippe tuas ultro ferietur ad aras,
quas statuam, ludosque traham tibi carmine sacros.

X. THE DARK VALLEY

their twitching limbs; another with high zeal
leads hounds down from the mountains and when they
are limp with plague, he makes them drink marshwaters;
this one drives mighty bears and sluggish asses
out of their dens into the waves, and swims
among them with an iron hook; this one,
roving the back ways, casts a spell on linxes,
vexing the poor beasts to and fro with famine.
I would not even wish my verse to tell you
the entire evil: we live against our will
calling for death all day. Now of yourself
be mindful; the retreating stars announce
Phoebus' approach, from whose sight I am banished.
Polipus finally, while he perchance
will climb an oak tree seeking doves, believe me,
will fall and his arrival swell our uproar;
the sisters thus spin out his thread, and he
will leave you in your fields, your chains thus loosed.

DORILUS: Divinity long honored in the forests,
O Pan, I pray, be present, let that day
come to me: from the flock a fatter lamb
you may be sure will gladly be struck down
upon the altars which I'll raise to you,
and I'll prolong your sacred games with song.

XI. PANTHEON

AUCTOR. Est tibi Phebus amor, Clio, quem lata per arva
insequeris, noctesque fugis fuscosque recessus;
Phebus amat lauros, quas inter sepe labores
deposuit sacros: nec te sedisse parumper
5   has subter virides, fervent nunc arva, pudebit.
Decantanda michi veniunt tua carmina Mopso;
sis fautrix, mecumque chelim tu tange Arethuse:
Mopsus enim pellet nebulas a carmine flabris.
Rupis in absconso, Berecinthia, montis agrestem
10   en tibi texebat septam sociatus Aminta
Glaucus, et ardentes lenibant murmure curas.
Ecce secus Tybrim fulvos per prata iuvencos
ac olidas virga cogebat pulchra capellas
Mirtilis, et Glaucum placida sic voce precatur:

MIRTILIS. – Glauce pater, si lenta salix tibi vimina prestet
usque opus inceptum peragas, si semper Amintas
subsidium prestans his tecum vivat in antris,
sis lenis nostrisque fave, mi candide, votis:
suscipe quos cernis tauros, has tolle capellas;
20   cornibus insignis frons illis, spargere harenam
spectabis pedibus, lactisque has esse feraces;
da fontes cantuque fove, da pascua cunctis.

GLAUCUS. O nimium dilecta michi, iam, Mirtilis, ecce
non cythisum salicesve vides, non aspera dumis
25   sunt spineta meis; humiles ex vallibus agnis
herbas porto senex paucis. Nam spernimur altis

XI. PANTHEON

AUTHOR: Phoebus is your beloved, Clio, whom
you follow after through the wide farmlands,
fleeing the nights and dark recesses; Phoebus
loves laurels, oft the prize for sacred labors;
nor will it shame you to have briefly sat
beneath these green boughs now while the fields are hot.
Your songs I sing to Mopsus; be my patroness,
and with me touch the lyre of Arethusa.
Mopsus will clear the song of mists with breezes.
    In a hidden spot on the cliff, Cybele,
Glaucus was weaving you a rustic fence
accompanied by Amintas, and they soothed
their burning cares with murmurings. Behold
beside the Tiber fair Mirtilis came
driving her tawny heifers and smelly goats
across the meadows with a rod, and thus
begged with a gentle voice:

MIRTILIS: "O father Glaucus,
so may the supple willow give you withes
until you have completed the work begun,
so may Amintas, helping you, live always
beside you in these caves, my shining one;
be pliant and be gracious to my prayers:
please take the bulls you see here, take these goats;
the bulls are crowned with horns, they paw the sand;
the goats are rich with milk. Give them springwater,
favor them with a song, give them all pasture.

GLAUCUS: Mirtilis, my already dear beloved,
you don't see any clover or willows here,
nor are there sharp thornbushes in my brambles;
an old man now, I carry from the valleys
some humble grass for a few lambs. I'm scorned

| | in silvis Rhodopes; me spernunt archades omnes.
| | Preterea, Cacus si viderit, omnia passim
| | distrahet in iugulum, dum tristes impleat iras.
| MIRTILIS. | Heu! satis hinc video: refugis, mi Glauce,
| | [quod optem,
| | immemor Alcidis nostri, qui carneus olim,
| | cortice dum parvo vectus torpentia circum
| | litora Iordanis spectares nunquid ad hamum
| | venisset piscis studio detentus inani,
| 35 | te traxit gregibusque suis prefecit amatis.
| | An tibi quos gessit soli gessisse labores,
| | stulte, putas? Cunctis voluit prodesse creatis.
| | Tolle igitur: novi quantum tibi prata favoris
| | iam servent; hec leta magis quam dudum Aracinthum
| 40 | viderit Amphyon seu natus Apolline colles
| | Ysmari et Amphrisum Phebus vel thessala pastor,
| | prospicies pecori. Nec desunt munera cantu.
| | Stat bicolor mirtus qua tu sub rupe sonantis
| | Tarpeie michi vinctus eris, nostrosque per omne
| 45 | tempus in amplexus venies. Quid carmina servas?
| | Dic, age; iam patulas aures armenta revolvunt;
| | et tu, magne comes, stipulis fac dicta secundes,
| | ut sonet omnis ager: tibi sit mea laurea munus.
| GLAUCUS. | Mirtilis, en vincor; dabimus tibi carmina. Aminta,
| 50 | expedias calamos: surgant ad sydera versus. –
| AUCTOR. | Inde pium summa reserans dulcedine pectus,
| | sic cantare Iovem cepit genitumque sacrumque
| | flamen, ut ethereo resonarent carmine valles.
| | Hinc quibus una tribus deitas connexa moretur
| 55 | legibus explicuit, silvis plaudentibus; inde

XI. PANTHEON

                in the tall forests of Mount Rhodope;
                all the Arcadians scorn me; and if Cacus
                should see it, he'll devour all things around
                until his gloomy rage is satisfied.

MIRTILIS: Alas! I see from this that you refuse,
                my Glaucus, what I wish, forgetful quite
                of our Alcides who once in the flesh–
                while you, in a small boat by Jordan's shores,
                were looking whether any fish had come,
                detained by vain desire, to the hook–
                drew you to him and placed you at the head
                of his beloved flocks. Or do you think,
                fond man, the labors which he undertook
                were done for you alone? He wished to help
                all creatures. Therefore listen: yes, I know
                how much favor the meadows show you now;
                but you will see these fields richer in cattle
                than Amphyon saw those of Aracinthus,
                Apollo's son the hills of Ysmarus,
                and Phoebus in his shepherd's guise Amphrisus
                or meadows of Thessalia. And a song
                will not lack its reward. I'll crown you with
                bicolored myrtle close beneath the rock
                of echoing Tarpeia, and you'll come
                to dwell in my embrace forevermore.
                Why then reserve your songs? Tell me, please do.
                The herds now turn their spreading ears; and you,
                great comrade, make the pipes accompany
                your words so that the whole field may resound.
                And let my laurel here be your reward.

GLAUCUS: Mirtilis, I'm won over; I will sing.
                Prepare the pipes, Amintas; let the verses
                rise to the stars.

AUTHOR: Thereupon opening
                his pious breast with sweetness consummate,
                thus he began to sing of Jove and the son
                and holy wind, so that the vales resounded
                with heavenly song. Hence to the applauding woods
                he told by what laws three parts are connected
                into one deity; then who created

quis terras undasque maris celumque serenum,
nocturnos ignes dederit superosque priores
et Phebi radios, Veneris Trivieque reflexus;
fluminibus valles qua lege et litora ponto,
60 qua flores pratis et densis arbuta lucis
sint concessa prius; quo post hec ordine campis,
montibus ac celsis fluviisque animalia surgant
atque ferant gressus; quis se per inane volucres
viribus extollant, quis se reptilia sulco
65 proserpant humili, quis sulcent equora pisces;
quis mentes parcasque viris, quis semina glebis
crediderit primus, sevus quis sanguine terras
innocuo primus macularit, et inscia primus
iussit ut in silvas irent armenta gregesque;
70 quis primus placidas pecori componeret umbras,
quisve ferox primus ferrum molliverit igne,
quisve prior stipulis dederit discrimina vocum.
Acrius hinc culpam cecinit Lycaonis avari,
turbatumque Iovem terris, silvasque ferasque
75 et pecudum genus omne simul sub gurgite mersum,
et cimba tenui vectum cum semine rerum
Deucaliona pium, pariter natosque nurusque.
Hinc lapides iactos hominum reassummere formas,
atque giganteam rabiem, cui ponere Olympum
80 vertice pindareo parvum, vel Pelion Osse;
deiectos colles tandem vanosque superbi
balatus pecoris, colles saltusque petitos
narrabat varios pastoribus atque capellis;
Archipatris pugnas sublataque cornua tauris,
85 Silvanoque sacrum, quod nondum viderat etas
ulla, pium, magnos servans sub cortice sensus;
qualiter hinc etiam campos liquisset avitos,
et magni promissa Dei partumque secutum
post risum sterilis vetule, grandesque paratus

XI. PANTHEON

the lands, the seawaves, and the sky serene,
who made nocturnal fires, Phoebus' rays,
the first heavenly bodies, the reflections
of Venus and Diana; by what law
valleys are granted to rivers, shores to the sea,
blooms to the fields, and trees to the serried groves;
then by what order animals arise
and set forth in the fields, on lofty mountains,
and in the rivers; by what power the birds
rise up into the air, how there crawl forth
reptiles in humble furrows, and how fish
swim in the seas; who first entrusted minds
and fates to men, and seeds unto the soil,
what cruel man first with innocent blood defiled
the earth, who first commanded herds and flocks
to go unwitting into pasturelands;
who first arranged a soft shade for the cattle,
or what fierce man first softened iron with fire,
or who first gave the reedpipes different notes.
More sharply after this he sang the crime
of greedy Lycaon, and Jove's great anger,
the forest beasts and every kind of cattle
all sunk together underneath the water,
and in a frail boat pious Deucalion
transported safely with the seeds of things,
and his sons also with him and their wives.
Then how thrown rocks take on the shapes of men,
the giants' madness which did think it slight
to place Olympus on Pindarus' peak
or Pelion on Ossa; then at length
he was recounting those great hills cast down,
the empty bleating of the prideful flock,
the various hills and sloping mountain pastures
sought out by goats and shepherds; then the fights
and raised horns of the bulls of Archipater,
Silvanus' sacred rite, unseen before,
keeping great meanings underneath the bark;
then how he even left ancestral fields,
the great God's promises and then the birth
after the sterile aged woman's laugh,
and how at heaven's command a man was ready

ut genitum iussu superûm mactaret ad aras,
Orbatos hyrcos merito flammasque typheas
e celo lapsas silvis vacuasque paludes,
et Cinaram bromio captum vigilasse duabus
monstrabat natis; aris tum numine raptum
inter se varios claros genuisse gemellos;
hinc siliquas quibus egra fames compressa furentis
est apri, fraudesque pie Sophronidis orbo,
agnum prepositis dum finxit pellibus hyrcum;
exilium pastosque greges munusque receptum
et reditum claudi, visos et in astra volatus,
et luctam in somnis habitam Stilbonis agrestem
et clunem tactum pariter nomenque secundum,
pastorumque dolos et sevas crimine flammas
invidie, puerumque datum memphitibus auro,
visa Pharath nexusque graves dubiosque solutos;
hincque pelusiacis prefectum messibus Argum
pinguibus, et steriles quo restaurasset aristas
iure vel effetos Memphim traxisset amicos,
tristeque servitium superûm post fata nepotum.
Inde Foroneum quem sustulit Ysis ab amne,
nyliacas pestes et nectos gurgite capros,
errores duros, damnatas sydere harenas
ac inopes campos, nimium querulosque subulcos,
et saxo latices lapsos et ab ethere panes,
iussa Iovis dum tecta sibi dum sacra parari
vellet, et absconsos alta sub nube recessus,
celso et ydumeo descriptas vertice leges,
illisas scopulo postquam conflatus Osyris;
vulnera serpentum, serpentis et irrita visu,
et, canibus campis telis arcuque fugatis,
agros post equa concessos sorte colonis.

XI. PANTHEON

to slaughter his own son upon large altars.
Then he described the goats' deserved bereavement
and the Typhaean flames that fell from heaven
onto the woods, the empty swamps, and how
Cinaram, drunk, spent nights with his two daughters;
then how someone whom power divine had snatched
from off the altar sired famous twins
at variance with each other; then the rinds
by which the raging boar's sick hunger is
suppressed, the tricking of a blind old man
by pious Sophronis when with skins imposed
she made a goat appear to be a lamb;
the exile, pastured flocks, payment received,
and the lame man's return, his vision of
flights to the stars, the dream of rural wrestling
by Stilbon and likewise his buttocks touched
and second name received; the shepherds' fraud
and envy's flame made savage by a crime,
the boy sold for gold coin to the Egytpians,
the Pharoah's vision and grave knots and doubts
resolved; then Argus placed in charge of all
the rich Pelusian harvests, by what law
he made up for the sterile ears of grain
or drew his hunger-weakened friends to Memphis,
and then the grandsons' bitter servitude
decreed by gods. Then Foroneus raised
from out the stream by Isis, and the plagues
of Nile, the goats drowned in the water,
hard wanderings, the sands doomed by the sun
and barren fields, the plowboys too complaining,
and liquid fallen from a rock and bread
from heaven, the commands of Jove who wished
to have prepared a house and sacred objects,
recesses hidden under a high cloud,
the laws inscribed atop the lofty peak
of Idumea, dashed against the rock
after Osyris' forging; wounds from serpents
made void by the beholding of a serpent,
and, dogs having been driven from the fields
with spears and bow, the farmlands after granted
to the inhabitants by equal lot.

	Pastorum veteres cantabat et inde palestras,
	serta ducum, baculos, sedes et frondea tecta
	cespite pre viridi, structum de marmore templum
125	et morbis assumpta malis armenta gregesque,
	pingue solum fuso grandi persepe cruore,
	aggere nudatas silvas et vellera rapta
	orbatumque ducem pecoris per compita Tygris;
	disperosque greges septas complesse forenses,
130	orsa deûm sensu complexa et somnia vatum,
	sacra hominum polluta malis reducesque magistors,
	ac ulmis frustra cecinit post premia fixa.
	Substitit hic paulum sumpturus pectore vires
GLAUCUS.	exhaustas cantu Glaucus; post: – O! precor, – inquit -
	romulides, maiora canam; date carmina, nymphe. –
AUCTOR.	Inde satum Maia celo per nubila lapsum
	cepit, et in Danis tegulas penetrasse canoras;
	cumque patris iussu sacros narrasset amores,
	consensu primo Danis, mirabile dictu!
140	virginis in gremio verbum sine semine carnem
	factum cantabat, magnum super omnia! nec non
	virginis infractum decus inde fuisse pudoris
	virginei nascente Deo. Fides ista, precor, sit.
	Hinc pedibus pulsare solum cantusque movere
145	vidisses satyros festasque agitare choreas,
	et faunos nymphasque simul latiasque puellas
	floribus et minio sertisque virentibus omnes
	insignes, dextris et tangere cimbala doctis;
	et dulci quodam tinnitu psallere celum
150	ac fulgore novo totum splendescere, et ultro
	tum varios pratis circum diffundere odores
	atque novis radiis flavum fervescere solem
	et placidam Phebem fratri coniungere currus;
	rore polos humidos, et claro Iuppiter imbre
135	arentes quondam placide perfundere terras;

XI. PANTHEON

He sang the shepherds' ancient wrestling matches,
the winners' wreaths, the staffs, and on green turf
the seats and leafy shelters, and the temple
built up of marble, and the herds and flocks
possessed by grim diseases, and the soil
oft fattened with abundance of spilled blood,
the forests stripped to make a mound, and fleeces
plundered, the leader all bereft of sheep
at Tigris' crossroads; and the flocks dispersed
to fill the foreign folds, things undertaken
according to the judgment of the gods
and prophets' dreams, the sacred things polluted
by human evils, the return of masters,
and prizes hung upon the elm in vain.

GLAUCUS: Here Glaucus paused a while to gather strength
into his breast exhausted by the song;
then "O! I pray" he said, "that I may sing
things even greater, Romans; nymphs, give song."

AUTHOR: Then he took up how Maia's son descended
from heaven through the clouds to penetrate
the tuneful home of Danae; and when he
had told of holy love, at father's bidding,
then first, Danae consenting, he did sing–
wondrous to tell!–the word in virgin's womb
made flesh without a seed, above all things
most great! the virgin's honor thus unbroken
by birth divine from virgin modesty.
May there be faith in that, I pray!
                    Thereat
you would have seen the satyrs' feet strike ground
and hear them sing and stir up festive dances,
and fauns and nymphs and Latian girls together
all decked with flowers and cinnabar and wreaths,
with skilled hands play the cymbals; and all heaven
ring sweetly with stringed instruments and shine
with splendor new, and also varied scents
diffuse about the fields, the yellow sun
grow warm with bright new rays, and peaceful Phoebe
rejoin her brother's chariot; the poles
all wet with dew, and gently Jupiter
pouring clear rain on the once thirsting lands;

ludere capreolos, cantu dulcesque volucres
arbustis certare, ignes emittere montes,
letari valles, grandes insurgere cautes;
surgere tum dumis ramos bicoloris olive,
160   serpentes hederas, lauros et crescere palmas.
Quid cedros Libani, crinitas dicere pinus
litoris adriaci, quid vites usque Falerni,
quarum antes gemmas effeti fundere visi,
molliri sentes valide, iuncique palustres
165   extolli et salices vitree? quid cuncta repandam?
Omnia letitia gaudent et carmine certant.
Solus in absconso Plutarcus tristior antro
flet misere, stauratque domos et limina sera
firmat, ut in cassum temptet post vulnera Codrus
170   ingressum, sevasque iubet vigilare sorores.
Ipse tamen Glaucus, dum cerneret omnia secum
letari, faciles fundebat pectore voces;
et sese ceptis referens, cantabat odoros
pastores puero portantes thura sabeos
175   advenisse quidem celeri ad presepia passu,
sydere dante viam montana per ardua claro.
Huncque per exustas latum referebat harenas
virginis in gremio genitricis ad usque canopos,
et rabidum fugisse lupum, mestosque dolentum
180   balatus ovium cesos ob nequiter agnos;
hincque globos legum solventem voce Ligurgum
pastorum in medio puerum, gesta atque priorum.
Inde Nathan fluvio lotum monstrasse futuris
quo lavacro porcos mundaret sorde vetusta;
185   in bromiumque thetim versam, pulosque carones,
compositos ignes ventos fluctusque tumentes
Asclepii iussu, manesque umbrasque sepultas
ad superos remeasse iterum firmabat; et huius
ostensum dudum quibus artibus usque dolentes

XI. PANTHEON

the young kids leap, sweet birds compete in song
among the trees, the mountains issue fires,
the vales rejoice and mighty rocks arise;
then from the brambles olive branches spring,
while twisting ivy, palms and laurels grow.
Why shall I mention cedars of Lebanon,
the crested pines of Adriatic shores,
Falernus' vines, whose tender rows appeared
to bring forth gems, tough briars now made soft,
and marsh reeds rising up and glistening willows?
Why should I tell them all? All things rejoice
with utter gladness and compete in song.
Only Plutarcus in his hidden cave
weeps wretchedly and gloomier than ever
builds homes and fortifies his doors with bars
so that the wounded Codrus may in vain
attempt to enter, and he orders too
the cruel sisters to keep watch.
                                           Meanwhile
when Glaucus saw all things rejoicing with him,
he kept pouring sweet tunes out from his breast;
and turning back to what he had begun,
was singing how, made sweet with Sabean scents,
the shepherds bringing incense to the boy
arrived indeed with swift step to the manger,
a bright star guiding them across steep mountains.
And he told how the boy was brought across
the burned sands in a virgin mother's lap
as far as the Egyptians, how he fled
the raging wolf, and the grieved sheep's sad bleating
for lambs unjustly slaughtered; then a boy
amid the shepherds with his word explaining
the mass of laws Lycurgan and the deeds
of former men. He spoke then of how Nathan,
washed in a stream, showed to future people
how he by such a washing would cleanse pigs
of ancient filth; of water turned to wine,
and bankers driven out, and fires, winds,
and swelling waves calmed by Asclepius' orders,
and ghosts and buried shades brought back to life;
and it was shown by what arts of this man

190 purgentur vicio pecudes, oleumque veternum
quo lapse iuvenum firmetur robore vires.
Inde Palem glandes, quas nusquam terrea quercus
gesserit in vitam, posuisse labantibus egris
in cenam pueris, et iussa extrema dedisse
195 Actheona pium, cecinitque hunc fraude Menalce
post epulas, lotis pedibus precibusve peractis,
obiectum canibus, quos inter pessima passum
plurima cantabat, mortique dedisse tropheum
de se, iam nimiis laceratum morsibus, ob quod
200 conscissos lapides tractosque in viscera fontes,
concussos motu montes lucosque revulsos,
ethere et in terris sparsas in luce tenebras,
territa per silvas pecora atque armenta ducesque,
auditum mugire solum, veteresque parentum
205 surrexisse animas tumulis silvisque revisas.
Herculis hinc durum monstrabat voce laborem,
hostia dum scopulis firmata refringere Cachi
est ausus, raptosque boves excerpere furi;
necnon interea subdebat in ordine cantu,
210 post triduum laceros artus consurgere vivos
Ypoliti, et silvis iterum gregibusque revisum
insignem lauro et palmata veste triumphi:
mirum grande nimis, sed quid non Iuppiter ingens,
dum voluit, potuit? Post hec, ad sydera motu
215 ascendisse suo Phebum, clarosque relictis
infusos ignes sociis quos traxerat ante;
hosque per Arturum missos serosque britannos,
ethiopas fuscos et Gangis fulgida rura.

GLAUCUS. – O tibi, nympha decus, quot surgere leta per agros
220 purpureos flores et candida lilia cernes
mixta simul croceis! quot surgere leta per agros

XI. PANTHEON

                even the cattle long with vice afflicted
                may still be purged, and by what aged oil
                the failing powers of young men be strengthened.
                He sang how for the sickly tottering boys
                Pales had placed upon the table acorns
                which no oak anywhere on earth had born,
                and pious Actaeon gave his last commands,
                and after dinner by Menalcas' fraud,
                after the feet were washed and prayers were finished,
                he was thrown to the dogs, to suffer there
                so many dreadful things, and Glaucus sang
                how that man made himself into death's trophy,
                now wounded with innumerable bites,
                at which the rocks were rent, springs swallowed up
                in bowels of the earth, the mountains shaken
                with tremor, groves torn down, and darkness scattered
                throughout the air and over lands in daytime,
                and sheep and herds and leaders terrified
                throughout the woods, the ground was heard to groan,
                and ancient souls of ancestors from tombs
                rose up and were again seen in the forest.
                Then with his voice he showed the labors hard
                of Hercules, when he dared break the doors
                blocked up with rocks and take the stolen cows
                from that thief Cacus; in his ordered song
                he set moreover how Hippolytus'
                gashed limbs after three days rose up alive,
                and how he reappeared to flocks and forests
                bedecked with laurel and in robes of triumph
                adorned with palms: immeasurable wonder,
                but what could mighty Jupiter not do
                when he so wished? Then how by his own motion
                Phoebus ascended to the stars, and how
                bright flames poured down on comrades left behind,
                the flames which he himself had worn before;
                these men sent to the north, the western British,
                dark Ethiop, and shining fields of Ganges.

GLAUCUS: O lovely nymph, how many crimson blooms
                and white and yellow lilies mixed together
                will you rejoice to see rise up for you
                throughout the lands! how many sacred temples

templa deûm, sacras laudes et munera cernes,
et quos pulchra coles campos replerier omnes
elysios et dulce solum regionis avite!
225 Hinc Codrus veniet, postquam resoluta iacebit
igne novo tellus, agnis seponere capros,
atque dabit rebus finem requiemque bubulcis.
Sed iam tempus adest rivos claudamus, Aminta. –

AUCTOR. Dum cecinit Glaucus, tacuit sine murmure Tybris;
230 Mirtilis auratos frugum fluviique recentis
immemores tenuit tauros, quos flumine vivo,
iam Glauco reticente, simul se mergier undis
spurciciem veterem tergentes, atque renatos
misceri sese gregibus per pascua Glauci
235 vidisses, plausuque novo concedere carmen.
Hesperus occeanum cantu detentus Olympo
respuit et seras concessit montibus umbras.
Ite domum, pueri, pastas revocate capellas;
ipse legam lauros: vati vos plaudite, colles.

XI. PANTHEON

               will you rejoice to see throughout the lands,
               and gifts and sacred praises; you'll see filled
               all the Elysian fields which you are tending
               and the sweet soil of your ancestral region!
               Hither will Codrus come, after the earth
               lies melted with new fire, to divide
               the goats from lambs, and he will give an end
               to things and give the plowboys rest. But now
               it's time for us to close the streams, Amintas.

AUTHOR: While Glaucus sang, the Tiber murmurless
               was hushed; Mirtilis kept the gilded bulls
               unmindful of their food or of fresh water,
               whom you would see –with Glaucus fallen quiet–
               now plunge themselves at once into the stream
               of living waters, washing off old dirt,
               and mingle, born anew, with Glaucus' flocks
               throughout the pasture, answering the song
               with fresh applause. Detained upon Olympus
               by Glaucus' singing, Hesperus disdained
               the sea and brought late shadows to the mountains.
               Go home, boys, call again your pastured goats;
               I'll bind the bays; you, hills, applaud the poet.

XII. SAPHOS

CALIOPES. Quid, puer, has inter lauros, stultissime, queris,
nunc has nunc illas carpens? Temerarie, nescis
sacrilegum violare nemus, nisi conscia Quiris
optatas frondes merito concesserit ante?
ARISTEUS. O scelus! ex minimis tris forsan captus odore
excerpsi. Seu nympha loci seu sis dea, nostras
excute tu quercus ac omnes collige glandes.
CALIOPES Cogis ut in risum veniam. Sic, obsecro, quercus
equiparas lauris? Non illas Iuppiter olim
10 extulit in tantum, quanquam sibi prisca dicarit
illas religio. Nescis, stolidissime, porcis
serventur glandes et laurea serta poetis,
quos nemori fontique sacro pulchrisque Camenis
et cytharis plectrisque suis prefecit Apollo?
ARISTEUS. Ergo sacrum Phebi nemus hoc, pulcherrima virgo?
Nescius optatum teneo. Quis denique prestet
quo visurus eam laudatam carmine Mopsi
egregiumque gregem vatum nymphasque canentes?
CALIOPES. Quid queris, nemorisque mei quid conspicis umbras?
ARISTEUS. Ut videam Saphon. Nostin? Da, nympha, recessus
quis nunc lenta diem vertat ludendo per herbas.
CALIOPES. Quid tibi cum Saphu, cum sis puer atque subulcus?
ARISTEUS. Heu! quid? Quid iuveni credis cum virgine pulchra?

XII. SAPHOS

CALIOPE: What seek you, foolish boy, among these laurels,
plucking now these, now those? Do you not know,
bold fellow, that to violate this grove
is sacrilege unless, conscious of merit,
Juno before has granted the wished-for leaves?

ARISTEUS: A wicked crime! that captured by the scent,
I've picked perhaps three of the smallest leaves.
If you're a nymph or goddess of the place,
come shake my oaks and gather all my acorns.

CALIOPE: You'll make me laugh. Pray, do you thus compare
your oaks with laurels? Though in ancient cults
they're consecrate to Jove, he did not raise
them high as these. Don't you know, stupid dolt,
acorns are served to pigs, and laurel wreaths
to poets whom Apollo put in charge
of grove and sacred fount and lovely Muses
and of his lyres and plectra?

ARISTEUS: Then is this
grove sacred to Apollo, lovely maiden?
Unwittingly I've gotten what I wished for.
Who will inform me then where I may see
that lady praised by Mopsus's song and by
the flock of poets and the singing nymphs?

CALIOPE: What do you seek and why do you peer in
among the shadows of my holy grove?

ARISTEUS: I look for Saphos. Don't you know her? Tell
in what recess she, lingering, spends the day,
at play among the grasses?

CALIOPE: What do you,
a boy and swineherd, have to do with Saphos?

ARISTEUS: Alas! What do you think a young man has

	Uror et amplexus cupio, turmasque reliqui,
25	invisam ut videam, nec quorsum querere novi.
CALIOPES.	Tu cupis amplexus Saphu? Nunc sydera lambant
	quos trahis ipse sues, volitentque per ethera vulpes,
	grux trahat ac anser pariter per rura quadrigas!
	Si memini, tu nuper haras mundare solebas,
30	et scabiem morsusque canum seu vulnera veprum
	nunc manibus purgare palam, nunc gurgite turpi,
	unguine nunc vario succisque potentibus atque
	galbaneis fumis nigrique bituminis offa;
	viribus ellebori stillaque dolentis amurce
35	vel potu tristes alvi depellere sordes,
	ac herbis variis formare volutabra porcis:
	et nunc Saphon amas? Expectet te quoque Pallas!
ARISTEUS.	Erras; Argus erat. Sed quid non Saphon amarem?
	Me Galathea diu, me quondam Phyllis amavit,
40	et mollis lanugo genas nunc serpere cepit,
	tradidit et calamos nobis Pan doctior olim
	et cantus docuit; nec plebis fece creatus:
	Cyrenes genitrix est nobis, thessala nympha.
	Nomen Aristeus; glandes et mella vetusti
45	archados accipio nemoris: te nosse putabam.
CALIOPES.	Nunc ego te teneo. Sic est, novisse decebat.
	Ysmarius tu grandis eras, tu Critis es Yde!
	Non ego te vidi pridem vulgare canentem
	in triviis carmen, misero plaudente popello?
ARISTEUS.	Vidisti, fateor. Non omnibus omnia semper
	sunt animo. Puero carmen vulgare placebat.
	Illud Lemniadi claudo concessimus; ast nunc

XII. SAPHOS

to do with such a wondrously fair maiden?
I'm burning and desire her embrace;
I left the crowds, not knowing where to seek,
that I may see her who has not been seen.

CALIOPE: Do you desire the embrace of Saphos?
Now may those pigs you drive be licked by stars,
may foxes fly, and may the crane and duck
draw side by side the four-horsed chariots
across the countryside! As I recall,
you recently cleaned pigsties and sometimes
with your hands openly healed mange, or dog-bites,
or bramble scratches, now with filthy water,
now with sundry ointments and strong draughts,
with smokes from galbanum and lumps of coal;
with hellebore, a drop of painful oil-lees,
or with some other drink you would expel
the stomach's bitter wastes, and make a place
with different grasses for the pigs to roll;
and now you're Saphos' lover? Pallas too
may be just waiting for you!

ARISTEUS: You are wrong:
that's Argus you described. Why shouldn't I
love Saphos? Long ago once Galathea
could love me, Phyllis loved me too, and now
soft down has started creeping on my cheeks,
and learned Pan once handed me his pipes
and taught me songs; nor was I lowly born:
my mother's the Thessalian nymph Cyrene.
My name is Aristeus; and I gather
acorns and honey from the ancient forest
of my Arcadia; I thought you knew.

CALIOPE: Ah, now I place you. Yes, I should have known.
You were the great Ismarian, you're Critis
from Ida! Didn't I see you before
singing a vulgar song beside the crossroads,
with the wretched rabble all applauding?

ARISTEUS: You saw it, I confess. But everyone
does not always maintain the same intentions.
A vulgar song did please me as a boy;
I've granted it to the lame god of Lemnos.

	altior est etas, alios que monstrat amores.
CALIOPES. 55	Ecastor! memini, nuper dissolvere linguam vix poterat Bathos; subito nunc culmina poscit Parnasi, stolide captus fervore dearum, factus Aristeus. Sed quid non fecit Olympus?
ARISTEUS.	Quid loqueris nunc ipsa tibi? Da, nympha, precamur, virginis antra mee; crucior, me fervor adurit.
CALIOPES.	Querere credo putes Phyllim seu forte Lupiscam, quas nemorum pomis trahitis quandoque per umbras. Hec dea, magna quidem, paucis et cognita dudum.
ARISTEUS. 65	Meonius pastor potuit vidisse Tonantis consortem natasque duas sub quercubus altis, exuviis nudas; quid non ego cernere Saphon?
CALIOPES.	Sic illis visum. Dic, tu quo noveris illam?
ARISTEUS. 70 75 80	Minciadem Silvanus heri, qua Sorgia saxo erumpit Vallis currens per devia Clause, convenit, placidaque simul sedere sub umbra ylicis antique. Quos postquam fronde virenti umbrasse esculea frontes et carmine vidi certantes ambo ferrent super ethera cantum, accessi: et tacitus mediis vepretibus altis delitui, porcis Gethe siliquisque relictis. Laudibus hi Saphon, resonantibus undique saxis, vocibus et calamis pariter, super astra ferebant. Miratus, fateor, confestim a Phyllide mentem diverti, sensique novos ambire furores intentum modulis pectus; captusque repente exquiro Saphon, cupiens quibus ipsa moretur antra videre oculis. Quid si tu forsitan esses? Nam gestu facieque deam verbisque fateris.

XII. SAPHOS

	But now my greater age sees other loves.
CALIOPE:	By Castor! I remember recently Bathos could scarcely loosen up his tongue; now suddenly, becoming Aristeus, he's asking for the summit of Parnassus, snared foolishly by love for goddesses. But what has great Olympus not accomplished?
ARISTEUS:	What are you saying to yourself? Tell, nymph, I beg, which are my maiden's caves; I'm anguished, this ardor burns me up.
CALIOPE:	I think you mean to look for Phyllis or perhaps Lupisca, whom you with apples do sometimes allure among the shadows of the wood. This goddess is great indeed and has for some time now been known to only few.
ARISTEUS:	The Lydian shepherd could see the consort of the Thunderer and his two daughters, naked of their clothing, beneath tall oaks; so why can't I see Saphos?
CALIOPE:	So it seemed best to them. How do you know her?
ARISTEUS:	Silvanus yesterday met Minciades where springs the Sorge to run through calm Vaucluse, and in an ancient holmoak's quiet shade they sat together. When I saw that they had shaded their brows with green oak leaves and raised, in rival song, their voices to the sky, then I drew near, and silently lay hidden among high brambles, having left the pigs and husks to Gaetha. These men equally with voice and pipes raised Saphos to the stars with praises, all around the rocks resounding. Wonderstruck, at once I turned my mind from Phyllis, I confess, and felt new furors pass through me, all attentive to the music. And captivated suddenly, I search for Saphos, longing to behold myself the caves in which she dwells. What if by chance you're she? For by your gesture, face, and words you do reveal yourself to be a goddess.

CALIOPES.	Non ausim, iuvenis, Saphon me dicere, cum sim obsequiis iniuncta suis. Si inspexeris illam,
85	longe aliud dices. Verum tibi maximus instat ante labor. Nimium celsos intratis amores precipites, cum turpe nimis sit vertere gressus.
ARISTEUS.	Quid Saphos, si tanta tibi reverentia vultus? Non equidem silvis Phyllis, non Delia celo
90	pulchrior. Ast nobis nomen, pulcherrima virgo, pande genusque tuum, si nostras venit ad aures.
CALIOPES.	Caliopes vocitor, magni Iovis inclita proles, castalii nemoris custos fontisque sonori; ut reor, omnino vestris incognita silvis.
ARISTEUS.	Imo equidem memini: grandis sic ante canebat Minciades, grandisque simul Silvanus in antro. Tu silvas resonare doces, tu maxima Saphu voce refers concepta sacri tibi pectoris hausta. Sed dic quas teneat sedes pulcherrima Saphos.
CALIOPES.	Panis nata dei celsum tenet optima Nyse Saphos, gorgonei residens in margine fontis. Huius sydereos oculos faciemque serenam concessum paucis dudum vidisse bubulcis; laurea serta tegunt et velum frontis honeste.
105	Cuius in obsequium circumsumus inde sorores Pyerides omnes; sibi cantat pulcher Apollo.
ARISTEUS.	Quid montes habitat Saphos? quid respuit urbes? quid faciem formosa tegit renuitque videri?
CALIOPES.	Hec, sibi dum vigilat, nemorum mediatur honores,
110	atque sedens fuscos Plutarci visitat ortos, concipiens nigre fletus et dissona silve; vel pelagi secreta notat lucosque sub undis, Phorcinidumque choros trahit et persepe napeas;

XII. SAPHOS

CALIOPE: I wouldn't dare, young man, to say I'm Saphos,
since I'm one of her servants. If you viewed her,
you'd say far otherwise. Truly enormous
labor lies before you. And although
it's very shameful to turn back one's steps,
you enter headlong into loves too high.

ARISTEUS: What's Saphos like, since your own face appears
worthy of reverence? Phyllis in the woods
is truly not more lovely, nor fair Delia
in the sky. Tell me, beautiful maiden,
your name and birth, in case I've heard of it.

CALIOPE: I'm called Caliope, a famous offspring
of mighty Jove, and guardian I am
of the Castalian grove and sonorous fountain;
I think I'm quite unknown within your woods.

ARISTEUS: No, truly I remember that the great
old Minciades used to sing of you,
together with Silvanus in the cave.
You teach the forest to resound, your voice
bears forth the great things Saphos has conceived
and drawn out for you from that sacred breast.
But say where does the loveliest Saphos dwell?

CALIOPE: Pan's dearest daughter, Saphos stays upon
the heights of Nysa, dwelling by the brim
of the gorgonean spring. The sight of her
bright starry eyes and of her face serene
has rarely been allowed to any peasants.
Laurels wreathe and veil her honest face.
On her we sister Muses all attend;
to her the handsome god Apollo sings.

ARISTEUS: Why does Saphos dwell on mountain peaks?
Why does she spurn the cities? Why does she
prevent her lovely face from being seen?

CALIOPE: Guarding herself, she meditates the forest's
honors, and while sitting still she visits
Plutarcus' blackened gardens, taking in
the dark woods' dissonance and lamentations;
or she observes the secrets of the sea
and groves beneath the waves, and leads out choruses
of Phorcinides often and of nymphs;

115	vel petit elysios colles et gramina leta conspicit et placidos flores frondesque virentes ac avium cantus et pulchri sydera celi, visaque sublimi complectitur omnia plectro, et viridis complexa libri sub tegmine ponit. Anne putas, vulgus stolidum seu garrula turba
120	auritos tondens asinos permitteret ista? Non equidem; clamore gravi, dum stringeret hyrcos, omnia turbaret. Montana ergo ocia dulci pace sibi plena expetiit mea fulgida diva; et quia quos querit frustra lasciva puella
125	Chyroni, flores pedibus calcamus euntes vere novo, Saphos celso se condidit antro atque sacros lauro texit castissima vultus.
ARISTEUS.	Vidi ego conflantem carmen celeste Aracintho pastorem celebrem primo, tandemque cicuta
130	sublatum; et latiis se pulsum vidit ab arvis qui penos septis contriverat ante leones. Sat vidisse oculis semel est mirabile quodque.
CALIOPES.	Sic est, sic sanctum nimio contemnitur usu. Preterea vultu quidam carpsere minaci
135	innocuam, maculisque piam depingere frontem, si possent, ausi, que postergasse necesse est.
ARISTEUS.	Imo age, nympha, precor; maculas ostende [nefandas.
CALIOPES.	Mendacem et stupris fedam morumque ruinam hanc plures dixere deam, scenasque colentem
140	dixerunt alii mimamque ambire theatra; soccos nonnulli damnant veteresque coturnos; hi, superûm fidibus dicunt quia cantet amores et facie ficta gestus designet avitos, pellendam patria, quasi regnans occupet urbes;

XII. SAPHOS

or else she seeks the Elysian hills and sees
the happy meadows, peaceful blooms, green leaves,
the birdsongs and the stars of lovely heaven,
and all things seen she then encompasses
with her sublimest lyre, placing them
under the cover of a green-hued book.
Think you the stupid mob or gabbing throng
shearing their long-eared asses would permit her
to do these things? Indeed not; while the mob
with noisy shouts were gathering in their goats,
they'd throw everything into sheer confusion.
Mountain leisure, therefore, sweet with peace
my shining goddess seeks out for herself;
because those flowers which the wanton girl
begs Chiron for in vain, we in the spring
tread careless underfoot, Saphos has hidden
herself in a high cave and covered up
her chastest face with sacred laurel boughs.

ARISTEUS: One time I saw on Aracinthus' slopes
a famous shepherd blow a heavenly song
yet finally be carried off by hemlock;
and he who had destroyed the Punic lions
within the sheepfolds, later saw himself
expelled from Latin farmlands. To have seen
everything once is wonderful enough.

CALIOPE: It's true: the holy is scorned with too much use.
Moreover certain folk with threatening mein
have dared to slander this innocent lady
and try to paint with stains her pious brow,
which of necessity she turned away.

ARISTEUS: Go on, nymph, please; what stains unspeakable?

CALIOPE: Many have said this goddess is a liar,
foul with stupidities, the ruin of conduct;
others have said she cultivates the stages
and goes into the theaters as a mime;
some folk condemn the ancient socks and buskins;
these say, because she sings upon her lyre
the loves of gods and with a feigning face
portrays ancestral deeds, that she must be
banned from the fatherland, as if she ruled

145	syrenam vocitant alii lucrique voracem,
	cum nequeant renuantque suos cognoscere cantus.
	His etiam commota, volens sua culmina servat.
ARISTEUS.	Dum porcam Cereri, Bacho dum cedimus hyrcum,
	forte graves vino ludentes talia quidam
150	eructant curanda parum, pereuntque per auras.
CALIPOS.	Non sic conati nemorum maculare priores.
ARISTEUS.	Qui, precor? An sano tanta est insania cuiquam?
CALIOPES.	«Ericolas» tales merito dixere veterni.
ARISTEUS.	Non satis accipio qui sint. Tu, credo, Platoni,
155	nympha, putes nunc verba loqui magnove Ligurgo:
	rusticus et paucis assuetus, nympha, rudisque.
CALIOPES.	Qui nuper raptas pecudes ex ore luporum
	dentibus excerpunt, magnos audentque boatus
	vendere simplicibus; qui sese noscere causas
160	infecti pecoris, fontes herbasque salubres,
	et celi mutare vices nemorumque fatentur;
	qui superûm sedes describunt voce superbi,
	et sentire deûum sensus causasque moventes
	in silvas fulmen, sacra atque piacula dicunt.
ARISTEUS.	Quid, precor, agricolis est cum pastore? Per agros
	ille boves terram cogit rescindere aratro,
	hic cogit virga pecudes in pascua; cogit
	vinitor ut certo consistant ordine vites,
	lac premit iste manu quod sumpsit ab ubere pingui
170	rancidulus: nil ergo videt de iure bubulci
	rusticus, et pastor nescit de more bufulci.
	Nullum sorte sua contentum liquit Erinis;

XII. SAPHOS

and occupied the cities; others call her
a siren and a greedy one for wealth,
as they're unable and unwilling too
to understand her songs. Still vexed by these,
she voluntarily keeps to her peak.

ARISTEUS: While offering a pig to Demeter
or goat to Bacchus, jesting drunkenly
perhaps some people burp forth things like these
not to be heeded as they fade in air.

CALIOPE: Not so. The woods' best men have tried to stain her.

ARISTEUS: Who, pray? Have sane men such insanity?

CALIOPE: "Lovers of strife" the ancients called such men
deservedly.

ARISTEUS: I don't sufficiently
grasp who they are. I think, nymph, you believe
you're talking now to Plato or Lycurgus;
I'm rustic, used to few and simple things.

CALIOPE: Those men who from the wolves' mouth recently
extracted cattle snatched up by those teeth,
and dare sell thunderclaps to simple folk;
those men who claim to recognize the causes
of sickness in the cattle and to know
the healthful springs and grasses, and profess
to alter heaven's and the forest's fortunes;
and those proud men who with their voice describe
the gods' abodes and say that they perceive
the gods' intentions and what causes make
the lightning strike our woods, and all the sacred
and expiatory rites.

ARISTEUS: What has a shepherd
to do with farmers, pray? The latter drives
his oxen through the fields to cleave the earth,
the former drives his sheep into the pastures,
one with a plow, one with a little rod;
the vintner sets the vines in certain order;
one man makes smelly cheeses of the milk
he takes from the rich udder; thus the rustic
sees nothing of the plowboys' ways; the shepherd
is ignorant of habits of the farmers.
Erinys has left nobody content

	hinc peragunt rixas tauri sevique leones.
	Sed da, queso, viam qua possim lenius alta
175	scandere Parnasi Saphonque videre canentem.
CALIOPES.	Turbavere quidem vestigia longa viarum
	et nemorum veteres rami cautesque revulsi,
	implicite sentes pulvisque per ethera vectus;
	velleris atque fames et grandis cura peculi
180	neglexit latos montis per secula calles.
	Hinc actum ut, scrobibus visis, in terga redirent
	iam plures peterentque suos per pascua fines.
ARISTEUS.	Non ego convertar facilis, nam sepe nivosi
	conscendi rupes pedibus scopulosque Lycei.
185	Omnia continui superant, michi crede, labores.
CALIOPES.	Vicit et ingenium vires: non talia quivit
	exuperare labor. Frustra sudavit in altum
	ferreus Arpinas, calamis et voce sonorus.
ARISTEUS.	Mens illi non ista fuit, nec carminis ardor.
190	Nascimur in varios actus, quos optima virtus
	si sequitur, facili ducetur ad ultima cursu.
CALIOPES.	Si tibi tantus amor fontis Saphuque videndi,
	accipe consilium: nam quenquam ducere nobis
	ipsa quidem vetuit Saphos, et lege perenni.
195	Solus inaccessum potuit conscendere culmen
	nuper Silvanus, nobis nec carior alter
	Minciadis post fata fuit; non pastor Opheltis,
	aonii pecoris stragem qui carmine pinxit.
	Hunc adeas; dabit ipse tibi quibus usus amicis
200	et quibus ipse viis conscendit culmen amatum.
ARISTEUS.	Ibo quidem, et geminos mecum portabo suellos,
	Silvanum si forte queam divertere donis.

XII. SAPHOS

                 with his own lot; hence bulls and savage lions
                 still carry on their strife. But show me, please,
                 the way by which I may more easily
                 climb high Parnassus and see Saphos singing.

CALIOPE: Old branches of the woods and fallen rocks
                 and tangled briars and the wind-blown dust
                 have marred the lengthy traces of the paths;
                 and greed for fleeces and the great concern
                 for wealth have caused the wide paths of the mountain
                 to be neglected now for centuries.
                 Hence it has come about that many men,
                 seeing the gulleys, have turned back already
                 and sought their object in the pasturelands.

ARISTEUS: I will not easily be turned, for often
                 I've climbed Lycaeus' snowy crags and cliffs
                 on foot. Persistent efforts conquer all,
                 believe me.

CALIOPE: And intention has been more
                 than power to perform; such things mere effort
                 could not surmount. Firm Arpinas in vain
                 was sweating towards the height with voice and pipes.

ARISTEUS: He did not have my passion nor my will.
                 We're born with various bents, which if pursued
                 with one's best valor, lead one to the goal
                 in an easy race.

CALIOPE: If you have so much love
                 to see the fount and Saphos, take my counsel:
                 Saphos herself has by eternal law
                 forbidden us to lead anyone to her.
                 Only Silvanus recently was able
                 to climb up to the inaccessible peak,
                 nor have we ever loved another more
                 since Minciades died, not even Opheltis
                 who sang the slaughter of Aonian sheep.
                 It's him you should approach; he will acquaint you
                 with all the friends and paths by which he managed
                 to climb at last to the beloved peak.

ARISTEUS: I'll go indeed and take with me twin piglets
                 in case Silvanus can be won with gifts.

XIII. LAUREA

DAPHNIS. Ocia nunc celebras, Stilbon, mirabile visu!
et qui scabrosas ambire sueveris alpes
candidulos manibus tractans hinc inde lapillos
torrentis vitrei, recubas iam segnis in umbra.
STILBON. Rupe sub hac celsa nuper versutus Amiclas
forte recensebat capros et pulchra Phaselis
frondosas salicum carpebat ab aggere virgas
falce, gregum raris cupiens innectere septis.
Hi fessum tenuere pecus, tenuere magistrum,
10 et quos debebant edos michi forte dederunt.
Sed tu quid valles peragras, qui lentus in antris
nunc calamis, nunc voce deos mulcere solebas?
Ardua non rapidi librat, dic Phebus Olympi?
DAPHNIS. Librat. Non homini semper datur equa voluptas.
15 His umbris equidem tecum refovebo capellas
quas habeo fessas, dum scendat mitius astrum.
STILBON. Imo age, da rivos hyrcis umbrasque capellis,
et mecum, mi Daphni, sede: placideque, precamur,
dic que te cure curvatum fronte fatigent.
DAPHNIS. Gargaphias memini valles, dum sibilus aure
is me lenis agit: zephyrus sic omnia circum
complebat. Tunc ipse meam cantare solebam
Elpida, qua silvis visa est nec pulchrior ullis.
STILBON. Elpis nota michi, sed non, quam forte recenses;
25 hec Crisidis comes: et tua que fuit, obsecro, Daphni?

XIII. THE LAUREL WREATH

DAPHNIS: Now you're at leisure, marvelous to see!
You, Stilbon, who were wont to cross rough Alps,
dragging from here and there with busy hands
those dazzling gems from out the icy torrent,
now lazily recline beneath the shade.

STILBON: Beneath this towering cliff the dexterous
Amiclas recently was counting goats
while fair Phaselis with her sickle gathered
some leafy willow wands along the banks,
wishing to weave them into the fence's gaps.
They kept the weary flock, they kept the leader,
but gave to me the kids they chanced to owe me.
But why do you roam the valleys, who were wont,
lingering in your caves, to charm the gods
now with your pipes, now with your voice? Does Phoebus
not poise upon the heights of steep Olympus?

DAPHNIS: Yes. Equal pleasure is not always given
to every man. But in these shades with you
I will indeed refresh my tired goats,
until the sun is milder in descent.

STILBON: Go on, do, offer streamlets to the kids
and shade to goats, and sit with me, my Daphnis;
and calmly, pray, tell what cares curve your brow.

DAPHNIS: That gentle whistling in the air reminds me
of the Gargaphian valleys: zephyrus
thus often filled the region all around.
Then I myself would sing about my Elpis,
the fairest seen of any in the forests.

STILBON: I know an Elpis, but perhaps she's not
the one you mention; she's Crisis' companion.
But which, I ask you, Daphnis, was your friend?

DAPHNIS.	Incola Parnasi, Nyse sociata napeis.
STILBON.	Cecus amor, cecique sumus quicunque sequentes!

           Aonias colit iste deas, quibus ultima rerum
           pauperies coniuncta manet semperque manebit,
30   celitibusque diis prefert suadente Dyone!
           Silvestres bacas dat laurus et alga cubile,
           pallentesque legunt versus et murmura criptis.
           Tytirus ismenus Tybris cantavit ad undas
           pastores tyrios et fractos vulnere tauros
35   argolicos, victusque fame post vendidit agnam,
           nec potuere sitim latices sedasse Talie.

DAPHNIS. Sunt olee molles et poma recentia mensis
           addita nunc vestris et strata cubilia fronde
           silvis in mediis, servat dum Nursia ludum;
40   sed qui meonias aurum faciebat harenas
           ac dives latius potator parthicus auri
           quas habuere dapes, dum flexit nubila vultus?
           Vivimus immunes, monstri nec pendimus iras,
           contenti paucis, lauroque innectere crines.

STILBON. Rara refers equidem, duris et debita fatis.
           Si vacat, enumera quot pavit Taurus Aminte
           quotque greges Mopso Pindus, quot Menalus Argo,
           quot Polibo Eurotas, Phorbanti quotque Erimantus;
           Alcidis numera pompas tumulosque canopûm:
50   deficiet tempus; fulgent monimenta priorum.
           Vos stolido montes fertis volitasse boatu
           saxaque dyrcetum, fluvios undasque sequaces
           in fontes rediisse suos quercusque revulsas,
           castaliis nymphis cythara cantantibus olim.

XIII. THE LAUREL WREATH

DAPHNIS: A dweller on Parnassus, her companions
the nymphs of Nysa.

STILBON: Blind is love, and blind
are we whoever follow it! This man
worships Aonian goddesses to whom
the direst poverty is ever joined
and always will be, and prefers them to
the heavenly gods at Aphrodite's urgings!
They eat wild laurel berries, sleep on weeds,
and with pale faces utter poetry
and murmurs full of secret messages.
The Theban Tytirus sang by Tiber's waves
of Tyrian shepherds and Argolian bulls
broken with wounds, but hungry afterwards
he sold a ewe, nor could he quench his thirst
with Thalian waters.

DAPHNIS: On our tables are
ripe olives and fresh apples, and our beds
are strewn with leaves amid the woods, while Nursia
plays on; but he who turned Maeonian sands
to gold, and he, the wealthy Parthian,
who drank gold –what were their meals like, although
their glance could move the clouds? We live immune,
nor fear a monster's wrath, content with little,
and glad to bind our hair with laurel boughs.

STILBON: You speak of rare events due to hard fates.
If you have time, enumerate the flocks:
how many Taurus pastured for Amintas,
how many Pindus kept for Mopsus too,
how many Menalus for Argus, and
Eurotas for Polibus, and how many
Erimantus for Phorbantis; count
the number of Alcides' retinue,
and all the burial mounds of the Egyptians.
There won't be time enough; the monuments
of our ancestors shine. With foolish shouting
you say that mountains and Boeotian rocks
have flown, that rivers and attending waves
have turned back to their sources, and that oaks
have been uprooted when Castalian nymphs

DAPHNIS.	Sic orbare procos Crisis hec male cognita novit,
	dum voluit miseros. Sed, ne vertantur in iram
	iurgia, cantemus carmen sub iudice certo.
	Tuque ligus, tyrenus ego: tibi fistula collo,
	suntque michi tenues stipule; cantabimus ambo.
STILBON.	Credis ut effugiam forsan? Michi tradidit Hermes
	compertos calamos; sumus et cantare parati,
	archadios quanquam dicas habuisse magistros.
	Et quod non audes, munus certaminis ipse
	deponam vitulam, qua non est pinguior ulla
65	armentis, etiamsi clamitet inde noverca.
DAPHNIS.	Est michi grex parvus, nec possum munera tanti.
	Dux gregis est hyrcus: tibi sit, si victor abibis.
STILBON.	Te dignum ponis munus; non, hercle! recuso.
	Est michi quam credas ars maior; victor abibo.
70	Sed quis erit, queso, iudex certaminis huius?
DAPHNIS.	Non video in ripa purgantem vellera Critim
	nunc ovium, lappasque gregis tribulosque levantem?
	Criti, tibi dico, nobis nunc, quesumus, assis,
	et nostros animo medius fac collige versus.
75	Ardua res agitur, magno sub munere, nobis.
CRITIS.	Dicite, namque adero donec sua vellera siccet
	hoc pecus. En sedeo; dulces dat parvulus amnis
	tinnitus medios inter labendo lapillos,
	atque tacent volucres. Stilbon, tu dicito primus,
80	hinc Daphnis: vicibusque suis det carmina quisque.
STILBON.	Hos calamos tibi, sacra, damus, si vicero, quercus.
DAPHNIS.	Tuque, virens semper, nostros, mea laurus, habeto.

XIII. THE LAUREL WREATH

were singing with a lyre.

DAPHNIS: Thus does this Crisis,
ill recognized, know how to leave her suitors
bereft when she desires to make them wretched.
But lest our argument be turned to anger,
let's sing a song with someone sure as judge.
You are Ligurian and I a Tuscan:
your pipes hang from your neck; I have slim reeds.
we both shall sing.

STILBON: You think I'll run away?
Hermes gave me the pipes that he invented;
I'm ready too to sing, though you may say
you had Arcadian teachers. And I'll set –
what you don't dare – a calf to be the prize
than which there is no fatter in the herd,
despite its mother's crying loudly for it.

DAPHNIS: My flock is small, and prizes of such value
I cannot give. The leader of the flock's
a goat; let it be yours if you are victor.

STILBON: You set a worthy prize, by Hercules!
I don't refuse. I'll be the one to win.
My skill is greater than you think it is.
But who, I ask, will judge our competition?

DAPHNIS: Isn't that Critis I see washing fleeces
along the riverbank, and taking burrs
and prickles from the sheep? Critis, I say,
come to us now, we ask you, and compare
our verses as a neutral party, do.
A difficult task we have engaged upon
with great rewards at stake.

CRITIS: Say on, with you
I'll stay until this sheep has dried its fleece.
I'm sitting down; sweet murmurs makes the stream
slipping among the stones; the birds are hushed.
Now Stilbon, you speak first, then Daphnis answer;
let each give songs in turn.

STILBON: You sacred oak,
I'll give these pipes to you if I'm the winner.

DAPHNIS: And you, my evergreen laurel, shall have mine.

STILBON. Noster amor Crisis est, nostros levat ipsa labores;
 ipsa vias nemorum florum distincta corollis
85 ostendit, stipulisque meos describit amores
 frondibus, ut videam veniens quod pergat in antrum.
DAPHNIS. Currit in amplexus, quotiens libet ire per umbras
 etherei nemoris, nostros mea lesbia Saphos:
 atque volens pario lapidi michi carmina celte
90 imprimit et duris mandat mea nomina tophis.
STILBON. Carpatie valles servant sub iudice Protheo
 mille michi vitulos, totidem pinguissima Cyrnos
 hyrcos cum gregibus nutrit; premit ubera Dilos,
 congerit Alopis census onagrosque fatigat.
DAPHNIS. Menalus et nobis lunata fronte iuvencos
 bis totidem; his fontes Silvanus monstrat et herbas,
 Parnasusque biceps Musis cantantibus auget
 lanigeras agnas et grandia premia servat.
STILBON. Iungere delphynes, magnas et cogere frenis
100 balenas nullos voluit docuisse Thalasson
 nos preter, quos sepe manu superasse sonoros
 tritonas vidit, natas et vincere Phorci.
DAPHNIS. Ponere nos docuit fines aliquando Thalasso
 Phebus, et agrestes phytonas vincere telis
105 et stipulis grandes in rixas vertere divos,
 dum nemus omne suum lustramus pectine vates.
STILBON. Massicus arva serit, servat Garganus aristas,
 vina ligus noster, dicteus retia tendit,
 mella dat ybleus suppletque armenta britannus,
110 et, si thura petam, Libanus dabit optima nobis.
DAPHNIS. Quis celum primus dederit, quis sydera celo,
 quis frondes silvis prestet, quis semina rerum,
 fortunas nemorum cantataque damna tropheis
 designat radio Pallas pulcherrima nobis.

XIII. THE LAUREL WREATH

STILBON: My love is Crisis who makes light my labors;
adorned with flower chaplets she marks out
the woodland paths, and with a reed writes down
her love for me on leaves so I may see,
when I come by, into which cave she's heading.

DAPHNIS: My Lesbian Saphos runs to my embrace
as often as I please to wander through
the airy woodland shadows, and with zeal
she prints for me engraved songs on marble
and to the hardened ground commits my names.

STILBON: Carpatian dells under judge Proteus
maintain a thousand calves for me, and Cyrnos
most fertile, nourishes as many goats
and flocks of sheep. Dilos presses the udders;
collecting the wealth, Alopis tires the asses.

DAPHNIS: Menalus keeps twice as many heifers
with crescent brow for me; Silvanus shows them
the springs and grasses; and twin-peaked Parnassus
with singing Muses makes the ewes grow wooly
and offers great rewards.

STILBON: Thalasson wished
to teach no one but me to yoke the dolphins
and drive great whales with reins, me whom he often
saw vanquish by hand the sounding tritons
and conquer Phorcus' daughters.

DAPHNIS: Phoebus once
taught me how to set limits to Thalasson,
to overcome with arms the savage pythons,
and with my reeds to set the gods a-quarreling
while his whole grove we brighten with a song.

STILBON: A Massican plants the fields, and a Garganian
keeps watch over the best, and our Ligurian
provides the wines, a Cretan holds the nets,
a Hyblaean gives honey and a Briton
supplies the herds, and if I want some incense,
a Lebanese will send the very best.

DAPHNIS: Who first established heaven and gave it stars,
leaves to the forest, and the seeds of things;
the fortunes of the woods and the defeats
proclaimed by trophies, lovely Pallas weaves

STILBON. Novit yperboreus que gignat maximus Athlas,
quidque ferat Meroe fervens Scathinavia novit
nostro opere; ac undas volucres miscemus Hybero
Gangis, et ethyopum boreas cognoscit harenas.
DAPHNIS. Ferrea vox nobis, annis invictaque laurus.
120 Cantaber hinc noscat facimus quos non videt yndos,
ac orco mersos superas revocamus ad auras,
et magnum placidis superamus cantibus annum.
STILBON. Palmite pampineo Cereris sacra cinget Eleusis,
Cinthius aut rapiet buxos et timpana Bachi,
125 ac olidus paphie Veneri mactabitur hyrcus,
si Mopsi calamis tenuis superetur Amiclas.
DAPHNIS. Dum cingent ulmos hedere parientque corimbos,
margine Penei dum surgent undique lauri,
litore dum bicolor nascetur mirtus amato,
130 a tenui Bavio grandis vincetur Amiclas.
STILBON. Phorcinidum leti naute cantamus amores,
at tristi torpent scrobibus cum murmure vates;
Eolus inde favet, ceptis favet inde Palemon;
Libetrides rident versus, rident Aganippe;
DAPHNIS. Heroum leti vates cantamus honores,
at nautas miseros scopulus terit, unda fatigat;
Libetrides servant carmen, servant Aganippe;
Eolus inde rapit miseros, rapit inde Palemon.
STILBON. Scis flevisse deas fidibus stipulisque canoris,
140 confractis parva ventis surgente favilla;
romuleus Mavors quandoque volumina mille
solvit et in cineres iussit volitare papiros.

XIII. THE LAUREL WREATH

for me with artful shuttle.

STILBON: By my work
the Hyperborean has learned what things
great Atlas can bring forth, the Scandinavian
has learned what burning Meroe bears; and I
mix Ganges' fleeting waves into the Ebro,
acquaint the north with Ethiopian sands.

DAPHNIS: I have a voice of iron and a laurel
unconquered by the years. Hence I inform
the Spaniard of the Indians he can't see,
and those submerged into the underworld
I call again into the upper air,
outlasting the great year with gentle songs.

STILBON: Eleusis with a young vine leaf will crown
the sacred things of Ceres, Cynthius
will steal the flutes and drums of Bacchus, or
a stinking goat be slain to Paphian Venus
if Mopsus' pipes surpass the slim Amiclas'.

DAPHNIS: While ivies circle elms and bring forth berries,
while laurels grow along the river margin,
while two-toned myrtles spring up on the shore,
low Bavius will conquer great Amiclas.

STILBON: Glad sailors, we shall sing the loves of seanymphs,
while with a gloomy murmur in their graves
the poets lie; Aeolus favors us,
and Palaemon favors the undertakings.
The muses laugh at verses, yea they laugh
the Aganippeans.

DAPHNIS: Glad poets, we
shall sing the heroes' honors, while a rock
wears out the wretched and wave-wearied sailors.
The muses preserve our song, the Aganippeans
preserve it; but the wretches there are snatched
by Aeolus, they're snatched by Palaemon.

STILBON: You know the goddesses have mourned their lutes
and reeds melodious when a few small sparks
rose on the broken winds; from time to time
the Romulean Mars has quite destroyed
a thousand scrolls and ordered the papyrus
to fly up into ashes.

DAPHNIS. Romuleus nuper cilices dispersit Amintas,
montanos faciens solitos innare carinis;
145 sic ligurum veniet qui calcet colla superbus
anguis, et eripiat male partos undique capros.
CRITIS. Iurgia pastorum non est compescere parvum:
et tu dignus eras vitula, tu dignus et hyrco.
Sat dictum, pueri: duras componite lites;
150 ibo ego nunc agnis tonsurus forfice lanam.

XIII. THE LAUREL WREATH

DAPHNIS: Romulean
Amintas recently dispersed Cilicians,
making the mountain men embark on ships;
and so a serpent proud will come to trample
the necks of the Ligurians and snatch
away from everywhere the ill-born goats.

CRITIS: It's no small thing to calm the shepherds' quarrels:
you're worthy of the calf, you of the goat.
Enough's been said, boys; end your harsh disputes;
I'll go with shears to clip the wooly ewes.

XIV. OLYMPIA

SILVIUS. Sentio, ni fallor, pueri, pia numina ruris
letari et cantu volucrum nemus omne repleri.
Itque reditque Lycos blando cum murmure; quidnam
viderit ignoro: cauda testatur amicum.
5 Ite igitur, iam clara dies diffunditur umbris,
precantata diu; quid sit perquirite, quidve
viderit inde Lycos noster, compertaque ferte.

CAMALUS. Dum nequit in somnum miserum componere pectus,
imperat ex molli recubans, heu! cespite mestus
10 Silvius, et noctis pavidas lustrare tenebras
vult pueros, longo fessos in luce labore.

SILVIUS. Camale, dum primos terris prestabit Hyberus
nocturnos ignes, currus dum Delia fratris
ducet ad occasum, dum sternet cerva leones,
15 obsequium prestabit hero sine murmure servus.
O Terapon, stabuli tu solve repagula nostri;
pone metum: videas catulus quid viderit, oro.

TERAPON. Festina, fac surge, senex! Iam corripit ignis
iam veteres quercus et noctem lumine vincit;
20 uritur omne nemus, fervens iam flamma penates
lambit, et occursu lucis perterritus intra
festinus redii. Lambit iam flamma penates!

SILVIUS. Pastorum venerande deus Pan, deprecor, assis;
et vos, o pueri, flammis occurrite lymphis.
25 Siste parum, Terapon, paulum consiste. Quid istud?

XIV. OLYMPIA

SILVIUS: Unless I am mistaken, boys, I hear
the holy rural deities rejoicing,
and all the wood is filled with song of birds;
Lycus runs to and fro with coaxing whimper;
I don't know what he's seen, but his tail wags
as for a friend. Go, then; by now bright daylight,
long preannounced, diffuses through the shadows.
Find out what's there, or what has Lycus seen,
and bring back a report.

CAMALUS: When wretched Silvius
has been unable to compose his breast
in sleep, he gives commands from where he lies
on the soft turf, alas! and wants us servants,
weary with long day's labor, to examine
the nighttime's fearful shadows.

SILVIUS: Camalus,
when Ebro lends to earth the night's first stars,
when Delia drives her brother's chariot westward,
and when deer strike down lions, then a servant
will do his master's bidding without grumbling.
O Therapon, you go unbar the stable;
don't fear; see what the pup has seen, I pray.

THERAPON: Hurry! Get up, old man! Already fire
has seized the ancient oaks and overcome
the nighttime with its brilliance; all the woods
are burning, hot flame licks the very house,
and terrified by what just struck my eye,
I hastened back inside. Flames lick the house!

SILVIUS: O venerable god of shepherds, Pan,
I pray, be with us! You, boys, run with water!
But wait a moment, Therapon, hold on.

	quid video? Sanusne satis sum? dormio forsan? Non facio! Lux ista quidem, non flamma vel ignis. Nonne vides letas frondes corilosque virentes luminis in medio, validas ac undique fagos
30	intactas? Imo nec nos malus ardor adurit.
TERAPON.	Si spectes celo, testantur sydera noctem: in silvis lux alma diem. Quid grande paratur?
SILVIUS.	Sic natura vices variat, noctemque diemque explicuit mixtos terris; nec lumina Phebe
35	nec solis radios cerno! Non sentis odores insolitos silvis, nemus hoc si forte sabeum fecisset natura parens? Quod inde recentes nox peperit flores? quod insuper audio cantus? Hec superos ambire locos et pascua signant.
OLMYPIA.	Salve, dulce decus nostrum, pater optime, salve! Ne timeas, sum nata tibi. Quid lumina flectis?
SILVIUS.	Nescio num vigilem, fateor, seu somnia cernam, nam coram genite voces et dulcis ymago stant equidem: timeo falli, quia sepe per umbras
45	illusere dii stolidos. Nos claustra petamus.
OLYMPIS.	Silvi, quid dubitas? an credis Olympia patrem ludat et in lucem sese sine numine divûm prebeat? Huc veni lacrimas demptura dolentes.
SILVIUS.	Agnosco: nec fallit amor, nec somnia fallunt.
50	O nimium dilecta michi, spes unica patris, quis te, nata, deus tenuit? Te Fusca ferebat, calcidicos colles et pascua lata Vesevi dum petii, raptam nobis Cibelisque sacrato absconsam gremio, nec post hec posse videri;
55	quod credens merensque miser, mea virgo, per altos

XIV. OLYMPIA

	What's that? What do I see? Am I quite sane? Perhaps I am asleep; no, I am not! That light indeed is neither flame nor fire. Don't you see how the hazeltrees are green and leaves look fresh amid the burning light, and all the sturdy beechtrees are unharmed? It's true, nor do we feel the harsh heat burn.
THERAPON:	If you look up, the stars show that it's night: yet in the woods is nourishing light of day. What great event is being thus prepared?
SILVIUS:	Nature has changed her ways, and has unfolded mixed night and day together for the earth; yet I see neither moonlight nor the sun! Don't you smell fragrances unusual as if our parent nature had by chance made this wood now Sabaea? What fresh flowers has night brought forth? And what songs do I hear? They signify that gods are walking here.
OLYMPIA:	Hail, my sweet jewel, dearest father, hail! Be not afraid. I am your daughter. Why thus bend aside your eyes?
SILVIUS:	I do not know whether I wake or dream, I do confess, for lo the very voice and sweetest image of my own daughter. But I am afraid to be deceived, for often during darkness the gods delude old fools. I'll check the folds.
OLYMPIA:	Why doubting, Silvius? Do you believe Olympia would mock her father thus and show herself to you without god's will? I've come to take away your mournful tears.
SILVIUS:	I'm certain: neither love nor dreams deceive me. O dearest darling, sole hope of your father, what god has kept you from me, daughter mine? Fusca was telling me that while I sought Chalcidian hills and the wide pasturelands of Mount Vesuvius, you were snatched away and hidden within Cybele's sacred lap, not to be seen again. Believing it, and wretched in my woe, I groaned and wept

	te montes umbrasque graves saltusque remotos
	ingemui flevique diu nultumque vocavi.
	Sed tu, si mereor, resera quibus, obsecro, lustris
	te tenuit tam longa dies? Dic, munere cuius
60	intertexta auro vesti tibi candida flavo?
	que tibi lux oculis olim non visa refulget?
	qui comites? Mirum quam grandis facta diebus
	in paucis: matura viro michi, nata, videris!
OLYMPIA.	Exuvias quas ipse michi, venerande, dedisti,
65	ingenti gremio servat Berecinthia mater;
	has vestes formamque dedit faciemque coruscam
	Parthenos, secumque fui. Sed respice nunquid
	videris hos usquam comites: vidisse iuvabit.
SILVIUS.	Non memini vidisse quidem: nec pulchrior, inquam,
70	his Narcissus erat, non talis denique Daphnis
	qui dryadum spes leta fuit, non pulcher Alexis.
OLYMPIA.	Non Marium Iulumque tuos dulcesque sorores
	noscis, et egregios vultus? Tua pulchra propago est.
SILVIUS.	Abstulit effigies notas lanugine malas
75	umbratas vidisse meis. Iam iungite dextras,
	amplexusque meos ac oscula leta venite
	ut prestem, satiemque animam! Quas, Pan, tibi laudes,
	quas, Silvane, canam? Pueri, nudate palestras
	et ludos agitote patrum. Stent munera fagis
80	victorum suspensa sacris, paterasque parate
	spumantes vino, lectum cantate Lyeum
	et sertis ornate lares; altaria surgant
	cespite gramineo; Trivie mactate bidentem
	candidulam, Noctique pie sic cedite fulvam;
85	fer calamos pueris, Terapon, fer serta puellis.

	for you, my maid, a long time through high mountains, deep shadows, distant groves, and called your name repeatedly. But tell me, if I'm worthy, in what woods have you stayed so long, I beg you? Whose gift is your white robe with gold inwoven? What light, not seen before, shines from your eyes? And who are your companions? I'm astonished how much you've grown in such short time! You look grown up enough for marriage, o my daughter.
OLYMPIA:	The garment which you gave me, reverend father, our Berecynthian Mother still preserves in her large lap. These clothes the Virgin gave me, this beauty also and this shining face, and I have been with her. But look again at my companions: have you never seen them? You will be pleased that you've seen them before!
SILVIUS:	Truly I don't remember having seen them, nor was Narcissus fairer than they are, nor even Daphnis, happy hope of dryads, nor fair Alexis!
OLYMPIA:	Don't you recognize your Marius and Iulus and my sisters and their distinguished faces? Lo, they are your own sweet lovely offspring!
SILVIUS:	My sons' cheeks shadowed with down impeded recognition of their known faces. Come let us clasp hands, and let me offer hugs and happy kisses and satisfy my soul! What praises, Pan, what praises, o Silvanus, shall I sing you? You boys, now strip for wrestling and lead on our fathers' games. Let the rewards of victors be hung on sacred beeches, and prepare the foaming bowls of wine; sing of glad Bacchus and deck the gods with garlands; raise up altars of grassy turf; and slay for Trivia a white sheep piously, for Night a dark one. Bring reedpipes for the young lads, Therapon, bring garlands for the girls.
OLYMPIA:	O Silvius,

OLYMPIA. Sunt, Silvi, calami, sunt serta decentia nobis,
et, si tanta tibi cura est deducere festum,
ignotos silvis modulos cantabimus istis.
SILVIUS. Imo, silva silet, tacitus nunc defluit Arnus
90 et silet omnis ager: pueri, vos atque silete.
OLYMPIA. Vivimus eternum meritis et numine Codri,
aurea qui nuper, celso dimissus Olympo
Parthenu in gremium, revocavit secula terris;
turpia pastorum passus convitia, cedro
95 affixus, leto concessit sponte triumphum.
  Vivimus eternum meritis et numine Codri.
Sic priscas sordes, morbos scabiemque vetustam
infecti pecoris preclaro sanguine lavit:
hincque petens valles Plutarci septa refrinxit,
100 in solem retrahens pecudes armentaque patrum.
  Vivimus eternum meritis et numine Codri.
Morte hinc prostrata, campos reseravit odoros
Elysii, sacrumque gregem deduxit in ortos
mellifluos victor lauro quercuque refulgens,
105 optandasque dedit nobis per secula sedes.
  Vivimus eternum meritis et numine Codri.
Exuvias in fine sibi pecus omne resummet;
ipse, iterum veniens, capros distinguet ab agnis,
hosque feris linquet, componet sedibus illos
110 perpetuis celoque novo post tempora claudet.
  Vivimus eternum meritis et numine Codri.
SILVIUS. Sentis, quam stulti latios cantare putamus
pastores calamis, perdentes tempora vocum!
Menalios vidi iuvenes per dorsa Lycei,
115 treitium et vatem solitum deducere cautes
carmine, nec quenquam possum concedere tanti,

XIV. OLYMPIA

                we have already pipes and comely garlands;
                and if you care so much to celebrate,
                we'll sing tunes that these woods have never heard.

SILVIUS: The woods are hushed, and quiet flows the Arno,
                and every field is still; servants, keep silent.

OLYMPIA: We live eternal life by Codrus' merits
                and by his power divine, who recently,
                sent down from heaven to a virgin's lap,
                brought back the golden age; who having suffered
                the shepherds' shameful mocking, to a cedar
                affixed, then freely granted death a triumph.
                  We live eternal life by Codrus' merits
                and by his power divine. Thus ancient filth,
                diseases, and old mange of an infected
                flock, he washed away with his bright blood;
                then seeking out the valleys of Plutarcus,
                broke down those pens, led back into the sun
                his fathers flocks and herds.
                  We live eternal life by Codrus' merits
                and by his power divine. With death prostrated,
                he opened up Elysium's fragrant fields,
                and led the holy flock into the gardens
                where honey flows; with oak and bays resplendent,
                the victor gave us dear abodes forever.
                  We live eternal life by Codrus' merits
                and by his power divine. At last each sheep
                will reassume its skin; coming again,
                he'll separate the goats and lambs himself:
                leave one for wild beasts, for the other make
                perpetual dwellings, and with a new heaven,
                he'll put an end to time.
                  We live eternal life by Codrus' merits
                and by his power divine.

SILVANUS: What fools we are
                to think that Latian swains are piping music
                when they just lose the meters of their tunes.
                I've seen Arcadian youths upon the ridges
                of Mount Lycaeus, and the Thracian poet
                whose singing used to move the very stones,
                but I cannot concede so much to any

ut similem natis faciam. Que guctura! que vox!
quis concentus erat! stipulis quis denique flatus!
Non equidem nemoris custos regina canori
120   Caliopes, non ipse deus qui presidet antro
gorgoneo equiparet. Flexere cacumina quercus,
et tenues nymphe tacitos petiere regressus
in lucem, mansere lupi catulique tacentes.
Preterea, o iuvenes, sensistis carminis huius
125   celestes sensus? Nunquam michi Tytirus olim
cantavit similes, senior nec Mopsus apricis
parrasius silvis: sanctum et memorabile totum est.
Virginibus nivee dentur mea cura columbe,
ast pueris fortes dederat quos Yschiros arcus.

OLYMPIA. Sint tua; nil fertur quod sit mortale per oras
quas dites colimus; renuunt eterna caducum.

SILVIUS. Quas oras, mea nata, refers? quas, deprecor, oras?
Nos omnes teget illa domus, somnosque quietos
herba dabit viridis cespesque sub ylice mensam;
135   vitreus is large prestabit pocula rivus;
castaneas mites et poma recentia nobis
rustica silva feret, teneros grex fertilis edos
lacque simul pressum. Quas ergo exquiritis oras?

OLYMPIA. Non tibi, care pater, dixi, Berecinthia mater
140   exuvias gremio servet quas ipse dedisti?
Non sum que fueram, dum tecum parvula vixi,
nam numero sum iuncta deûm; me pulcher Olympus
expectat comitesque meos; stat vertere gressus
in patriam: tu vive, pater dulcissime, felix!

SILVIUS. Heu! moriar lacrimans, miserum si, nata, relinquis.

XIV. OLYMPIA

as to esteem him equal with my children.
What tone! what voice! what harmony there was!
what tune breathed from the reeds! The forest's keeper,
the queen of song, Caliope, indeed
would not compare, nor would the very god
presiding over the Gorgonean cave.
The oaks bent down their tops, and slender nymphs
sought silent hidingplaces near the light;
the wolves were tame then, and the dogs were silent.
Moreover, boys, did you perceive this song's
heavenly senses? Never has Tytirus
sung anything like this, nor older Mopsus
in the sunny woods though he's Arcadian.
It is completely memorable and holy!
Let snowy doves be given to the virgins
at my expense; and to the boys be given
strong Ischirian bows.

OLYMPIA: You keep them, father;
for nothing mortal touches the rich shores
that we inhabit; but eternal things
renounce the transitory!

SILVIUS: What shores, daughter,
do you refer to? Which are they, I pray?
That home will shelter all of us; the grass
will give us quiet sleep; beneath the oak
the sod will be our table. Crystal streams
will generously fill our drinking cups,
the rustic wood will bear for us ripe chestnuts
and freshest apples, and the fertile flock
will bring forth tender kids and furnish cheese.
What shores then do you seek?

OLYMPIA: Did I not tell you,
dear father, that the Berecynthian mother
holds in her lap the clothes you gave to me?
I am not as I was when as a child
I lived with you; for I have joined the gods;
the beautiful Olympus now awaits me
and my companions. It is time to turn
our steps towards home. Farewell, you sweetest father!

SILVIUS: Alas! I shall die weeping if you leave me

OLYMPIA. Pone, precor, luctus; credisne refringere fatum
nunc lacrimis? Omnes silvis quotcunque creati
nascimur in mortem: feci quod tu quoque, Silvi,
post facies. Noli, queso, lacerare deorum
150 invidia eternos annos; tibi crede quietem
post funus, laudesque pias michi reddito celo,
quod moriens fugi mortem nemorumque labores.
Separor ad tempus; post hec me quippe videbis,
perpetuosque trahes mecum feliciter annos.
SILVIUS. In lacrimis oculos fundam tristemque senectam.
Heu! quibus in silvis post anxia fata requiram
te profugam, ex nostris bis raptam viribus oris?
OLYMPIA. Elysium repeto, quod tu scansurus es olim.
SILVIUS. Elysium, memini, quondam cantare solebat
160 Minciades stipula, qua nemo docitor usquam;
estne, quod ille canit, vestrum? Didicisse iuvabit.
OLYMPIA. Senserat ille quidem vi mentis grandia quedam,
ac in parte loci faciem: sed pauca canebat,
si videas quam multa tenet, quam pulchra piorum
165 Elysium sedesque deûm gratissima nostrum.
SILVIUS. Quos tenet iste locus montes? quibus insitus oris?
Que non Minciades vidit seu sponte reliquit,
da nobis. Audire fuit persepe laborum
utile solamen: veniet mens forte videndi.
OLYMPIA. Est in secessu pecori mons invius egro,
lumine perpetuo clarus, quo primus ab imis

                    in misery, my daughter!
OLYMPIA: Cease from grief,
            I beg you; do you think that with your tears
            you can break fate? All creatures in the woods,
            as many as were made, are born to die.
            I've done what you too, Silvius, will do.
            I pray, do not wish to berate with envy
            the gods' eternal years. Believe that rest
            awaits you after death; give pious praises
            to heaven on my behalf, because in dying
            I did escape from death and woodland toils.
            I'm parted from you for a little while;
            but truly you will see me after this
            and gladly live with me through endless years.
SILVIUS: My sorrowful old age and my two eyes
            will melt in tears! Alas! within what forest
            shall I look for you after troubled death,
            my fleeting one, twice snatched out of my arms?
OLYMPIA: Elysium I return to, whither you
            at one time will ascend.
SILVIUS: Sometimes the Mincian,
            I do recall, would sing of an Elysium
            with reeds on which no one has been more skilled.
            Is what he sang of yours? I'd like to know.
OLYMPIA: Indeed with force of mind he did perceive
            great things, the partial nature of the place;
            but if you see, you'll know that he sang few
            of all the many beauties which the Elysium
            of faithful spirits holds, and the abodes
            most pleasing to our gods.
SILVIUS: Among what peaks
            is this place set? or on what shores? Do tell me
            the things the Mincian poet did not see
            or left unsung on purpose. Listening
            has often been a useful comforter
            of troubles; maybe I will gain desire
            to see the place.
OLYMPIA: Far off there is a mountain
            impassible to sickly sheep, and bright
            with light perpetual, where Phoebus first

insurgit terris Phebus, cui vertice summo
silva sedet palmas tollens ad sydera celsas
et letas pariter lauros cedrosque perennes,
175 Palladis ac oleas optate pacis amicas.
Quis queat hinc varios flores, quis posset odores
quos lenis fert aura loco, quis dicere rivos
argento similes mira scaturigine circum
omnia rorantes, lepido cum murmure flexus
180 arbustis mixtos nunc hinc nunc inde trahentes?
Hesperidum potiora locus fert aurea poma;
sunt auro volucres picte, sunt cornubus aureis
capreoli et mites damme, sunt insuper agne
velleribus niveis claro rutilantibus auro,
185 suntque boves taurique simul pinguesque iuvence,
insignes omnes auro, mitesque leones
crinibus et mites gryphes radiantibus auro.
Aureus est nobis sol ac argentea luna,
et maiora quidem quam vobis sydera fulgent.
190 Ver ibi perpetuum nullis offenditur austris,
letaque temperies loca possidet. Exulat inde
terrestris nebula et nox et discordia rerum.
Mors ibi nulla manet gregibus, non egra senectus,
atque graves absunt cure maciesque dolorque;
195 sponte sua veniunt cunctis optata. Quid ultra?
Dulcisono resonat cantu mitissimus aer.

SILVIUS. Mira refers; sanctamque puto sedemque deorum
quam memoras silvam. Sed quisnam presidet illi?
Et comites, mea nata, refer ritusque locorum.

OLYMPIA. Hac in gramineo summo sedet aggere grandis
Archesilas, servatque greges et temperat orbes;
cuius enim si forte velis describere vultus,
in cassum facies: nequeunt comprendere mentes.
Est alacer pulcherque nimis totusque serenus.
205 huius et in gremio iacet agnus candidus, ex quo
silvicolis gratus cibus est, et vescimur illo;
inde salus venit nobis et vita renatis.

uprises from below, upon whose peak
a forest raises tall palms to the stars
and happy laurels too and longlived cedars
and Pallas' olives, friends of hoped-for peace.
Who can report the varied kinds of flowers,
the fragrances born on the gentle breeze,
or who can tell the streams that flow like silver,
bedewing all around with wondrous bubbling,
winding its way with gentle murmuring
among the trees on this side and on that.
The place bears golden apples better than
the Hesperides'. Golden birds are there,
and bucks with golden horns, and gentle does,
and lambs whose snowy fleeces shine with gold;
plump heifers, cows, and bulls, all marked with gold;
tame lions and tame gryphins, both their manes
all radiant with gold; our sun is golden,
our moon is made of silver; larger stars
shine there than here for you. Eternal spring
uninjured by northwinds, and temperate weather
possess the happy regions, banishing
all fogs and night and elemental discord.
No death awaits the flocks, nor sick old age;
and heavy cares are absent, absent too
are poverty and pain. But all that's wished for
comes freely unto everyone. What more?
The gentlest air resounds with dulcet song.

SILVIUS: You speak of marvels, and I think that wood
you mention is the gods' own sacred dwelling.
But who rules over it? And tell me, daughter,
who are your comrades there? What are the customs?

OLYMPIA: Atop the grassy summit of this mountain
great Archesilas sits and keeps the flocks
and regulates the heavens, whose appearance
if you should wish me to describe, you'd wish
in vain; no mortal mind can comprehend it.
He's full of life and beauty, totally
serene, and in his lap a white lamb lies
from which comes pleasing food foor woodland dwellers;
and we are fed by it. Thence comes our health
and life for those reborn. From both alike

Ex his ambobus pariter sic evolat ignis,
ut mirum credas; hos lumen ad omnia confert:
210 solatur mestos et mentis lumina purgat,
consilium miseris prestat viresque cadentum
instaurat, dulcesque animis infundit amores.
Stat satyrum longeva cohors hinc undique supplex,
omnis cana quidem roseis ornata coronis,
215 et cytharis agni laudes et carmine cantat.
Purpureus post ordo virûm venerabilis, inquam,
et viridi cunctis cinguntur tempora lauro.
Hi cecinere Deum stipulis per compita verum,
et forti sevos animo vicere labores.
220 Agmen adest niveum post hos, cui lilia frontes
circumdant; huic iuncta cohors tua pulchra manemus
natorum. Crocei sequitur post ordo coloris
inclitus, et magno fulgens splendore sonora
voce deûm laudes cantat regique ministrat;
225 quos inter placido vultu cantabat Asylas,
dum silvis assumpta prius sum monte levatis.
SILVIUS. Ergo, precor, noster montem conscendit Asylas?
Emeruit, nam mitis erat fideique vetuste
preclarum specimen: faciat Deus ipse revisam!
230 Sed dic, tene, precor, novit dum culmen adires?
OLYMPIA. Imo equidem applaudens iniecit brachia collo,
et postquam amplexus letos ac oscula centum
impressit fronti, multis comitantibus, inquit:
– Venisti, o nostri soboles carissima Silvi!
235 «De Libano» nunc «sponsa veni» sa crosque hymeneos
cantemus, matremque viri, mea neptis, honora –
meque trahens, genibus flexis, quo pulchra sedebat
Parthenos, posuit. Leta hec suscepit in ulnis
ancillam, dixitque pie: – Mea filia, nostris
240 ecce choris iungere piis sponsique frueris

XIV. OLYMPIA

flies out a fire such as you would think
a wonder; this bears light to all things there,
consoles the mournful, cleanses the mind's eyes,
advises the sad, restores the strength of those
who fall, and pours sweet love into our souls.
On either side of them a longlived band
of satyrs kneel, each white head crowned with roses,
and all with lyres sing praises of the lamb.
And after them a venerable rank
of men in crimson, with green laurel wreaths
their temples girt: these at the crossroads sang
the true god with their pipes, and with strong spirit
endured most cruel hardships. After these
a snowy rank with lilies round their brows,
to whose throng we are joined, your pretty offspring.
There follows next a famous yellow order:
with sonorous voice and shining with great splendor,
they sing the praise of gods and serve the king;
among whom with a tranquil face Asylas
was singing when I, taken from the forest,
was first led up the mountain.

SILVIUS: Then has our
Asylas climbed the mountain? He deserved it,
for he was gentle and a bright example
of ancient faith. God grant that I may see him
again! But say, when you approached the summit,
did he know who you were?

OLYMPIA: Indeed he did,
rejoicing threw his arms about my neck,
and after glad embraces and a hundred
fond kisses on my brow, a throng about him,
said, "Have you come, our Silvius' dearest offspring?
Now let us sing 'Come, bride of Lebanon'
and sacred wedding hymns, and you, my grandchild,
do honor to the mother of the groom."
And leading me, he placed me with bent knees
where sat the lovely Virgin. Happily
she took me in her arms as her handmaiden,
and with affection said, "My daughter, here
you'll join our holy chorus and enjoy
your spouse in everlasting marriage. Here

eternis thalamis, et semper Olympia celo,
que fueras terris Violantes, inclita fies –
inque dedit vestes quas cernis. Si tibi narrem
quos cantus tunc silva dedit, quos fistula versus
pastoris lyrici, credes vix; omne per antrum
insonuit carmen montis, tantusque refulsit
ignis, ut exuri dixisses omnia flammis,
et totum rosei cecidere per aera flores.

SILVIUS. Que sit Parthenos nobis superadde, precamur.
OLYMPIA. Almia Iovis genitrix hec est et filia nati,
splendens aula deûm, celi decus, inscia noctis,
ethereum sydus, pastorum certa salutis
spes custosque gregum requiesque optat laborum.
Hanc fauni nympheque colunt, hanc grandis Apollo
laudibus extollit cythara dominamque fatetur;
que residens solio patris veneranda vetusti
a dextris geniti tanto splendore refulget,
ut facie silvam montem collesque polosque
letificet formosa nimis, cui candida circum
agmina cignorum volitant matremque salutant,
luminis eterni sponsam genitamque cientes.

SILVIUS. Et vos quid, pueri, plaudunt dum gucture cigni?
OLYMPIA. Nos pueri legimus flores factisque corollis
cingimus intonsos crines letisque choreis
ambimus silvam fontes rivosque sonoros,
et mediis herbis ludentes vocibus altis
Parthenu placide meritos cantamus honores
et geniti laudes pariter. Quis gaudia silve
enumerare queat, quis verbis pandere? Nemo.
Induat ut volucres pennas quibus alta volatu
expetat et videat, opus est: sunt cetera frustra.

| | you'll be known always as Olympia
| | who were on earth Violante." Then she gave me
| | the clothing which you see. If I could tell you
| | what songs the forest then produced, what tunes
| | the reedpipes of melodious shepherds breathed,
| | you scarcely would believe it. Every cave
| | upon the mountain echoed with the song,
| | and such a fire shone that you'd have said
| | that everything was burning up in flames,
| | and rosy flowers fell throughout the air.
SILVIUS: Please tell me more; who is this virgin queen?
OLYMPIA: The nourishing mother of Jove is she, and daughter
of her own son, bright palace of the gods,
the gem of heaven, ignorant of night,
star of the upper air, sure hope of safety
for shepherds, the protector of the flocks,
and wished-for rest from labors. Fauns and nymphs
all worship her, Apollo with his lyre
exalts her with fine praises and proclaims
that she's his ruling lady. Venerable,
sitting upon the ancient father's throne
beside her son's right hand, with such bright splendor
she shines that she exhilarates the forest,
the mountain, hills, and poles with her fair face.
Around her fly white rows of swans, saluting
the mother, calling her both bride and daughter
of the eternal light.
SILVIUS: And what do you do,
my children, while the swans with voice approve her?
OLYMPIA: We children gather flowers, and make wreaths
to gird our uncut hair; in merry bands
we wander through the forest, by the springs
and tuneful streams. And playing in the grasses
we sing out loudly well-deserved honors
unto the gentle Virgin and the praises
of her fair son. Who could enumerate,
who could reveal with words the forest's joys?
No one! But he must like a bird don wings
with which by flight to seek the heights and see;
the rest is all in vain.

SILVIUS. Sunt optanda quidem: sed quis michi Dedalus usquam
qui tribuat pennas agiles nectatque lacertis,
ostendatque viam facilem doceatque volatum?
OLYMPIA. Pasce famem fratris, lactis da pocula fessis,
assis detentis et nudos contege, lapsos
erige, dum possis, pateatque forensibus antrum:
hec aquile volucres prestabunt munera pennas,
atque Deo monstrante viam volitabis in altum.
SILVIUS. Quo tendis? quo, nata, fugis, miserumque parentem
implicitum linquis lacrimis? Heu! cessit in auras
ethereas, traxitque simul quos duxit odores.
In mortem lacrimis ibo ducamque senectam.
Vos, pueri, vitulos in pascua pellite: surgit
285 Lucifer et mediis iam sol emittitur umbris.

SILVIUS:	I wish indeed
I had them! but who'll ever be for me
a Daedalus and give me agile wings,
and tie them on with laces, and point out
the easy way and teach me how to fly?
OLYMPIA:	Feed your brother's hunger, to the weary
offer cups of milk, visit the prisoner,
clothe the naked; when you can, raise up
the fallen, let the entrance of your cave
be open to all; these services will lend
you feathered eagle wings, and you will fly
up to the height with God showing the way.
SILVIUS:	Where are you going? Whither do you flee
and leave your mournful father drowned in tears?
Alas! she's gone into the upper air
and drawn with her the fragrances she brought.
In tears I'll die and live out my old age.
You servants, drive the calves into the pastures;
the morning star is rising and already
the sun is shining forth amid the shadows.

XV. PHYLOSTROPOS

PHYLOSTROPUS. Lusimus et sertis nimium nymphisque vacatum est;
instat hyemps, sydusque malum, mi Typhle, minatur
exitium pecori: non cernis summa Cephei
iam texisse nives et silvas ponere frondes?
TYPHLUS. Quid montes spectem? Video flavescere campos,
et cantu rauce quatiunt arbusta cicade.
PHYLOSTROPUS. Falleris. Ast veniant segetes cantentque volucres:
nonne puer Yacintus erat puer et Ciparissus?
Florebat iuvenis, cecidit dum pulcher Adonis,
10 et victor florebat herus calidonius apri.
Exarsere novi pratis iam frigore flores,
et cereris grando plenas vacuavit aristas.
Est mutanda quidem sedes, dum tempora cedunt.
TYPHLUS. Quis neget incautos quosdam cecidisse puellos?
15 Ast ego si varios timeam quos astra minantur
armentis casus, nusquam michi pascua tuta.
Hic gelidi fontes, hic pascua pinguia. Quid plus?
Celum mite satis pecori, corilique frequentes,
glandifere quercus et celse vertice pinus;
20 novimus hic omnes saltus et lustra ferarum.
Quid potius queram? Dissolvet more vetusto
sol glaciem pelletque nives, frondesque redibunt.
PHYLOSTROPUS. Hesperidum tibi poma Crisis fontesque Ticini
spondet et apricas penei litoris umbras,

XV. PHYLOSTROPOS

PHYLOSTROPOS: We've played and wasted too much time on wreaths
and nymphs; approaching winter and ill stars,
my Typhlus, threaten death unto the sheep.
Do you not see how snow already whitens
the mountain peaks and how the woods are leafless?

TYPHLUS: Why shall I look at mountains? I do see
the fields grow golden, and the hoarse cicadas
shake the trees with song.

PHYLOSTROPOS: You are deceived.
But let the birds sing and the crops come in:
for wasn't Hyacinthus just a boy
and Ciparissus too? The fair Adonis
was flourishing with youth when he was felled;
the Calydonian master of the boar
was flourishing with youth and victory.
Now hail has wasted the full ears of grain.
We must move on, while still the year allows.

TYPHLUS: Who will deny that certain careless fellows
perished as boys? If I feared everything
the stars might threaten to befall the flocks,
I'd never have safe pastures. Here the springs
are cool, the pastures rich. What more is wanted?
The climate's mild enough for sheep. The hazeltrees,
the acornbearing oak, and lofty pine
grow densely. We have learned here every grove
and every wild beast's lair. What should I seek?
The sun will melt the ice as usual
and banish snow; the leaves will all return.

PHYLOSTROPOS: Thus Crisis promises to you the apples
of the Hesperides, Ticinus' springs,
and sunny shades of the Penean shore

25	murmure sic blando, et lacrimis versuta Dyones, heu! pedibus laqueos et collo vincula nectit. Si sors illa tuum feriat caput impia, que iam pervigilem lucis Daphnim subtraxit et Argum, cognosces lacrimans quid nunc mea verba resultent.
TYPHLUS.	Quid tandem, si vita placet? Sunt ocia nobis exoptanda diis, et spes maiora reservat.
PHYLOSTROPUS.	Non prius humentem cantu secedere noctem excubitor premonstrat avis, quam: –Surgito, Typhle! - inquit amica Crisis – Pete pascua, solvito septas!
35	Surgis iners, gelidas tenebrosa per invia valles innixus baculo queris tectusque galero. Hinc imbres quatiunt miserum, lubricumque fatigat inde solum; nunc terga tibi, nunc pectora nudat infestus boreas, pelles iniuria vincit
40	etheris adversi. Veniet sed mitior estas: insomnes noctes, radios dabit illa diurnos, intentos stimulis culices; et mungere capras, lac palmis pressare tuis, fluvioque lutosos nunc purgare greges manibus, nunc vellera lappis.
45	Quas animo fesse pecudes morboque iacentes iniciant curas taceo: spes omnia suadet. Nam tibi parta domi requies stratumque cubile, seu validas nemorum superare securibus ulmos, carpare seu messes, seu terram vertere rastris
50	cogeris, in reditu. Sunt hec, precor, ocia, Typhle, exoptanda diis? Non te Crisis optima linquit insudare iocis iuvenumque intrare palestras; non, dum sacra diis fumant altaria ruris, femina nulla minus voluit pensare labores,
55	non ut grata tue servet male parta quieti, sed mechis quos ipsa novos exquirit anela.
TYPHLUS.	Quos nequit amplexus sibi summere, damnat iniquus

XV. PHYLOSTROPOS

with her alluring murmur; and Dyone,
crafty with tears, alas! ensnares your feet
and binds your neck in chains. If that dread lot
should smite you, that ill hap which stole away
the watchful Daphnis from the woods and Argus,
you'd learn with weeping what my words now say.

TYPHLUS: So what, if life is pleasing? we have leisure
the gods might envy, and hope for greater things.

PHYLOSTROPHOS: Nor sooner does the crowing cock announce
that damp night is retreating, than "Rise up,
Typhlus!" your girlfriend Crisis says, "Head out
for pasture, open up the pens!" You rise
still sleepy, take your walking stick and cap,
and seek the frozen vale through pathless darkness.
From overhead rains batter you, poor fellow,
while underfoot the slippery ground exhausts you.
The keen northwind lays bare your back or chest;
the blasts of hostile wind quite overcome
the skins you wear. Yet milder summer will come:
it will bring sleepless nights and heat by day,
and goad you with persistant gnats; you must
go milk the goats, make cheeses with your palms,
now in a stream wash off the muddy flocks,
now clean their fleece of burrs. I will not mention
what worries seize the mind when weary sheep
lie down with illness; hope is all-persuasive.
Even if rest awaits you at your home
with bed prepared, you're forced on your return
to chop with axe the sturdy forest elms,
or gather in the crops, or hoe the earth.
Are these your leisures envied by the gods,
pray tell, my Typhlus? Your excellent Crisis
does not leave you free time to sweat at sports
or enter the young men's wrestling arenas;
no, since the sacred altars raise their smoke
to rural gods, no woman has less wanted
to think of work; and all your hard-earned pleasures
she has no wish to save for *your* repose
but for her lovers, ever seeking new ones.

TYPHLUS: The unjust envious man condemns forthwith

	invidus extemplo. Quot mechos, queso, puelle
	usquam novisti, mordax Phylostrope? Narra.
PHYLOSTROPUS.	Quod nolles audisse petis. Quot sydera celo,
	testantur veteres fagi, testantur et antra
	silvarum flammas Crisidis, cripteque scrobesque;
	quotque lupis misere nudos canibusque reliquit.
TYPHLUS.	Ex multis unum saltem, si dicere plures
65	forte piget, numera; Crisidis iam pande lupanar.
PHYLOSTROPUS.	Non piget, et clades pariter narrabimus, ut quis
	sit finis videas mechis, cultoribus atque.
	Auro qui nuper Pactoli tinxit harenas
	et frigios pavit vitulos, dilexit, et atro
70	tandem succubuit potato sanguine tauri.
	Tymbreique ducem pecoris non dente molosus
	ex ulnis huius movit, silvasque ruinis
	argolicis turbo delevit missus ab antris?
	Pastorem eoum, cui Ganges grandis et Yndus
75	potavere greges et longus culmine Taurus
	pavit, in arthoos flexus seu versus in austrum,
	e gremio Crisidis carpsit sus feta caputque
	sanguine respersit putrido, truncumque cadaver
	exhibuit scithicis corvis milvisque ferisque.
80	Silvarum predo pregrandis et arbiter olim
	pharsalicus Crisidem tenuit; post liquit amatam,
	adversis haustis deceptus iaspide succis.
	Nec tu Dametam gratum vidisse negabis
	infande iuveni: cui dum Pan iussit abiret
85	exul in externos agros, concessit eunti
	nec lacrimas, ommitto greges, non, pessima, vestes,
	sed solum nudumque solo canibusque reliquit,
	ni pia tunc gremio Cibeles cepisset amico:
	et miserum risisse senem potuere subulci.

XV. PHYLOSTROPOS

	embraces that he can't have for himself. How many lovers of this girl, pray tell, have you known of, jealous Phylostropos?
PHYLOSTROPOS:	You ask for what you do not want to hear. As many as the stars up in the sky: the ancient beechtrees and the woodland caves, the grottoes and the ditches all bear witness to Crisis' loves; and just as many times she left them naked to the wolves and dogs.
TYPHLUS:	From all those cases tell me one at least, if you're perchance ashamed to tell me more; lay open now the brothel of my Crisis.
PHYLOSTROPOS:	I'm not ashamed; I'll tell you several so that you may perceive what end's reserved for an adultress and her worshippers. The man who recently tinted with gold Pactolus' sands and pastured Phrygian calves made love to her and finally succumbed, from drinking bull's blood. Didn't the hound's [sharp tooth remove the leader of the Thymbrian sheep from his elm tree, and from Argolian caves a catastrophic storm destroy the forests? A bearing sow plucked from the lap of Crisis the eastern shepherd, whose flocks the great Ganges and Indus watered and vast Taurus pastured upon its peak, both to the north and south; she splashed his head with foul blood and displayed his corpse to Scythian crows, kites, and wild beasts. A mighty robber, once Pharsalian lord, possessed this Crisis but departed later deceived by swallowing deadly jasper juice. You won't deny she found Dametas pleasing, vile girl; but when Pan ordered him to go an exile into foreign fields, she granted no tears at his departure, not to mention no flocks, no clothes, that wickedest of women, but left him naked on the ground for dogs, had not pious Cybele taken him into her friendly lap; the farmboys laughed

90	Quid numerem multos? Dudum Crisis impia nobis obtulit obscenos, quercus has inter, amores.
TYPHLUS.	Me miserum! quotiens ursis et ab ubere natos eripui, quotiens tremulis pendentia ramis mala tuli Crisidi, quotiens pullosque palumbis
95	subtraxi, cursuque pedum iaculisque coronas quesivi mechis, video. Nunc pulchra Dyones sola meas placido servabit pectore curas.
PHYLOSTROPUS.	Corporis exitium fugies mentisque ruinam, si blandam fugias nimium sevamque Dyonem.
TYPHLUS.	Quid meruit quia bland fuit? Dilexit amantem.
PHYLOSTROPUS.	Quid meruit? Cernis quot gignant arbuta frondes? Tot mala, tot mestis dedit ista pericula silvis. Hec Nysi crinem dicteos iecit in agros, Pasiphen tauro stravit Mirramque nefandis
105	ignibus incendit, privavit vellere Phasim quondam dyrceo, flammas contorsit in Ydam, lumina turbavit Mopso; sic Cyrcis honores, abstulit Alcidi clavam. Quid multa recensem? Plura petis? Satis ista quidem: tu nescius erras,
110	dum lacrimis credis, dum summis et oscula diris delinita malis. Has pestes mitte, precamur; hostes pelle, precor, diros, ne forte morentur sedibus his captos, pluvius dum surgat Orion.
TYPHLUS.	Auribus ecce lupum teneo: quos damnat amores
115	hos cupio, timeoque dolos et temporis ortum. Premia quis linquat Crisidis? quis grata Dyonis basia et amplexus ac dulces reprobet ignes? quisve nives imbresque graves celumque superbum

XV. PHYLOSTROPOS

| | at that old wretched man. Why should I list
| | so many? Not long since impious Crisis
| | offered to me among these very oaks
| | her obscene loves.
TYPHLUS: | Ah wretched me! how often
I've snatched the bear cubs from their mother's teat,
how often from the trembling boughs I've plucked
apples for Crisis, and how often snared
the pigeons and young doves, and by footracing
or throwing sought rewards for Crisis' lovers?
I see it now. Now only fair Dyone
will get attentions from my peaceful breast.
PHYLOSTROPOS: You'll shun both body's wreck and mental ruin
if you avoid the charming, cruel Dyone.
TYPHLUS: What ill has she deserved for being charming?
She has well loved her lover.
PHYLOSTROPOS: What deserved?
You see how many leaves the trees bring forth:
so many evils and so many dangers
has she brought to the mournful woods. She threw
into the Cretan fields a hair of Nisus,
spread out Pasiphae to the bull, and kindled
poor Myrrha with unspeakable desires,
deprived Phasis of the once-Theban fleece,
whirled flames on Ida, troubled Mopsus' eyes,
stole Circes' honors and Alcides' club.
Why tell so many things? Do you want more?
This is enough indeed: ignorantly
you err when you believe her show of tears,
or when you take her kisses that cajole
with frightful evils. Send away these plagues,
I beg you; drive away the cruel foes,
lest they delay their captives in these dwellings
until Orion brings the winter season.
TYPHLUS: Alas, I hold the wolf here by its ears:
these loves which he condemns I do desire,
yet fear deceits and fear the rising storm.
Who'd leave Crisis' rewards? Who would reprove
Dyone's pleasing kisses and embraces
and her sweet fires? yet who may bear the snows

120		perferet, et ventos et duras etheris iras? Sed quid dimoveor? Nunc primum perdere frondes vidimus has fagos, nivibusque albescere montes. Que tulit Alcidamas, que passus grandis Osyris, non ego ferre queam? Stipulis et carmine vitam ducere consilium: Crisis assit et alma Dyones;
125		illa legat flores, imponat et altera sertum.
	PHYLOSTROPUS.	Decidet iste calor; pratis armenta peribunt; infames stolidum rapient per devia nymphe, teque Trinos Penosque trahent Thlipsisque Lipisque in scotinas silvas, famuli pastoris Averni.
	TYPHLUS.	Etatis placidos ludos, dum credis, amice, teque simul perdis. Memini, cantabat inesse pastor Epy, silvis quondam famosus apricis, interitum menti pariter cum corpore cunctis.
135	PHYLOSTROPUS.	Typhle, precor, sanusne satis? Dic, improba credis dicta senis damnata diu, cum dicat Ariston et samius cantet pastor cantentque bubulci omnes romuleos qui mulcent pectine saltus, eternas hominum mentes a numine lapsas ethereo? firmetque Soter, qui sanguine silvas
140		infectosque greges pridem purgavit, in altum scandere non sontes et letis sedibus uti, sic alios post fata focos intrare typheos? Hos ego, si possem, mecum, mi Typhle, volebam effugeres rupesque novas scopulosque videres.
	TYPHLUS.	Quid faciam? Ridenda michi, Phylostrope, suades: certa sinam, non certa sequar? Quis, queso, sequatur?
	PHYLOSTROPUS.	Quid certum, dic, Typhle, tenes? Rapit omnia tempus:

XV. PHYLOSTROPOS

and heavy rains and arrogance of heaven,
the winds and cruel angers of the air?
But why am I so moved? Is this the first time
that we have seen these beech trees lose their leaves
and mountains white with snows? Shall I not bear
what Alcidamas bore, what great Osyris
suffered? It is my plan to lead my life
with pipe and song: let Crisis be with me
and fond Dyone; let one bind the flowers
and let the other one set on the wreath.

PHYLOSTROPOS: This heat will soon diminish; then the herds
will perish in the fields; out of the way
disreputable nymphs will snatch the fool;
the servants of the shepherd of Avernus,
Thlipsis and Lipis, will drag you away
with Trini and Peni into the dark woods.

TYPHLUS: And you friend, thinking thus, lose both yourself
and pleasant pastimes. I recall that Epy,
once famous in the sunny woods, sang how
death comes for everyone to mind and body.

PHYLOSTROPOS: Typhlus, I pray, are you quite sane? Please say,
do you believe these old man's wicked sayings
long since condemned, when Ariston declares
and Samos' shepherd and the farmboys sing
who charmed the Romulean groves with song
that the eternal minds of men descend
from heavenly divinity? And when
the Saviour, whose blood cleansed long ago
the forests and infected flocks, confirms
the innocent ascend on high to enjoy
the blessed seats, while others after death
enter Typhoean fires? These I wished
that you would flee from with me, if I could,
my Typhlus, and you'd see new cliffs and crags.

TYPHLUS: What shall I do? Phylostropos, you urge me
to things ridiculous. Shall I then leave
what's certain and pursue uncertain things?
Who, pray, would do it?

PHYLOSTROPOS: Typhlus, tell me what
it is that you consider certain? Time

	quas Amon vestit silvas, denudat Orion,
	et sub sole cadit quicquid sub sole creatum est.
150	Verum ego perpetuos fontes umbrasque perennes
	ut videas teneasque loquor, pestesque furentes
	Chyronis fugias preponens firma caducis.
TYPHLUS.	In siculis Arethusa iugis hec pascua servat?
PHYLOSTROPUS.	Non equidem, nostris nemus hoc plus distat ab oris.
TYPHLUS.	Quis colit hoc igitur? Trax foran, forte canopus?
PHYLOSTROPUS.	Surgit silva virens celi sub cardine levo,
	aspera dumetis et saxo infixa rubenti.
	Presidet insignis magnusque Theoschyrus illi
	pastor, et emissos lambunt de rupe liquores
160	selecte pecudes pauce domitique iuvenci,
	ac herbas tenues carpunt quas undique prestat
	ipse lapis, dum longa quidem ieiunia solvant
	quod mortale solum fecit per inania pingue.
TYPHLUS.	Quid frustra signare locum nemus atque laboras?
165	An visurus ego veniam, Phylostrope, silvas
	huius, queso, senis, cuius rapuisse iuvencam
	iamdudum memini, leges ritusque suorum
	iam pedibus calcasse meis manibusque nefastis
	carpendas porcis olim iecisse Dyonis?
170	Non veniam; timeo vires irasque frementis.
	Preterea in saxum fecundas ducere capras
	precipis, ut pereant macie scabieque geluque!
	Non faciam; potius nostris est vivere silvis.
PHYLOSTROPUS.	Non hominis mores nosti; miserebitur ultro
175	si dicas peccasse, sibi veniamque preceris.
	Quid Glaucus fecit, quid post hunc magnus Amintas?
	Sed sine deveniam quo tendit sermo priorum,

XV. PHYLOSTROPOS

snatches all things: the woods which Amon clads
Orion strips; and under heaven perishes
whatever was created under heaven.
But I speak of perpetual fonts and shades
perennial, so that you may perceive
and gain them, and may flee the raging plagues
of Chiron, setting things that are quite firm
ahead of failing ones.

TYPHLUS: Does Arethusa
maintain these pastures on Sicilian ridges?

PHYLOSTROPOS: No, no, this grove is farther from our shores.

TYPHLUS: Who tends it then? The Thracian or Canopian?

PHYLOSTROPOS: A green wood rises under the left pole
of heaven, rough with thickets and infixed
with ruddy stone. The notable and great
Theoschyrus presides above as shepherd;
the few selected sheep and well-tamed calves
lap waters there that issue from the rock,
and crop the tender grasses which spring forth
from out the very stone, till they undo
long fasting, for he made the barren soil
grow rich throughout the wasteland.

TYPHLUS: Why in vain
do you make efforts to describe to me
the place and forest? Will I come to see,
Phylostropos, the woods of this old man,
whose calf I long ago remember stealing,
whose laws and rites I've trampled underfoot,
and with unholy hands his gatherings
have thrown to Dyone's pigs? I will not come;
I fear that raging man's great strength and anger.
Moreover, it means leading fertile shegoats
up to a rocky precipice, that they
may die from hunger, mange, and icy cold!
I won't; it's better to live in our forests.

PHYLOSTROPOS: You have not learned his ways; he will have mercy,
moreover, if you say that you have sinned
and pray to him for pardon. What did Glaucus
attain, or after him the great Amintas?
Let me proceed to where the speech of ancients

et demum, si iure potes, premissa refelle.
Hinc faciles scandunt scabrosi culmina montis,
letaque comperiunt que dixi pascua fronde
fontibus ac umbris longoque patentia tractu;
non ibi fessa gelu pereunt armenta, nec auster
aut pinguem boreas adversis flatibus orbem
concutiunt, non dira lues astrumve malignum
infundunt pestes: zephyrus sacer omnia mulcet.
O! tibi si referam quas nutriat illa puellas
silva parens, nymphasque deas dryadesque frequentes,
illico damnabis Crisidem turpemque Dyonem;
sponte quidem dices: – Satyros dimitto iocantes
et faunos cantusque avium placidosque colores
herbarum florumque simul. – Tu forte videbis.

TYPHLUS. Iam cupio: sed, queso, refer quis sibilus auri
detulit ista tue, seu si tu forsan adisti.

PHYLOSTROPUS. Archades ac ytali firmant priscique sicani
pastores, quibus ante datum conscendere culmen.

TYPHLUS. Que nova lux oculis venit, Phylostrope, nostris!
Iam foveas et putre solum rupesque cadentes
insidiasque graves et sevi gurgitis iras
et pecoris pestes video, nymbosque minantes.
Assis, pulchra Pales, supplex tua numina posco.
Optime, da veniam, pater, oro Theoschyre, lapso.
Heu michi! quo fugiam? Gelidas has linquere valles
infectosque greges cupio, silvasque remotas
querere, si possim duras fregisse cathenas
quas posuere truces pedibus colloque puelle.

PHYLOSTROPUS. Vir nuper fueras Poliphemi tractus in antrum
obicibus fractis, et nunc es femina mollis.
Frange, trabes animo forti postesque revelle,

XV. PHYLOSTROPOS

has tended, and after that, if you can rightly,
refute what has been said. From here they easily
ascend the summits of the rugged slope,
and find the happy pastures that I spoke of,
with leaf and stream and shade, extending far.
There flocks don't die worn out by freezing cold,
no south or north winds shake the fertile world
with hostile blasts; no deadly pestilence
or baneful star pours out it plagues; instead
a sacred breeze caresses everything.
Oh if I tell you of the girls that forest
so kindly nourishes, nymphs, goddesses,
and thronging dryads, you'll immediately
condemn that Crisis and shameful Dyone;
indeed you'll freely say, "I here renounce
the playing satyrs, fauns, and songs of birds,
and pleasant colors of the grass and flowers."
Perhaps you'll see.

TYPHLUS: Now I desire it.
But say what whistling bore this to your ear,
or whether you perchance were there yourself.

PHYLOSTROPOS: Arcadian, Italian and Sicilian
shepherds of old confirm it, who were granted
to climb the peak.

TYPHLUS: What new light to my eyes
has come, Phylostropos! Now I do see
the pitfalls, crumbling earth, and falling rocks,
the dangerous snares, the cruel whirpool's wraths,
the plagues of sheep, and clouds that threaten storm.
Be present, lovely Pales; I a suppliant
call on your powers divine. I pray, grant mercy,
Theoschyrus, best father, to one fallen.
Alas for me! for whither shall I flee?
I long to leave these frozen valleys and
infected flocks, to seek the woods remote,
if I can only break the iron chains
which savage girls placed on my neck and feet.

PHYLOSTROPOS: Before you were a man dragged in the cave
of Polyphemus with its broken bolts;
now you're a weak, soft woman. Break the beams

210		reddito teque tibi; pueris aliena sinamus, et nostro meliora gregi nobisque petamus.
	TYPHLUS.	Me quoque terret iter durum vertexque levatus; deficient vires. Non est presummere sani, quod non perficias, hominis; desistere mens est.
215	PHYLOSTROPUS.	Nondum fregisti laqueos: tua lumina circum obscene volitant volucres; obsiste, repelle: est iter in primis durum, parvoque labore vincitur inceptum. Vires prestabit eunti ipse Soter; nunc surge, precor; sol vergit in undas.
220	TYPHLUS.	Urgeor, insistam; tu primus summito callem, Laurea, sis felix, et vos estote, capelle; imus ut ex syrio carpamus litore palmas.

XV. PHYLOSTROPOS

                    with a strong mind and tear away the doors,
and give yourself back to yourself; let's leave
unsuitable behavior to young children,
but for our flock and us seek better things.

TYPHLUS: The journey's difficulty frightens me
and the high elevation; my own strength
will not suffice. It's not for a sane man
to undertake what he cannot accomplish.
I think I'd better give it up.

PHYLOSTROPOS: You haven't
yet burst your bonds. Around your eyes there fly
ill-omened birds; resist, drive them away.
The journey's hard at first, but the beginning
is overcome with just a little effort.
The Saviour will lend strength as you proceed;
Now rise, I pray; the sun sinks in the waves.

TYPHLUS: I will press on; I'll enter on the journey;
but you go first. My laurel tree, farewell,
and farewell, goats, to you; we go in order
that we may pluck palms from the Syrian shore.

XVI. AGGELOS

APPENNINUS. Angele, quis, queso, pecus hoc, fortassis Apollo
vallibus Amphrisi pavit, dum pastor honores
perdidit ethereos? Videas, non invidus illud
fascinet et pereat: metuunt mala murmura pingues!

ANGELUS. Appennine, reor, tibi pinguis ludit in arvo
taurus, et umbroso recubant sub colle Lycei
nunc paste feteque boves; sis letus et, oro,
parcius ignoscas miseris: fortuna secundis
invidet, et celsas excerpsit turbine fagos.

APPENNNINUS. Peccavi, fateor. Sed tu que pascua queris
cum grege tam modico? Fallor? Ter quinque capellas,
nec plures, per rura trahis: consistere mecum
si libet, hic poteras; vepreta hic grata capellis,
hic fontes, hic antra novis iam tecta corimbis.

ANGELUS. Iussus in id venio, non solum iungere parvum
hic pecus hoc vestris, ast ut tibi largiar omne:
nil equidem maius potuit nunc mittere pauper
Cerretius. Dic, oro, senem novistis etruscum,
hos inter montes et pinguia pabula, nostrum?

APPENNINUS. Iam vidisse senem memini, nostrisque sub antris
nonnunquam duros solitum recreare labores;
dumque ravennatis ciclopis staret in antro
et fessus silvas ambiret sepe palustres,

XVI. THE MESSENGER

APPENNINUS: Angelus, who was pastor of this herd?
Perhaps Apollo in Amphrisus' valleys
when as a shepherd he left godly honors?
May you be careful that no envious man
bewitch it till it die; the wealthy fear
such evil murmurs!

ANGELUS: I think, Appenninus,
that your fat bull is sporting in the field;
beneath Lyceus' shady hill recline
your pregnant, pastured cows; may you have joy,
and, pray, don't be too hard on the afflicted;
for fortune envies those who are well off,
and picks out lofty beechtrees in the whirlwind.

APPENNINUS: I wronged you, I admit it. As for you,
what pastures seek you with a flock so modest?
Am I mistaken? Thrice five ewes, not more,
you're leading through the countryside; you could
stop here with me, if so it pleases you.
Here are thornbushes pleasing to the goats,
here springs, here caves decked with fresh ivy berries.

ANGELUS: As I'm invited, I'll come in, not only
to mix this small herd briefly here with yours,
but rather give it all to you; indeed,
no greater gift could poor Cerretius send.
Pray tell me, did you know our old Etruscan
when he was in these mountains and rich pastures?

APPENNINUS: I now remember having seen the old man
sometimes refresh himself from rugged labors
within our caves; we saw him other times
within the cave of the Ravennan cyclops
and when he often walked the marshy forests

    vidimus, atque henetûm dum venit cernere colles.
25   Sed pecus hoc claudum, servans vix pellibus ossa,
    quid michi? Silvano decuit misisse; videret
    et morbi causas, leta et medicamina morbis.
    Non archas siculusve fuit, non ysmarus olim,
    non ytalus pastor, cui tantum iuris in agris
30   alma Pales dederit. Fauni nympheque sedentes
    assurgunt homini; silve placidique recessus
    antraque pastorum, fontes, quid multa? deorum
    tecta patent tusco, et patuere silentia Ditis.
    Angele, huic potuit pecus egrum mittere noster.

ANGELUS. Erubuit munus tam parvum mittere tanto
    pastori, sueto tauros deducere regum
    syderosque greges, quanquam nil sanctius usquam
    diligat aut optet celsis preponere silvis:
    si calamis, si voce canat, si forte susurro
40   murmuret ipse, sibi semper Silvanus in ore
    Cerretii resonat, semper Silvanus ubique,
    et pater et dominus, spes gradis et unica semper;
    teque fidemque tuam colit, Appennine, secundum.
    Nunc ego per dulces nuper tua cura napeas,
45   Appennine, precor, parvum ne respue munus:
    sunt tenues, fateor, nec multum lactis habentes,
    sed predulce quidem; pomisque favisque Menalce,
    si gustent latii, si gustes ipse parumper,
    prepones. Queso, parvum ne respute munus.

APPENNINUS. Da sordis causam; dabitur fortasse mederi.

ANGELUS. Pascua sunt nobis Cerreti montis in umbra,
    heu! sterili nimium, nullis frondentia lucis;
    nec salices capris surgent, nec surgit ybiscus,
    Lambere muscosas silices rarumque vetustis

XVI. THE MESSENGER

or came to see the hills of Veneto.
But this lame herd, that scarcely with its skin
can hold its bones together, why for me?
He should have sent it to Silvanus, who
would understand both the disease's cause
and the effective medicines for it.
There has been no Arcadian, no Sicilian,
no Ismarian, nor Italian shepherd
to whom nourishing Pales gave so much
rural authority. The seated fauns
and nymphs rise up for him; the shepherds' caves
and peaceful haunts, the woodlands and the springs,
—why list them all?— the houses of the gods
lie open to the Tuscan, and as well
the silences of Dis. To him our friend
could send a sickly herd, my Angelus.

ANGELUS: He blushed to send so small a gift to such
a mighty shepherd, wont to lead the bulls
of kings and flocks as numerous as stars,
although there's no one he esteems more holy
or hopes to set above the lofty forests.
Whether Cerretius plays his pipes or sings
or murmurs, in his mouth Silvanus's name
is always sounding, everywhere Silvanus,
both lord and father, sole great hope, always;
second it't's you he cherishes, Appenninus,
and your devotion. By sweet nymphs you loved,
I pray you not to scorn a gift that's small.
They're thin, I grant, and do not have much milk,
but they are very tasty; you'll prefer them,
if Latins or if you yourself will taste them
just briefly, to Menalcas' beans and apples.
I beg you not to scorn a gift that's small.

APPENNINUS: Tell me the reason why they are so meager;
perhaps their plight can be alleviated.

ANGELUS: Our pastures in the shade of Mount Cerretus
alas! are sterile, and not green with groves;
no willows grow for goats, nor does hibiscus.
A crippling hunger forces the poor goats
to lick moss-covered rocks and the wild thyme

55	immixtum conchis serpillum carpere cogit
	egra fames miseras; illis hinc squalida pellis,
	hinc macies tristisque color seteque cadentes;
	Elsa brevis fluvius post his precordia saxum
	fecit, et attonitas vacuavit sanguine fibras.
60	Tu pingues facili facies, ceptoque favebit
	consiliis herbisque suis Silvanus et undis.
APPENNINUS.	Invitis nobis tenet hec nunc pascua vester
	Cerretius. Scabris quidnam grandevus in arvis
	inserit aut sevit? Quid credit, solvere rastris
65	exhaustas glebas grandique labore colonûm
	emunctas prosit? Timeo non seva Dyones
	occupet insanum. Senis est dimittere mores
	nonnunquam iuvenum; lusit Galathea potentem
	viribus, enervem faciet quid lusca Dyones?
ANGELUS.	Absit; nulla seni talis nunc cura, doletque
	obsequio quondam nimiumque vacasse Liquoris.
	Sed quid vis faciat, patrios ni spectet in agros?
	Nil gregis est illi, nec sunt sibi pascua, si sit;
	torpendum est igitur seu vomere vertere glebas.
APPENNINUS.	Angele, iam, nosti, non omnia novimus omnes:
	teque latet, video, quoniam persepe remotum
	Cerretium dudum vel viva voce vocarit
	Silvanus, carosque greges tacitosque recessus
	quos ligurum saltus, quos servant pascua ruris
80	Anseris antiqui quos servant pinguis et ingens
	Euganeus venetûmque palus prestare paratus.
	Que cupias maiora, precor? Venere sicani
	dicteique duces, cyprii magnique quirites
	et satyri faunique omnes nympheque deeque
85	hunc inter fedas undas audire canentem;
	Panque deus calamos posuit stupefactus amicos:
	et pauper noster longum sprevisse videtur!
	Quid, si tantus amor, quid, si reverentia tangit,

XVI. THE MESSENGER

                mixed sparsely with embedded ancient seashells;
hence come their ragged coats, hence come their thinness
and sorry color and their molting hairs;
then Elsa's shallow stream afterwards made
their stomachs hard and flushed out bloodstained entrails.
You'll easily fatten them, and our Silvanus
will help you with his counsels, herbs, and waters.

APPENNINUS: Against my wish Cerretius keeps those pastures.
Why does the old man plant or sow in wasteland?
What profit does he think that it may bring
to rake a soil exhausted and worn out
by farmers' heavy labors? I do fear
lest cruel Dyone hold him, that old madman.
Old men should put away their youthful habits;
When he was strong, still Galathea mocked him;
now that he's weak, how will Dyone treat him?

ANGELUS: Far be it; no such care is his right now.
It grieves him that he once spent too much time
in service to Lycoris. What should he do
if not look after his paternal fields?
No flock is his; and if a flock, no pastures;
he must be idle or else plow the soil.

APPENNINUS: My Angelus, you realize already
that we don't all know everything: I see
that you are unaware that very often
Silvanus has called faraway Cerretius
at length and with a loud voice, being ready
to offer him fine flocks, quiet retreats,
which are assured by the Ligurians' glade,
the rural pasturelands of ancient Anser,
the rich and powerful Euganeus,
and the Venetian marsh. What greater things
could one desire, I ask ? Sicilian, Cretan,
Cyprian leaders have come, great knights and satyrs
and fauns and all the nymphs and goddesses
to hear him singing mid the dirty waters;
and Pan divine, struck dumb, has laid aside
his cherished reeds; and yet it seems our pauper
has scorned him for a long time! If he's moved
by so much love and reverence, why does

		negligit oblatum? Veniat, durosque relinquat
90		agrestes patriisque sinat dare semina sulcis.
	ANGELUS.	Ignaros quotiens, heu! fallit ceca voluptas?
		Dixisti nuper: «Non omnia novimus omnes»,
		et merito. Nostro seva si rusticus Amon
		peste boves mediis pingues consumpsit in arvis,
95		pectoris ardentis multum sibi cessit Apollo.
		Quem tacitum mitemque vides et rura colentem,
		noluit Egonis nuper describere dulces
		pellibus is pecudum quos ipse canebat amores,
		dum maiora legit, dum se maioribus aptum
100		extimat. Et dudum, dum fervidus omnia campis
		sol raperet, sacra Cereri consedimus ambo
		ylice sub viridi; tunc primus verba facesso,
		convenioque senem: – Dic, – inquam – cernere concas
		has putres sterilique solo decerpere credis?
105		Quid non Silvanum sequeris iam sepe vocatus? –
		Ille diu corilos tactius prospexit, et inde:
		– Omnia qui profert nil dat, michi maximus Egon
		iam dixit. Midas pridem, dum fortior etas,
		iusserat illud idem: cuius dum credulus intro
110		festinus silvas, Gaurum Baiasque saluto
		fontibus insignes, et pascua credo parari,
		non tauris, parvo pecori parvoque subulco,
		hospes suscipior placidi Stilbonis in antrum.
		Ast Midas patitur; nec tandem pabula dantur,
115		nec vocor ut veniam sumpturus prandia secum.
		Miror et indignor pariter, mecumque revolvo:
		– Quid nunc, si lucos intrassem iniussus apricos,
		aut si maturis tenuissem messibus apros,
		vel si vinetis olidos crescentibus hyrcos
120		liquissem? Nullis veniebam candidus undis,

XVI. THE MESSENGER

     he disregard the offer? Let him come,
     let him abandon the hard country folk
     and cease to sow seeds in his father's furrows.
ANGELUS: How often does blind pleasure, alas! deceive
     the ignorant. You said just now and rightly
     that we don't all know everything. If his
     fat cows the rural Amon has consumed
     with pestilence amid the fields, Apollo
     has granted much within his ardent breast.
     He whom you witness tilling, mild and silent,
     was recently unwilling –for he chooses
     and thinks himself best fit for greater things–
     to write on sheepskins the sweet loves of Egon,
     which Egon by himself was wont to sing.
     Some time ago, while hot sun cleared the fields,
     we both sat under Ceres' sacred oak;
     then first I spoke, and called to the old man:
     "Say, do you plan to sift out crumbling shells
     and then collect them from the sterile soil?
     Why don't you go to your Silvanus as
     you have by now so often been invited?"
     For quite a while he looked in silence at
     the ivyberries. "'He who offers all
     gives nothing,' once great Egon said to me.
     First Midas, in my younger days, did offer
     the selfsame invitation: while I hasten
     all trusting to his woods, and while I'm greeting
     Gaurus and Baia famous for its springs,
     and while I think a pasture is made ready,
     not one for bulls but just for a small flock
     and modest herdsman, I am taken in
     as guest by tranquil Stilbon. And yet Midas
     does nothing; even after a long time
     no pastureland is given, nor am I
     summoned to come and take my meals with him.
     I'm equally astonished and indignant,
     and think, 'What now if I had come unbidden
     into the sunny groves, or if I had
     kept boars among the ripened grains, or left
     some smelly goats among the growing vines?
     But I came honestly, since when I'm scorned

postquam despicior sic accersitus et insons.
Pascua sint Mide que spectat lata Vesevus,
meque meus tenuis letum prospectet agellus.—
Flecto gradum volucer repetens vestigia retro.
125 Menalios persepe lupos ursosque coegit
in laqueos exire suos sudoribus Archas,
post hec captivos nemori solvebat aperto,
iam satur. Heu! votis misere sic angimur omnes,
et si succedant satis est: hinc linquimus ultro.
130 Quid, si Silvanus faceret? Non dulcius esset,
queso, mori? Tentare deos stultissima res est.
Pan nobis pregrande dedit, nec spernere munus
est animus: paucis contentor munere Panis.
Silvestres corili pascunt, dat pocula rivus,
135 dant quercus umbras, dant somnos aggere frondes,
cetera si desint, lapposaque vellera tegmen
corporis effeti, quibus insita dulcis et ingens
libertas, que, sera tamen, respexit inertem. –
Conticui. Quis iure queat prevertere dictum?
140 Tu tamen interea parvum iam suscipe munus.
APPENNINUS. Sat dictum. Fiat, sit nostrum. Caludicet esto,
nam pregnans video, prolem sperasse iuvabit
et cepisse novam. Surgunt ex montibus altis
sydera; sis mecum. Nostro hoc tu iungito, Solon.

XVI. THE MESSENGER

although invited and quite innocent.
Let Midas have the rich wide pasturelands
beneath Vesuvius, and let my sparse
small field keep me content.' I turn my step,
and swiftly retrace my tracks. Frequently Archas
with effort forced Menalian wolves and bears
to pass into his snares, after which, sated,
he'd loose his captives in the open woods.
Alas! thus we're all wretchedly made anxious
by wishes: it's enough if they come true;
from then on we relinquish them quite gladly.
What if Silvanus now should do as Midas?
Wouldn't it be sweeter then to die?
To tempt the gods is a most foolish thing.
Abundantly has Pan given to me,
and I do not intend to spurn his gift:
I am content with little. By Pan's gift
the silvan ivyberries offer food,
the stream gives drinks, the oaks give cooling shade,
a heap of leaves gives rest, if other things
are lacking, and a burr-infested fleece
offers a cover for my weakened body.
To these is added sweet, great liberty,
which, although late, has looked at last upon
an artless man." I had no answer. Who
could rightly contradict what he had said?
But you meanwhile accept his little gift.

APPENNINUS: Enough is said. So be it: it is mine.
Perhaps that ewe is limping now because,
as I perceive, she's pregnant; I'll enjoy
having awaited offspring and then gotten
a newborn. From the high peaks stars are rising;
stay with me. Solon, join this flock with ours.

Notes

Historical Background

As about half of Boccaccio's eclogues treat specific historical situations, it is very helpful to have a brief summary of the events involved. Two main areas concerned our writer: the aftermath of King Robert's death in Naples, and the coronation of Charles IV of Bohemia as the new Roman emperor.

Naples

In 1343 – roughly two years after Boccaccio's return to Florence – King Robert, praised by both Petrarch and Boccaccio as a wise ruler and a great patron of both scholarship and the arts, died, leaving his kingdom to his granddaughter Joan. Joan was married to a cousin, Prince Andrew, brother of the King of Hungary. In time, as Joan demonstrated little affection for her husband and was rumored to be involved with another cousin, Louis of Taranto, the barons of the realm, who had sworn their allegiance to Joan and not to Andrew, took advantage of occasions to manifest their insubordination to the Hungarian prince. Andrew's brother, King Ludwig of Hungary, angered at the offenses to his family honor, determined to have Andrew crowned as king. The barons feared harsh punishments for their past behavior and conspired to prevent the coronation. On the very eve of the grand event, in 1347, while in the city of Aversa, Andrew was called from his bed at night and strangled. The body was thrown from a window as if the prince had fallen accidentally.

In the morning when the body was found, the obvious murder outraged the population, not to mention the victim's brother. Some rumors implicated the unloving queen in the crime. Hoping to assuage the demands for justice and to forestall worse vengeance, the nobles commissioned Hugo, Count of Avellino, to investigate the event and bring to trial all suspects. Within a short time he had jailed, tortured, and executed several people of whom three were held chiefly responsible for the crime: these were Roberto Capanni, Grand Seneschal of the Kingdom, his niece Sancia, Countess of Marcone, and his mother Filippa of Catania. Perhaps the fact that Filippa had risen from her beginnings as a Sicilian washerwoman to be Queen Joan's chief attendant, and that her Ethiopian husband, Roberto's father, had risen from the status of a kitchen servant to that of Seneschal, encouraged the selection of these scapegoats from among those involved in the conspiracy. Boccaccio in his life of Filippa (*De casibus* 9.26.11) probably expressed common sentiments when he exclaimed, "How ridiculous to see an Ethiop from a workhouse of slaves and from the odors of the kitchen offering royal services to King Robert, going ahead of the young noblemen, and presiding over the court, and giving laws to men of power!" In any case, King Ludwig was not at all satisfied by these judicial proceedings, and commenced an invasion to complete the punishment of the guilty.

The ruling house of Anjou was a leader of the Guelf faction in Italy; the king of Hungary, on the other hand, was the son-in law of the future emperor Charles IV of Bohemia. Some feared his coming was a prelude to an invasion by Charles. Therefore, understandably, Pope Clement VI came to the defense of Joan and her cousin Louis. Papal warnings against any threat to church territories suggested to many that King Ludwig might be excommunicated for his invasion. Furthermore the pope sent envoys to the lords of Mantua, Verona, Bologna, Forlì, Rimini, and Ferrara, exhorting them to forbid passage to the Hungarian king. Despite these efforts, however, King Ludwig passed without opposition or hostility as far as Romagna. Indeed, he even attracted considerable sympathy and reinforcement along the way, and arrived in January 1348 in Aversa with two or three times as many men as had started out from Hungary.

Although Louis of Taranto wanted to organize a resistance to the invasion, the barons and other princes of Naples refused to support his obvious personal ambitions. Seeing herself helpless, Joan sailed by night for her territories in Provence, hoping also to negotiate aid from the Pope. Her situation was extremely delicate, for she was not only a suspect in her husband's murder, but was also pregnant by Louis. Two days later, Louis, accompanied by the faithful and shrewd Niccola Acciaiuoli, similarly fled from Naples, heading for Niccola's native Florence, where they hoped to find help. But Florence refused him entry into the city for fear of reprisals from King Ludwig. The two exiles turned to Avignon.

Louis's brother Robert, along with their cousins Charles and Robert of Durazzo, went with a great entourage to meet King Ludwig at Aversa. After showing them hospitality, at the end of a festive dinner King Ludwig suddenly arrested all the princes. Charles he accused triply: of conspiring against Andrew, of marrying a woman promised to himself, and of plotting to take over the kingdom by betraying Ludwig once the latter had gotten rid of Joan and Louis. King Ludwig had Charles decapitated in the same royal residence where Andrew had died; then he massacred his followers, and sacked the homes of Charles and the other princes. Charles's wife Maria and their children barely escaped, fleeing on foot in the dark. Despite Neapolitan gestures of welcome, Ludwig held all the inhabitants in suspicion. Dividing up the royal properties among himself and his followers, he appeared more as a pillager than a bringer of justice. Furthermore, in his vengeances against the killers of Andrew, he arrested and tortured many people who had been maliciously accused by personal enemies. Thus he earned the reputation of a bloody monster. Finally he made it clear, in his demands to the Pope, that revenge had been a pretense for his assertion of claims to the Sicilian throne. As a result of all of this, the initial sympathy of the Italians soon turned to horror. Boccaccio displays this change of heart in his *Eclogues* very clearly.

The Neapolitans revolted. Meanwhile Niccola Acciaiuoli arranged for the pope to receive Joan and Louis and, at last, to authorize their marriage in the spring of 1348. In May, when plague had broken out in Naples, King Ludwig, fearing lest the Venetians block his return northward because of an old territorial quarrel, left in secret haste for his own kingdom. Niccola began to arrange for the return to Naples of the royal couple. In June, Joan, in desperate need of money, sold the land of Avignon to the papacy. By mid-August she and Louis were ecstatically welcomed home.

Hungarian troops were still stationed all around them, however, and several years of fighting ensued. Joan was further oppressed by the increasing efforts of her husband to wrest from her the royal powers even though he was not officially king. In the spring of 1350 Ludwig launched a second invasion. Meeting strong resistance and running out of funds, he soon negotiated his departure in exchange for a papal investigation into Joan's role in the murder of Andrew. For a large sum of money, he also released the Neapolitan princes who had all this time remained his prisoners. A papal inquiry cleared Joan of any guilt for Andrew's death. But in a sudden coup, possibly planned by Niccola, Louis seized total control of Naples, forcing Joan to renounce her powers. On Pentecost of 1352 Louis, assured of peace with Hungary, was crowned King of Naples.

Niccola was rewarded for his invaluable services by advancement to the post of Grand Seneschal, not to mention numerous grants of land and titles of nobility. Petrarch in February 1352 wrote him a letter of congratulations. But if Boccaccio's eighth eclogue refers to Niccola as is generally supposed, we can see that his views of Niccola's success were vastly different from those of his admired friend. Matteo Villani in his *Chronicles* (3.9) insists on praising Niccola's valor, fortitude, and nobility of spirit despite what he calls the envious criticism of fellow Florentines. Clearly the success of this merchant – who, having gone like Boccaccio and many other Florentines as a youth to Naples to do business, had risen to the highest post besides the king and truly ran the kingdom – caused very mixed emotions in his native city.

But Boccaccio had personal reasons for feeling angry at Niccola Acciaiuoli. After several years of vain attempts to attract Petrarch to the Neapolitan court to be its illustrious man of letters, Niccola turned his invitation to Boccaccio, whom he had known since both were youths. Arriving in the autumn of 1362, Boccaccio found himself not honored but ignored, ill housed, and treated like a servant. He left in a rage the following spring and explained his departure in a furious letter to Francesco Nelli, claiming that Niccola, despite his literary pretensions, had been disappointed at Boccaccio's refusal to write flattering lies. The historian Léonard has suggested that the impoverished and self-doubting Boccaccio was jealous of his old acquaintance; although there may be some truth to that, Boccaccio's ultimate celebration of the life of poor but independent liberty suggests a real disgust with the whole system of patrons and courts and their political rather than literary demands on a writer.

The Roman Emperor

The biggest political threat to the Florentines during the writing of these *Eclogues* was the expansion of Visconti power throughout northern Italy. Florence, Siena and Perugia in the early 1350's formed a league against archbishop Giovanni de' Visconti, the tyrant of Milan, and sought aid from two sources: the pope and Charles IV. Although the Florentines were traditionally Guelf, the papal curia was so well paid by the Visconti that Pope Clement VI reconciled himself with the archbishop, annulling some current proceedings against him and legitimizing his occupation of Bologna. Putting aside traditional suspicions, the Tuscan league turned to Charles IV, offering money and soldiers if he would attack and overthrow the Milanese ruler. They also offered to acclaim him the rightful future emperor on condition that he maintain their own laws and liberties. Five ambassadors sent to Charles to urge him into action included Boccaccio's friend Pino de' Rossi. But negotiations got nowhere because of Charles's lack of money and distrust of the Tuscan Guelfs.

At the end of 1352 Pope Clement died and was replaced by Innocent VI. The Tuscans and Visconti published a treaty in which neither side had much faith. Boccaccio paid a semi-official visit to his former patron and friends in Forlì and Ravenna in the summer of 1353, probably to pursue discussions about the Visconti. He was horrified to learn that Petrarch had just decided to accept Visconti patronage and to live in Milan. From Ravenna Boccaccio wrote an outraged letter of protest that after having praised liberty and condemned Visconti tyranny Petrarch could make such a move.

When the Visconti offered Charles aid towards his coronation, Charles decided to seize the opportunity to enter Italy as a peacemaker and friend to all. In February 1354 the pope promised to effect the coronation. Boccaccio was sent to Avignon to express Florentine misgivings at Charles's imminent descent into Italy and to seek papal protection for the Florentine liberty and laws; he was also to sound out the pope's attitude towards the impending event.

By autumn the German king began his journey south. Now every Italian faction sought imperial support against its local enemies; but Charles wisely refrained as much as possible from taking sides, and even disappointed the Italian Ghibellines by his refusal to favor their causes.

By agreement with the Visconti, he visited their territory as a tightly guarded guest –"submitting his person, and his honor, and his imperial dignity beyond due measure to the judgment and power of the tyrants," writes Matteo Villani (4.38) – and on Epiphany of 1354 received at Moncia a crown of iron. The Visconti entertained him and his small, unarmed escort with a display of their armed forces, causing people to remark that the prophecy had been fulfilled which said the eagle would be subject to the viper; for the viper was the Visconti coat-of-arms. Worried at a possible alliance of imperial and Visconti forces, the Florentines hastened to fortify their city while negotiating with Charles, who continued his journey towards Rome. While other states offered their submission to the king, the Florentine envoys carefully avoided calling him by any imperial title until they could assure the maintenance of Florentine liberties. Nonetheless, Charles showed the Florentine envoys benevolence and even special favor in order to allay their fears. Finally he accepted to exchange a promise of Florentine freedom for one hundred thousand florins. Afterwards the Florentines found out to their chagrin that Charles had already promised to the pope the same things for which the Florentines now had to pay; but Charles had seen a good opportunity for making some much-needed money for his trip.

Meanwhile Cola di Rienzo returned to Rome that August, welcomed by the fickle populace, and was trying to gather money and forces to control the powerful Roman families. By October he had mismanaged his affairs sufficiently that the opposing families stirred the people against him, and he was cut down by a mob as he tried to escape in disguise. The end of his Roman Republic came just in time for the coronation of the new Roman emperor.

Secretly arriving in Rome on Holy Thursday 1355, Charles visited the Roman churches disguised as a pilgrim. On Easter Sunday he made his official entry with a solemn procession to St. Peter's. There he was crowned by the cardinal of Ostia. Normally two other cardinals would also have been in attendance, but the pope had refused to pay their way, and they had declined to go at their own expense. Otherwise, however, there was no lack of festivity. Villani reports (5.3) that five thousand German and Bohemian knights and nobles and more than ten thousand Italians attended the coronation. According to agreements with the pope, the new emperor lodged outside the city and immediately headed back to his own kingdom.

He paused for a while in Pisa, where, to Boccaccio's disgust and at the request of Niccola Acciaiuoli, he gave a laurel crown to Zanobi da Strada, an insignificant writer who had put his talents to Niccola's service. While the emperor was in Pisa, a fire broke out in his residence, and his cousin suddenly died apparently from eating an eel. The empress felt extremely nervous and was glad to continue northward. All Visconti lands were shut now to the emperor and posted with armed guards. After a two-hour wait, he was permitted to lodge with a few unarmed followers in Cremona, and similarly the next day at Soncino. This humiliating circumstance further hastened his journey home. Villani sums up the situation (5.54): "he returned having received the crown without one sword-stroke, and with his purse full of money which had been empty when he came, but with little glory of valorous actions and with plenty of shame for the abasement of the imperial majesty."

Partial family tree of the House of Anjou
(from E.G. Léonard, 1944, p.4)

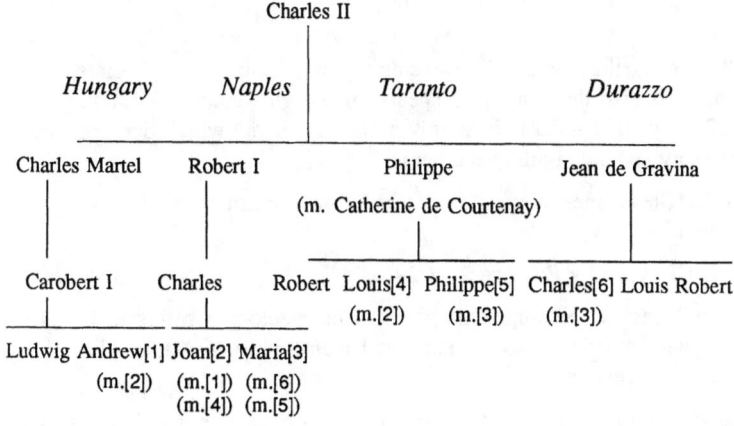

Notes on the Eclogues

Line numbers refer to the Latin text.

I Galla

Damon is the name of an exemplary friend, usually associated with Pythias; it is also the name of a speaker in Vergil's eclogue 8, and appears in 3.17 as well. Tyndarus is simply a classical name which does not seem to have any special significance here.

1-4. These lines suggest Boccaccio's own return from Naples to Florence in 1341.

10. Cf. Vergil's Eclogue 2:28-29.

13. Alcestus: although this name in later eclogues refers to Louis of Taranto who married Queen Joan and became king of Naples, here it is merely some Tuscan.

atra cupido: probably the desire for wealth; cf. lines 6-7 which may refer to commercial travel. Thus the two speakers would represent the two loves –of Crisis (money) and of Dione (lust) – rejected at last in Eclogue 15.

32-34. Cf. Vergil's Eclogue 5:16-18.

35-36. Between these two lines was originally another verse: "...annis/dum primo calamos volui subflare palustres,/ has..."(when first I wished to play the reed pipes) (Hecker, p.47).

41-42. Cf. Ovid's *Metamorphoses* 10.547-552, the tale of Venus and Adonis.

55. Mount Ugo is near Florence. Hecker (p.47n.) suggests that Egon may indicate King Robert.

60. Galla: the name of the nymph reminds one of Vergil's tenth eclogue in which Gallus laments the infidelity of his woman.

84-5. Cf. Vergil's Eclogue 10.29-30.

99-101. Cf. Vergil's Eclogue 1.59-63.

115-19. Cf. Dante's first poem to Giovanni del Virgilio, lines 20-23, where Dante praises Giovanni as a Orphic poet capable of moving wild animals and even trees and streams.

II Pampinea

This eclogue is based in general on Vergil's second and tenth eclogues, which similarly present a long lover's complaint. In the tenth, the monologue is followed, as here, by a brief narrated closure referring to Hesperus; but Vergil used a narrative opening as well, whereas Boccaccio begins at once with Palemon's speech. It may be noted, however, that many of Boccaccio's ideas and phrases come from Ovid's *Metamorphoses* as well as from a variety of Vergilian eclogues. Palemon is the name of a speaker in Vergil's third eclogue; Pampinea seems to be a name invented by Boccaccio and used repeatedly in other works (*Comedia delle ninfe, Decameron*). It is a Latin word meaning "garlanded with vine leaves." Most of the other names are drawn from Vergil, though not solely from the eclogues. Boccaccio's spellings are not always classical; thus *e.g.* he writes Liquoris for Lycoris, Testilis for Thestylis.

2. Silvanus: a woodland deity, mentioned in Vergil's Eclogue 10.24.

2-3. fontibus ursos/segnes immisi cf. Vergil's Eclogue 2.59: "immisi fontibus apros."

45-47. Cf *Metamorphoses* 1.508-10, in the pleas of Apollo to the fleeing Daphne.

63-64. Corydon and Alexis are the names of complaining lover and beloved in Vergil's Eclogue 2.

73-74: Cf. Vergil's Eclogue 1.16-17, "saepe malum hoc nobis, si mens non laeva fuisset,/de caelo tactas memini praedicere quercus." Also Eclogue 9.15: "monuisset ab ilice cornix." The crow was "pulsa" or driven away by Minerva for reporting bad news (Ovid, *Metamorphoses* 2.563).

85: Lidonnici (1914, p.318) suggests that Nasilus may refer to Ovid, who is certainly one of the obvious "teachers" in this poem, as in other writings by Boccaccio. If so, the line is perhaps to be connected with lines 97-99 which declare Palemon's skill at storytelling, and with 116 which implies that he can sing. Perhaps there lurks behind Palemon the figure of the Ovidian love poet who, for all his skill in poetry, languishes unrequited and outdone by rivals.

100. Glaucus appears as a name in the *Georgics* and *Aeneid* although not in the *Eclogues* of Vergil. The story of the seagod by that name is told in Ovid's *Metamorphoses* 13.898 ff. Perhaps the names of the rivals Palemon and Glaucus were associated for Boccaccio because both are the names of seagods, even though that reference seems irrelevant to the poem at hand.

112. Delia: Diana.

157. Alpheans: Pisans.

159. The ending, with evening compelling the singing herdsman to drive the flock homeward, may be compared to the ending of Vergil's Eclogues 6 and 10.

III Faunus

The only thing Boccaccio's letter to Fra Martino tells us about this eclogue is that Faunus represents Francesco degli Ordelaffi, the Ghibelline ruler of Forlì, who is called Faunus here because of his love for hunting. In the autumn of 1347 Francesco indeed left Forlì to join forces with King Louis of Hungary, who was on his way to invade Naples. By May 1348, however, he returned to Forlì because it had been attacked by Count Asturgo di Durfort, a Guelf acting on behalf of the Church; Francesco's refusal to pay certain taxes which the church claimed were due —a defiance exacerbated perhaps by his support of King Ludwig of Hungary rather than the papally supported Queen Joan— had occasioned the attack. Boccaccio, in a letter to Zanobi da Strada in 1348 (Masséra, p.128), wrote that he was preparing to accompany his employer Francesco towards Naples, not as a fighter but as an observer (cf. lines 125-7); it is possible, however, that he never actually got as far as Naples, for all the events narrated in the *Eclogues* are reported at second hand rather than directly witnessed.

Pamphylus is the name of the successful lover in Boccaccio's Eclogue 1, and Palemon the name of the lamenting lover in Boccaccio's Eclogue 2; but there is no necessary connection between those characters and these. The original version of this eclogue had presented a dialogue between Moeris, representing Checco da Mileto de' Rossi, and Menalcas, representing Boccaccio. In revision, the figure of Menalcas was split into two contrasting figures, Pamphylus and Palemon. Palemon seems to be Boccaccio both in his weaving of verses pleasing to Petrarch and in his preparations for departure at the end. Yet Pamphylus' suggestion that they all sing was also originally Menalcas', i.e. Boccaccio's. And it was originally Moeris, i.e.

Checco, rather than Palemon who complains that public duties prevent him from writing poetry. Thus the identifications, clearly autobiographical in the early version, have become more confused, perhaps intentionally more fictionalized, in the revision. Possibly one of Giovanni del Virgilio's students, Checco de' Rossi became a secretary to Francesco degli Ordelaffi, with whom Boccaccio too was residing in 1347-8. Checco (or Cecco or Francesco) knew the pastoral correspondence of Dante and Giovanni del Virgilio, and Boccaccio wrote to him hoping to initiate a similar exchange. We have two poems from each; it is Boccaccio's second poem that was revised and included in the *Buccolicum carmen* as no. 3. There is also a sonnet by Boccaccio addressed to Checco ("Voglia il ciel, voglia pur seguir l'editto") with a replying sonnet from him.

1. Cf. Vergil's Eclogue 1.1. The first eleven lines were added in revision, the original version beginning: "Tempus erat placidum."

4. Cf. Vergil's Eclogue 6.17; Servius glosses "attrita ansa" by explaining that the handle is worn thin from much drinking.

12-13. Cf. Petrarch's Eclogue 2.5: "pastores somnus habebat."

16. *acanthus*: cf. Vergil's Eclogue 3.45, in which a cup is described as bearing a picture of Orpheus and a border of acanthus; thus the plant is associated with poetry. Similarly, Servius glosses a reference to acanthus in the *Georgics* 2.119 by saying that the plant is evergreen like the olive or laurel; this could easily suggest a possible substitution of acanthus for laurel as the sign of immortal poetry. Boccaccio probably wished to distinguish his modest work from the truly laurel-winning poetry of Petrarch, whose coronation is mentioned here.

18-19. Mopsus: Petrarch. Boccaccio had recently read Petrarch's "Argus" eclogue, which had much influence on this poem. Palemon's act of weaving a garland pleasing to Mopsus can thus be understood as Boccaccio's composition of this very eclogue in imitation of Petrarch's. Boccaccio also refers here to Petrarch's coronation with the laurel crown on the Capitoline in Rome, on April 8, 1341; the "worthy men" were the senator Orso dell'Anguillara, who placed the crown on his head, and Stefano Colonna the Elder, who delivered an accompanying eulogy of the poet. The name Mopsus seemed appropriate for Petrarch because in Vergil's Eclogue 5, Mopsus sings the lament for the death of Daphnis; thus Boccaccio clearly recognized the Vergilian model for Petrarch's poem, though he chose not to follow it himself.

21. Testilis: a personification of Forlì, foreseeing the disastrous consequences of his departure and criticizing his irresponsible adventuring. The

name appears in Vergil's ecl.2.10 and also in Boccaccio's 2.149.

26-27. Allobrogian wolves: agents of Avignon. The Allobrogi were inhabitants of Gaul near the Rhône; Ricci (p.664-65) suggests that they represent papal legates in church territory in Romagna, which includes Forlì.

28. Molossian hounds: popular sporting dogs, here standing for soldiers; the whole hunting scene represents war.

48. Amintas: possibly Dante. The name appears frequently in Vergil's eclogues (2, 3, 5, 10).

55. Duty to the flock represents public duties which interfere with Palemon's leisure for poetry.

58. Cidypes: this name too is Vergilian but from the *Georgics*. Possibly someone historical is meant here, but if so, he is unidentifiable.

67-9. The area is the Kingdom of Naples, separated from Sicily (Pelorus) by the Tyrrhenian and Ionian Seas.

70. Argus: King Robert of Naples, d. 1343. Petrarch's "Argus" eclogue uses the same name for him. Donato degli Albanzani (to whom Boccaccio's own eclogues are dedicated) later glossed Petrarch's poem by commenting that Argus signifies "prudent, wise, discreet, and all-seeing." Thus the hundred-eyed Argus represents the providential guardian.

76. Nysa: Parnassus; although the two mountains are actually distinct, they could be confused.

77. Amphrysian shepherd: Apollo.

79. Cf. the Dream of Scipio in Cicero's *Republic* as commented on by Macrobius, who explains that the souls of good men return after death to the stars.

82. Alexis: the young Andrew, husband of Queen Joan. In truth, King Robert left his crown to Joan, his granddaughter, and not to Andrew. Andrew and his brother, the king of Hungary, were cousins to the ruling line of Naples.

84. *pregnant wolf*: probably Joan, accused and later absolved of involvement in her husband's murder. Torraca (pp.168-69) suggests that the wolf is not Joan but Sancia di Morcone, also pregnant at the time and definitely implicated in the murder, but this seems less likely and has not been generally accepted.

85. The darkness represents Andrew's nighttime murder.

86. *throat*: Andrew was strangled.

89. Boccaccio reports two different rumors, making explicit that both are merely what he has heard. One maintains that the queen was directly responsible (she had little affection for her husband and was already involved with another cousin, Louis of Taranto). The other instead focuses blame on the barons (lions and boars) who, having sworn loyalty to Joan, resented the imminent coronation of Andrew.

90. *harsh himself*: Matteo Villani writes in his chronicles (1.9) that the barons, having sworn fealty to Joan and seeing her care little for her husband, grew bold and treated him without much honor; "Whereat the noble spirit of the young man, seeing himself offended and disrespected by his subjects, was easily angered. And as the insults multiplied in various ways, both from his wife and from his barons, through youthful lack of control he uttered words of threat, sometimes to the queen, sometimes to the barons, because of which, along with the other matters mentioned already, as the time of his coronation drew near, he hastened his cruel and violent death." Boccaccio in his *De casibus*, Bk.9 "De Philippa Cathinensi") similarly notes: "certain of the kingdom's nobles feared the already known severity of the young king against them and his perhaps deserved anger, and foresaw their own punishment if he should become king; conspiring secretly against him, they set to work to prevent his coronation."

95. Tytirus: not Vergil, as in Eclogue 1, but King Ludwig of Hungary, the brother of Andrew.

96. Hyster: Danube.

108. Chalcidians: founders of Cumae near Naples. Hence, Neapolitans.

109. Eridanus: Po river.

118-120. These lines seem to have been added after 1359, when Francesco lost his whole state to the church through the victory of Cardinal Albornoz.

125. Boccaccio seems to refer here to his own imminent departure with Francesco.

127. Crisis in Eclogues 13 and 15 clearly signifies wealth; the name is derived from the Greek χρυσος or gold. Possibly, therefore, Palemon is asking Pamphylus to take care not of his girl but of his property.

IV Dorus

Boccaccio in his letter to Fra Martino writes: "The title of the fourth eclogue is Dorus for this reason: because it treats of the flight of Louis King of Sicily; and since one can believe that it is most bitter to a king to have left his own realm, as is plainly perceived in the course of the eclogue, I named it after bitterness, for the Greek "doris" means "bitterness" in Latin. The speakers are Dorus, that is the king himself set in a bitter situation, and Montanus, who can be taken to mean any inhabitant of Volterra, for Volterra is situated on a mountain, and the king, coming to them, was taken in by the Volterrans; the third speaker is Phytias, by whom I mean the Grand Seneschal who never deserted him, and I call him Phytias on account of his wholehearted friendship towards the king: and I take its meaning from the name of Phytias Damon's friend, about whom Valerius writes where he treats of friendship." Boccaccio's consistent error about the meaning of the Greek "dorus" can be seen similarly in his explanation of the name Dorilus in Eclogue 10 and in his derivation of Pandora (*Genealogia* 4.45) from "pan, which is 'all,' and doris, which is 'bitterness'."

Hortis (p.14) observes that Boccaccio has portrayed the different characters of Louis and Niccola: the one fearful and self-pitying, the other calmly continuing to advise him, comforting him yet not allowing him vain hopes. Very interesting in this regard is a letter written later by Niccola Acciaiuoli to his cousin, the bishop of Florence, about the events at hand: "When the king of Hungary first arrived in this kingdom, because of the inconstancy of the subjects (to speak politely), it was expedient that madam the queen and my lord the king, whose welfare I so faithfully and constantly embraced, abandon the realm; and as the princes and nobles and almost all the people wanted to obey the said king of Hungary, I alone, leaving everything which I possessed in this kingdom – which was no small amount– followed their [the king and queen's] fortune...As madam the queen was pregnant and without apostolic dispensation, and my lord was an inexperienced youth, it behooved me alone, for lack of anyone better than I who had followed their fortunes as I did, to provide for them solicitously and with the greatest shrewdness to resolve the most cruel, harsh, and destructive plight of my aforesaid masters." (Léonard, 1932, 2.78-9.) One can see in this letter both the remarkable qualities of Acciaiuoli that earned him his success, and the self aggrandizing manner that ultimately repelled Boccaccio.

6. Cf. Boethius' *Consolation of Philosophy* 2.5 (prose) and Dante's *Convivio* 4.13.11-12.

18. Alphean: Pisan.

IV Dorus 215

19. redcapped residents: the cardinals at Avignon.

22-28. Niccola Acciaiuoli had indeed hoped that his relatives in Florence could help arrange for Florentine aid to the king. But the Florentines, afraid of retribution from Ludwig of Hungary, refused even to allow him to enter the city.

43. Campania is the region around Naples. The Volscians were ancients inhabitants of Latium, i.e. the region around Rome.

44-45. The Lucanian, Samnite, Bruttian, and Calabrian regions are in southern Italy, between Campania and Italy's southern tip and across to the Adriatic.

46. Daunus: in Apulia, on the Adriatic. Pelignus: in central Italy.

47. Argus: King Robert of Naples, as in Eclogue 3.

49. Although King Robert wrote a number of speeches and a brief treatise on the poverty of Christ and the Apostles, he is better known as a patron of writers and scholars than as a writer himself. However, Boccaccio here praises his literary abilities along with everything else. Petrarch's *Rerum memorandarum libri* 1.37 praises King Robert for his interest in and support of literature and scholarship; it was he who had "examined" Petrarch and sponsored his laureation.

53. Alexis: Prince Andrew, as in Eclogue 3.

54. the woods: the barons who had sworn fealty to Joan and resented Andrew's efforts to control them.

55. cruel death: by murder.

56. Niccola Acciaiuoli arranged for the marriage in 1347 of his master, Louis of Taranto, with Queen Joan, Robert's heir (Liquoris). The matter was delicate, for Joan was still under suspicion of complicity in her first husband's murder, and was already pregnant by Louis. Nonetheless, thanks to close ties between the ruling house of Anjou and the Pope, a dispensation was granted. The marriage, which took place very shortly before the invasion, did not legally make Louis king of Naples; however, in time he subdued his wife and took over the power. In Vergil's tenth Eclogue Lycoris, abandoning her former lover, has run off to the north with a new beau; perhaps Boccaccio gives the name to Joan because of her switch from Andrew to Louis and their flight into France.

57. Joan was the granddaughter of King Robert. Louis certainly did not yet have grandchildren of his own.

59-60. Naples was founded in ancient times by the Chalcidian settlers of Cumae.

61. Erinys: one of the furies; Erinyes was a name for the Furies in general. Dorus here suggests that an internal power struggle in Naples encouraged the invasion of King Louis of Hungary to take advantage of the situation.

62. Polyphemus: King Ludwig of Hungary. In eclogue 3 he is called Tityrus. The name Polyphemus may come from two possible sources at once. Dante, in his second pastoral epistle to Giovanni del Virgilio, refuses the invitation to Bologna saying that he is afraid of savage Polyphemus and recalling the giant's cruel violence against Acis (75-81); i.e. Dante is afraid of Bologna's Guelph ruler. Vergil's description of the horrible man eating giant Polyphemus in *Aeneid* 3.616-61 would also by itself provide a likely source.

63. The king of Hungary was a cousin of both Louis of Taranto and Joan.

64. Hyster: Danube.

65. Reference to the murder of his brother Andrew and the uncertainty of who was responsible for it.

66. Note that even Louis here calls the King of Hungary's anger "iusta" or righteous.

72. Paphus: Charles of Durazzo, Duke of Calabria, another cousin in the royal family, who was summarily beheaded by King Ludwig of Hungary.

74. King Ludwig of Hungary also deceitfully captured the remaining Neapolitan princes, brothers of Charles and Louis, and sent them as prisoners to Hungary.

84. Probably a reference to churches. Ceres, goddess of agriculture, might possibly signify Mary; Lyceus, one of Apollo's names, might signify Christ; perhaps specific churches are intended.

92-93. Corydon and Amintas are names from Vergil's *Eclogues*. It is hard to tell whether they are meant to refer to anyone particular; but given the generality of Montanus, I doubt it. In Eclogue 8 Coridon is Zanobi da Strada; however, that is clearly not the identity here.

99. *shepherds and flocks*: the nobles and populace.

105. Nays is Maria, sister of Queen Joan and widow of the recently beheaded Charles of Durazzo. She fled by night with her two babies to the

monastery of Santa Croce and from there escaped disguised in a monk's habit, going finally to France until Naples was safe for her return.

116-121. There is little evidence to allow us to identify these persons. Some commentators have suggested that Paphus is Charles of Durazzo, as in line 72; on the one hand, it would seem foolish of Boccaccio to use the same name twice in the same poem for two different men; on the other hand, the identification as Charles seems equally foolish given the announcement of his death in that previous line.

139. They landed at Talamone, a port belonging to Siena, and went from there to Acciaiuoli property near Florence. After the Florentines had refused them admission, they sailed for Provence and finally arrived in Avignon to seek papal aid.

145. The prophecy of a swift return, etc., was clearly written after the events foretold had transpired, perhaps as a later addition to the poem. Otherwise, we must assume–as is quite possible–that eclogues 4-6 were written all together rather than as the events were occurring. This latter assumption would reinforce the idea that Boccaccio had in mind a sequence and not just isolated eclogues.

149. *one head*: a very puzzling part of the prophecy. Lidonnici (1914, p.181) suggests that it represents Joan's sale of Avignon to the papacy in order to raise enough money for the return. I don't quite see how this interpretation works, but have no alternative to offer.

V *The Falling Forest*

Boccaccio wrote to Fra Martino: "The fifth eclogue is entitled 'The Falling Forest' because it treats the decline and in some sense the fall of the city of Naples after the flight of King Louis, whom I mentioned before. Speaking in a pastoral manner, I call the city a 'forest,' for just as wild animals live in the woods, so do men in the cities; and in the same manner I sometimes call men 'sheep,' 'goats,' and 'cows.' There are two speakers, Caliopus and Pamphylus. By Caliopus I understand someone reciting excellently the damages done to the desolate city, for 'caliopes' in Greek is 'good sonority' in Latin, which good sonority in someone can be nothing other than speaking in a proper order. Pamphylus can be understood as any Neapolitan you prefer who loves his city wholeheartedly, since 'pamphylus' in Greek means 'all love' in Latin." Lidonnici (1914, p.322) has suggested that Pamphylus may represent Boccaccio, geographically removed but emotionally close to Naples and anxious for news. As Caliope is the muse of epic poetry, Boccaccio seems to conceive this eclogue partly as a grand historical poem and shows the process whereby history becomes poetry. Surely the fall of Troy provides a model for the theme.

2. Chalcidia: The Chalcidian peninsula was the original home of the settlers of Cumae, whose descendants founded Naples. Thus the beloved nymph as well as the forest is identified with the city.

6. Pelorus: the northeastern promontory of Sicily.

20-22: His fear of vengeful harm from Bavius' dog is analogous to the fear expressed in ll. 126-27.

27. Parthenope: a siren who gave her name to the ancient site of Naples.

33. Libistrian: in North Africa. Cf. *Aeneid* 5.37.

34. Ercinia: in Germany.

40. While the sun was entering the zodiac sign of the ram, i.e. in spring.

56. Tytirus: presumably King Robert. The contrast between the good old days under King Robert and the evil times since then is modeled on Petrarch's "Argus" as well as on reality.

57. Ciclops: King Ludwig of Hungary; cf. his appellation "Polyphemus" in Eclogue 4 and below, 5.126.

70-72. Cf. Vergil's Eclogue 1.24-25 describing Rome.

94. *ruddy lord of gardens*: Priapus.

110. Lidonnici suggests in his notes (p.322) that this may refer to the outbreak of plague in Naples in 1348.

113. Alcestus and Liquoris are Louis of Taranto and Queen Joan; cf. 4.56.

116. Note the recurring refrain; cf. line 77. Chalcidia's speech is 90 lines long; the refrain first occurs in her 50th line.

121. *crime*: Boccaccio suggests as before that the calamities in Naples are a direct result of criminal activities such as the murder of Andrew.

126. Polyphemus: King of Hungary.

131. Licisca: a dog.

VI Alcestus

Boccaccio writes, "The sixth eclogue is called Alcestus because it speaks of the return of the aforesaid king to his own kingdom; I call the king Alcestus so that through this name it may be perceived how he assumed near the end of his life the manners of an excellent and virtuous king: for Alcestus derives from 'alce,' which is 'virtue,' and 'estus,' which is 'fervor.' There are two speakers, Amintas and Melibeus, by which nothing deep is intended." Both speakers' names appear frequently in Vergil's eclogues. The king is, of course, Louis of Taranto. If Boccaccio named him here for his behavior near the end of his life, then the eclogue must have been written not at the time of the events but rather much later; Louis died in May 1362.

The structure of this eclogue, with its shift from lament to rejoicing, bears analogy to two of Vergil's eclogues: the fifth, which has as the subject of its pair of songs a figure generally interpreted as Caesar and thus shares the political topic of Boccaccio's poem; and the eighth, which includes the theme of return and the use of a recurring refrain but is focused on love rather than politics. However, both the songs within Boccaccio's eclogue follow the shift from sorrow to joy rather than standing in contrast to each other, one in sorrow and one in joy. The mutual praises and gifts of the two singers continue the imitation of Vergil's fifth eclogue.

8. This is clearly a reference to the previous eclogue, suggesting a continuous reading of this part of the sequence.

12. King Ludwig of Hungary, partly to escape from the plague which had broken out and partly to avoid being cut off from Hungary by the Venetians, suddenly left Naples and returned to his own kingdom, leaving his troops behind.

19-20. Various mountains around Naples.

21. Vulturnus: the river running through Campania.

26. baneful revolution: evil astrological influences.

32-34. Cyrceus, Garganus, Appenninus: all mountains in southern Italy.

40. Euboean: of Naples.

43. Cf. Dante's *Inferno* 2.127-29.

47: Phoebus and Pales: probably meant to imply Christ and Mary.

55. Orion: a winter constellation, associated with bad weather; cf. lines 1-3.

62-63. Cf. Vergil's Eclogue 7.4-5.

64. Yollas: Petrarch. The name appears in Vergil's Eclogues 2 and 3, but not in a context applicable here.

69-71. Phyllis' loves: possibly a reference to Boccaccio's eclogues 1 and 2; Lidonnici (p.202) suggests it may refer to Queen Joan's recent marriage to Louis. Phytias: Niccola Acciaiuoli, whose great trials are the subject of eclogue 4. Thus Boccaccio may be offering here a brief catalogue of his own work so far, demonstrating the variety of its themes. However, the catalogue is also based closely on Vergil's eclogue 5.10-11.

72. Stilbon: Zanobi da Strada, court poet at Naples and secretary to Niccola Acciaiuoli. Stilbon is a name of Mercury, known for his piping to Argus in Ovid's account. Boccaccio also associates the name in eclogue 13 with merchants, whose patron Mercury is; Hortis (p.19) suggests that the name is used here to imply criticism of Zanobi for abandoning poetry to pursue more lucrative jobs at the royal and papal courts.

79. "puer" (boy) seems odd for Amintas to say to Melibeus, since the latter describes himself as an old shepherd in 1.24. But it could be explained by a difference in social class.

85. Parthenopean: of Naples. Daunia: Apulia.

87. Vulturnus: see line 21.

91-93. Probably the imprisonment of the Neapolitan princes by the King of Hungary.

100-01. Cf. Vergil's Eclogue 5.45-47 and 76-77.

109. The return of Astraea: cf. Vergil's eclogue 4.6. Like Vergil's fourth eclogue, Amintas's song is an anticipatory celebration of future good rather than a panegyric for any good done by Louis so far.

118. Dis: the underworld.

126. Tyrrhenian: Etrurian or Tuscan. The identity of Asylas and Damon is hard to ascertain. Phytias is, as before, Niccola Acciaiuoli.

136-37. Cf. Vergil's Eclogue 10.73-74.

137. Arnus: the Arno, hence Florence. In Eclogue 4, Boccaccio described the Florentines' refusal to aid Louis of Taranto in his time of greatest need.

141-44. Cf. Vergil's Eclogue 5.81 and 16-18.

145-46. These lines acknowledge Petrarch as the model towards which

Boccaccio's rustic singers aspire. At the same time, Boccaccio's shepherds express considerable satisfaction in their own verses.

147-48. The gift of cups made by a master craftsman: cf. Vergil's eclogue 3.36-37.

155-58. The gift of the staff: cf. Vergil's Eclogue 5.89-91.

159-66. Lidonnici notes (p.204-5) that even this most celebratory of political eclogues ends with apprehension of new troubles. If, as he suggests, the final threat refers to the plans of Charles IV to enter Italy and receive the imperial crown, then Boccaccio would be continuing to link eclogue to eclogue even across shifting topics. But more likely the ending expresses simply an anxiety that the troubles are not yet over for Naples, as indeed they were not; for the King of Hungary had left many troops stationed in Neapolitan territory, though outside the city. Matteo Villani's chronicle (I.20) ends his chapter on the return of the royal couple similarly with the Neapolitans' grave apprehensions of continuing war and devastation.

VII The Quarrel

"The seventh eclogue is entitled The Quarrel because it contains the quarrels between our city and the emperor. There are two speakers, Daphnis and Florida. By Daphnis I mean the emperor, for Daphnis, as may be read in Ovid's greater work, was the son of Mercury and the first shepherd: thus too the emperor is wont to be the first among the shepherds of the earth, that is among kings. Florida is Florence." This is the full extent of Boccaccio's comment in his letter to Fra Martino. The title probably derives in part from Servius' gloss to Vergil's third eclogue, described as "plenam iurgii" (full of quarreling). Certainly that eclogue provided the model for the trading of insults and accusations, including the charge of stealing part of the flock. Its reference to a gift of golden apples (70-71) was also picked up for Boccaccio's ending. The use of Daphnis for the emperor may derive not only from Ovid's *Metamorphoses* (4.277) but also from Vergil's fifth eclogue, in which the dying Daphnis was generally understood as Julius Caesar. If Ovid's context is alluded too, however, there Daphnis is turned to stone by the wrath of a jealous mistress – an outcome devoutly to be wished by the Florentines.

Boccaccio was sent by Florence to Avignon in 1354 to find out what the Pope's attitudes and plans were with regard to the possible descent of Charles IV into Italy to be crowned emperor at Rome. Although both Dante and Petrarch had written letters exhorting various German emperors to reestablish the imperial seat at Rome, Boccaccio showed no interest in a Roman world empire. Rather he expressed the Florentine anxieties that an imperial presence too near by would threaten Florentine autonomy. Both Naples and Florence shared a Guelph allegiance. Zumbini ("Egloghe," p.123), noting that the emperor's speeches in this eclogue borrow phrases from Dante, suggests that the replies of Florida may be read as Boccaccio's political answers to Dante. Boccaccio's scorn for the barbaric northerners and his criticism of the Florentine use of mercenaries also demonstrate some similarity to Petrarch's "Italia mia" canzone. On the other hand, Boccaccio makes no mention at all of Cola di Rienzo's recent effort to reestablish the Roman republic, much celebrated in Petrarch's fifth eclogue. Eclogue nine continues the topic of this poem.

6-8. Phaselis: Lidonnici (p.323) suggests that the lines indicate Florentine attempts to regain Lucca, which had been bought by the Visconti and then shifted to Pisan rule; he identifies Lupiscus with some member of the Visconti. Phaselis appears again in lines 11-14, lamenting Daphnis' theft of a sheep. Charles, having taken control of Pisa temporarily, accepted 30,000 florins from Pisa in return for letting them keep Lucca; the Lucchese, who had hoped to be liberated from Pisan domination, were dismayed, as were the Florentines. Perhaps Phaselis represents Lucca or its former rulers, whose sheep or jurisdiction has been stolen by Charles. In that case, the earlier reference to Phaselis would fit Lidonnici's suggestion fairly well.

9. Cf. Vergil's Eclogue 7.7-8. Perhaps the preceding line was also in Boccaccio's mind, given the association of Charles with the frigid north.

11-14. Charles took control of Pisa in an effort to be a peacemaker among Italian factions.

17. Circius: a north-west wind. Ercinia: Germany; cf. 5.34-5.

19. Elis: Pisa was the name of a capital city in the province of Elis, in the Peloponnesus, and near the river Alpheus. Hence also the use of "Alpheans" for Pisans.

21. Galatea: Rome, cf. line 39. As Galatea means "milk-white" and Lusca "one-eyed," Charles is contrasting the two states as two women, fair and ugly.

33. Fragile laws: a jibe at the inability of Charles to enforce laws even within his own Germanic territories.

38. Molossian hounds: soldiers, as in eclogue 3. Charles actually left Germany with a very small force of three hundred knights, although Italian states along the way contributed to his escort.

VII The Quarrel

39-41. Preparations for the imperial coronation at Rome.

54-55. A reference to the existence in ancient times of Roman emperors from Germany. Cf. lines 62-65.

56. The imperial eagle.

57. Lidonnici (p.324) identifies the wolves as Visconti, in keeping with his interpretation of the name Lupiscus, from *lupus* or "wolf." The Florentines had in fact previously approached Charles for aid against the Visconti, but he had refused to get involved. Thus Daphnis's patronizing offer of protection for Florence, especially in the light of his treatment by the Visconti (see below, lines 119-120), would certainly ring false to contemporary Florentines.

70. Golia: unidentifiable, and perhaps not intended to be really referential.

75. Florence made ready her fortifications and supplies for war while at the same time sending envoys to negotiate with Charles once he was truly in Italy. Florentines feared that their resistance to his coming might provoke some retributive attack, but Charles, short of money, was glad to avoid expensive wars and to negotiate a payment from Florence instead.

77. The lily was a symbol of Florence, appearing on the florin.

81-86. Criticism of the use of mercenaries, many of whom were, in fact, from Germany.

104-5. Phrygian pastor: Pope Innocent VI; Osyris, the Visconti, whose insignia was a serpent. Both were initially resistant to Charles' descent into Italy, but were ultimately persuaded to support it. To suggest that they were punished, however, is a gross misrepresentation, as Florida is quick to point out.

114-15. Canopus, in Egypt, represents the territory held by the Visconti, continuing their identification with the Egyptian Osyris. Camander and the Mysian hills refer to papal territories, continuing the pope's "Phrygian" epithet. There is perhaps an ironic allusion to *Metamorphoses* 15.826-30 where Cleopatra threatens vainly that the Roman empire will serve Canopus; for Charles as emperor really was in a sense subservient to the Visconti, despite his formal authority over them.

119. The door marked with a serpent is Milan, where Charles, compelled to enter with almost no escort, was treated to a display of Visconti military might. Matteo Villani (4.38) comments: "he made a pact at once with the rulers of Milan, submitting his person and his honor and his imperial dignity

beyond due measure to the power and authority of the tyrants, putting trust in them, either from naiveté or from mad counsel, but not from sure and clear judgment;.." The pact was that he would give them the right to hold the crown at Moncia, and would leave them as his vicars all their current power throughout the lands that they had managed to possess; in return the Visconti would contribute to his expenses. Describing Charles' closely guarded visit to Milan as a "courteous prison," Villani claimed that an old prophecy was thus fulfilled that said the eagle would be dominated by the serpent.

120. The iron crown conferred on Charles by the Visconti at Moncia (January 1355) is referred to scornfully as a rusty one. Charles' sluggishness in the Venetian fields may refer to the events during the spring and summer of 1354. When the Venetians reaffirmed an anti-Visconti league with other Lombard states, Giovanni Visconti attacked unsuccesfully. The Lombard League sent ambassadors to Charles urging him to come to Italy to oppose the Visconti; but Charles, as Matteo Villani writes (4.25), "did not dare, even when sollicited by the powers and money of the Lombard League, to take up arms against him [Visconti].."

127. Frogs: cf. eclogue 9 where Florence is represented by Batracos or Frogs.

131. Arnus and Alpheus: the rivers of Florence and Pisa.

134-37. Hesperidian apples: these golden apples from mythology here represent the 100,000 florins which Florence paid to Charles in return for an assurance of their own liberties and privileges despite their formal submission to his rule. The hero of Thirinthia is Hercules, raised at Tiryns.

138. Insubrians: Milanese. On Charles' return to Germany from Rome, he found the Visconti cities all locked to him, and was finally permitted to enter a town for the night on condition that he come in alone without any armed escort. This Visconti show of power soon after the coronation at Rome shamefully demonstrated the real weakness of the new emperor.

VIII Midas

Boccaccio's letter to Fra Martino explains his title thus: "Midas was a most avaricious king of Phrygia, and since in this eclogue the subject of conversation is a certain very avaricious lord, I was pleased to call him and to entitle the eclogue 'Midas'. There are two speakers, Damon and Phytias, that is two very close friends such as they were, about whom Valerius writes in the abovementioned section [on friendship]." He gives no further

VIII Midas   225

clues about the object of his harsh attack, undoubtedly because he was not eager to have it deciphered. Most commentators, however, have assumed that it concerns Niccola Acciaiuoli and an invitation from him to Boccaccio in 1355; lines added later merge this occasion with the disastrous visit of 1362. The curious insertion of this diatribe in between the obviously paired eclogues 7 and 9 suggests that it may be the center of a symmetrically arranged sequence. In that case the obviously late arrangement of pieces might detract from assuming that its placement implies a date of 1355; however, the two inferences are not incompatible. Lidonnici (p.325) suggests that Damon may represent Maghinardo dei Cavalcanti, a Florentine resident in Naples, who in 1362-3 took Boccaccio into his own home from Boccaccio's disgraceful lodgings at the court. It has also been suggested, however, that this eclogue shows Boccaccio being dissuaded from showing up at the court in the first place, thus referring to the 1355 visit and rendering indeterminate the identification of the friend. Branca ("Profilo," p.104) suggests Barbato da Sulmona as a friend Boccaccio might have stopped to visit on his way to the court.

2. Midas: Niccola Acciaiuoli, who is again referred to as Midas in eclogue 16. Lupisca: perhaps Niccola's sister Andrea. Niccola also had a sister named Lapa, whose name might have suggested Lupa; Léonard thinks Lapa may be the sister meant in this attack (*Boccace et Naples*, p.77). When Bocaccio came to Naples in 1362, he brought as a gift the *De mulieribus claris* dedicated to Andrea. Torraca (*Per la biografia*, p.174) suggests that she was not grateful for the offering and did not look out for Boccaccio during his miserable sojourn. Moreover, as the wife and mother of two convicted conspirators in Prince Andrew's murder, she may well have been implicated in that crime.

7. Minerva's task: weaving.

10. Marsian: the name of two peoples, one the ancient inhabitants of Latium, the other a German tribe; it is not clear whom Boccaccio means. Aufidus is a river in Apulia. Thus the two servants demonstrate Midas's wealth and power.

20-23. Cf Vergil's Eclogue 1.11-15.

30. Orion: winter.

34. nymph: Hortis, Lidonnici, and Léonard all identify her as Caterina di Courtenay, the widow of Filippo di Taranto (King Robert's brother) and the patroness of Niccola who launched his career at court; she was rumored to be his lover. Torraca (*Per la biografia*, p.172) objected that Caterina was dead in 1346, long before even the 1355 date; but his objection has

not persuaded subsequent scholars. Indeed the past tense of "residebat" (dwelled) may imply that she is dead.

36-40. Besides implying a sexual relationship, Damon implies also that Niccola bought her love by making a loan from his banking firm. Niccola in his will left 500 florins to the bank to unburden his soul from the guilt of having used bank funds "more for the end of my honor and glory than for the profit and advantage of the company" (Léonard, *Boccace et Naples*, pp.17-28,21-22). This may or may not corroborate Damon's accusations.

43-44. The deaths of King Robert and Prince Andrew, who are referred to consistently under these names, sets the involvement with the nymph some time before 1343, when Caterina was still alive. While Niccola was rapidly advancing his career, Boccaccio, having abandoned the business world, was pursuing the study of canon law, a pursuit he was later to term another waste of time.

47-51. Niccola arranged for the marriage of Joan (Melalces) and Louis (Ametus), a marriage which required special papal dispensation because of the suspicion that Joan had been involved in the murder of her first husband. As Joan had initially married Andrew from the Hungarian branch of the family, and her sister had married a cousin of the Durazzo branch, the Taranto line was obviously discontent. (See the genealogical chart in "Historical Background".) Niccola was clearly working to promote the interests of Louis, the son of Caterina and his own pupil. Thus Niccola might well be held in suspicion for instigating or at least encouraging Andrew's murder in order to set Louis on the throne, enhancing his own career in the process.

52-55. After the royal couple had fled from the invasion by the King of Hungary, Niccola arranged for their return and was rewarded with the highest titles in the realm as well as with profitable properties.

56. Originally Niccola was, like Boccaccio, a Florentine youth who had come to Naples as an apprentice in the banking business. Léonard suggests that the contrast between Niccola's astounding and rapid success and Boccaccio's long drawn-out floundering caused Boccaccio to envy his former companion and therefore to paint an unjustly malicious portrait of his character. (See both *Boccace et Naples* and "Nicolas Acciaiuoli Victime de Boccace.") It must also be noted that Boccaccio's literary friends around Naples – Barbato da Sulmona, Giovanni Barrili, Paolo da Perugia– were from King Robert's time, therefore supporters of Joan rather than of Louis. The latter two had even been in the service of Prince Andrew. Thus the friends most likely to keep Boccaccio informed about events in Naples were politically diffident about the seizure of increasing power by Louis through

VIII Midas 227

Niccola's aid. (See Léonard, *Boccace*, pp.51-2.)

65. Lycurgus: famous lawmaker of ancient Sparta.

67. sulphurous hills: volcanic region around Naples. Lyaeus is Bacchus; thus the fields are the wine-producing areas.

98-101. Niccola often invited Petrarch, in vain, to come as court poet and add glory to his patron's image. He settled instead for the mediocre writer Zanobi da Strada, whom he persuaded the new emperor Charles IV to crown with laurel, outraging Petrarch's admirers. His invitations to Boccaccio were another demonstration of his desire to illustrate his court with famous writers; but his subsequent neglect of Boccaccio revealed a deeper lack of interest in literature. Boccaccio in his furious letter to Nelli wrote that Niccola liked to talk about books as if he had read them when he had not, and that he kept his library, of which he was proud, locked up so that it was no use to anyone. The idea of trying to capture and possess the Muses by mere power derives from the tale of Pyreneus in Ovid's *Metamorphoses* 5.269-93. The old Ascraean is Hesiod; Niccola tried to be a writer himself, composing in French a romantic account of the adventures of an order of knights of the Holy Spirit which his master Louis had established.

108. Cf. Vergil's Eclogue 3.5.

122-3. Damon suggests that the criminal acts of Niccola are allowed by God as vengeance for the murder of Andrew. The royal pair are criticized for their inability or unwillingness to control him.

127-29. Boccaccio implies that he suffered Niccola's disdain because he was unwilling to turn his writing to the false glorification of an unworthy man. Turn the brambles into bays may mean false praise of Niccola's writing, or may simply be a parallel expression for the undue exaltation of Niccola himself.

132-33. Cf. Vergil's Eclogue 1.16-17 and 9.15. Boccaccio seems to have Vergil's first eclogue frequently in mind during the writing of his eighth, identifying himself with the weary wandering Meliboeus.

135-36. Coridon: Zanobi da Strada was employed by Niccola from 1349 (although actually arriving at Naples in 1352) until 1355, when, leaving Naples, he became secretary to Niccola's brother Angelo Acciauoli, the new bishop of Monte Cassino. Niccola rewarded him for his years of service by arranging for his coronation with laurel. Lines 135-36 indicate that Zanobi has already been crowned and departed. He died in 1361, before the final additions to this poem. Phytias accuses him not only of writing mediocre and flattering verses but even perhaps of having a homosexual relationship with Niccola; Zanobi was known for his virginity with regard to women. Boccaccio in his letter to Iacopo Pizzinga (1371) wrote that he would like to be able to list Zanobi along with Dante and Petrarch but that Zanobi, "content with having pleased one man alone with a few verses, as if regretting the honor he had received, drawn by desire for money, departed to the western Babylon [Avignon] and fell silent."

144-45. Parrhasian Lycaeus is a mountain in Arcadia known as the home of Pan. Since Phytias identifies his homeland as Arcadia (line 25-26), the allusion here is to Certaldo; cf. its description in eclogue 16. The Stymphalian lands were famous for vicious birds of prey which Hercules was given the labor of killing.

146-49. Silvanus is clearly Petrarch, whom Boccaccio visited on his return from Naples in 1363. It was Petrarch's name for himself in his first eclogue. Amiclas appears as another name for Petrarch in his eclogue 8, which, like Boccaccio's 8, announces his withdrawal from the patronage of a corrupt court (Avignon) despite the favors of his patron Cardinal Giovanni Colonna (1347). Is this similarity coincidental? Boccaccio first saw Petrarch's *Bucolicum carmen* in 1359, after he had presumably written the initial version of this eclogue. Nonetheless, he could have decided on its placement in the sequence after becoming acquainted with Petrarch's work. Perhaps, however, Boccaccio simply considered that eight, traditionally a number of justice, suited his topic. Petrarch's eighth is not his central eclogue. In any case, either Boccaccio is using both names to designate the same poet, or else one of them is another literary friend, perhaps Barbato da Sulmona, whom Boccaccio visited before continuing on to see Petrarch.

153-54. This prophecy might have been written after the death of King Louis in May 1362, when Niccola was accused by the papal curia of improperly appropriating funds due to the church. Perhaps, however, the prophecy is simply wishful thinking, reinforced by the theme of justice implicit in the number 8.

IX Anxiety

Boccaccio wrote to Fra Martino that he called the eclogue "Anxiety" "because it is almost entirely about the anxiety of our city at the imperial coronation." The two speakers are thus characterized: "By Batrachos I mean the manner of the Florentines, for we talk a great deal but are worthless in fighting; and so is Batracos, because "batracos" in Greek is "frog" in Latin; for frogs are very noisy and very timid. Archas furthermore I take as any foreigner, and so I intended no particular meaning to the name."

The name seems clearly suggested by the Arcadia from which he comes. Lidonnici (p.327) further suggests that Archas may represent the ancient glory of Greece to form a pair with the Latin glory celebrated in Batracos' speech. Hecker (*Boccaccio-Funde*, pp.71-72) has observed that the autograph manuscript, beginning with this eclogue, which is the first with a Greek title, includes marginal glosses by Boccaccio to explain the meanings of Greek names used in his verse.

3. Parthenian peak: in Arcadia.

4. these shores: Florence. The fat sheep are prosperous citizens.

13-18. These lines, inspired by Vergil's Eclogue 4.21-2, offer a pastoral translation of Florentine commerce to "spots remote" and the return of merchants who bring their plentiful profits into Florence from abroad. This is perhaps an ironic version of Vergil's "gens aurea" (golden race).

20. Amarillis: Rome. According to Lidonnici (p.327), Giovanni del Virgilio's eclogue to Mussato (line 7) uses the name this way and was glossed "idest Roma" by Boccaccio in his transcription of it (Cod.Laur.29.8). Boccaccio used the name to stand for Rome also in his pastoral letter to Petrarch ("Ut huic epistole"). The original source for this idea is Vergil's Eclogue 1.30: "postquam nos Amaryllis habet, Galatea reliquit," which Servius interpreted as Vergil's leaving Mantua for Rome.

25-26. Circius: Charles IV, King of Bohemia, came to Rome to be crowned emperor in 1355. Circius is the name of a northern wind; so too Charles came from the north.

32. Etruscan: Tuscan.

36. Albula: Tiber river.

38-41. Hortis (*Studi*, p.39) suggests that the roosters or "galli" represent the French kings, since the wolf seems clearly to refer to Rome. However, he offers no gloss on the foxes. The Rutulians were ancient inhabitants of Latium; thus the reference to Rome seems at least double.

51 ff. The long disquisition on the laurel was inspired perhaps by Petrarch's coronation oration, although in this eclogue, as suits the context, the examples of laureates are almost all generals and political leaders rather than literary men. Nonetheless, the depreciation of the laurel by the coronation of Zanobi may have inspired Batracos's speech as much as Florentine scorn for calling a northern barbarian the Roman emperor.

The very mention of laurels within an eclogue might already be considered a mixing of high and low styles (Alastair Fowler, *Kinds of Literature*,

Cambridge, Mass., 1982, p.240). The *Rota Virgilis* for example, lists terms properly associated with the three styles: the low style, clearly pastoral with its mention of "pastor otiosus, Tityrus, Meliboeus, ovis, baculus," should refer to the beech tree; the middle style uses fruit trees; while the high or epic style is granted the cedar and the laurel. (See Edmond Faral, *Les arts poétiques du 12e et 13e siècle*, Paris, 1962, p.87.) The *Rota Virgilis* scheme of stylistic levels was cited in turn by John of Garland (*Parisiana Poetria*, New Haven, 1972, pp.38-41). Boccaccio and Petrarch both speak frequently of the laurel in their eclogues, imitating Vergil's own ambitious raising of pastoral potentials in the central three eclogues. The medieval rhetoricians who divided the styles according to Vergil's three works ignored Vergil's own mixing of categories: pastoral episodes in the *Aeneid* and cosmic myths or grand historical events in the *Bucolics*.

58. Linternus: Scipio, from the name of his villa. The Lybian plagues are the Carthaginian invaders.

62. Rustic Arpinas: Marius, of plebeian origin, conqueror of the Cimbrians and Teutons. Cf. Boccaccio' *De casibus* 6.2 and *Genealogia* 15.7.

66. Opheltes: Pompey, the conqueror of Asia. Boccaccio's eclogue 12.197 uses the same name possibly for Lucan, who wrote about Pompey. The flocks brought to Rome (Tarpeia's rock) would be prisoners of war. Reference to Pompey's victory over the Cilicians recurs in 13.143-44.

74. Daphnis: Julius Caesar, as in Vergil's eclogue 5 according to many interpreters. The Allobrogians and Aeduans are inhabitants of transalpine Gaul.

80. Corigillus: Claudius Drusus, called Germanicus, a Roman general very successful in Tiberius' wars against the Pannonians and Germans; see Valerius Maximus 5.5.3. The Hyster is the Danube, cf. 3.96.

81. Smyrnian: Homer. Venetian: Vergil. Etruscan: Petrarch or Dante. Three poets finally end the list of generals, several of whom are noted for their victories against the very northerners that have now outrageously produced the latest emperor. Tyrian is perhaps a substitution for Tyrrhenian *i.e.* Tuscan.

85-86. Hercules.

87. Jason.

97-98. The sheep and hounds are Italian citizens and German soldiers.

101. The one-eyed shepherd: Hannibal.

IX Anxiety   231

103. Byrsian: Carthaginian.

104-7. Possibly a reference to the forced resignation from consulship in 215 B.C. of M. Claudius Marcellus, famous for his leadership in the Campanian battles against Hannibal. (Livy 23.31.)

111. The anti-Visconti league of Italian states had previously invited Charles to come to Italy and help defeat the Visconti, but Charles had refused to take on such troubles.

113. benighted: because unenlightened by Christian revelation.

115. The man of Mars: the Roman, Mettius Curtius, who saved Rome by riding into a chasm that had opened in the Forum and thereby placating the gods of the underworld. (Livy 7.6 and Valerius Maximus 5.6.2.) The following series of references are all to men who saved Rome, but who might not have bothered had they foreseen the current ignominious event.

118. Cackling geese saved Rome from a surprise attack (Livy 5.47).

119-21. Decius and Publius Mus, who died in defense of Rome (Livy 7.21 and 8.10; Val. Max. 5.6.5-6).

123. Ercinia: Germany.

125. Cimbrians: northerners.

133. Offspring of Amintas: possibly Alexander the Great. Archas' point seems to be that as Rome stole the ancient glory of Greece, so now Roman glory is similarly being snatched away by another newcomer.

135-36. *I.e.* the Greeks made laws for the Etruscans, or perhaps for the Italians in general. Boccaccio comments in his "De Fluminibus" about the Eurotas that "its banks abounded in laurel and it was therefore held sacred to Apollo."

141. Egon: the pope.

143. Daphnis: the emperor, who from the Guelph viewpoint of the Florentines is second to the pope.

144-56. The division between Guelphs and Ghibillines. Batracos notes the traditional Florentine allegiance to the pope, and expresses the fear that Guelphs may suffer reprisals from the new emperor. However, the final lines of this speech sound almost comically exaggerated. Batracos is not necessarily expressing Boccaccio's own attitudes, as his satiric name for the Florentines makes clear. Rome is the mother of Florence.

164-70. The commercial dispersion of the Florentines, described as a wonderful creator of wealth at the beginning of the eclogue, is now characterized as the cause of Florence's military weakness.

172-9. Boccaccio's implication that Rome was reluctant to crown Charles, or that there was little festivity at the event, is contradicted by contemporary historical accounts (Zumbini, "Egloghe," p.125). For an account of the coronation, see Matteo Villani, 5.2; e.g.: "furono ricevuti nella chiesa con grande tumulto di stromenti, e allegrezza e festa di catuna gente" (they [the royal couple] were received in the church with a great clamor of instruments, and with joyfulness and festivity by all the people). The pope, however, urged Charles to leave Rome immediately after the coronation, which he did.

190-91. These lines may have been added later, after Charles's brief return to Italy in 1368-9. (Hecker, p.61 and n.4; and Lidonnici, p.210).

192. Pales: Virgin Mary; cf. eclogue 6.47, and also Petrarch's eclogue 1.11-12.

X The Dark Valley

Boccaccio's letter to Fra Martino explains that the title refers to the poem's description of those in hell, "who are forever devoid of light." "By Lycidas I mean a certain former tyrant, whom I call Lycidas from "lyco" which in Latin is "wolf"; and as the wolf is the most rapacious beast, so are tyrants the most rapacious men. Dorilus in truth is a certain prisoner sunk in persistent grief, named from "doris" which means "bitterness," but I made it the diminutive Dorilus so that a plebean man might not be called by the same name as a king." This final note refers us back to eclogue 4, in which Dorus was the name assigned to the troubled Louis of Taranto.

The identification of both characters has occasioned much perplexity. Zumbini ("Egloghe," p.133), Carrara (*Poesia pastorale*, p.120), Grant (*Neo-Latin*, p.101) and Bergin (*Boccaccio*, p.260) have all suggested that Dorilus, being a poet, might indicate Boccaccio himself. One could support the notion by pointing out that Lycidas' speech beginning with line 55 is similar to the dead husband's rebuke of Boccaccio in the *Corbaccio*: the combination of mature age and poetic studies should have taught him how to live properly and avoid delusions. This eclogue, following one on the imperial coronation in 1355, was probably composed close to that date and thus close also to the date of the *Corbaccio*. But Boccaccio was never, so far as we know, imprisoned by a tyrant, nor had his goods confiscated. Zumbini's identification of Polipus with Niccola Acciaiuoli does not really fit the text. Carrara (p.120) tried also a different approach, by which Polipus and Lycidas would refer not to specific historical persons but, respectively, to "poverty, or ignorance, or cupidity, or the bonds and necessities of daily life" and "someone who could have helped Dorilus raise himself, through either his protection or his example." Cavallari (*Fortuna di Dante*, Firenze, 1921, p.429-30) hesitantly proposed that the poet Dorilus might represent Dante; but this seems unlikely. Hortis (*Studi*, pp.43-44) suggested that lines 6ff. refer once again to the marriage of Joan and Louis still unsanctified when Ludwig of Hungary invaded the kingdom; he tentatively identified Lycidas with Francesco Ordelaffi, driven out by Cardinal Albornoz in 1359 and sheltered by Bernabò Visconti, called Plutarcus because of his wealth. This all seems equally unconvincing and inappropriate. Lidonicci too (pp.227-28) supported the Neapolitan references of Dorilus' complaint, identifying Polipus with Acciaiuoli, and Dorilus possibly with Boccaccio: not imprisoned but stuck into the dismal lodging described in his famous letter to Nelli; Nelli is the Hylas who is prospering while Dorilus suffers. However, the eclogue predicts that Dorilus will be liberated after Polipus dies, whereas Boccaccio left Naples quite freely long before Acciaiuoli's demise. Lycidas, Lidonicci claims, is King Robert, unhappy about the behavior of his desendants. But had Boccaccio any reason to describe Robert as one of the damned, especially as a thief and pederast? Lidonnici admitted that there is no mention of any homosexual affair involving Robert; the theft of sheep from Micon he glossed as Robert's possession of Naples, considered by the pope a feudal territory of the papacy. But why should this be theft? The pope looked favorably on King Robert's family. Moreover, for Boccaccio to put Robert in hell for ruling Naples simply does not fit at all with his previous lavish praises for Robert's rule, even if one grants Boccaccio's ambivalent alignments with regard to later events.

Torraca (*Per la biografia*, p.180-84) argued for the identification of Lycidas with Ostasio da Polenta, who fraudulently took possession of Ravenna during the absence of its lord, his cousin. Eclogue 16.23 refers to Boccaccio's visiting the "marshy..woods" of Ravenna, using the same word "palustres" mentioned by Lycidas in 10.26. Lycidas' lament over the madness of his offspring fits the murder by one of his sons of the other two. Dorilus, according to Torraca, is ser Menghino Mezzani, a literary man imprisoned by Ostasio's son Bernardino, the eclogue's Polipus. Torraca claims that the eclogue's lines 58-67 even imitate a few lines of Meghino's epitaph for Dante. At all events, the eclogue remains obscure, and if it did refer to a tyrant still in power, Boccacio may have wanted the protection of that obscurity.

It is worth noting, nonetheless, that besides historical representation, the eclogue offers a reworking of several literary models. Carrara (pp. 120-1) noted a certain analogy with the dialogue between the poet Dante and the infernal sodomite Brunetto Latini. Both Brunetto and Lycidas act as counselor or "maestro" to the poets for whom each seems to feel some personal bond. Of course the visit of a warning figure to someone imprisoned and perilously sunk in grief recalls Boethius' *Consolation of Philosophy*. Although Boccaccio replaced the positive figure of Philosophy with the negative example of "a certain tyrant," both have come to bring the sufferer some consolation. In the *Corbaccio*, already mentioned as an analogous text, the visiting ghost, who is suffering purgatorial and not infernal pains, is similarly concerned with teaching the narrator to improve his spiritual state. Thus Carrara was partly right to suggest that we read the poem as a moral rather than historical allegory, even though specific details do seem to point to real persons. The physical imprisonment and deprivation of Dorilus is matched and outweighed by the spiritual bondage and loss of Lycidas and the rest of the damned.

1-3: the four seasons are indicated by appropriate constellations: Amon is the Ram; Chiron is Sagittarius, the centaur.

6-11: the striking of a special tree does seem to indicate the death of a leader; Petrarch's eclogue 2.12-13 uses a similar image for the death of King Robert, or perhaps of Andrew as Bergin interprets it (*Petrarch's Bucolicum Carmen*, p.220) cf. Boccaccio's eclogue 5.78-9. The trembling sheep of line 9 would represent the citizens, and the shepherds the nobility who, perhaps having been discovered in conspiracy, have hidden in fortified places.

13: i.e. preparing for a wedding. Lidonnici suggests that the name may refer to a goldsmith; similarly Phytias in line 16 might mean a close friend of the speaker, cf. the use of Phytias in Petrarch's Eclogue 2, and in Boccaccio's 4 and 1.57.

16-17: the outrages enacted by the centaurs derives from Ovid's *Metamorphoses* 12.210ff., where the centaurs turn a wedding feast into a scene of carnage; cf. the forceably interrupted wedding in this eclogue, lines 13-14, as well as the turmoil of the flocks just above.

19-20: the dark, comfortless cave is surely a prison. Without myrtle or ivy signifies without his beloved (myrtle being an attribute of Venus) and, perhaps, without poetry or books; cf. Servius's glosses on ivy in Vergil's Eclogues 4.19 and 7.25, as well as the response of Lycidas in lines 55-61.

25: Plutarcus: Pluto, ruler of the underworld.

34: Polipus one assumes to be the same as "he whose rustic freedom has ceased" and who has been causing the previously recounted troubles of 11ff. The similarity between his name and that of Polyphemus in eclogues 3 and 4, as well as the parallel disasters of a leader's death followed by civic disruption suggested to Hortis and Lidonnici that Neapoliitan affairs were again the subject.

43. Cf. *Aeneid* 4.698-9, where Iris releases Dido's soul to Hades by cutting a lock for Proserpina.

35-36: cf. *Aeneid* 8.362-65, where Evander invites Aeneas into his humble dwelling.

46: Micon cf. below 1.143.

53: fettered for no crime cf. Boethius, *Consolation of Philosophy*, I prose 3. Boethius too had his goods confiscated (prose 4).

64-6: Argus is Hesiod, Mopsus Homer, Tytirus Vergil. The blindness of Homer and confiscation of Vergil's lands should be examples to Dorilus of poets who remained productive rather than sunk in despair despite their hardships.

75: Archas, the Arcadian, is Mercury, who was born on the summit of mount Cyllene in Arcadia. Thus he is also called Cyllenius, as above in line 41.

76:Trenaros, or Taenarus, is a promontory in Laconia thought to be an entrance to the underworld. Boccaccio's "Accessus" (64) to the *Esposizioni* of Dante's *Commedia* cites Seneca's *Hercules furens* as a source for this name for hell.

86: Pelorus: Sicily. Thymbrean: in Asia Minor. Eridanus: river Po.

102-03: Perhaps the animals represent the souls of sinners. Boethius (4.prose 2) describes how the vices turn men into a variety of beasts: avarice makes one a wolf, intemperate anger a lion, foul lust a pig, etc. Cf. the *Corbaccio* (ed. Ricci, Torino, 1977), pp.17-18.

109: Fusca, meaning dark or swarthy, may be intended here as the wife's proper name. Cf. Petrarch's eclogue 11. If Boccaccio took the idea for this name from Petrarch, then the poem might date from 1359 rather than the date closer to 1355 suggested above; however, the two Fuscas have almost nothing in common.

111-13: cf. *Aeneid* 6.274-275.

130-31: Diomedes' horses were flesh-eating; cf. *Teseida* 8.120 and gloss. The oxen of Geryon, which it was one of Hercules' labors to capture, were guarded by a giant and a two-headed dog; Boccaccio has multiplied this dog into a whole pack. Cf. The subsequent reference to hydras, again a multiplication from Hercules' labor of killing one hydra.

139-41: Lycidas' association with wolves may be appropriate to his crime of theft if we recall that for Boethius the greedy man becomes wolf-like. Cf. also the derivation of Lycidas's name.

143: Micon cf. line 46.

147-8: Hercules' twelfth labor was to bring up Cerberus from the underworld; while doing so, he also rescued Theseus, who had tried to carry off Proserpina. There is an implicit allusion to Christ's harrowing of hell, as the subsequent lines clarify.

150: Pan is God or Christ.

151: Archesilas: God, from the Greek *arche* or ruler. Cf eclogue 14.200.

165: the subject "we" following the list of suffering animals reinforces the idea that the animals represent sinners.

170: The sisters are the three fates, who spin out men's lives.

XI Pantheon

About the eleventh eclogue Boccaccio wrote, "..it is called Pantheon from 'pan,' which is 'all,' and 'theos,' which is 'god,' because its discourse is all about things divine. In this one alone the author speaks, reciting some things said by certain interlocutors, who are two: Mirtilis and Glaucus. By Mirtilis I mean the Church of God, which I name from 'myrtle' because the myrtle has two-colored leaves, for the lower sides are blood-red and the upper sides green; so that we may perceive through those colors the persecutions and tribulations once suffered by holy people and their most sure faith concerning the heavenly mercy promised them by Christ. By Glaucus, moreover, I mean the apostle Peter; for Glaucus was a fisherman, and having tasted a certain grass he suddenly threw himself into the sea and was numbered among the marine gods; thus too Peter was a fisherman, and having tasted the teachings of Christ, he threw himself into the waves, that is into the threats and terrors from enemies of the Christian name, preaching the name of Christ, because of which he became a god, that is a saint, among the friends of God in heaven." This use of Glaucus in a Christian sense was undoubtedly inspired by Dante's *Paradiso* 1.67-72.

The eclogue as a whole is clearly modeled on Vergil's sixth, in which

Silenus, begged by two boys and a naiad, at last agrees to sing a series of myths beginning with the creation. Vergil similarly recounts indirectly the songs of Silenus. His poem ends too with the evening star summoning the boys to drive home their sheep, although Boccaccio has reinterpreted Vergil's final phrase to make the evening star itself reluctant to move on. Glaucus' song within Boccaccio's poem is divided in two equal halves representing the Old and New Testament. The invocation to the second half, echoing the "maiora canamus" from Vergil's fourth eclogue, associates the narration of Christ's birth with the famous Vergilian poem. Just as Vergil had with that phrase announced a shift from the Theocritan idyll to a new kind of eclogue dealing with nobler themes, so too Boccaccio announces his new use of the eclogue for treating subjects of divinity. In a sense, although the preceding eclogue was already otherworldly in its description of hell, that one had summed up the vices and sorrows of the first nine poems; now the theme turns in a more hopeful direction, away from evil and looking towards heaven.

As it is not clear just when Boccaccio composed this poem, we do not know whether he had yet seen the rest of Petrarch's pastoral sequence. If so, he might have been impressed by Petrarch's sixth eclogue, which is a hostile dialogue between St. Peter and the current pope. Nonetheless, Boccaccio's poem is completely different in content, for instead of attacking the contemporary state of the church, it presents the church in the lovely figure of Mirtilis and retells the stories of the Bible. Whereas Petrarch's poem forms part of a series of eclogues about the problems with contemporary leadership both secular and spiritual, Boccaccio's functions within a series of eclogues on completely otherworldly and doctrinal matters. Only lines 25-29 hint at the failings of contemporary society, and these allusions are swiftly brushed aside in Mirtilis' response.

One other possible model for this poem is Theodulus' single "Ecloga" from the ninth or tenth century, which had served as a school text and was thus fairly well known (*Theoduli eclogam*, ed. Joannes Osternacher, Ripariae prope Lentiam, 1902). It is a singing match between Pseustis (Falsehood) and Alithia (Truth), in which the former sings scenes from pagan mythology and the latter scenes from Scripture; thus it participates in a tradition that, associating Moses with Musaeus, considered the Greek myths a garbled version of earlier books of Scripture. In pitting the two against each other, it is quite different from Boccaccio's poem, where Greek myths directly signify Judaeo-Christian stories without any suggestion of their falsehood. Moreover, there is almost no overlap between the two authors in their selection of paired events, the two exceptions being the use of Deucalion and Pyrrha for Noah and the use of Pelion and Ossa for the tower of Babel. Theodulus, drawing from only the Old Testament, includes a number of episodes omitted by Boccaccio, and reassigns others to different myths. Boccaccio, perhaps combining this with Vergil's fourth eclogue, developed the idea of using classical poetry to sing about Christ. Thus classical myth is no longer seen as an intended but garbled version of Scripture; rather, while on the one hand it is read more historically as not really about Biblical matters (thus in the *Genealogia* the secret wisdom of the ancient poets includes historical, moral, and scientific meanings but not Biblical ones), on the other hand it is used by the new Christian poet to mean new things in a purely constructed manner.

The New Testament narration follows closely the content rehearsed by Boccaccio as his credo in the *Genealogia* 15.9, a chapter significantly on the topic: that "it is not improper for certain Christians to study pagan antiquity." Long before in the pastoral *Comedia delle ninfe fiorentine* 39, Boccaccio had set into the mouth of Lia, the nymph representing Faith, a credo using classical names to signify Christian things: e.g. Pluto for Satan, Ceres and Bacchus for the bread and wine of the communion, Cybele for the church. Even earlier, the *Filocolo* 1.1 had referred to Christ and Satan as "the son of Jove" and "Pluto," while Juno, as Jove's bride, represented the church. In sum, the method of this eclogue had already a long usage in Boccaccio's works.

1. Clio: one of the nine muses, usually the muse of history. Boccaccio's *Genealogia* 11.2, however, says this about her: "We indeed say that the nine muses represent the stages of learning and knowledge [doctrinae atque scientiae modos]. The first is this Clio as the first thought of learning [prima cogitatio discendi]. For Clios in Greek means fame, and since no one seeks knowledge unless he may advance the worthiness of his fame, therefore the first is named Clio, i.e. the thought of pursuing knowledge." The passage is taken almost verbatim from Fulgentius, whom he cites (*Mitologiarum libri* 1.15).

Clio's love for Apollo may perhaps be glossed as the desire for enlightenment or truth. Apollo is invoked near the beginning of Dante's *Paradiso* 1 (line 13), the same canto which refers to Glaucus, and is connected with "l'amato alloro" (15) cf. Boccaccio's line 3: "Phebus amat lauros" (Phoebus loves laurels). Dante's *Convivio* 3.12 also explicitly associates the sun with God as the intellectual light that makes all things intelligible. Clio as the historical muse might be especially suited to this poetry of Truth.

3-4: The suggestion that by writing a poetry of sacred truth one might deserve to win the laurel crown is another indirect echo of *Paradiso* 1.22-33.

4-5. nor will it shame you: cf Vergil's eclogue 6.2, addressed to a different Muse. Together with line 7 the verses mean that the poetry of truth (or Truth) should not be ashamed to take on the lowly pastoral mode.

6. Mopsus: Petrarch, as usual. This might imply, but by no means necessarily, that Boccaccio had read Petrarch's *Bucolicum carmen* and was responding to it, in hopes that Petrarch will like the new developments. But cf. 3.18 and 53, written when Boccaccio had as yet read only Petrarch's "Argus". Petrarch is in any case the audience for whom Boccaccio is composing these Latin poems in a classical genre.

7. the lyre of Arethusa: Arethusa is a spring in Syracuse, Sicily, which was the birthplace of the pastoral poet Theocritus. Hence, the line invokes the muse to help the poet sing pastoral verses. Cf. Vergil's eclogue 6.1.

8. Petrarch will suggest any corrections or improvements to the poem at hand.

9. Cybele was worshiped on Mount Berecinthus, hence she is the Berecinthian. (See *De montibus*.) *Genealogia* 3.2 refers to Cybele as one of the names for the mother of the gods (deorum mater). Thus the author addresses his song to the Virgin Mary. Cf. Boccaccio's comment in the *Corbaccio* that he had always especially venerated the Virgin, and the addressing of his previous fictions to a human Maria. *Corbaccio* (ed. Ricci, p.16): "..you always, whatever the condition of your life, have had a special reverence and devotion for Her in whose womb was enclosed our salvation...and in her, as in a fixed goal, you had always entire hope."

10. The construction by St. Peter of what is presumably a sheepfold might suggest the building of a –perhaps spiritual church. But the weaving of slender twigs was also used by Vergil (Eclogue 10.70-71) to refer to the making of pastoral verses. Cf. Boccaccio's first eclogue to Checco, line 29, "Me quoque texentem silvestri vigmine septam," (..me also weaving a pen of forest twigs) which is clearly a reference to the writing of pastoral poetry. In this light, Peter's activity as a writer makes him a precursor for Boccaccio's own pastoral verses on religious topics.

Amintas is St. Paul; cf. line 16, and ecl.15.176.

12-14. Mirtilis, or the church, is clearly located in Rome even though the Papal court was still in Avignon.

15. The church calls Glaucus "father" because Peter was the first pope.

25-27. The number of true believers is few. Although Rhodopes is really a mountain in Thrace, the name is chosen as a pun for the river Rhone, or Rhodanus; thus it refers to the papal curia at Avignon.

28-29. Cacus, the thief from *Aeneid* 8.190 ff., ought to be read together with the reference to Hercules (Alcides) in line 31, which clearly indicates Christ. According to the *Aeneid*, Hercules found the cattle stolen and hidden in a cave by the monstrous, semihuman Cacus, and destroyed the monster as well as well as bringing back the lost animals. Thus Cacus signifies the devil, as also in lines 206-08, although in line 167 he is given a different name. Perhaps there is also an implicit allusion to the King of France who has stolen the pope and cardinals from Rome, and would make war if there were any attempted restoration. As in eclogue 10, a combination of moral and historical readings might be possible.

31. Alcides, see note to 28-29.

32-35. See Matthew 4:18-20 and Luke 5:1-11.

40-41. Cf. Vergil's eclogue 6.29-30. Amphrysus: where Apollo, disguised as a shepherd, kept the flocks of Admetus in Thessaly.

44. Tarpean rock: Boccaccio in *De montibus* identifies this Roman site as the Capitoline hill. Cf. Petrarch's laurel coronation on the Capitoline in 1341.

47. comrade: Amintas, cf. 49-50.

56-65. Cf. Vergil's Eclogue 6.31-40.

67-72. Cain and his descendents. See Genesis 5.21-22: Jubal is the first musician; Tubal-cain the first forger of brass and iron.

73. Lycaon, in Ovid's *Metamorphoses* 1.210ff., is a murderer, the first human whose crimes are specifically recounted; his tale is told by Jupiter as an example of the pervasive wickedness of humans and as a demonstration of the existence of divine retribution: Lycaon becomes a wolf, but Jupiter tells the tale to justify causing the great flood which will destroy mankind.

75-8. The flood. Deucalion is Noah. For the story of how he and his wife renewed the human race by throwing stones, see Ovid's *Metamorphoses* 1.318ff.

79-83. The tower of Babel, the confusion of tongues, and the dispersion of human tribes (Genesis 11). For the story of the giants' attempt to reach heaven by piling up mountains, see *Metamorphoses* 1.151-62.

84-90. Archipater is Abraham; Silvanus, the classical woodland god, is Jehovah (*Genesis* 12:7-8). 84 may refer to Abraham's prosperity (13.2),

XI Pantheon 241

or to the strife between the herdsmen of Abraham and Lot (13.7). God's promise of a child to the aged Sarah and the laugh it caused (17.15-18.15; 21.1-7). The sacrifice of Isaac (22.1-19).

91-94. The fall of Sodom and Gomorrah, and Lot's seduction by his daughters (19.12-38). Cinyras was the father Myrrha, who lay with him without his knowing (*Metamorphoses* 10.298ff.).

95-98. Isaac bore Esau and Jacob; Esau sold his birthright to Jacob for a meal (25.19-34). Rebekah dressed Jacob in skins to make the blind old Isaac mistake him for his hairier brother; thus Jacob received the father's blessing (27.5-29). Sophronis is a Greek word meaning temperate or self-controlled; why Boccaccio thought it appropriate as a name for Rebekkah remains unclear to me.

99-102. Jacob's departure, his work as a shepherd for Laban, and his marriage to Laban's daughters (28-29). The dream of Jacob's ladder (28.11-17). Jacob's wrestling with an angel, who touched his thigh, making him lame, and gave him a new name: Israel (32.24-32). Stilbon, the name given to Jacob, is one of the names of Mercury; Boccaccio reserved this name of the messenger of the gods for use specifically in the context of Jacob's divinely inspired dreams.

103-08. Joseph sold by his brothers to Egyptians, his interpretation of the Pharoah's dream, his administration of crops reserved for the years of famine, his aid to his own family (37, and 38-47). Argus was the name used by both Petrarch and Boccaccio for King Robert of Naples; it seems to be associated for them with the idea of a just and benevolent ruler, in this case Joseph as administrator.

109-110. The servitude of the Jews in Egypt; Moses taken from the stream by the Pharoah's daughter, named here after an Egyptian goddess as the rulers of Egypt claimed to be its gods. Phoroneus was a mythical Argive king who gave laws to his people (*Genealogia* 7.23), thus representing the lawgiver Moses.

111-121. The plagues in Egypt, the Egyptians (goats) drowned in the Red Sea, the Jews' wandering in the desert, water struck from a rock, manna fallen from heaven, God's orders for the building of a temple; the writing of the ten commandments, and Moses' smashing the tablets of law when he saw the golden calf forged by his brother Aaron at the people's insistence (the idol, rather than Aaron, is given the name of the Egyptian god); the serpent bites healed for those who beheld a serpent of bronze set up in the camp, the invasion and possession of the promised land.

122-24. The temple of Solomon and holy rites, here presented as the ancient celebratory games of the Greeks.

125-31. The Babylonian captivity. Nebuchadnezzar blinds the last Hebrew King, Zedekiah (*Jeremiah* 52.11). The dispersal of the Jews into foreign lands. The prediction of these evils by the prophets.

135. "maiora canam": cf. Vergil's Eclogue 4.1.

136. Maia's son is Mercury, who as Jove's messenger represents the angel Gabriel.

137. Danae, visited by Jupiter in the form of a rain of gold, represents the Virgin Mary beloved by God.

153. The moon is in conjunction with the sun, thus making a new moon.

159-60. Symbolic plants: the olive of peace, the ivy and laurel of immortal life, and the palm of victory.

167. Plutarcus, as in eclogue 10, is Satan; his name is derived from Pluto, ruler of the underworld.

169. Codrus was a king of Athens who, hearing an oracle that the Athenians would be vanquished by the Dorian invaders if his own life were saved, sacrificed himself successfully for the salvation of his people (Valerius Maximus, *Factorum et Dictorum Memorabiblium Libri* 5.6.ext.1). Thus he represents Christ. Christ is called by a series of seven different names in this poem, but Codrus begins and ends the list.

170. the cruel sisters: the Furies.

173-76. The three kings bring gifts to the baby Jesus.

177-80. The flight from Herod (the wolf), and the slaughter of the innocents.

181-2. Jesus in the temple; Lycurgus was a famous ancient lawgiver.

183-84. Nathan, the prophet who anointed Solomon king of Israel (1 *Kings* 1.32-35), stands for John the Baptist. Christ's baptism in turn takes on the allegorical meaning of Christ's cleansing mankind from sin through baptism.

185. Carones, perhaps a mistaken form of Chronos, is another name for Saturn, who taught the Italians how to make coins from metal (*Genealogia* 8.1) and whose temple in Rome was the public treasury. Thus he represents the moneychangers driven from the temple.

187. Asclepius, the famous ancient healer, son of Apollo, who brought

the dead Hippolytus back to life, represents Christ as healer of the sick and resurrector of the dead.

192-194. Pales, a rural god of shepherds, is Christ; the acorns represent the bread of the last supper, because in the simple golden age men ate acorns instead of making bread. The ancient Pales, who in other eclogues represents the Virgin Mary, was considered variously male or female.

194-95. Actaeon is again Christ, who will be killed by his own people. Cf. lines 197 and 199 where Christ is described as thrown to the dogs and covered with bites.

195. Menalcas is Judas, possibly so named for the malicious Menalcas of Vergil's third eclogue, esp. 10-15.

206-07. Christ's harrowing of hell; cf. lines 28 and 31.

211. Hippolytus, representing Christ, was resurrected from death; see note to line 187.

212. The use of laurel in connection with Christ's triumph over death provides a religious context for Aristeus' pursuit of the laurel in the following eclogue.

215-16. Phoebus as the sun which rises again after it has set represents the resurrected Christ. Moreover the fiery nature of the sun is associated with the Pentecostal descent of flames on Mary and the apostles.

217-18. The apostles are sent out in all directions to preach.

219-24. The spread of Christianity throughout the world. The crimson blooms may represent martyrs, and the lilies virgins.

225-27. The second coming and last judgment. For Codrus, see note to line 169. It is appropriate that the final sabbath be accompanied by the eighth name for Christ, a recurrence of the first name, according to traditional meanings of eight as renewal (the octave) and as the completion of time, measured in sevens. On seven as the ages of history and eight as the number of eternity and final judgment, see Hugo of St. Victor, *Exegetica*, *PL* 175.22; Isidore of Seville, *Liber numerorum*, *PL* 83.189; Rabanus Maurus, *Comment. in Genesim* I,9, *PL* 107.464.

228. Cf. Vergil's Eclogue 3.111.

231-35. Baptism of the faithful after hearing the story of Christ. Cf. Book V of the *Filocolo*.

236-38. Cf. Vergil's Eclogue 6.85-6 and 10.77.

XII Saphos

Boccaccio wrote to Fra Martino: "The twelfth eclogue is entitled Saphos because the whole discourse of the eclogue is about this Saphos, whom I understand as representing poetry because Sappho, a certain girl of Lesbos, was the most worthy in poetry in her era. The speakers are two, Caliope and Aristeus. By Caliope, as was said elsewhere, I mean "good sonority," because in the good declaration regulated by poetic meters almost the whole force of poetry seems to consist. Aristeus represents me eager to arrive at poetry, and I name myself "Aristeus" after a certain Aristeus whose tongue had an impediment up until his adolescence so that he could barely express anything fully enough; at last, the knot being loosed from his tongue, he became eloquent." The change in Aristeus' ability to speak can be read as analogous to Boccaccio's change from vernacular to Latin poetry, as lines 51-55 imply.

The "elsewhere" with regard to the derivation of Caliope is Boccaccio's *Genealogia* 11.2, where she is the last of the nine muses who all together represent the production of poetry from cogitation through memory and invention to the final pronunciation of the poem. Caliope is translated there "best voice." Boccaccio also cites, among various interpretations, that of Macrobius' *Somnium Scipionis* according to which eight muses are matched to the eight heavenly spheres while the ninth accords the harmony of them all; thus she is not only the ninth but the supreme muse. Together Clio of the preceding eclogue and Caliope here represent the first and last of the nine Muses.

By this time Boccaccio had certainly read Petrarch's entire *Bucolicum carmen*. The whole eclogue is similar in theme to Petrarch's third, about Stupeus' love for Daphne; but whereas Petrarch's poem celebrates his triumphal winning of the laurel crown and connects it to ancient Roman glory, Boccaccio's poem, not tied to any particular place or history, presents a self-portrait which is not only much humbler but even humorous in places, despite his serious love for poetry. This deprecating self-image is a response not only to Petrarch's but also, perhaps, to his own ambitiousness in the preceeding eclogue, which ends with a reference to the laurel crown.

3. grove: *Genealogia.* 11.2 explains that the grove represents the tranquil solitude necessary for meditation.

17. Mopsus: Petrarch; his song is perhaps a reference to Petrarch's eclogue 3.

22. swineherd: Caliope identifies him with the lowest of the pastoral

XII Saphos

vocations, which were from best to worst: cowherd, shepherd, goatherd, and swineherd. Lines 74 and 201 confirm the truth of her assessment.

39. Phyllis seems to be the typical name for the peasant-class object of erotic love. It might, therefore, represent the common, vulgar throng who loved his vernacular writings. Petrarch used the name Galathea in his eleventh eclogue to represent Laura; but Boccaccio is obviously not giving it that elevated status here. It recurs frequently in Vergil's eclogues. Boccaccio's first eclogue is a love complaint to the "wanton Galla," and his early epistolary eclogue to Checco di Mileto refers to "the wanton Galathea" as the poet's beloved. Youthful loves may again imply youthful attempts at a lower kind of writing, more sensual and less intellectual.

41. Pan as the poetic mentor of more learned poetry stands in contrast to Nasilus, probably Ovid, as the teacher in eclogue 2.86.

43. *Genealogia* 7.27 tells of a Cyrene, mother of Aristeus after being raped by Apollo. She is the sister of Daphne, and both are daughters of the river-god Peneus. Peneus' river flows through Thessaly, which Boccaccio calls "famous for the songs of poets and for historical writings."

Genealogia 5.13 discusses Aristeus at some length, with reference to Vergil's *Georgics* 4.317-ff. This chapter also links Aristeus with Bathos (cf. line 55). Aristeus became ruler of Arcadia, and the first to establish the use honey; he also taught his people how to press oil from the olives. These details, although unglossed by Boccaccio, are highly suggestive of poetic and intellectual activity, especially as the words for honey (meli) and song (melos) were easily confused. Thus the namesake of Boccaccio's persona is not quite so poor a figure as it might seem.

47. Ismarian: Orpheus, from the mountain where he used to sing. Critis: the name means "judge" or "critic;" Ida is the site of the judgment of Paris. Hence Critis is Paris, and Aristeus is mocked for choosing erotic poetry over the poetry of wisdom.

48-9: Cf. Vergil's Eclogue 3.25-7: "non tu in triviis, indocte, solebar/ stridenti miserum stipula disperdere carmen?" (Didn't you, unlearned, used to spoil a wretched song on squeaking reeds at the crossroads?)

52. the lame god of Lemnos: Vulcan; i.e. Aristeus has burned his earlier works. Cf. Boccaccio's letter to Pietro di Monteforti (ed. Corazzini, p.356) and Petrarch's *Seniles* 5.2 in re Boccaccio's apparently aborted intention to burn his poetry. Probably he did burn some of his poems, and perhaps with good reason; all poets have produced efforts of which they are not proud. However, he certainly did not destroy much of his earlier vernacular writing.

63. Lydian shepherd: Paris, cf. line 47. Here the erotic implications are impishly expanded.

67. Minciades is Vergil, Silvanus Petrarch. The Mincius is the river of Vergil's native Mantua. Silvanus is Petrarch's pastoral name for himself.

67-68. The Vaucluse near the head of the Sorge was Petrarch's favorite residence.

71-72. The song contest between Vergil and Petrarch may refer to the composition of either eclogues or epics, since Petrarch vied with Vergil in both forms. The pastoral verse seems more appropriate here as an inspiration to Aristeus. On the other hand, the loftiness of their poetry may imply epic as well. In any case, Aristeus learns from them about the possibility of a truly lofty poetry.

93. grove: see note to line 3; fountain: Boccaccio explains in *Genealogia* 11.2 that the Muses' fountain "not only delights the eyes of the beholder but also by a certain hidden power draws his mind into meditation and instills a desire to compose."

97-98. See introductory note about Caliope.

100. Nysa: according to Boccaccio's *De montibus* it is the other peak of Mt. Parnassus. *Genealogia* 1.4 not only credits Pan with being the inventor of musical pipes but also interprets his name and body as a symbol for created nature ("natura naturatam") or the universal body of nature, whose pipes signify the celestial harmony of the spheres. Boccaccio further cites Macrobius that Pan is the sun (regulating the planets represented by his pipes) and hence "the father of all mortal life." His love for Syrinx too is glossed as a love for the harmony of the spheres. Thus he can well represent the source of that lofty poetry of wisdom to which Aristeus/Boccaccio aspires.

101. gorgonean spring: the Hippocrene spring struck forth by the hoof of Pegasus, who in turn was born from the blood of the Medusa or Gorgon. Both Pegasus and the spring are sacred to the Muses.

110. Plutarcus' gardens: the underworld.

113. Phorcinides: daughters of the sea-god Phorcus.

117. There is almost a pun on "complectitur" and "plectro".

118. The green book within which all these divine secrets are contained seems to be nature itself, seen as a work of harmonious art. There is a merging of metaphors here of the audible (music) and the visible (book); the visible world contains harmonies which can be heard not by the ear but

by the mind or soul.

119-20. The reference to asses' ears suggests Midas' poor judgment in music. The phrase "auritos asinos" is also a borrowing from Ovid's *Amores* 2.7.15 ("auritus asellus"), in which the poet claims he is being unjustly accused of having an affair with his mistress's slave, only to admit in the following poem that it is true. Like Midas the Ovidian speaker has chosen a less worthy object of love, and like Aristeus he is rebuked for his vulgar love.

125. Chiron: the centaur, a winter constellation, hence winter.

129. a famous shepherd: Socrates.

130-31. Scipio Africanus. These two examples demonstrate the truths which Caliope has just expressed and is about to reiterate: that the worthiest are not appreciated by the mob, and that familiarity breeds contempt.

138-145. These lines recapitulate traditional accusations; cf. Boccaccio's refutations of such objections in the fourteenth book of his *Genealogia*.

157-64. Caliope lists the detractors of poetry. 157-59: perhaps merchants. 159-61: medical doctors; cf. Petrarch's *Invectivum contra medicum*, a defense of poetry against one such detractor.

162-4: the clergy.

165-173. The general meaning of Aristeus' reply seems to be that people in different professions are ignorant of each other's work, but also envious that the others may be better off. This envy, sprung from malaise about oneself and total incomprehension of others, is the cause for attacks such as the ones against poetry.

181-85. A less confident response is given in the *De casibus* III, 14, 10-11: "I wish to be and take great pains that I may be a poet. Whether I will arrive at the summit only God knows. I think that I do not have sufficient strength for so long a climb when along the way many passes, and cliffs almost insurmountable intervene. However, many ignorant persons have the opinion that the summit of poetry can be reached very easily" (trans. Louis Brewer Hall, *The Fates of Illustrious Men*, New York, Frederick Ungar, 1965, p.106).

184. Lycaeus: mountain in Arcadia where Pan is said to have been born.

188. Lidonnici (p.338) identifies Arpinas as Cicero, who tried in vain to write poetry; Arpinum was his birthplace. Boccaccio's *Genealogia* 14.7

calls Cicero "a philosopher rather than a poet" and cites Cicero's defense of Archias "that while other arts are matters of science and formula and technique, poetry depends solely upon an inborn faculty, is evoked by purely mental activity, and is infused with a strange supernal inspiration" (trans. Osgood, *Boccaccio on Poetry*, p.41.)

195-96, with 176-80. In the letter to Iacopo Pizzinga (1372) Boccaccio similarly praises Petrarch for ascending Parnassus by a path long overgrown and thus clearing the way for others.

197. Opheltis: Lucan, whose Pharsalia describes the civil war between Caesar and Pompey. Boccaccio rates him beneath Vergil and Petrarch.

201-02. It is typical of Boccaccio to end by poking fun at himself as someone earnest but naive and woefully outclassed by those whom he wishes to join.

XIII The Laurel Wreath

Boccaccio writes that he named this eclogue for "the laurel wreath, which is the mark of poets, and for this reason: because it speaks especially about the honor-bringing of the art of poetry. There are three speakers: Daphnis, Stilbon, and Critis. By Daphnis I mean any distinguished poet, since poets are honored with that crown, i.e. laurel, with which conquerors and triumphant emperors used to be honored; and they were the first shepherds, as was Daphnis... Stilbon represents a certain Genoan merchant with whom I long ago had an argument in Genoa, a city to which I refer several times in this eclogue; I call him Stilbon after Mercury, the god of merchants, who is also called Stilbon. "Critis" in Greek is "judge" in Latin, and he represents someone taken on as judge of the aforesaid argument." Hortis (*Studi*, pp.55-56) and Lidonnici (p.298) agree that the argument must have taken place in 1365 when Boccaccio passed through Genoa on his way to Avignon on official business from Florence. The original Genoan merchant has not been identified, but his particular identification is not important; he serves as a foil for Boccaccio's defense of the literary career, just as the medical doctor did for Petrarch's *Invectivum contra medicum* (begun in 1352). One can see in these debates between poets and merchants or doctors the Renaissance version of the old debate poems between clerics and soldiers; the issue is still the conflict between the intellectual class and the class socially and materially in power. Thus the contrast in lines 81-82 between the laurel and the oak is one between poetry and power.

Carrara (*Poesia pastorale*, pp.123-4), Grant (*Neo-Latin*, p.105), and

Bergin (*Boccaccio*, p.264) have pointed out the close resemblance between this eclogue's song contest and that in Vergil's eclogue 3: both are hostile – using a song contest as a substitution for an argument, and both use alternate quatrains. Carrara links Boccaccio's eclogues 12 and 13 as a pair modeled intentionally after eclogues by Petrarch and by Vergil, the two masters named in 12. Certainly 13 does continue the topic of 12: the celebration of poetry and its separation from the vulgar crowd. The role of Crisis, moreover, connects it forward to eclogue 15.

1-4. Suggestive of the opening of Vergil's Eclogue 1.

Lidonnici (p.263) notes the parallel between Daphnis' surprise that the once-active Stilbon is now at leisure, and Stilbon's surprise that the usually sedentary Daphnis is now wandering about.

14. Cf.12.60-61.

20. Boccaccio's *De fontibus* tells us that the Gargaphia, in Boeotia, is a spring sacred to Diana and Hecate. Surely it represents some region of Italy, perhaps near Naples or perhaps the Elsa valley by Certaldo (see following note).

23. Elpis: Hortis (p.72) observes that Boccaccio appended a note in the margin of the autograph manuscript identifying Elpis as the Greek word for "hope". This would identify her also with Fiammetta, whom Boccaccio used to sing about both at Naples and in Tuscany. Fiammetta is most clearly identified with hope in the pastoral *Comedia delle ninfe fiorentine*.

24-26. Hope is known to both merchant and poet, but they are different hopes. Crisis represents wealth, her name being derived from the Greek word for gold, cf. 3.127 and 15.23ff. The nymphs of Nysa are the Muses.

27. blind love ("cecus amor"): the merchant's condemnation of the poet's love for impoverished muses is couched ironically in the phrase used by Vergil to denounce Pygmalion's muderous greed for money: "auri caecus amore" (*Aeneid* 1.349).

33. Theban Tytirus is Vergil, whose native Mantua was founded by the daughter of the Theban Tiresias. Vergil is called Tytirus also in 10.66-67, and the Tytirus of Vergil's first eclogue was frequently identified with the poet. The shepherds and bulls are the Trojans and Italians at war in the *Aeneid*.

36. Thalian waters: the muses' fountain.

45-46. Midas turned everything he touched to gold but was therefore unable to eat; Crassus, who fought against the Parthians, had molten gold poured down his throat because of his greed as governor. Cf. Dante's *Purgatorio* 20.116-17, where the avaricious call out: "Crasso,/dicci, chè il sai, di che sapore è l'oro?" (Crassus, tell us, for you know it, how does gold taste?) Boccaccio's *Amorosa Visione* 13.5-12 places Midas and Crassus side by side in the Triumph of Riches.

58. Ligurian: from Genoa.

83-90. Stilbon sings of his love for wealth; Daphnis for Saphos, the figure of lofty poetry from eclogue 12. Note the contrast between the ephemeral leaves on which wealth sets her mark and the lasting monuments of poetry.

91. Proteus tended Poseidon's flocks of seacows. Vergil sets his residence on the island of Carpathos, between Crete and Rhodes. Cyrnus is Corsica.

95. Maenalus is a mountain in Arcadia, favored resort of Pan. It is associated with song as is Arcadia generally: cf. lines 61-62 and Vergil's Eclogue 10.31-33, which also mention Pan. The mountains of the poets are contrasted to the valleys of the merchants; cf. the debate eclogue in *Comedia delle ninfe fiorentine* 14.

98. The great rewards of poetry are to be set against the collected wealth of Stilbon's previous fourth line.

99-102. Thalasson is named from the Greek word for ocean. The merchant's mastery over the ocean creatures symbolizes successful commerce.

107. Massican: in Campania. Garganian: in Apulia.

111-14. The poet's song is associated with the tapestry woven by Pallas in competition against Arachne (see Ovid's *Metamorphoses* 6.1ff.); it celebrated the power of the gods. Boccaccio mentions both religious and historical topics, both of which are treated in his own previous eclogues. He omits amatory topics because he is setting forth only the loftiest and most serious poetry in response to the merchant's scorn. Arachne's tapestry, in contrast to Pallas's, had depicted the gods' erotic adventures.

119, 122. The lasting quality of art as opposed to wealth is again emphasized, cf. lines 89-90.

123-26. A series of inappropriate offerings match the apparent absurdity of poetry's victory over business. Mopsus, usually a reference to Petrarch, might stand for any great poet. Cf. line 130. Although Lidonnici (p.339) suggests that Amiclas means poverty, I find this doubtful. Vergil in *Aeneid* 10.563-4 mentions a Latian people called "the silent Amyclae," ruled by the richest man in all Ausonia. The combination of wealth and silence is obviously Boccaccio's point with regard to the merchants.

130. Daphnis boasts that not only can the great Mopsus beat Amiclas, but even the lowly Bavius can best him. If Mopsus stands for Petrarch, the lowly Bavius is probably Boccaccio himself, in his usual posture of humility towards his admired friend.

133. Aeolus and Palaemon: ruler of the winds and seagod.

139-42. Although usually Daphnis' verses respond to Stilbon's, here Stilbon replies to the previous lines about shipwreck by describing the destruction of supposedly immortal poetry by war and fire.

143-44. Lidonnici (pp.144-45) identifies Amintas as Pompey, conqueror of the pirate stronghold Coracesium in Cilicia; this victory is mentioned also in eclogue 9.71-72. The ancient town would be analogous to Genoa as a powerful seaport.

145-6. The serpent is the insignia of the Visconti of Milan who will conquer the Genoans, referred to rather unkindly as goats rather than sheep or cows. Genoa's struggle with the Visconti, underway in 1363, was ended in 1367 when the Genoans agreed to pay a large yearly sum to the Visconti. If these lines were written in 1365, as suggested above, Boccaccio is predicting in mid-struggle that the Visconti will have the upper hand. It is also possible, of course, that the lines of "prophecy" were added later, just as the lines about the emperor's second descent into Italy in eclogue 9.185-92.

XIV Olympia

Boccaccio's letter interprets "olympos" as "splendid or full of light" and hence as the Greek name for heaven, suitable to an eclogue which "discusses at length the quality of the heavenly region." "By Silvius I mean myself, whom I name thus because I first had the idea for this eclogue while in a certain forest. 'Camalos' in Greek is 'lazy' or 'sluggish' in Latin, because in him are demonstrated the manners of a lazy servant. I cannot tell you the meaning of 'Terapon' because I don't remember it, unless I look again at the book from which I took it, and so forgive me: you know that human memory is fallible, and especially that of old men. By Olympia I mean my little daughter who died at an age in which we believe the dying become citizens of heaven; and therefore I have changed her name from Violante, as it was while she was alive, to 'heavenly' or 'Olympia.' " In a letter to Petrarch in 1367, Boccaccio mentions that his daughter had died at the age of five and a half. It is not known for certain in what year she died; Ricci (Boccaccio, *Opere*, p.675) suggests 1355 while Boccaccio was presumably again in Naples (cf. lines 51-54). However, the eclogue was probably written at least a few years later. Therapon is a Greek word meaning servant.

Although Boccaccio claims that he named himself Silvius simply because he thought up this poem while in the woods, nonetheless it is worth noting the resemblance to Petrarch's pastoral name for himself in his first eclogue. Petrarch's accompanying letter (X,4) claims similarly that he chose the name Silvius because of his love for the woodland retreat; yet the eclogue clearly sets the forest-dweller against the holy monk as an earthly against a heavenly orientation. In Boccaccio's poem too, the dialogue is clearly between an earthly and a heavenly perspective, and the pair of names indicates that difference. Possibly both Petrarch and Boccaccio were inspired by the lines from Dante's *Purgatorio* 32.100-02, in which Beatrice says to Dante:

"Qui sarai tu poco tempo silvano;
e sarai meco sanza fine cive
di quella Roma onde Cristo è romano."

(Here you will be for a little while forester; and you will be with me endlessly a citizen of that Rome of which Christ is a Roman.) The forest in the eclogues becomes the world of temporary things, counterposed to the eternal.

One of the most startling and novel features of this eclogue is its setting at night, so that the eclogue ends not with the usual evening but, in reverse, with the coming of dawn. The nighttime setting makes this scene suggestive of an annunciation to the shepherds. For despite his identification with Boccaccio, Silvius seems to represent someone who has only vaguely heard about heaven and needs instruction in the basic doctrines of salvation. Night and forest combine to represent the world without divine light.

Another novelty of Boccaccio's treatment is that the mediating female has been changed from beloved, as for Dante and Petrarch, to a very young daughter, thus eliminating the erotic desire so prevalent in those other poets and replacing it with a truly touching paternal affection.

The poem can be compared to Petrarch's 11, in which the death of the beloved is lamented by Niobe and Fusca (dark), who are comforted by a personification of religion named Fulgentia, a name similar in meaning to Boccaccio's "olympos." Niobe too is a parental figure, but lacks the human reality of Boccaccio's self projection. In any case, the "Olympia" draws much more heavily from Dante than from Petrarch, and especially from Dante's descriptions of the Earthly Paradise. Boccaccio, still trying to fit this matter into the pastoral mode, clearly prefers the fields and forests of the Earthly Paradise to the more abstract patterns of light in Dante's heavenly paradise.

XIV Olympia

8-22. The introductory theme of the willing and reluctant servants can be read as a parable outlining Silvius' options as a servant of God. The blind desire for present comforts makes man reluctant to attend to divine commands and even to divine messages of hope. In a more literal mode the servants provide, along with the opening description of the dog, a comic and familiar beginning which sets off the lofty magnificence and strangeness of the heavenly vision.

12. I.e. when stars rise in the west.

13. Delia: the moon-goddess; her brother: Apollo, the sun god.

16-17. Sabaea: famous Arabian source of perfumes.

33-39. The bright light suddenly illuminating the forest, the expression of curiosity about it, and the accompanying music, all reflect the signs at the approach of the divine pageant in *Purgatorio* 29.16-23. This and other echoes of *Purgatorio* 29 in the "Olympia" have been pointed out by Ricci (pp.686-88) and Labagnara (*Il poema*, pp.96-100).

51. Fusca: the name means dark, as indicative of one in mourning; it refers no doubt to Violante's mother, who Ricci (p.674) suggests was Bruna di Ciango da Montemagno. The name Bruna, meaning dark-haired, would thus be included in the punning name Fusca.

53. Cybele's lap: the earth.

65. Berecynthian mother: Cybele, from her birthplace. Cf. 11.9.

78-85. The classical forms of celebration are contrasted to the Christian song which follows, enlarging the theme from Boccaccio's personal consolation and salvation to the world's.

91. Codrus: Christ; cf. 11.169 and 225. The four stanzas refer, quite clearly, to Christ's birth and death, his redemption of mankind, the harrowing of hell, and the final judgment. Note the use of a refrain, as in Eclogue 6 and Vergil's Eclogue 8; neither Dante nor Petrarch made use of this Vergilian feature, but cf. John of Garland's bucolic example in the *Parisiana Poetria*, pp.24-27.

116. The Thracian poet: Orpheus.

120. Caliope: muse, especially of epic poetry. The god: Apollo.

125-26. Tytirus: Vergil. Mopsus: Homer. Cf. 10.65-66.

153. Cf. John 16:16-20.

160. The Mincian: Vergil, from the river Mincio that runs through

his homeland. His description of Elysium occurs in the sixth book of the *Aeneid*. Silvius' question is reminiscent of *Purgatorio* 28.139-41:

Quelli ch'anticamente poetaro
l'età de l'oro e suo stato felice,
forse in Parnaso esto loco sognaro.

(Those who in ancient times wrote poetry about the golden age and its happy state, perhaps on Parnassus dreamed of this place.)

170-80, 190-92. This description is inspired by Dante's of the Earthly Paradise in *Purgatorio* 28.1-33, 97-102.

201. Archesilas: God, from the Greek word for ruler; cf. 10.151.

205-7. The lamb of God is, of course, Christ, who feeds and restores the blessed through the communion. This eclogue includes Christ both as shepherd (97-109) and as sheep, traditional images befitting the pastoral mode.

213-26. The streaming light and various ranks of heaven, distinguished by color of robe and flowery crown, reflect the description of the streaming candelabra and its following procession in Dante's Earthly Paradise, *Purgatorio* 29. (See also Revelations 21:23 for the Lamb as a source of light.) But whereas Dante's figures represent books of the Bible and the virtues, Boccaccio's represent the souls of humans in various categories. The satyrs, described as old, may be the Old Testament prophets and writers. The men in crimson are apostles and martyrs who were persecuted for spreading the word of God. Their crimson robes indicate their sufferings; the laurel crowns signify their hard-won immortality and their ultimate victory over earthly persecutors. The white group seem to represent those who died young and innocent, or perhaps the virginal; the white of both garment and lilies indicates their purity. The yellow group seems to represent all the other blessed. For similar categories and colors, see eclogue 11.220-21.

225. Asylas: Boccaccio's own father. Boccaccio had written about him considerably more critically in the *Amorosa Visione* 14.34-45, where the father is depicted clawing ineffectively at the mountain of coins and jewels in the triumph of Riches; that image may have resulted from an ironic combination of the recent bank failures in Florence and the father's persistent attempts to channel Boccaccio away from an impoverished life of scholarship and poetry into a career, like his own banking business, that would make some money. Nonetheless, even there, Boccaccio, an illegitimate child, gratefully identifies him as "he who had freely and gladly nourished me as his son." By the time of this eclogue, Boccaccio has apparently come to

appreciate his father's seeming opposition as an effect of paternal love, or perhaps has allowed the tender feelings of his own fatherhood to overflow towards his parent as well as towards his child.

231-34. Boccaccio's father apparently accepted his own illegitimate son's illegitimate children with a love not diminshed by social distinctions.

235. Asylas greets Olympia's entrance to heaven with the same words that greet the arrival of Beatrice in Dante's pageant, *Purgatorio* 30.11; the phrase comes from the Song of Solomon 4.8.

250. Daughter of her son: cf. *Paradiso* 33.1.

260. Swans: *Genealogia* 3.22 refers to swans as being sweet singers and as signifying "lauticam muliebrem" or womanly splendor.

263-65. Cf. *Purgatorio* 28.40-42: Matelda singing and gathering flowers.

275-77: The traditional acts of charity.

285. The Christian sun shines forth dispersing the night shadows with which Vergil ends his first and last eclogues –and *Aeneid* as well. This line and Silvius' response to Olympia's hymn (112 ff.) together suggest the supremacy of Christian over classical poetry, reversing the arguments of Petrarch's first eclogue. Possibly it was not by chance that Boccaccio expressed this overgoing of the Vergilian eclogue in a poem drawing heavily from *Purgatorio* 28-30, where Dante's Vergil vanishes to be replaced by Beatrice.

XV Phylostropos

Boccaccio writes: "The fifteenth eclogue is called Phylostropos because it treats of a calling back from the enticing love of earthly things to the love of heavenly ones; for Phylostropos is derived from 'phylos,' which is 'love,' and 'tropos,' which is 'conversion'. There are two speakers, Phylostropos and Typhlus. By Phylostropos I mean my glorious teacher Francesco Petrarca, by whose admonitions I have often been persuaded to abandon delight in temporal things and direct my mind to eternal ones, and thus he turned my loves, even if not completely, yet considerably towards the better. Typhlus I want to be understood as myself and anyone else clouded by the mist mortal things, since 'typhlus' in Greek means 'blind' in Latin." Thus Boccaccio in his last two eclogues before the envoy, but especially in this one, presents himself as a representative of Everyman, a role well known from Dante's *Commedia* but not apparent in the bucolics of Vergil or Petrarch.

The structure and content of the poem are partially close to Petrarch's ninth eclogue, a dialogue between Philogeus (Earth lover) and Theophilus (God-lover). Theophilus calls Philogeus "blind" (line 84), describes the labors and troubles of the farmer, and condemns the dangerous desire for possessions. For Petrarch, however, it is the plague that sets the context for this discussion. Philogeus, lamenting worldly loss and death, immediately accepts Theophilus's suggestion to seek true safety on high; there is no real opposition between the two figures, both of whom "speak for Petrarch," as Bergin has noted (*Petrarch's Bucolicum*, p.235). From the start Philogeus is already complaining of life's harshness and instability, whereas Boccaccio's Typhlus must be taught with difficulty to see that he is not as well of as he believes.

Writing at a farther remove from the plague, Boccaccio drew instead on the traditional debate between winter and spring, moralizing the seasons to make winter represent sin and death, and combining this structure perhaps with the winter motif of Vergil's final eclogue. The movement from winter to eternal spring in the "Phylostropos" parallels the movement from night to dawn in the preceeding eclogue, and the themes of both are very similar. In 14 the Boccaccio-Everyman figure must be consoled for earthly sorrows by the promise of heavenly recompense; in 15 he must be warned away from earthly joys by the peril of damnation and the promise of God's mercy.

Vergil's tenth eclogue is a source not only for the winter theme coming appropriately at the end of a sequence but also for the celebration of the author's friendship with another poet. In Vergil's 10, Vergil himself describes fondly but critically the amorous obsession of his friend Gallus; Boccaccio humbly puts himself in the position of the one at fault, and gives his friend Petrarch the role of critic and advisor. This was not the first time that Boccaccio had put Petrarch in that position. At the beginning of Book 8 of the *De Casibus* Boccaccio describes how, when he was feeling sluggish and reluctant to keep working, a vision of Petrarch appeared to him and admonished him to greater efforts for both Fame and God.

We are readier to believe Boccaccio's temptation to sins of concupiscence than to those of greed. Nonetheless, his letter to Zanobi, "Longum tempus effluxit," describes the shamefully recurring allure of a profitable career: "comfortably enough, in my judgment, I had accorded myself with Seneca in moderate poverty; but recently the thin whistle of more jocund fortune suddenly shattered my resolve and drove me back into the former snares from which I had already been freed,..." Petrarch at the end of his letter *Seniles* I.5 gently chides Boccaccio for frequently complaining about his financial straits.

Petrarch did in fact address several moralizing letters to Boccaccio in his later years, when Petrarch tended to be writing more about faith and salvation. Hortis (*Studi*, p.61) and Fracassetti (Petrarch's *Lettere senili*, vol.I, p.52) both associate this eclogue with Petrarch's *Seniles* I.5 (1362), his response to the warnings of Pietro Petroni that death was imminent and that literary studies ought to be abandoned as evil. Petrarch's advice that one should always be mindful of one's mortality and his defense of learning as an aid rather than an impediment to salvation do seem fitting to the speeches and citations of Phylostropos in this eclogue. However, the issue may well have reinforced Boccaccio's decision to turn the forms of classical poetry to explicitly Christian use and to follow Dante as a prime example of how literature can be made conducive to salvation.

Dante certainly provides another source for the poem. For example, the persuasion that the ascent will get easier as one climbs comes from Vergil's exhortation to Dante at the bottom of Mount Purgatory (4.88-90). From the same canto comes the encouragement of the guide going first (23, 29). This poem is the third of what Carrara called Boccaccio's "bucolic otherworld" poems (*Poesia*, pp.128-29). Inverting Dante's order, Boccaccio follows the description of Paradise (Eclogue 14) with a description of the difficulties and urgency of a purgatorial ascent from fallible to lasting joys. Just as the *Amorosa Visione* ended with the narrator at the beginning of such an ascent, so too the eclogue sequence offers this as its final image before the dedicatory envoy.

1. wreaths and nymphs: poetic ambition as well as erotic pursuits are criticized as temporal rather than eternal concerns. Cf. lines 23-24: the laureled Penean shores are part of Crisis's treacherous promise.

8-10. Hyacinth: killed accidentally by Apollo during a game of quoits (Ovid, *Metamorphoses* 10.162ff.). Ciparissus: turned by grief into a cypress while a youth (*Metamorphoses* 10.106ff.). Adonis: killed in youth by a boar (*Metamorphoses* 10.708ff.). The Calydonian master of the boar: Meleager, whose mother caused his death shortly after he killed the famous boar *(Metamorphoses* 8.26ff.).

23-24. Crisis: wealth, from the Greek word for gold. Cf.3.127 and note. Boccaccio's letter to Petrarch "Ut huic epistola" (1353) accuses Petrarch of allowing himself to be seduced by Crisis in going to work for the dreaded Visconti. The Hesperidean apples were golden. Ticinus: a river in the Alps with golden sands, according to Boccaccio's *De fluminibus*. Peneus: thanks to the myth of Daphne, Boccaccio's *De fluminibus* describes its shores as abundant with laurels; thus dreams of poetic success are mingled with dreams of wealth.

25. Dyone: concupiscence, from the name of Venus's mother and thus also sometimes of Venus. Cf. Dioneo in the *Decameron*.

28. Daphnis: Caesar, as in Vergil's Eclogue 5; Argus: here Alexis rather than King Robert. Both are examples of sudden death by murder.

68-70. Crassus: Pactolus's golden sands are proverbial, so that Crassus's gilding of them demonstrates his inordinate wealth. Bull's blood signifies gold, which Crassus was forced to drink at his death, because of the veins of gold in Mt. Taurus, as Lidonnici explains (p.342).

71-73. Thymbrians and Argolians are Trojans and Greeks. Perhaps Boccaccio also had in mind the murder of Polydorus by the king of Thrace when Polydorus came to him with Priam's treasures for safekeeping; this scene at the beginning of *Aeneid* 3 contains the much quoted phrase: "quid non mortalia pectora cogis, auri sacra fames!" (To what do you not drive the hearts of men, accursed hunger for gold!)

74-79. Cyrus, ruler of Persia, was killed by Tomyris, Queen of the Massegetae (the sow), who submerged his cut-off head in a bucket of blood and threw his corpse to the birds of prey.

80-82. Mithridates, called Pharsalicus because he was defeated by Pompey, hero of the *Pharsalia*. Betrayed by his own son, he poisoned himself. The deceit may refer either to his son or to the poison which, because he had accustomed himself to toxic draughts, took effect with terrible slowness.

83-89. Lidonnici (p.342) suggests that Dametas refers to Zanobi, who left Italy to work for the papal curia in Avignon and died soon thereafter of the plague. Pan had been used to represent the pope in Boccaccio's "Ut huic epistola" letter to Petrarch and also in Petrarch's Eclogue 12. Cybele certainly indicates death, cf. 14.53 and 65. Boccaccio was scornful of Zanobi's choice to pursue a well-paying job rather than devote himself to scholarly study and literature. In his letter to Iacopo Pizzinghe, Boccaccio described Zanobi's career: "drawn by the lust for money he went away to western Babylon [Avignon] and fell silent." Thus the pursuit of wealth is perilous to literary activity as well as to salvation. However, the lines may refer to someone else dying destitute in exile.

90-91. Petrarch too received offers of lucrative positions, including in 1361 or 1362 a post as apostolic secretary which, unlike Zanobi, he refused (*Seniles* 1.4). See also above, note to lines 23-24, in re Petrarch's seduction by Crisis.

103. Scylla, in love with her father Nisus's enemy, pulled out the hair on which her father's life depended; the conquering beloved, however, was so horrified by her patricide that he had her drowned. (*Metamorphoses* 8.6ff.)

104. Pasiphae, in love with a bull, became mother of the Minotaur. Vergil's Eclogue 6 treats her story at some length (45-60).

104-05. Myrrha, in love with her own father, found a way to sleep with him without being identified (*Metamorphoses* 10.208ff.)

105-06. Phasis: the river of Colchis, where the golden fleece hung till Jason stole it. It is not clear why Boccaccio calls the fleece Dircean or Theban; possibly the episode of Jason's sowing serpent teeth which turned into armed men associated it for Boccaccio with the founding of Thebes, which includes a similar episode.

106-07. Mt. Ida stands for Troy, burned because of Paris's abduction of Helen. Mopsus is the blinded Samson of the Old Testament. Circe was frequently interpreted allegorically as the lust which turns men into beasts until vanquished by reason. *De casibus* 1.18.14 and 17 similarly list the blinding of Samson along with the fall of Troy, the disgraceful feminization of Hercules, and the transformations of men by Circe as examples of the dire effects of lust.

108. Alcides, i.e. Hercules, set aside his club and donned woman's attire to spin for his beloved Omphale.

122. Alcidamas: perhaps Alcides. Both he and Osyris continued to exist as gods after their deaths.

128. Hecker (*Boccaccio-funde*, p.72) observes that Boccaccio glossed these Greek names himself: "Trinos [threnos] grece luctum, Penos grece dolor et labor, Thlipsis grece mestitia, Lipis grece anxietas." The name Trini thus means grief or mourning, Peni pain and suffering, Thlipsis sorrow or affliction, and Lipis anxiety.

132. Epy: Epicurus. Cf. Petrarch's eclogue 7, where the name is used for the corrupt pope's concubine, the worldly values to which he is bound in unholy alliance. Epicurus denied the existence of an immortal soul, maintaining that the mind died along with the body.

135-36. Ariston: Plato, son of Ariston. Samos's shepherd: Pythagoras. The farmboys: various Roman writers, including Cicero and Vergil.

142. Typhoeus was a giant who, having rebelled against Zeus, was buried beneath Mt. Etna. Obviously to a Christian he is analogous to Satan.

148. Amon: the Ram, i.e. springtime; Orion: a winter constellation.

152. Chiron: Sagittarius, a winter zodiac sign, astrological home of Saturn, the bringer of disease and death.

153. A nymph and stream near Syracuse, incidentally the original home of pastoral poetry.

158. Theoschyrus: from the Greek *theos kouros*, the son of God.

159. The water which Moses struck from a rock with his staff in the desert was considered an event analogous to or fulfilled by the blood from Christ's side where he was struck by a lance.

161-63. For the wasteland made to flourish cf. *Isaiah* 51.3. Boccaccio's *Comedia delle ninfe fiorentine* 14.49-51 and 109-11 contrasts in a pastoral dialogue the nourishing grasses sprung from mountain rock with the rich-seeming lowland grasses that have kept the sheep hungry and empty.

166-67. Cf. 10.143. Lidonnici (p.276) rejects Carrara's suggestion that the line refers to Boccaccio's seducing a nun ("Un peccato del Boccaccio," *Giornale Storico di Letteratura Italiana* 36, p.123); it seems rather to be a general indication of wrongdoing.

169. Cf. pearls before swine.

176. Glaucus: Peter, as in eclogue 11. Amintas: Paul, cf. 11.10. Both sinned against Christ but were forgiven.

200. Pales: possibly the Virgin Mary, as in 6.47 and 8.192; but in 11.192 it stands for Christ. The Roman deity of herds and shepherds was of either sex.

204-05. Cf. Boethius's *Consolation of Philosophy*, 3.5m.1-4 and 3.10m.1-4.

XVI The Messenger

Boccaccio writes: "The sixteenth and last eclogue is entitled Aggelos, as announcer and leader of the preceeding ones and as the one that offers them to the friend to whom I sent them; for 'aggelos' in Greek is what we in Latin call 'messenger.' There are two speakers: Appenninus and Angelus. By Appenninus I mean my friend to whom I am sending them, whom I call 'Appenninus' because he was born and raised at the foot of the Appennine mountains. By Angelus, as I said, I mean the eclogue itself leading and speaking as a messenger."

The friend is Donato degli Albanzani (c.1326-c.1411), a grammarian and humanist, the younger friend of both Boccaccio and Petrarch, and author of the first commentary on Petrarch's *Bucolicum carmen*. Petrarch dedicated to him his "De ipsius ignorantia," and Donato became the godfather of Petrarch's grandson. Near the end of *Seniles* 3.1 Petrarch describes him as "sweet, genuine, and affectionate." In the *Genealogia* 15.13, Boccaccio notes that he was not in the habit of dedicating his works to kings or indeed to anyone, but that the dedication of the eclogues had been requested by Donato, "a poor but upright man, and my particular friend." After the death of Petrarch and Boccaccio, Donato was invited to the Este court as tutor to the young prince Niccola III, who upon his ascension to power made Donato his chancellor. It is for this court that Donato translated into Italian Boccaccio's *De mulieribus claris* and Petrarch's *De viris illustribus*. The humanist chancellor Salutati referred to Donato as one of the most distinguished men of his time.

1-4. The opening lines are obviously ironic. The first line echoes that of Vergil's third eclogue.

5-9. Given Donatus' poverty, these lines are perhaps ironic as well, and thus a fitting reply. However, Ricci suggests (*Opere*, 612) that the reference, not ironic, is to Donato's poetry, none of which seems to have survived.

11. Thrice five ewes: the fifteen previous eclogues.

13-14. As the poems are a flock, the bushes, springs, and berries indicate a place that welcomes literary efforts.

18. Cerretius: Boccaccio, who names himself after his hometown Certaldo. Cf. *Filocolo* 5.42, where the site is identified by a "cerreto" or oak grove and by the Elsa. The old Etruscan is again Boccaccio.

20-24. These lines review the occasions when Boccaccio and Donato were in the same place and could see each other: in Casentino (near Florence) at Donato's home; in Ravenna; and in Venice in 1363 while Boccaccio was visiting Petrarch. Donato was teaching in Ravenna from 1351-56, and Boccaccio spent several months there in 1353 at the court of the local ruler; thus Torraca (*Per la biografia*, pp.186-90) dates the eclogue reference to that time. Donatus moved to Venice in 1356.

26. Silvanus: Petrarch would be better able to emend these verses.

30. Pales: the Virgin Mary, cf. 15.200 and note.

46. Rossi ("Boccaccio autore," p.47) notes the contrast between Boccaccio's sheep and the milk-rich one of Dante's first eclogue (58-59: "ovis

gratissima..lactis abundans") or Vergil's sheep with swollen udders (eclogue 4.21-2). Vergil's line does not particularly refer to poetry, but Dante's does allude to his own *Commedia*; thus Boccaccio is once again self-denigrating in comparing himself with Dante. It may astonish modern readers that Boccaccio could describe his eclogues as thin in meaning but pleasurable.

47-49. Clearly Menalcas refers to another writer whom Boccaccio considered inferior. Zanobi has been suggested.

53-54. Boccaccio plays on the words "salices" (willows) and "silices" (rocks).

55. Seashells: cf. the description of Certaldo in *Filocolo* 5.8.

60-62. A request for corrections from both Donatus and Petrarch.

66. Dyone: erotic passion, cf. 15.25 and passim.

68. Galathea: probably a general rather than specific allusion to early loves. Cf also Vergil's Eclogue 1.30-35; the preceding lines are imitated later in this poem (see 138 and note).

71. Cf. Vergil's Eclogue 10.2 where Lycoris is the name of the faithless beloved.

75. Cf. Vergil's Eclogue 8.63: "non omnia possumus omnes" (we can't all do everything).

76-78. Petrarch did indeed invite Boccaccio several times to stay with him; see *Seniles* 1.5 and 3.1. Boccaccio had in Dante's eclogue to Giovanni del Virgilio a literary precedent for an eclogue about the refusal of an invitation.

79-81. Petrarch's own income is assured by benefices in four places: Parma, Teano in Campania (Anser was a poet, contemporary with Vergil, who was given a villa in that region), Monselice in the Euganean hills (the most profitable of the four), and Padua.

82-83. The Sicilian leader is King Robert; the Cyprian is Pietro di Lusignano, King of Cyprus.

85. dirty waters: at Venice.

93-95. Boccaccio lacks external goods, but has been endowed with internal talents.

97-100. Egon is probably the pope; cf. 9.141. Boccaccio refers to turning down a job as papal secretary because it would interfere with his other, more important studies and writings. Ricci (*Opere*, 699) suggests that "maiora" refers to the *Genealogia*. Since Boccaccio visited the papal court in 1365, Lidonnici infers that this poem dates from about 1366; cf. 145 note. Boccaccio also turned down offers from Niccolo Orsini, Hugo di Sanseverino, and King James of Maiorca. His letter of reply to Orsini (1371) is similar in sentiment to this poem: (Corazzini p.320): "for my old age accustomed to liberty does not allow me now to take on a yoke. A little patch of land is my home, but with slender victuals it suffices me."

108. Midas: Niccola Acciaiuoli; cf. eclogue 8.

113. Stilbon: Mainardo de' Cavalcanti, an old friend to whom Boccaccio later dedicated the *De casibus virorum illustrium*, which had originally been intended for either King Louis or Niccola Acciaiuoli.

125-27. Arcas was king of Arcady, and Maenalian means Arcadian; but I cannot identify the allusion.

132. Pan: God.

138. Cf. Vergil's Eclogue 1.27. The Boccaccio figure, still struggling against his bonds in Eclogue 15, is now at liberty –including from Dyone and, one infers, from Crisis. Moreover, the final eclogue fulfills the ideal expressed but unaccomplished in Eclogue 1.8-10.

132-39. Boccaccio's letters to Petrarch ("Ut huic epistola") and to Zanobi ("Longum tempus effluxit") both declare his choice of poverty with liberty over money with service to some lord. The letter to Petrarch, expressing outrage at Petrarch's acceptance of patronage from the Visconti (1353), is couched in pastoral language with some of the same names as in the eclogues: Pan, Silvanus, Egon, Crisis, etc. Similarly pastoral is a passage from *De casibus* 1.16.7-8 in praise of poverty and the intellectual life: "Oh, how beautiful and sacred a thing it is to engage in simple tasks with you [poverty]; to love the country; to honor solitude; putting aside abundance to contemplate ideas celestial under the trees by the silvery streams. Let others seek greatness. A small house serves me, secure with you, Diogenes, with the families of Fabricius and Curius" (trans. Hall, pp.37-38).

142. pregnant: either because it contains deeper meanings or because it will encourage others to produce further Latin poetry, especially bucolic poems.

145. Solon: Donato's son, who was so named. His death in 1368 makes it likely that the eclogue was written before then.

The Garland Library of Medieval Literature

Series A (Texts and Translations); Series B (Translations Only)

1. Chrétien de Troyes: *Lancelot*, or *The Knight of the Cart*. Edited and translated by William W. Kibler. Series A.
2. Brunetto Latini: *Il Tesoretto*. Edited and translated by Julia Bolton Holloway. Series A.
3. *The Poetry of Arnaut Daniel*. Edited and translated by James J. Wilhelm. Series A.
4. *The Poetry of William VII, Count of Poitiers, IX Duke of Aquitaine*. Edited and translated by Gerald A. Bond; music edited by Hendrik van der Werf. Series A.
5. *The Poetry of Cercamon and Jaufre Rudel*. Edited and translated by George Wolf and Roy Rosenstein; music edited by Hendrik van der Werf. Series A.
6. *The Vidas of the Troubadours*. Translated by Margarita Egan. Series B.
7. *Medieval Latin Poems of Male Love and Friendship*. Translated by Thomas Stehling. Series A.
8. *Barthar Saga*. Edited and translated by Jon Skaptason and Phillip Pulsiano. Series A.
9. Guillaume de Machaut: *Judgment of the King of Bohemia*. Edited and translated by R. Barton Palmer. Series A.
10. *Three Lives of the Last Englishmen*. Translated by Michael Swanton. Series B.
11. Giovanni Boccaccio: *Eclogues*. Edited and translated by Janet Smarr. Series A.
12. *Les Cent Nouvelles Nouvelles*. Translated by Judith B. Diner. Series B.
13. *Waltharius* and *Ruodlieb*. Edited and translated by Dennis M. Kratz. Series A.
14. *The Writings of Medieval Women*. Translated by Marcelle Thiébaux. Series B.
15. *The Rise of Gawain (De ortu Waluuanii)*. Edited and translated by Mildred Day. Series A.

16, 17. *The French Fabliau:* B.N. 837. Edited and translated by Raymond Eichmann and John DuVal. Series A.
18. *The Poetry of Guido Cavalcanti.* Edited and translated by Lowry Nelson, Jr. Series A.
19. Hartmann von Aue: *Iwein.* Edited and translated by Patrick M. McConeghy. Series A.
20. *Seven Medieval Latin Comedies.* Translated by Alison Goddard Elliott. Series B.
21. Christine de Pizan: *The Epistle of the Prison of Human Life.* Edited and translated by Josette A. Wisman. Series A.
22. *The Poetry of the Sicilian School.* Edited and translated by Frede Jensen. Series A.
23. *The Poetry of Cino da Pistoia.* Edited and translated by Christopher Kleinhenz. Series A.
24. *The Lyrics and Melodies of Adam de la Halle.* Edited and translated by Deborah Nelson; music edited by Hendrik van der Werf. Series A.
25. Chrétien de Troyes. *Erec and Enide.* Edited and translated by Carleton W. Carroll. Series A.
26. *Three Ovidian Tales.* Edited and translated by Raymond J. Cormier. Series A.
27. *The Poetry of Guido Guinizelli.* Edited and translated by Robert Edwards. Series A.
28. *Meier Helmbrecht.* Edited by Ulrich Seelbach; introduced and translated by Linda B. Parshall. Series A.
29. *Pathelin and Other Farces.* Edited and translated by Richard Switzer and Mireille Guillet-Rydell. Series A.
30. Wolfram von Eschenbach: *Titurel.* Edited and translated by Sidney M. Johnson and Marion Gibbs. Series A.
31. Gerald of Wales (Giraldus Cambrensis): *The Life of St. Hugh of Avalon.* Edited and translated by Richard M. Loomis. Series A.
32. *L'Art d'Amours.* Translated by Lawrence Blonquist. Series B.
33. Boccaccio: *Ameto.* Translated by Judith Serafini-Sauli. Series B.
34, 35. *The Medieval Pastourelle.* Selected and edited by William D. Paden, Jr. Series A.
36. Thomas of Britain: *Tristan.* Edited and translated by Valerie Roberts. Series A.
37. *Graelent* and *Guingamor:* Two Breton Lays. Edited and translated by Russell Weingartner. Series A.
38. Heinrich von Veldeke: *Eneit.* Translated by J. W. Thomas. Series B.
39. *The Lyrics and Melodies of Gace Brulé.* Edited and translated by Samuel Rosenberg and Samuel Danon; music edited by Hendrik van der Werf. Series A.

40. Boccaccio: *Life of Dante*. Translated by Vincenzo Bollettino. Series B.
41. *The Lyrics and Melodies of Thibaut de Champagne*. Lyrics edited and translated by Kathleen Brahney; music edited by Donna Mayer-Martin. Series A.
42. *The Poetry of Sordello*. Edited and translated by James J. Wilhelm. Series A.
43. Boccaccio: *Il Filocolo*. Translated by Donald S. Cheney and Thomas G. Bergin. Series B.
44. *Le Roman de Thèbes*. Translated by John Smartt Coley. Series B.
45. Guillaume de Machaut: *The Judgment of the King of Navarre*. Translated and edited by R. Barton Palmer. Series A.
46. *The French Chansons of Charles D'Orléans*. Edited and translated by Sarah Spence. Series A.
47. *Pilgrimage of Charlemagne* and *Aucassin and Nicolette*. Edited and translated by Glyn Burgess. Series A.
48. Chrétien de Troyes: *The Knight with the Lion*, or *Yvain*. Edited and translated by William W. Kibler. Series A.
49. *Carmina Burana*. Translated by Edward Blodgett and Roy Arthur Swanson. Series A.
50. *The Poetry of Bernart de Ventadorn*. Edited and translated by Tilde Sankovitch. Series A.
51. *Ysengrimus the Wolf*. Edited and translated by Gillian Adams. Series A.
52. *Medieval Debate Poetry*. Edited and translated by Michel-André Bossy. Series A.
53. Boccaccio: *Il Filostrato*. Italian text by Vincenzo Pernicone; translated by Robert P. apRoberts and Anna Bruni Seldis. Series A.
54. Guillaume de Machaut: *La Fonteinne amoureuse*. Edited and translated by Brenda Hosington. Series A.
55. *The Knight of the Parrot*. Translated by Thomas E. Vesce. Series B.
56. *The Story of Meriadoc, King of Cambria (Historia Meriadoci)*. Edited and translated by Mildred Day. Series A.

For Product Safety Concerns and Information please contact our EU representative GPSR@taylorandfrancis.com
Taylor & Francis Verlag GmbH, Kaufingerstraße 24, 80331 München, Germany

www.ingramcontent.com/pod-product-compliance
Lightning Source LLC
Chambersburg PA
CBHW060623250426
43670CB00056B/1777